Muhammad

◆

IN

EUROPE

ʾMuhammad

◆——◆

IN
EUROPE

◆——◆

MINOU REEVES

WITH A BIOGRAPHICAL CONTRIBUTION
BY P. J. STEWART

NEW YORK UNIVERSITY PRESS
Washington Square, New York

First published in paperback in the U.S.A. in 2003 by
NEW YORK UNIVERSITY PRESS
Washington Square
New York, NY 10003
www.nyupress.org

Library of Congress Cataloging-in-Publication Data
Reeves, Minou.
Muhammad in Europe : a thousand years of western myth-making /
Minou Reeves : with a biographical contribution by P.J.Stewart.
p.   cm.
Includes bibliographical references (p.   ) and index.
ISBN 0-8147-7533-0 (cloth : alk. paper)   ISBN 0-8147-7564-0 (pbk)
1. Muhammad, Prophet, d. 632. 2. Islam—Relations—Christianity.
3. Christianity and other religions—Islam. I. Stewart, P.J.
II. Title.
BP75.R375 1999
297.6 3--dc21
99-22794
CIP

Jacket design by Garnet Design
Typeset by Samantha Barden

Printed in Lebanon

To my brothers
Mehrdad and Mehran

Contents

Acknowledgements

The concept of this book derives from my work on my earlier study of the position of women in Islam, *Female Warriors of Allah: Women and the Islamic Revolution*, but the impetus to write it was given by a discussion with my old friend and colleague Professor Rüdiger Görner of London University, who was convinced that it was important to record the story now told in this volume. I am deeply grateful to him for this initial and continuing support and encouragement.

My researches at Cambridge University were especially supported by the late Mr Bahman Vessal of the Faculty of Oriental Studies, who contributed significantly to my thinking. Mr John Cooper, also of the Faculty of Oriental Studies of Cambridge University, tirelessly encouraged and advised me as the work progressed and I am deeply indebted to him. I should also like to thank the staff of Cambridge University Library, Birmingham Central Library and Selly Oaks Colleges Library of Birmingham, who were helpful beyond the call of duty. Their assistance in tracking down the many, diverse sources of this study was invaluable.

The writing of four scholars were of immense importance in helping me formulate my ideas and clarify the direction of my argument. They are Seyyid Hossein Nasr, whose insights into the spirituality of Islam and its founder, were an essential source of inspiration. The works of W. Montgomery Watt have stood the test of time and richly deserve the expression of my special gratitude. R.W. Southern's *Western Views of Islam in the Middle Ages* provided a vital yardstick for my assessments of perceptions of Muhammad in the West from the Middle Ages to the Reformation. Byron Porter Smith's *Islam in English Literature* gave me some essential clues to the reception of Islam in England.

A constant and thorough source of reliable reference was Udo Steinbach's *Der Nahe und Mittlere Osten. The Cambridge Encyclopedia of Islam* helped me trace the thread of Muhammad's reception in Europe through the ages.

Miss Sue Coll made many constructive suggestions in the early editing of the book. I am greatly indebted to Dr Philip Stewart of the Honour School of Human Sciences at Oxford University whose contribution to the biography of Muhammad was invaluable.

My profound thanks are also due to Mrs Emma Hawker for her undivided commitment to this book and her wise judgement in its editorial stages.

In my reflections and thoughts on early Christianity my long and fascinating discussions with my friend Mrs Hilda Pudsey were both inspiring and vitally informative. Throughout the gestation of the book my friends Liz Macfarlane, Kay Sanderston, Jane Alexander and Susanna Mitchell gave me unerring encouragement, including at times of difficulty when the way forward seemed unclear.

Another friend, Mary Isaacs, clarified my ideas on the Renaissance period, particularly in France. I am most grateful to her for those lively discussions. I also wish to thank Mrs Alison Latter, Bookshop Manager at the Centre for International Briefing at Farnham Castle who familiarized me with the most recent publications on Islam and particularly those published by my publishers Garnet and Ithaca Press.

Julie Ramsden of Aston University, Birmingham, assisted me unstintingly in the last stages of the typing and I am grateful for her special interest in the text. Last but not least, I must mention with deepest gratitude my husband, Professor Nigel Reeves, for his continuous perceptive advice, encouragement and contribution to the improvement of the text. In particular I owe to him the English translations of all the French and German literary and philosophical passages quoted in the book where no standard translations were available. I gained from him further insight into the stages of European history and thought that form the intellectual backdrop to this work during our many discussions and debates.

Preface

Several years ago when I was working on my book *Female Warriors of Allah: Women and the Islamic Revolution*, I encountered again and again Western portraits claiming to depict Muhammad's life and personality. They had been written by generations of European writers presenting Islam and its Prophet to a Western audience. Over the course of no less than thirteen centuries a stubbornly biased and consistently negative outlook had persisted, permeating deep levels of European consciousness. In the works of an overwhelming majority of European writers Muhammad was portrayed as a man of deep moral faults. Churchmen, historians, orientalists, biographers, philosophers, dramatists, poets and politicians alike had sought to attribute to Islam and especially to Muhammad fanatical and disreputable, even demonic characteristics. The unchanging nature of this portrayal was as striking as it was disturbing.

The trouble started with early medieval Christian polemicists. They chose not to attack Islamic theology, which was too seductive in its simplicity and clarity, and which raised too many awkward questions about Christian dogma. Nor could they cast doubt on the pious practice of ordinary Muslims. Instead, anticipating the worst excesses of tabloid journalism, they personalized the issue and attacked the Prophet of Islam, dispensing with all but the barest knowledge of any facts and inventing falsehoods. Muslims could not reply in kind, since they are told by the Qur'an to revere Jesus as a holy prophet.

Since then, Westerners of most ideological tendencies (but not, let it be said, Jewish) have inherited the assumption that there was something wrong with Muhammad's character and behaviour, which gave them licence to be at least patronizing and in many cases positively defamatory. Christians have claimed that Muhammad deliberately spread a false religion of his own invention, atheists that he pretended to have the support of God in order to manipulate people, liberals that he was an autocrat, authoritarians that he was a libertarian, feminists that he was an exploiter of women, male chauvinists that he was ruled by women, and so on. Most of these later writers simply repeated the fabrications of their predecessors, but Voltaire stands out for having invented new slanders.

From time to time a fresh start has been attempted by a Westerner ready to look again at the original sources – Sale, Carlyle, Rilke, Tor Andrae, Watt, Schimmel . . . However, more often than not these more balanced views have been thrust aside by the revival of the old calumnies. It was as if the clichés and prejudices had been planted so deep in the Western mind that nothing could displace them.

These images bear no resemblance to the Muhammad familiar to Muslims, seen by them as the noblest of men, kindest of husbands and fathers, most faithful and forgiving of friends, who humbly accepted the terrible burden placed on him by his God, patiently laboured through persecution, emigration and war to carry out his task, and who in victory was magnanimous towards his enemies.

I decided to trace this consistent tradition of distortion and to seek the reasons behind it. The account of Western portrayals of Muhammad is prefaced by two chapters setting out – as far as possible objectively and unadorned – the true story of Muhammad, based on original sources, with the emphasis on those aspects of his life and character that have been most maligned in the West. This biographical sketch is condensed, and avoids the temptations of elaborated detail and hypothesized mental states. In this respect I was most fortunate to receive expert assistance from the Qur'anic scholar and historian of Islam, Dr P. J. Stewart, who has scrutinized and revised the biographical account in the light of his long years of study in this area. I am deeply indebted to him for this important contribution to the clarity and historicity of Muhammad's biography.

The early biographical sources are of course all Muslim, just as the early sources for the life of Jesus are all Christian and those for Buddha all Buddhist, and allowances have had to be made for the devotional element in the Islamic view of Muhammad. The two chapters of the outline biography are followed by a separate chapter on spiritual content of Islam. Together, these three chapters provide the background against which Western accounts should be viewed.

The rest of the book traces the historical trail left by European images and fables. In following it, readers will find themselves on a journey through the evolution of European self-identification and political formation from the Crusades to the present day. They will continually encounter Muhammad and Islam as the defining foil to Western thought, sometimes as whipping-boy, occasionally as inspiring and reviving contrast, frequently as satanic menace.

Coming closer to the present day, it becomes plain to see how these images, so deeply rooted in the Western consciousness, have helped to ignite the suspicion and resentment towards the West that manifests itself in Islamic Fundamentalism. Far from being a recent phenomenon, this emerged in response to European colonialism in the Islamic Orient from North Africa to Indonesia, and most crucially to the establishment of Israel in the heart of the Near East.

Today the attraction of Islamic Fundamentalism reaches beyond revolutionary Iran, to Turkey, Egypt and – dramatically close to Europe – to Algeria. Its impact has been so great in recent years that, even as more balanced pictures of Muhammad and his religion have begun to appear in Western writings, they have been eclipsed by images of a radical, anti-Western and violent Islam that once again bears the hallmarks of the age-old prejudices. It is as if the wheel of history has turned full circle back to the age of the Crusades and Holy Wars.

This book, then, traces the story of Muhammad's reception in Europe, a story of rivalry and confrontation and yet at times of fascination for the exotic. By uncovering the clichés and distortions that have shaped the Western views of Islam and its founder, I hope that readers will be enabled to assess Europe's own part in the making of this turbulent relationship. By seeing the world of the other with empathy and openness – by relying on well-founded research and knowledge rather than on myth – it may be that confrontation can make way for mutual respect and tolerance. Unless the West begins to form a more sympathetic and wholesome view of Islam, the medieval rancour will continue, nurturing hatred, violence and political turmoil.

Muhammad's message was of friendship and unity, not contempt and war. Hatred did not feature in his plan of social and religious reform. His successors respected the freedom of conscience of their Christian and Jewish subjects. If Westerners will learn to respect Muhammad and Islam, they can hope to be respected in return.

Minou Reeves
Cambridge, January 2000

Introduction

The life of Muhammad and the founding of Islam were not at first perceived as a threat in the Christian world of Europe and north Africa. Indeed, they were scarcely perceived at all, hidden beyond a great desert. It was only in the border country of Ghassan that the news brought by caravans from Mecca was noted. Ominously, it was answered by an attempt to muster the northern Arab tribes against Islam – the move that provoked Muhammad's last three military expeditions.

Christians were preoccupied with the bitter struggles for political and doctrinal domination in the territories of the disintegrated Roman Empire. In its eastern half, ever since the year 380 CE, when Emperor Theodosius I had declared Orthodox Christianity to be the only tolerated religion, the state had been fighting against heretics and non-Christians. In what had been the West Roman Empire, barbarian invaders were battling with each other and against attempts by Byzantium to regain territory.

Immediately after Muhammad's death in 632 CE, Islam began to spread with extraordinary rapidity. In 634 CE his successors captured the Byzantine fortress of Bosra in Trans-Jordania. By 637 CE most of Syria had been conquered, and in 638 CE Jerusalem opened its gates to the Muslim Caliph Umar. In 641 CE Egypt and before long, other Byzantine possessions in north Africa yielded to the power of Islam. Within a decade of its Prophet's death, Islam held sway over most of the eastern and southern territories of the East Roman Empire. It had also taken over one of the greatest empires of all time, that of the Sassanids in Persia and Mesopotamia.

By 711 CE Islam extended throughout north Africa and the Arab Empire had reached Spain. In 846 CE the Muslims had pushed forward as far as Rome and had advanced well into Lombardy, and around the year 900 CE Sicily became theirs. If the Arab advance had not been halted in 732 CE after a battle fought between Charles Martel and the Muslim forces not far from Paris, the latter would have established their rule over large areas of France as well, though their defeat did not prevent them from holding positions on the coasts of Provence and Languedoc for several decades.

Islam had rapidly become a reality to the divided peoples of Western Europe and to the Byzantine Emperor. The sudden rise of the Arab Empire and the rapid spread of Islam are normally explained by the exhaustion of the two neighbouring empires of the East, the Persian and the Byzantine – by the disorders in their armies, disorganized and surprised by unexpected conquests – by the discontent of the Persians with their despotic rulers, or by the alienation of the Eastern churches from the Byzantine Emperor and Greek domination. However, many and varied as these reasons are, they cannot explain so complete a victory.

The triumph of Islam after Muhammad's death seems much more likely to have been its appeal as a religion. Islam accepted those who converted as equals in the sight of God, regardless of race, sex, or social status, and it gave to slaves the right to buy their freedom. Conversion was rapid and on a huge scale, yet there were no vendettas or recriminations against those who chose to remain Jews, Christians or Zoroastrians. On the contrary, in the old Roman Empire they were freed from the centuries-old imposition of Christian orthodoxy by the state. To the oppressed the advent of Islam came as a liberation, not a conquest. The expansion and popularity of Islam presented a huge and pressing dilemma for Christians. In practice it called for military action to protect Christendom against the lightning speed of Islam's conquests. In theory it required an urgent answer to the mystery of Islam's position in relationship to Christianity. Was Islam a heresy, a schism? Was it a parody of Christianity or a new religion, a separate school of thought which deserved respect and recognition? Or was it a joint work of Man and Devil? These were the anguished questions which medieval Christians asked themselves and which, in various guises, have continued to agonize Christian commentators and Western writers down to our own century.

Why were Muslims so impervious to the appeal of Christianity, when their Qur'an recognized Jesus as Messiah? There were those who hoped that it was indeed a sect, a branch of the Church, which needed enlightenment. But for centuries, attempts to baptize these stray sheep failed, a source of great anxiety and distress to many who then became bitter opponents of Islam, condemning it to literal damnation.

The first and most profoundly influential of such changes from hoped-for accommodation to outright rejection occurred in the early Middle Ages. Medieval scholars and churchmen preferred to give the easy answer to the question of what was Islam: that it was the work of one man, Muhammad, and that he was inspired by Satan. There was thus no need to answer awkward questions about the religion; defame its founder and you could forget the rest. Fantastic legends and fables began to emerge in order to frighten Christians away from the dreadful possibility of conversion to the other religion. It was asserted, for instance, that Muhammad had died not in the year 632 CE but in 666 – the number of the Beast in the Apocalypse, so he must be the Anti-Christ. With his name corrupted to 'Mahound', Muhammad became the 'Devil incarnate'.

Christian Europe considered Christianity to be the only true religion, at whose core was the unique teaching of the Holy Trinity. Once and once only in the history of mankind God had become incarnate in the person of a human being, in Jesus of Nazareth, in order to save the world from evil and sin. Thus Christians believed themselves to have been entrusted with the ultimate Truth which God had exclusively granted them. But Muhammad had denied the divinity of Jesus and the validity of the Trinity; he had even claimed that Jesus had been crucified in appearance only and had gone on to die a normal death. In rejecting the redemptive power of Christ's sacrifice, was not Muhammad as wicked as the Jews, whom Christians held responsible for having killed the physical incarnation of God?

To label Muhammad the 'Devil incarnate' was only the verbal expression of the contempt in which the early Christian world held him and his religion. The most destructive physical manifestation of this contempt and fear was the Crusades, during which hundreds of thousands of Muslims were massacred by Christian zealots. In 1095, inspired by Pope Urban II, who offered rewards on earth and a place in Paradise thereafter for their crusading deeds, tens of thousands of knights and peasants, rich and poor, old and young set out under the sign of the Cross for the Holy Land. Their task was to recapture the Holy City of Jerusalem from the infidel, but this was only the beginning of a series of crusading expeditions, designed to crush the power and influence of Islam. In this bloodthirsty era, peaceful conversion was decisively rejected in favour of force.

The Crusades finally proved to be a disastrous military failure for Europe, so that what could not be achieved by physical confrontation had to find an alternative sphere of conflict in vituperation. Muhammad as 'Devil incarnate', as 'false prophet', was to be the verbal assault weapon that the Christian West obstinately refused to lay down. As the power of Islam continued to grow – the banner being taken up after the Arabs by the Turks – Christian anger was further internalized and deepened. The fictitious picture of Muhammad as a man of unbridled sensuality and militance became established as a cliché preserved with remarkable continuity by later generations.

The Christian conception of Muhammad as 'impostor' and 'false prophet' was derived from an interpretation of the way the latter had lived and acted. Christians sought to demonstrate that Muhammad could not by definition have been a Messenger of God. In their eyes, the contrast with the pattern set by Jesus could hardly have been greater. Muhammad laid claim to no divine qualities or miraculous powers; moreover he married, fathered children, defended himself by force of arms against those who waged war on him and eventually presided over the city of Medina – in Christian eyes merely as its temporal, even profane, ruler.

For the medieval cleric and scholar, nourished on the core doctrines of Christianity – the separation of spiritual and temporal power, the notion of Christ's Kingdom as 'not of this world', the virtues of celibacy – Muhammad's example was contrary to all patterns of behaviour associated with religious devotion. Christian believers took no account of the similarity of Muhammad's life to that of some Old Testament prophets, who also married, had children, fought battles and ruled their communities, for Christians saw the main function of the prophets as having been to prepare the coming of Christ, whose new covenant had replaced the old.

The demonization of Muhammad lived on in new variations throughout the Renaissance and the Reformation. For example, Marlowe's Tamburlaine burns the Qur'an as the work of the Devil, and to Luther, Muhammad was second in wickedness only to the Pope (whom Luther cast in the role of Anti-Christ), and was cursed as the Son of the Devil. Humanism seemed powerless to overcome the deep-seated fear and prejudice.

Remarkably, the Enlightenment and the Age of Reason also failed to change the stereotype, with Voltaire fulminating against Muhammad as the embodiment of religious fanaticism. For him, Muhammad remained the impostor par excellence. The understanding with which Muhammad's religion is treated by the German humanist Lessing, though exemplary, is a rare exception even in an age that prided itself upon tolerance.

The late eighteenth and nineteenth centuries present a highly contradictory assessment of Muhammad. With Goethe, a rehabilitation in his early work of Muhammad as a figure of genius and of heroic proportions is followed in later years by a fascination with a hedonistic and heretical branch of Islamic mysticism. Yet, some twenty-five years before Goethe's orientally inspired work, Napoleon had invaded Egypt, marched on Jerusalem and massacred Muslims. In a quasi-revival of the Crusades, his design was to march through Syria and with a grand gesture retake Constantinople for Europe. The plan was thwarted in Syria, and Jerusalem was recaptured by the Muslims. But the French presence remained dominant in north Africa and the Middle East and already the seeds of long-lasting resentment amongst Muslims were sown. It was the beginning of European colonialism in the Islamic Orient.

In striking contrast, Carlyle's account of Muhammad, in his famous London lectures *On Heroes and Hero-Worship* in 1840, condemned the hostile attitudes of Europeans towards Muhammad and his religion, by celebrating the Prophet of Islam as an upright, sincere and great man of history.

The literary and philosophical interest in Islam and Orientalism aroused by the new accessibility of the Islamic East, took another turn, however, in Europe's celebration of the Orient's alleged culture of sensuality and cruelty. Byron, Shelley, Heine, Hugo, the painters Delacroix and Ingres all contributed to these unreal images of Muhammad's religion and of Islamic culture emanating from it. Hence the mainstream medieval pictures of Muhammad and of Islam lived on in new guises.

In the twentieth century the contradictory pattern continues. We find attraction to Islamic mysticism and a fascination with the Islamic Orient at the beginning of the century, with Islam depicted as a religion of natural simplicity and spiritual purity. In Germany it was Rilke who became deeply involved in Islam, celebrating it as a religion whose adherents did not need any intermediary to reach God; but most biographers remained divided in their views of Muhammad, seeing in him two personalities, an earlier sincere and thinking man and a later scheming, sensual, ambitious and belligerent despot, thus keeping alive the ancient belief that he was the antithesis to Christ. Indeed, even in the encyclopedias the old stereotype is often repeated in the form of the assertion of a fatal confusion in Muhammad's life between the religious and the secular.

But not all recent writers and biographers have followed this line. There has been a genuine attempt since the 1950s by European experts on Islam and their popularizers to review Muhammad and his religion afresh, returning to Islamic sources in place of the deeply engrained, prejudiced Western perspectives that had built up over so much time. These writers, translating the Qur'an into their own European languages, concluded from their analyses that, contrary to prevailing views, Muhammad had been devout and sincere.

Fatefully, however, much of this tentative understanding may have been disrupted by the publication of Salman Rushdie's fictional portrait of Muhammad in his novel *The Satanic Verses*. This publication appeared in Britain after a confrontation between the Islamic East and the West had been sparked off by the Islamic Revolution in Iran. Rushdie's novel reverts to the old, disparaging Western name of 'Mahound' for Muhammad and uses motifs drawn from the early European Middle Ages, adding some fictions of his own which proved to be as offensive as those of Voltaire. It is not much consolation to observe that the author relates these as the fantasies of the schizophrenic hero of the novel.

Few Westerners would have noticed this opaque novel if it had not been for Muslim reactions to its publication, culminating in the fatwa of Ayatollah Khomeini in February 1989. Overnight Rushdie became transformed into the hero and symbol of free speech in the eyes of Western liberals, who characteristically were less concerned with what he had said than with his right to have said it. One must hope that the dispute will recede into the past, his revival of medieval fictions will be forgotten and the negative image of Muhammad will at last be erased from the Western mind.

A note on the sources

The Qur'an itself is by far the oldest source of information about Muhammad, having come down in the form it took in his lifetime. It is invaluable not only for understanding Muhammad's task as the Messenger of God and his work as a social and religious reformer but also for reconstructing the history of the early Muslim community. Furthermore, it gives us some indication of how Muhammad lived as a man.

Next in importance are the narratives of the early Muslim historians who wrote about Muhammad's life in the two centuries following his death in 632 CE. These narratives are by no means biographies in the modern sense. They include what is called *Sira* (works that sought to preserve accounts of Muhammad's life), *Tafsir* (works that set out traditional interpretations of the Qur'an), and eventually *Hadith* (collections of sayings of and about Muhammad).

These early scribes lived in different parts of the rapidly expanding Islamic state and had to travel extensively, especially to Muhammed's birthplace, Mecca, and to his adopted city of Medina, in search of oral and written information. Oral traditions were derived from Muhammad's first companions and from his and their descendants and had been passed down from generation to generation. They had circulated throughout the Islamic lands. Notable amongst these scholars were the historians Muhammad ibn Ishaq and his later editor Muhammad ibn Hisham, Muhammad ibn Umar al-Waqidi and his secretary Muhammad ibn Saad. Abu Ja'far Al-Tabari was a scholar of encyclopedic knowledge who produced history, Tafsir and legal works. There were six authorized collections of Hadith, the most respected being that made by Muhammad ibn Ismail al-Bukhari.

Confronted with a baffling multiplicity of literature and oral traditions, these authors sought to eliminate all but the most reliable material. While ibn Ishaq and Al-Tabari attempted to reconstruct Muhammad's life and deeds chronologically, Ibn Saad's approach was more thematic, and Bukhari grouped Hadith by topic. Al-Waqidi, on the other hand, concentrated on military history.

The chief tool used by these and other scholars was the *isnad* – the chain of authorities reaching back to Muhammad or one of his companions. To be acceptable, an account of an event had to have a sound *isnad*, one transmitted by people of good and truthful character, each of whom had had the opportunity to meet his or her predecessor and successor in the chain. Inevitably, there are items that slipped through the net, and once an *isnad* had been confirmed as sound, unscrupulous people could attach it to fake evidence. However, the authors named above are recognized as the most reliable, precisely because they were such painstaking scholars. Al-Tabari, for example, accepted Ibn Ishaq as a historical authority but not as a legal one, considering him insufficiently critical of *isnads*. Ibn Ishaq for his part showed a healthy scepticism; if something seemed to him implausible, he would relay it with a comment to the effect that he could not vouch for it.

The picture of Muhammad that emerges from careful study of this literature is remarkably consistent and amazingly detailed – far more so than that of any previous religious founder. It tallies perfectly with the evidence of the Qur'an, which had been taken down at his dictation by his secretaries. Muhammad stands before us in the round, a real human being and not an icon or a disembodied voice. The dearth of information about his life before his mission, and even about his life as Prophet in Mecca, is compensated by the abundant evidence, gathered from hundreds of witnesses, concerning his life after the migration to Medina.

The contrast is enormous between the Muslim account of Muhammad and the scurrilous fabrications of medieval Christians and their spiritual descendants, as the following pages will show.

1

Muhammad the Prophet of Mecca

No mysteries surround the birth of Muhammad. He was born in Mecca, posthumous son of a merchant from one of the leading families in the town. Like practically all the free citizens, he was a member of the wealthiest and most influential tribe of Arabia, the Quraysh. They traced their ancestry back to their days as Bedouins, before they built the town towards the end of the fifth century CE. They had settled in the hot, dry valley in which stood the Kaaba, an ancient stone shrine. Their prosperity came partly from attending to the pilgrims who came from all over Arabia to visit it, and partly from organizing and financing camel caravans along the two trade routes that met there – from Ethiopia to Mesopotamia and from Syria to Yemen.

At the time of Muhammad's birth in about 570 CE, there were a dozen clans of Quraysh. Those that were descended from Muhammad's great-great-great-grandfather, Qusayy, the founder of Mecca, included Muhammad's own clan Hashim, the clan that was to produce one of his worst enemies, Abd Shams, and the clan to which he and some of his closest relatives were linked by marriage, Asad.

Muhammad's grandfather, Abd al Muttalib, son of Hashim, was one of the leading Meccans of his generation. He had been brought up by his mother's family in Yathrib after his father's early death, and had been brought back to Mecca by his uncle al-Muttalib, from whom he had inherited the privilege of feeding and watering the poorer pilgrims out of funds levied from the townsmen. He had added to his prestige by rediscovering the long-lost sacred spring of Zamzam by the Kaaba. His five wives had provided him with ten sons and six daughters. Muhammad's father Abdallah came somewhere in the middle of the family. He married Amina of Zuhra – a clan descended from Qusayy's brother. At the same time, Abd al-Muttalib married Amina's cousin and foster-sister Hala.

Amina was pregnant with her only son, Muhammad, when Abdallah died in Yathrib while on a trading trip. It was a grave handicap in Arab society to be born without a father, but the boy enjoyed the deep affection of his prestigious grandfather, who had himself been a fatherless child. However, Muhammad was soon sent to be suckled by a Bedouin woman, Halima of the tribe of Bani Saad, in accordance with the custom of Meccan families, who considered the desert air and way of life healthier for their infants.

Although Halima claimed that she had prospered ever since Muhammad had come to live with them, she brought him back to his mother when he was two years old. However, Amina was so impressed with his health and strength that she asked Halima to keep him longer. He spent several more months with his foster-mother, until one day she became anxious about him, following a mysterious visit from two strangers clad in white. This time Amina agreed to take him back, and he lived with her for the next four years, tended by the Ethiopian slave Baraka, inherited from Muhammad's father. In Mecca, he formed close bonds with his uncles and aunts and cousins, particularly with Hamza and Safiya, the son and daughter of Hala. It is possible that he returned to the Bedouin for short stays, and his childhood experience of the desert certainly marked him deeply, giving him self-reliance and a taste for solitude.

When Muhammad was about six, Amina took him with Baraka to meet his grandfather's relatives in Yathrib, where his father Abdallah had died and been buried and which, under the name of Medina, was in due course to become Muhammad's adopted home. This entailed a long and trying camel ride across the desert. Yathrib was a delightful contrast not only to the wilderness, but also to Mecca and its hot and stony valley. Instead, here was a cool, green oasis, in which fortified hamlets nestled amid fields and orchards and palm groves, stretching over a wide plain high in the mountains. The little boy was not to know that beneath this peaceful surface lurked tribal hatreds that were soon to lead to war.

For some weeks Muhammad enjoyed this earthly paradise. However, all too soon it was time to make the journey back. After three exhausting days in the desert the weather started deteriorating, and soon they found themselves amid vicious sandstorms and burning winds. Amina, whose health was not robust, was the first to feel the effects of the exposure. She fell seriously ill and when the caravan stopped for the night she died by the roadside. In the morning, Baraka and Muhammad transported her body to the nearby village of Abwa and there they buried her. Then they rejoined the caravan and returned to Mecca. Muhammad was filled with a deep sense of loss by his mother's death. He was now fully orphaned. Many years later, when he was exiled by his Meccan opponents, on his first pilgrimage from Medina to Mecca, he stopped at his mother's grave and cried bitterly, bringing tears to the eyes of his companions.

Muhammad inherited hardly anything from his parents: five camels, some goats – and Baraka, who became the most enduring mother figure in his childhood. She brought the orphan back to his grandfather, Abd al-Muttalib, whose household she joined to attend to Muhammad. The old man welcomed the boy like a son and, until his own death two years later, treated him with utmost love and tenderness – to the extent of making his own children jealous. During this time, Muhammad became familiar with the religious rituals of the polytheist Kaaba over which his grandfather presided. He watched the ceremonies, listened to the stories of the gods and goddesses and perhaps began already to long for something more sublime.

Abd al-Muttalib's death not only shattered Muhammad's emotional world, but left the clan Hashim without a prestigious head. It was to his eldest son Zubayr that the patriarch bequeathed his dignity and offices, but Zubayr lacked the charisma and inclination of his father and passed on the honour of provisioning the pilgrims to his younger brother Al Abbas. But while Al Abbas was able to retain some of the duties attached to the running of the Kaaba, including the guardianship of the Holy Well, he never attained any commanding position in Mecca. It was thus that the prestige of the House of Hashim began to wane, while the rival clans of Abd Shams and Makhzum rose in importance.

With his grandfather's death, Muhammad's home changed once again. This time from the luxury of his grandfather's house to the more modest lifestyle of his uncle Abu Talib. On his deathbed Abd al-Muttalib had called his son Abu Talib and entrusted him with the guardianship of Muhammad. Abu Talib was married and had two sons, Talib and Aqil, the latter being a couple of years older than Muhammad. Two other sons, Jafar and Ali, were born later, and there were three daughters. Abu Talib possessed many noble qualities but little property, and although he was respected as an honourable citizen of Mecca, he too, like his eldest brother, Zubayr, remained in the background. But he faithfully and kindly took care of the young boy, fulfilling his father's wishes.

Much of Muhammad's youth was spent as a shepherd tending camels and goats in the lonely hills and valleys around Mecca. There were no schools or libraries in Mecca, and its literature was an oral tradition. Wealthy merchants had their sons taught how to use a version of the Syriac alphabet to keep accounts and bills of lading, but Muhammad seems to have missed out even on this. However, he was well versed in the oral culture of Arabia, though he preferred plain speech to the fanciful language of the poets. The early historians Ibn Saad and Al-Tabari describe the young Muhammad as being of a refined mind and delicate taste, reserved and pensive, living within himself and not mixing with the Meccan youth who spent their leisure on wine, women and song.

There is a story that has captured the imagination of Muslims and which is consistent with his character. One day when Muhammad was tending his flocks with another Qurayshi youth in the hills outside the town, he wanted to find out what the young men of Mecca got up to at night. He asked his companion to look after his flock and set out. No sooner had he reached the first houses than he heard the sound of flutes and tambourines from a wedding. He sat down to watch but fell into a swoon, sleeping until the next day's sunshine wakened him. The same happened a second time, after which such thoughts left him.

The arrivals and departures of caravans were important events in the lives of the Meccans. Apart from the excitement of welcoming or bidding farewell to husbands, fathers, lovers or sons, there was the sheer financial importance of the caravans. Almost all Meccans had some kind of investment in the fortunes of the hundreds of camels which went out with hides, dates, raisins, fabrics and silver bars and came back with oil and perfumes and manufactured goods from Syria, Egypt and Persia, or spices and gold from Yemen. Abu Talib's trading never produced sufficient profits to afford him a life of ease and plenty. One morning, Muhammad, aged perhaps fourteen, is said to have accompanied his uncle to the assembly point of the caravans. When Abu Talib mounted his camel, Muhammad seized his hand and begged to be taken on the journey. His uncle had pity on the boy and granted his wish.

This trip made a strong impression on Muhammad. His longest ever journey had been to Yathrib, during which he had lost his mother, but this journey was far longer, to Bosra in Byzantine Syria, and was to last for several months. Bosra was a trade centre where Greeks, Syrians and Egyptians assembled to barter their goods with the Arabs of the peninsula. In exchange for raw hides from the desert, raisins from Taif and silver from Mecca, they supplied brocades and linen, oil and perfumes, spices, jewellery and luxury goods.

Bosra was very different from anything Muhammad had ever seen, a meeting place of cultures – Greek, Aramaic, Coptic and Arabic. He must have observed Christian churches with their crosses and images, their bells and hymns. Abu Talib's party is said to have camped near the cell of a monk or hermit called Bahira, and there are stories of prophecies he made about Muhammad.

Eventually, Muhammad started working in the caravan business. He soon learnt the trade of his ancestors and began to distinguish himself at it, gaining a reputation for hard work and honesty. We know virtually nothing for certain of this period, but we can suppose that Muhammad's life involved long and arduous journeys in the gruelling climate of the desert, guarding caravans against raiders and keeping the animals in good condition.

From what we know of him in later life, we must suppose that religious concerns already exercised Muhammad's mind. He had ample opportunity while travelling through the desert to marvel at the magnificence of its vast spaces, its huge mountains and its brilliant night skies, and to wonder at the miraculous presence of life wherever a little water could be drawn out of the parched ground. Back in Mecca, he no doubt visited the Kaaba and quietly rejected its idols, quizzing the pilgrims about their beliefs and comparing these with what he had heard about Judaism and Christianity.

When Muhammad was in his mid-twenties, something happened which transformed his entire life. His beloved aunt Safiya, daughter of his grandfather and of his mother's cousin and foster-sister Hala, had married Awwam, son of Khuwaylid of clan Asad. Awwam had a sister called Khadija, who was in her late thirties and had been married twice. She had inherited the estate and enterprise of her deceased husbands – both merchant bankers who had invested in caravans to Syria and Mesopotamia. She was a woman of exceptional intelligence and ability and was now running the business herself, with her own employees, cameleers, customers and creditors. She was looking for an experienced, trustworthy assistant to take a valuable consignment of goods to Syria.

She heard of Muhammad's reputation through Safiya and others, and made discreet contact with Abu Talib, who persuaded his nephew to offer her his services.

To assist Muhammad, Khadija sent her personal slave, an Ethiopian called Maisara, and he came back with glowing reports which confirmed the excellent results of the trading. She was so impressed that she put Muhammad in charge of all her caravans. Soon, her admiration turned to love. Accounts of his looks emphasize the particular beauty of his large eyes, with their long eyelashes, and of his wide mouth, with its engaging smile. He was of medium height, strongly built, with very black hair and beard. He was an attentive listener and a man of few words, but what he said always made sense.

Khadija could not hope that Muhammad would take the initiative. He was so much younger than she and had by all accounts no experience with women. Besides, he was her employee, respectful and modest. In the end, she sent a go-between, who discreetly sounded him out concerning his feelings about marriage in general and about his employer in particular. His replies were encouraging, so Khadija offered him her hand in marriage and he gratefully accepted.

There was still the problem of Khadija's family. According to Arab custom, even a mature woman of her status needed the consent of the head of her family. This was her uncle Umar ibn Asad, who might be loath to see his niece's wealth bestowed on an outsider. He is said to have fallen into a violent passion on hearing the news and to have declared that he would never consent to give away to 'that poor youth' a niece courted by the great men of Quraysh. But with Khadija's insistence, the old man became reconciled to the idea and eventually gave in. And so it was that Muhammad and Khadija were wedded, he being twenty-five and she nearly forty.

It was the beginning of an exceptionally happy marriage marked by deep and exclusive affection; an equal and respectful partnership the more unusual for the fact that women in Arabia had no rights and were often treated by men as casual playthings. Muhammad used to say of her that she was the best of all women of her time and that he would be with her in Paradise. She certainly deserved her reputation. When Muhammad began his task as prophet she stood resolutely by him, renouncing money and comfort and dedicating herself fully to his religious cause.

Khadija gave Muhammad four daughters: Zeynab, Ruqayya, Um Kulthum and Fatima. There was also at least one son, Qasim, who died in infancy, leaving Muhammad without a male heir. However, there was a boy in the family, Zayd ibn Harith, a slave whom Khadija had presented to Muhammad as a wedding gift. It is said that Zayd's father, a Bedouin from the north, traced him and wanted to ransom him. Zayd said he preferred to remain with Muhammad, who was so touched that he gave him his freedom and adopted him.

Slavery was commonplace in Arabia, as in the neighbouring empires, and Mecca, with its great wealth, had particularly large numbers of slaves, many of them African. They had no rights but could only expect to die as slaves, and the women were exploited sexually by their masters. Muhammad had a succession of slaves, all of whom he freed even before Islam made manumission practically obligatory. He set free his nurse Baraka when he married, and he found her a husband.

A second boy joined the family a few years into the marriage. Abu Talib's business had collapsed, and he was reduced to herding camels, unable to provide for his children. Muhammad and Khadija fostered his youngest son, Ali, while uncle Al Abbas took in Ali's teenage brother Jafar. Muhammad, who had known no father, was himself a model father and treated Ali and Zayd as kindly as if they had been his own children. Both prospered under his care and remained devoted to him all their lives, becoming pillars of Islam.

When Muhammad was about thirty-five, there occurred an event that showed the high regard in which he had come to be held. Flash flooding over the Meccan hills had undermined and damaged the foundation of the Kaaba, the shrine in the centre of Mecca. It was a windowless stone structure measuring about 40 by 35 foot and standing 50 foot high, built of local stone and standing on a base 2 foot high. In the wall near the south-east corner was fixed the sacred Black Stone. The clans came together to rebuild the sanctuary, but quarrels arose over who should lift the Stone into place. The clansmen were on the verge of coming to blows, when they decided to appeal for a solution to the first man who came into the sanctuary. This was Muhammad who had just returned from a journey and had gone straight to the Kaaba. He was hailed, 'Here is Al Amin, the trustworthy!'. Muhammad spread his cloak on the ground and asked for representatives of each clan to help place the Stone on it and together to raise it to the right height. With the agreement of all, he himself then moved the Stone into place.

Muhammad was leading a full and busy life as husband, father, businessman and respected citizen. He might have gone on like this indefinitely, but his spirit was restless, searching for ultimate meaning. He was deeply troubled by the injustice he saw around him – the callous treatment of the poor and the slaves, the neglect of orphans, the exploitation of women. His search for Truth was not confined to solitary meditation and self-denial, but extended to finding solutions to the plight of the oppressed.

Muhammad was not alone in his search for a deeper truth. Tradition has handed down the names of four men who shared his concerns, including a cousin of Muhammad's and two cousins of Khadija's. One of the latter was the learned Waraqa ibn Naufal, who had studied sacred texts and eventually became a Christian. Waraqa had been consulted by Khadija about her marriage to Muhammad but, unlike her guardian uncle Umar ibn Asad, he had given his approval at once, having heard from her about Muhammad's devout character. Waraqa found in Muhammad a genuine kindred spirit – a passionate believer in the unity of God.

Muhammad started to spend an increasing amount of time in solitude, climbing Mount Hira to devote himself to prayer and meditation. Khadija knew that he was experiencing new heights of spirituality and did everything she could to sustain him. Sometimes she would find him lost in thoughts, at other times he would expound passionately about his beliefs and doubts, quoting Waraqa's statements and seeking her advice. Khadija on her part fully appreciated Muhammad's agonies and had become a safe receptacle for the turbulence that had begun to agitate his soul, giving him what support she could. At this stage and for several more years after his call to prophecy, Muhammad's inner struggles went unobserved by the world, and Khadija, Waraqa and perhaps the other three monotheists were the only witnesses. The children were still too young to know of his spiritual strivings.

The steps by which Muhammad was transformed into an inspired Prophet, empowered to preach and summon his people to faith in the one God, can be traced in various sources, of which by far the oldest is the Holy Qur'an itself. According to al-Zuhri, the 'father of Arab historiography', Muhammad's widow Aisha said that his experiences began with true vision, which used to come like the dawning of the day. A later experience of this kind is described in Qur'an 53. 1–18:

> *By the star when it goes down,*
> *Your companion has not erred nor gone astray,*
> *Nor does he speak out of desire.*
> *It is nothing but revelation revealed,*
> *Taught by the Mighty of Power,*
> *Possessor of Strength. He stood*
> *On the highest horizon,*
> *Then drew near and came down*
> *So that he was two bow-lengths off or nearer,*
> *Then revealed to his servant the revelation.*
> *The heart has not lied about what he saw,*
> *So will you dispute with him about what he sees?*
> *Also he saw him on a second descent*
> *By the furthest zizyphus bush*
> *By which is the Garden of the Abode,*
> *When That which pervades covered the zizyphus;*
> *The eye did not flinch nor did it strain.*
> *He saw one of his Lord's greatest signs.*

After his first vision, Muhammad fell into a state of anguish, unsure of the real source from which it emanated. Khadija went on reassuring him that only God could have been his inspirer and that only a pure and pious man such as he could have been selected by God to undergo such an experience. She could well have tried to discourage him, for his withdrawal from normal life was beginning to affect his family's prosperity. Khadija's once flourishing business had declined considerably and the revenues were becoming less and less reliable. However, she had faith in his intuitive powers and in his worthiness to receive insight into the secrets of Creation. He needed all her support, for his mind at this time hung in suspense, doubting that his vision had a divine source. He spent increasingly long periods in his refuge in a cave on Mount Hira, where only Khadija was allowed to join him.

The Muslim mystical tradition of Sufism associates the following much later Qur'anic verse (2. 255) with Muhammad's awareness of divine reality and his longing to arrive at illumination:

> *There is no God but He, the Living, the Eternal One. Neither slumber*
> *nor sleep overtakes Him. His is what the Heavens and the Earth contain.*

Who can intercede with Him except by His permission. He knows what is before and behind men. They can grasp only that part of His knowledge which He wills. His throne is as vast as the Heavens and the Earth. God is the Patron of the Faithful. He leads them from darkness to light.

Some two years after the first visions, in or about 610 CE, when Muhammad was about forty, there occurred the most momentous event of all – the start of the coming of the Qur'an. The following is a brief account by Al-Tabari:

On the night whereon the Lord was minded to deal graciously with him, Gabriel came to Muhammad as he slept with his family in the cave of Hira. He held in his hand a piece of silk with writing thereon, and he said '*Iqra*' – 'Recite/Read!' Muhammad replied: 'What shall I recite?' [or 'I cannot read']. Whereupon the Angel did so tightly grip him that he thought death had come upon him. Then said Gabriel a second time 'Read!' And Muhammad, but only to escape the agony, replied, 'What shall I read?' Gabriel proceeded: *Qur'an 96. 1–5*

Recite in the Name of your Lord who created,
Created man from a clot of blood!
Recite! Your Lord is Most Bountiful,
Who taught by the pen
Taught man what he did not know.

When he had ended, the Angel departed. Muhammad awoke, and 'the words', he said, 'were as though they had been engraved on my heart'. He became distressed at the thought that he might be possessed of evil spirits, and he considered suicide; but as he rushed with the intention of casting himself down a precipice, he was arrested by the appearance of Gabriel, and stood for a long time transfixed by the sight. At last, the vision disappearing, he returned to Khadija who, alarmed at his absence, had sent a courier to Mecca in quest of him. In consternation he threw himself into her lap and told her what had occurred. She reassured him, saying that he would surely be a prophet and Waraqa confirmed her in the belief.

The history both of Muhammad as Prophet and of Islam begins with this extraordinary night near the end of the month of Ramadan, known to Muslims as the Night of Power. Despite their dramatic nature, its events were not sudden but were the culmination of years of meditation and yearning. However, when Muhammad saw what those years had led to, he was filled with fear and a sense of unworthiness. He did not push himself forward, but bravely accepted what was thrust upon him.

The verses that he was told to recite were the beginning of the long succession that gradually came to constitute *al-Qur'an* – 'the Recitation'. Later tradition claimed that Muhammad had been illiterate, and that this is the meaning of the word *ummi* in Qur'an 7. 157–8. It was believed that he became literate as the Angel Gabriel spoke to him and called upon him to recite after him the Qur'anic verses. However, the word *ummi* originally meant 'of the people' or 'indigenous', referring to the Arabs who now received the word of God in their own language, Arabic, like the Jews and the Christians before them in their own languages. So the Arabs also became a people of the Book. In the Qur'an Muhammad is often called the *ummi* prophet, the unlettered prophet, stressing the miraculous nature of his inspiration. During Muhammad's lifetime, the Qur'an remained primarily a body of recitations, but he employed a series of secretaries to write it down, himself indicating where each new passage was to be added. He presumably kept custody of the sheets or scrolls and may have recited from them, as suggested by Qur'an 98. 2:

A messenger of God reciting from sheets made pure.

The Qur'an consists of 114 suras – self-contained units varying in length between 3 very short verses and nearly 300 lengthy ones. Most suras came a bit at a time. Over 80 of them had been complete by the time Muhammad emigrated from Mecca. At every level, from that of the individual phrase or verse right up to the whole book, the Qur'an has a unique order, which constantly confounds the habits of ordinary thinking, being neither logical nor chronological but obeying some higher order.

The Qur'an is considered by Muslims to be expressed in the most perfect language – a unique form of Arabic that was neither the dialect of Mecca nor the inter-tribal lingua franca of the poets. The variety of parables, allegories, similes, metaphors, hyperboles and imagery make the Qur'an into a unique document, which translation cannot convey.

There can be no doubt that Muhammad experienced the Qur'an as something that reached him from God. Sometimes he longed for a revelation and none came, and at other times he was taken by surprise in the most awkward circumstances. Often he was told things that made his life more difficult. As for the language of the Qur'an, it is totally different from that of his sayings as reported in the hadith, which are cast in an easy conversational Arabic, full of earthy expressions and touches of humour.

In later centuries, learned theological arguments developed over whether the Qur'an was created or eternal. The majority opted for its eternity, but there have always been those Muslims who regard it as having come into existence as the Prophet's perception of eternal truths. All agree, however, on its inspired nature. Most serious Western students of the Qur'an accept their judgement.

There followed a difficult period for Muhammad. After the first verses, there was a period of perhaps two years when little or nothing further came. He began to despair. The Qur'anic verses that broke this silence may have been the following (93. 1–11), with their assurance that God is not displeased:

> *By the morning light,*
> *By the night when it is still,*
> *Your Lord has not left you nor is displeased.*
> *The last will be better for you than the first,*
> *And God will soon give you to be pleased.*
> *Did He not find you an orphan and shelter you?*
> *He found you straying and guided you.*
> *He found you needy and enriched you.*
> *So do not deprive the orphan,*
> *Nor scold the beggar;*
> *And proclaim the goodness of your Lord.*

After that, the revelations began to follow one upon another with increasing frequency. They were the fruit of his constant prayers and meditation, but when they happened they were so powerful, so magnificent that he was absolutely shaken. They drained him of all his energies. Their physical manifestation appeared in bouts of violent trembling and cold sweats, which overwhelmed him each time a new recitation was revealed. In these moments of prophetic inspiration Muhammad would beg Khadija to cover him up with a heavy garment until he had recovered.

The picture of Muhammad's mission and of the duty that God had laid upon him gradually unfolded as new Qur'anic passages succeeded one another throughout his time in Mecca. He is a bearer of glad tidings to those who will hear, a warner of the troubles that will overtake the ungodly. He is to call people to God, to preach the pursuit of virtue and the avoidance of vice. The Qur'an speaks repeatedly of the prophets who went before – Adam, Noah, Abraham, Ishmael, Isaac, Jacob, Joseph, Moses and Aaron, Jonah, Solomon, David and Jesus. The shrine of Kaaba, founded by Adam and rebuilt by Abraham and Ishmael, was a concrete link between Muhammad and former prophets.

Muhammad saw himself only as the latest in this series of prophets, not introducing a new religion but renewing the original and only true one – the religion of *islam* or 'submission'. In the Qur'an, Abraham and Ishmael, praying to God, beseech Him to make them *muslim* – submissive to God (2. 128). Jacob on his deathbed asks his children whom they will worship after him, and they reply that they will be *muslim* to the God of Abraham, Ishmael and Isaac (2. 133). Similarly, Joseph begs God to make him die *muslim*, united with the righteous (12. 101). The Western term 'Mohammedan' is a complete misnomer, suggesting a religion centred on the man rather than on his God.

The trying time of uncertainty and speculation was now to be left behind. For the rest of his life, Muhammad was a man with a mission. At first he sought only to convince his immediate family. Khadija is universally recognized as the very first to embrace Islam. She knew her husband's sincerity, his religious integrity and his simplicity of heart. She supported him unconditionally and at the expense of losing her wealth and privilege. Soon Muhammad's adoptive sons Ali and Zayd joined her in acknowledging Muhammad as Prophet. There was also his former nurse, Baraka; now a widow, she had returned as Umm Ayman, and her new faith was so strong that Muhammad married her to Zayd.

A Qur'anic verse called on Muhammad to warn his relatives. He invited the men descended from Abd al-Muttalib – some forty of them – to a meal at which he preached Islam. However, apart from Ali, only two of them are to be found in the lists of early converts: Ali's older brother Jafar and their cousin Ubayda. Some time later they were joined by Muhammad's childhood companion, Hala's son Hamza – the only one of his uncles to become a Muslim while Muhammad lived in Mecca. Abu Talib was unable to abandon the faith of his ancestors, though he gave Ali his blessing and assured Muhammad of his personal support. Another uncle, Abu Lahab, was positively abusive.

The first convert from outside Muhammad's immediate family was his friend Abu Bakr, for whom it was later claimed by some that he preceded Ali into the religion. Of him Muhammad used to say: 'No one I invited to the faith failed to display hesitation or perplexity except Abu Bakr'. He was an intelligent and successful Meccan merchant, two years younger than Muhammad. His nature was mild and sympathetic and his heart tender and compassionate. As soon as he became a Muslim, he set about bringing in other converts. At the time of his conversion he possessed about 40,000 pieces of silver. The greater part of his fortune was now devoted to the support of Muhammad and his family and to the freeing of slaves who were persecuted by their owners because of their attachment to the religion. Following Muhammad's example, he started leading an extremely frugal life. His faith in Muhammad is seen by the early Muslim historians as the greatest guarantee of the sincerity of Muhammad and his loyalty to his call. Abu Bakr was a highly respected man in Mecca and an authority on the history of the Arabs and of Quraysh, and he would have never committed himself to Muhammad if he had not been convinced of his sincerity.

Once Muhammad had begun preaching Islam openly, converts started coming in from every part of the clan system. Some of them were young cousins such as Saad ibn Abi Waqqas, the nephew of Muhammad's mother Amina, and Al-Zubayr, the son of Muhammad's aunt Safiya. One valuable ally was Uthman ibn al-Affan from the clan of Abd Shams, which produced some of Islam's earliest enemies. Another was al-Arqam ibn Abd-Manaf, whose clan, Makhzum, led the opposition. He provided space in his large house for the Muslims' activities.

Among the converts were many women who braved the hostility of their families and sometimes even their husbands to dedicate themselves to a spiritual life under the teachings of Islam. They found themselves accepted as equals in the new community, and in due course they were granted formal rights that they had never enjoyed in pagan society in such matters as marriage, divorce and inheritance.

Another weak and unprivileged group in pre-Islamic Arab society, who found Islam relevant to their plight, were the slaves, attracted by the message of social justice. Where money could be raised, they were freed. They included the African Bilal, later the first muezzin of Islam, and Abdallah ibn Mas'ud, whose mother had confessed to Islam before he had, and had been freed. Abdallah became inseparable from Muhammad and belonged to his circle of first companions. He admired Muhammad so much that he even watched over him when he was asleep. It is from Abdallah ibn Mas'ud that much of the tradition regarding the life of Muhammad was gathered.

Muhammad's teaching was revolutionary in the Meccan context, yet it concerned a set of values and principles underlying the code of ethics of any civilized community. It was about valuing the source of all existence and condemning such anti-social behaviour as homicide, assault, revenge, theft, deceit, defamation, evil language, corruption, greed, accumulation of wealth, adultery, prostitution, abuse of slaves, neglect of orphans and any exploitation of men and women. Instead, Islam encouraged such virtues as piety, justice, generosity, loyalty, peacefulness, forgiveness, modesty, patience, fairness to women and children, support for the sick and the poor, dutifulness towards parents, chastity and self-control.

With a following of oppressed women, restless slaves and poor people no longer content to be poor, Islam was already beginning to pose a threat to the rich and powerful. However, Muhammad's greatest offence in the eyes of the pagans was his condemnation of polytheism. It seemed that he threatened one of the two pillars of Mecca's prosperity: the flow of pilgrims to the Kaaba and to other shrines in which Meccans had an interest. The second pillar was trade. A hostile league started to build up against Muhammad, Khadija and the converts. It was headed by the leading man in Meccan politics, Abu al-Hakam, the man whom Muslims nicknamed 'Abu Jahl' – 'father of ignorance', of the clan Makhzum. He was supported by Abu Sufyan, a figure of increasing importance, and by many others of his clan, the Abd Shams, who had replaced the Hashim as the leading clan of Qusayy. Among those most hostile to Islam was Abu Sufyan's wife Hind, who became all the more virulent when her daughter, Umm Habiba, converted to Islam and married a Muslim cousin of Muhammad's. The building up of the movement against Muhammad was to a great extent due to her.

Against these enemies, Muhammad and Khadija enjoyed the protection of the clan Hashim who, although unwilling to acknowledge him as Prophet, was still well disposed towards him, with the notable exception of Abu Lahab and his wife, who joined the other enemies of

Islam in denigrating Muhammad, calling him *majnun* – 'madman', *sahir* – 'magician', *sha'ir* – poet' or *kahin* – 'soothsayer'.

To avoid provocation, the Muslims assembled secretly to worship in the wadis round the town. This was not enough to satisfy the opposition, and they began to be subjected to verbal abuse and to all sorts of other indignities. In view of the worsening situation, Muhammad encouraged his followers to emigrate to Ethiopia. He was confident that they would be safe under the protection of a Christian ruler, the Negus Armah. Eighty-three men are listed as having gone to Ethiopia, many of them with wives and children. This was a substantial proportion of the community of believers and included many of Muhammad's most active followers. Among others there were Muhammad's daughter Ruqayya, with her husband Uthman and seven of his close cousins, led by Jafar son of Abu Talib.

Muhammad had put many of his followers out of reach of persecution, but in doing so he had greatly weakened his own position. There were comforts even in this bleak time, the greatest of them being the surprise conversion of Umar, who had been a sworn enemy of Islam. He was the son of the zealous pagan Khattab who energetically opposed Muhammad the minute he heard of his religion. The historian Ibn Ishaq describes how one day Umar came out, girt with his sword, determined to kill Muhammad. On the way he met a man who, on hearing what Umar intended, objected that Umar's own sister, Fatima, and her husband, Said, had secretly become Muslims. Furious, Umar went straight to Fatima's house to confront her. At that moment the Muslim blacksmith Khabbab was reading the most recent Qur'anic revelation to them – sura 20. As Umar stormed in, he heard the dreaded sound. Fatima had hastily hidden the sheet but Umar discovered it and demanded to see it. What he read so moved him that he went straight to Muhammad to declare his submission to Islam. From then on he was one of Muhammad's closest and most powerful followers.

Muhammad's enemies kept up their pitiless pressure. They mocked him for not fitting in with their preconception of someone endowed with supernatural powers. Why did they not see him talking to angels? Why did he not work any miracles? Muhammad patiently explained that a prophet does not have to be superhuman. The Qur'an 18. 110 instructs him to:

Say: 'I am just a human being like you, except that to me is given the revelation that your god is God Alone.'

Throughout his life he impressed others precisely by his refusal to raise himself above his fellows or to claim miraculous powers. It may have been painful for him to accept that God had not granted him any, for he clearly believed that wonders had attended the lives of Moses and Jesus and other prophets, as recounted in the Qur'an. With one exception, he nevertheless refused either to promise or to claim any miracle. With all his adoring followers, many of them very simple men and women, he could easily have allowed rumours of supernatural events to develop. Instead he insisted on sober realism. When he was asked for miracles the Qur'an instructed him to reply:

Am I anything but a human being – a messenger? (17. 93)
The Unseen is only for God; so wait, and I shall be with you as one of those who wait. (10. 20).

The one miracle that Muhammad did claim was his receipt of the Qur'an. The very word for a Qur'anic verse, *aya*, means literally 'a sign' and is used also to mean 'a miracle'. The belief that the revelations were miraculous is expressed in the Holy Book itself, for example (10. 37–8):

This Qur'an is not such as can be produced by less than God, but it is the confirmation of what was before it and an exposition of the Scripture – there is no doubt in it – from the Lord of the worlds.
Or do they say: 'He produced it.'? Say: 'Then bring a sura like it; and ask help, if you can, of anyone less than God, if you speak the truth.'

There is however one event often understood as miraculous: Muhammad's Night Journey to Jerusalem and his Ascent into Paradise. Many versions exist, but their origin is to be found in Qur'an 17. 1:

Glory be to Him who carried his servant by night from the Sacred Mosque to the Furthest Mosque, whose precinct We have blessed, so that We might show him some of our Signs.

The story goes that he was sleeping beside the Kaaba one night when the angel Gabriel came to him with a winged steed called Buraq, which transported him to the Temple of Jerusalem. There he met Abraham, Moses and Jesus. A ladder came down from Heaven and Gabriel led Muhammad up. In the First Heaven he saw Adam reviewing the souls of his descendants, and he was shown the torments of the damned. They ascended to the Seventh Heaven, where Muhammad found Abraham again, who took him into Paradise.

The Night Journey has been accepted literally by many Muslims as a miracle. However, Ibn Ishaq understands it as a vision, and he quotes Aisha as saying: 'The Prophet's body stayed where it was, but God transported his spirit by night.' This is confirmed by Qur'an 17. 60, which commentators relate to the same experience:

We made the vision that We showed you only as a test for the people.

This vision is part of the basis for the great reverence Muslims feel for Jerusalem, the third holiest city of Islam, towards which at this time the faithful faced for worship.

One other Qur'anic passage is understood by many Muslims as describing a miracle but is better understood as referring to some striking visual phenomenon of atmospheric origin (54. 1–2):

The Hour is near and the Moon is split apart.
But if they see a sign they say: 'Passing magic!'

It is in this time of persecution that the affair of the 'Satanic Verses' is alleged to have occurred. This story, related by Ibn Saad and Al-Tabari, cannot be ignored, given the trouble that has followed publication of Salman Rushdie's novel of that name. It is now vehemently denied by many Muslims, as if acceptance of it as true would be deeply damaging to the reputation of Muhammad. In fact he comes out of the story very honourably, and Muslims should not fear its truth any more than their enemies should hope for it to be true. If it had been shameful, no Muslim would ever have transmitted it, nor would two of the most respected historians of Islam have recorded it.

The pagan leaders of Mecca are said to have proposed a compromise to Muhammad: if he recognised their three goddesses Al-Lat, Al-Uzza and Manat, as the 'daughters of Allah', they would make their peace with him. The story goes that they offered him great wealth and a young bride, but it seems unlikely that they seriously intended to raise him to a position where he might rival them. There is no reason to suppose that Muhammad would have been influenced by such material concerns, given his abstemious nature and his concern with spiritual values.

One day, according to Al-Tabari, as Muhammad was musing on the plight of his followers and longing for peace with his enemies, Satan is alleged to have put into his mouth,

> Have you thought on Al-Lat and Al-Uzza
> And on the third, Manat?
> 'Those are the exalted cranes, and their intercession is approved.'

When the polytheists heard this they were delighted, thinking that Islam had accepted their goddesses. However, Muhammad soon became aware of his own error and thus received the correct Qur'anic continuation (Qur'an 53. 19–20):

> *Have you thought on Al-Lat and Al-Uzza, and, third, on Manat? Is God to have daughters and you sons? This is indeed an unfair distinction. These are only names that you and your fathers have invented, for which God has sent forth no authority. They follow only conjectures and what their minds desire, although guidance has already come to them from their Lord.*

Another Qur'anic passage (22. 52–5) is said by Al-Tabari to have been given to console Muhammad for his mistake. Here is how it begins:

> *Never did we send a prophet before you but that, when he had a longing, Satan injected something into the longing; but God cancels what Satan injects, and God establishes his signs. God is knowing, wise.*

Those who would deny the story of the Satanic verses outright have also to explain the continuation of sura 53, following the correction, which is most naturally understood as a denial that the Meccan goddesses were angels capable of intercession (53. 26–7):

> *However many angels there may be in the heavens, their intercession is worth nothing unless God permits it for whom he pleases.*
> *Those who do not believe in the Hereafter name the angels with female names.*

Al-Tabari does not specify how long after the incident of the alleged Satanic Verses their Qur'anic abrogation happened. But he does attribute the first wave of returns from Ethiopia to the fact that news of peace with the pagans had reached Africa. This suggests that the supposed compromise lasted some time. Whatever did or did not happen, all possibility of any mutual accommodation was ended by the sura 109:

> *In the Name of God, the Merciful, the Forgiving,*
> *Say: 'You ungrateful ones,*
> *I do not worship what you worship,*
> *Nor do you worship what I worship,*
> *And I shall not worship what you worship,*
> *Nor will you worship what I worship.*
> *For you your religion and for me my religion.'*

The passions that have been raised over this story spring from the belief that, if true, it discredits Muhammad. Careful consideration shows otherwise. The Meccans wanted him to accept their idols as goddesses. They wanted their goddesses to have real power. The offending verse recorded by the historian, Al-Tabari, says merely that the intercession of the supposed angels is 'approved' (or, according to another version, 'hoped for'), which does not limit the power of God to ignore it. The abrogation that (alone) appears in the Qur'an over several verses rejects the idea that the idols are angels, being only a belief held by pagans (i.e. 'Those who do not believe in the hereafter').

If Muhammad did utter the offending verses, he is to be all the more admired for having seen that they had to be rejected, given that they did not diminish the uniqueness or power of God. He could have saved himself embarrassment by maintaining them and making clear the very limited nature of the compromise. Instead he had the force of character to admit to a mistake and to face the renewed hostility of the Meccans. In the short term this would have thrown into doubt his reliability as a transmitter of the Qur'an, but in the long term it strengthened confidence in him as a vigilant and courageous self-critic. There is therefore no mystery in the readiness of Al-Tabari and Ibn Saad to transmit the story.

Since he had refused to compromise, Muhammad's enemies built up the pressure, organizing a boycott of the clan Hashim. It was decreed that no one should trade with its members nor inter-marry with them.

This lasted two years, but it was doomed to failure, because not all Hashim were Muslims and not all Muslims were Hashim. Eventually the boycott was lifted at the request of non-Muslims who were too greatly inconvenienced by it.

Throughout this time, Muhammad had enjoyed the protection of Hashim under its head, Abu Talib, who, though not a Muslim, had a deep respect and affection for his nephew. In 619 CE Abu Talib died, to be succeeded by Muhammad's enemy, Abu Lahab. At first the new leader reluctantly agreed to give Muhammad continued clan protection, but he soon withdrew it. To make matters worse, Muhammad also lost his beloved wife, Khadija. Now he was bereft both of a protector and of his closest companion and supporter. He grieved for her.

In danger in Mecca, Muhammad started to explore the possibility of moving elsewhere. He travelled to the upland oasis of Taif, forty miles south-east of Mecca, to seek the protection of the tribe of Thaqif. Its leaders received him coldly, and when he left he was pursued by a hostile crowd. He returned dejected to Mecca, where he sought the protection of another clan to replace that of Hashim. After a couple of refusals he was given the necessary guarantees by al-Mutim, head of the clan descended from Hashim's brother Nawfal. His uncle Abbas meanwhile quietly exerted his influence to counteract that of Abu Lahab.

Although not completely devoid of protection in Mecca, Muhammad began spending much of his time away from the town, preaching at fairs and markets and centres of pilgrimage. It was with pilgrims at Aqaba near Mecca that he had his crucial success, converting six men from the tribe of Khazraj in Yathrib. The following year, 621, five of them returned with seven more Yathribis, two of them from the rival tribe of Aws, which had won a Pyrrhic victory in the latest round of their protracted war. They swore an oath of allegiance to Muhammad and of fidelity to the moral commandments of Islam. It was called a 'women's oath' because it made no mention of fighting.

The year 622 was the turning point in the history of Islam, and was later fixed as the beginning of the Muslim era. Seventy-five Muslims, including two women, made the pilgrimage from Yathrib and met Muhammad at Aqaba. They swore an oath of loyalty to him, undertaking to fight for his safety if necessary. Muhammad's uncle Abbas attended this meeting, wishing to assure himself of the guarantees being offered to his nephew.

Everything was now ready for the focus of Islam to move to Yathrib. In the course of the next three months some fifty Muslim men, most of them with their families, made the desert journey to join those who had gone there in advance. By the beginning of First Rabi, the third month of the year, it was time for Muhammad to follow them. With the help of Ali he had just had a miraculous escape from an assassination attempt, in which one representative from each clan of Quraysh was to stab him simultaneously so that no clan could risk vengeance. The next night he slipped out of Mecca secretly with Abu Bakr for companion. After hiding for three days in a cave near the town, the two men made their way with a Bedouin guide by little frequented routes to Yathrib, which was soon to be known as 'Madinat al Nabi' – City of the Prophet, or simply as Medina.

2

Muhammad's Rule in Medina

The Making of Islam

Muhammad's position

The Muslims of Medina had invited Muhammad in the hope that he would help to keep the peace between its two main tribes, Aws and Khazraj. At the same time, the immigrants from Mecca naturally looked to him as their leader. His position was therefore from the outset a political as well as a religious one. There was no contradiction between these roles, which all the great prophets before him, except Jesus, had combined.

It was essential that he be seen as neutral between Aws and Khazraj, and the first decision that would bear on this was where he set up house. After a few days based on the outskirts of the oasis he announced that his camel, Qaswa, would choose the place. After wandering round, the sensible beast, perhaps with some discreet prompting from her rider, set him down at the ideal spot in the heart of the oasis, just inside the Khazraj side of the frontier between the two tribes.

Over the next ten months, the Muslims built the Prophet's Mosque, which was to become, next to the shrine at Mecca, the holiest place of Islam, the model for all later mosques. They used no slaves but did the work with their own hands, with the eager participation of Muhammad. Built with sun-baked brick, the mosque took about ten months to complete. Its main feature was the courtyard, a rectangle aligned north-south, about 36 yards by 30. There was a covered area, with a roof of palm branches, thatched and daubed, resting on palm trunks. There was as yet no minaret; when the African freedman Bilal was made the first muezzin, with the task of calling the faithful to worship, he did so from the roof of a nearby house.

The Mosque was not just a place of prayer. When not in use for worship, its courtyard was a public space, in which Muhammad received visitors, presided over discussions and ministered to the refugees who arrived destitute from Mecca. When war broke out, it became the centre where operations were planned and, when there was fighting on the edge of the oasis, a hospital tent was erected there. Muhammad's family lived in rooms backing on to the east wall of the mosque, so his public life and his private life were intertwined to an extent rare before the advent of modern media. This makes all the more remarkable the fact that he was never found, even by his enemies, to have acted in any way contrary to his principles.

Muhammad's first concern was to consolidate the position of the Muslim community in Mecca – the *Umma*. This consisted of two elements: the immigrants from Mecca and the Medinan converts, who owed allegiance to their own clan leaders. He had a delicate diplomatic task to maintain the balance between the parties and to remain on good terms with the local headmen – some of them not yet Muslims – and also with the nomadic tribes in the surrounding desert. It was only gradually that he came to be recognized as the supreme head of the whole of Medina.

Muhammad and the Jews of Medina

Besides Aws and Khazraj, there were many Jews in Medina, mainly grouped in three tribes: Qaynuqa, who were allied to Khazraj, and Nadir and Qurayza, who were allied to the dominant Aws. Their settlements were in the south-west of the oasis, not far from the Mosque. Their origin is uncertain, but they had strong links with Syria and had quite probably come originally to escape from the Byzantine Empire, which operated a draconian policy of repression towards all religions other than Orthodox Christianity.

Muhammad expected to be well received by the Jews. They were fellow monotheists, and his message to the Arabs seemed to be identical to that brought to the Jews by Moses and their other prophets. From the outset, Muhammad insisted that he was not proclaiming a new religion, for he believed that he had been sent to restore the one true religion given to Adam. He was simply performing the task that God had given to previous prophets such as Noah, Abraham, Moses and David.

Two features of Islam at this time brought it closer to Judaism. In Medina, as before in Mecca, the Muslims faced towards Jerusalem for their worship, and they fasted on the tenth day of the first month, Ashura, corresponding to Yom Kippur. The first practice ceased when a Qur'anic verse, received dramatically in mid-worship, ordered them henceforth to face the Kaaba. The second was replaced by the fast of Ramadan. Hostile spirits claim that these changes show that Muhammad made up the religion as he went along, to suit circumstances, but they show only that Islam was instituted progressively, which Muslims have never denied.

A document known as the 'Constitution of Medina' and reproduced by Ibn Ishaq is very probably the authentic agreement drafted by Muhammad to regulate relations with the Medinans. With regard to the Jews, it states, 'The Jews . . . are one community with the believers (the Jews having their religion and the Muslims theirs)'. It requires Muslims and Jews to offer each other mutual support if attacked. A Qur'anic verse, 3. 64, invites the Jews to recognize what unites them with the Muslims and separates them from Christians (who have taken Jesus for a 'lord beside God'):

> Say: 'People of Scripture, come to fair terms between us and you: that we worship none but God, that we associate no partner with Him, and that we do not some of us take others as lords beside God.'

Another verse, 5. 5, proposes mutual acceptance of kosher and halal food and of Jewish and Muslim marriage partners:

> The food of those who were given the Scripture is lawful for you, and yours is lawful for them, and chaste women from among the believers and chaste women from among those who were given the Scripture before.

Instead of welcoming Muhammad, the Jews started to criticize. They argued that the Qur'an contradicted their own scriptures proving that Muhammad had erred, which led to heated debates. The Qur'an explained the recalcitrance of the Jews by saying that they had disobeyed God's commandments and corrupted the scriptures. Having gone astray, they had to be brought back to the right path, to the undivided monotheism of Abraham, the father of both the Jews and the Arabs. Abraham had considered himself to be simply the proclaimer of God's message, and Muhammad was renewing it. However, the Jews were unwilling to accept that a non-Jew could be a prophet, though they did not deny that the Arabs were descended from Abraham through his first-born, Ishmael.

Unfortunately, the Muslims' relations with the Jews of Medina were soon complicated by war with Mecca. Some of the Jewish leaders believed that by allying themselves with the polytheists they could rid themselves of Muhammad. The ruin that this brought upon them has often been interpreted as evidence of implacable Muslim hatred of the Jews. It was in fact the product of a unique set of circumstances; Islam was fighting for survival, and most Medinan Jews were on the side of its enemies, though there were exceptions, such as Rabbi Mukhayriq, who died fighting for the Muslims in the Battle of Uhud. Once Islam was safely established, it accepted and protected its Jewish subjects, allowing them to worship freely in their synagogues and to judge themselves by their own laws. When the Jews of Europe suffered Christian persecution, it was often to Muslim countries that they fled for safety.

Muhammad at war

It was not many months before open hostilities broke out between the Muslims and the Meccans. The immigrants in Medina had only such possessions and savings as they had been able to bring with them, and the pagans of Mecca had seized most of their property. They lacked the farming skills that were necessary to make a living from the land of Medina. Their natural response was to seek compensation from Meccan caravans by organizing razzias – the traditional Arab raids, whose object was to seize property rather than take life. This new departure was authorized by Qur'an 22. 39–40:

> Permission is given to those who are fought against, because they are oppressed – and God is powerful to help them;
> Those who have been expelled from their homes without justification except that they say: 'Our Lord is God'.

Even the eighteenth-century English historian and author of the *History of the Decline and Fall of the Roman Empire*, Edward Gibbon, no friend of Islam, sees no alternative for Muhammad at this moment, but to defend his faith against the violence of its enemies:

> In the state of nature every man has a right to defend, by force of arms, his person and his possessions; to repel, or even to prevent, the violence of his enemies. In the free society of the Arabs, the duties of subject and

citizen imposed a feeble restraint; and Mahomet, in the exercise of a peaceful and benevolent mission, had been despoilt and banished by the injustice of his countrymen. The choice of an independent people had exalted the fugitive of Mecca to the ranks of sovereign; and he was invested with the just prerogative of forming alliances and of waging defensive war.[1]

The leader of the first successful razzia disobeyed the Prophet's instructions and launched it on the last day of Rajab, one of the sacred months in which fighting was forbidden, killing two Meccans. At first Muhammad refused to distribute the booty, but a Qur'anic verse provided the justification (2. 217):

They ask you about fighting in the sacred month; say: 'Fighting in it is grave, but to block the path of God – being ungrateful to Him and to drive out people from the Sacred Mosque is graver with God, and persecution is graver than killing.'

Soon after, a larger caravan was on its way back from Syria, led by Abu Sufyan of the clan Abd Shams. Muhammad set out with more than 300 men: 83 immigrants, 170 Khazraj and 61 Aws. They had only 70 camels between them and had to take it in turns to ride. Meccan spies reported their movements, and Abu Jahl led out a relief force of nearly 1,000, including many relatives of the Muslims. In the event, the caravan evaded capture, but the relief force nevertheless attacked the Muslims at the watering place of Badr. To their own astonishment, although heavily outnumbered, Muhammad's men triumphed, thanks to their vastly superior discipline and dedication. Some 50 or more Meccans were killed, and nearly 70 taken prisoner. The dead included Abu Jahl, the commander of the army, and at least a dozen of the leading men of Mecca, whose administrative and commercial skills could hardly be replaced. The Muslims suffered only 14 dead.

The significance of Badr was both religious and political. On the religious front, it strengthened the faith of the Muslims in their cause, extending Muhammad's following even further. Many nomadic tribes who had sided with the Meccans now sent deputations to Medina to embrace Islam. Politically, the Battle of Badr made it clear that

---

1 Edward Gibbon, *Decline and Fall of the Roman Empire*, London 1872, p. 503.

Muhammad was capable of challenging the Meccans' supremacy. Their prestige and authority had been shattered by the defeat and Muhammad knew that now they would be desperate to reverse it.

The new leader of Mecca was Abu Sufyan, a long-standing enemy of Islam, but one whose intelligence and pragmatism were to allow him eventually to make peace. There was also a hopeful change in the leadership of the clan Hashim. Abu Lahab, one of the few Meccans who had not volunteered to fight at Badr, was killed in a subsequent quarrel, to be succeeded by Abbas. The latter was perhaps already secretly a Muslim and he saw that the fortunes of his clan were bound up with the success of his nephew.

Abu Sufyan spent the next year building up a force of 3,000 camel riders and 200 horsemen. They made their way to Medina and assembled near Mount Uhud, north-east of the oasis. Muhammad was persuaded, against his better judgement, to seek out the enemy, as they were destroying the crops. Under cover of darkness, the Muslims attained a dominant position on the slopes of Uhud. When battle was joined they came near to victory, although again outnumbered three to one. However, they had no cavalry, and the Meccan horsemen were able to outflank them. The Muslim position looked desperate when Muhammad was wounded and rumoured dead. Thinking he had already won, Abu Sufyan ordered a retreat to avoid further losses. His failure to drive home his advantage proved fatal to the Meccan cause.

The Muslims had lost 65 men, including Muhammad's dearest uncle, Hamza, killed by an assassin specially recruited by Abu Sufyan's wife Hind, whose father he had killed at Badr. She personally mutilated Hamza's body. On the other side only 22 had been killed. On the face of it, the Meccans had now avenged the disasters of Nakhla and Badr, for the combined total of dead were 79 Muslims and 73 polytheists. However, their object had been to destroy Muhammad, and in this they had failed. Still, the near-defeat posed grave problems for the Muslims: if Badr had been a sign of God's favour, was not this a sign that he had deserted them? Much of sura 3 was devoted to drawing the lessons and rebuilding morale.

A further lesson of Uhud was that not all who called themselves Muslims could be relied on. Following a disagreement about tactics on the eve of the battle, Abd-Allah ibn Ubayy, one of the main leaders of Khazraj, had left with his troops. Such people came to be referred to by the term *munafiq* – 'hypocrite' – and suras 4, 9 and 33 devote much attention to the problem they posed. Muhammad showed his wisdom and generosity of spirit by always giving such people the benefit of the doubt. He remained on good terms with Abd-Allah, after whose death he gave his own shirt for his shroud and personally presided over his funeral.

The two years that followed the Battle of Uhud were spent by the Meccans in preparation for a supreme effort to get rid of Muhammad. Abu Sufyan gathered an army of 10,000, including 6,000 Bedouin and 600 horsemen. Against this huge force, the Muslims had only 3,000 men and no more than three dozen horses. Muhammad decided to employ an original device suggested by a Persian convert by the name of Salman. His plan involved digging a deep trench across the open, northern side of the oasis – the other sides being protected by lava flows.

The Muslim strategy was a complete success. For about a fortnight the Meccan horsemen attempted to cross the trench, but only a few succeeded, and they were quickly driven back. The weather had become exceptionally cold and a severe storm began to blow, lowering the morale of the Meccan warriors. One morning, the Muslims looked out and found that much of the opposing army had disappeared overnight. Abu Sufyan had no choice but to withdraw his troops. Humiliated and exhausted, he led them back to Mecca.

Each of these three engagements had sequels for the Jewish clans of Medina, which had supported the Meccans. Soon after Badr, the Bani Qaynuqa were expelled from the oasis, after an incident in which some of them had subjected a Muslim woman to insulting behaviour. This however was only the culmination of a whole series of provocations. The expulsion was possible only with the cooperation of the leaders of Khazraj, whose allies these Jews were.

Soon after Uhud, the Bani Nadir followed Qaynuqa into exile because of a plot to assassinate Muhammad. Their leader Huyay had maintained clandestine contacts with Mecca and was perhaps the most bitterly anti-Muslim of all. He and many of his clan settled in the oasis of Khaybar, and they financed much of the Bedouin contribution to the Meccan war effort, promising them half the date harvest of Khaybar if they defeated the Muslims.

The most terrible punishment was that of the Bani Qurayza. Their leader, Kaab ibn Asad, had remained on good terms with the Muslims, and his clan had lent the tools for the digging of the trench that saved Medina from the final assault. However, when he saw the size of the Meccan army, he became convinced that Islam would be destroyed and that it would be madness to be on the losing side, so he agreed to a proposal from Huyay to let part of the Meccan army secretly into the Jewish fortresses. A double agent revealed this plan to Muhammad before it could be executed. When the Meccan army retreated, he feared that it was just a tactical move and that the agreement with Qurayza was about to be put into effect.

The Jewish tribe was immediately besieged. When they capitulated, there was controversy about their fate. They were allies of Aws, and some members of the tribe wanted them to be spared as the Bani Nadir had been. Muhammad asked Saad ibn Muadh, head of the Aws, to pass judgement. Saad condemned the men to be executed and the women and children to be enslaved. Though he may not have known it, he was applying the law of Moses to the followers of Moses (Deuteronomy, 20. 12–14).

This was not the end of the Jews in Medina. A few smaller groups remained, and indeed, when Muhammad died, his chain-mail armour was pledged to a Jewish pawnbroker in exchange for barley to feed the poor. There was no ethnic hatred towards Jews as Jews; on the contrary, many Muslims – including Muhammad himself – married Jewish women.

With the failure of the final Meccan effort in the Siege of the Trench, the danger lifted. Islam was never again at risk of annihilation and the more extreme defensive measures were abandoned. Among the first to benefit from the more relaxed situation were the Jews of Khaybar, including many of the Bani Nadir refugees. When they were besieged and defeated a year later, they lost title to their date palms but were allowed to stay, on condition that they pay half the harvest to the Muslims.

In his conduct of war, Muhammad imposed various restrictions on his men. They were not to kill women or children or non-combatants. Prisoners of war were to be treated well and given food, drink and clothing, until they were exchanged or ransomed, the exceptions being the men of Qurayza. Defeated parties who accepted Islam were allowed to retain their liberty and property. Mutilation of the dead and looting were prohibited. All this was a complete break with Arab tradition. It anticipated the Geneva Conventions by thirteen centuries.

Throughout these campaigns, Muhammad – a man in his 50s – showed tremendous physical courage and endurance. He led from the front and was personally at the head of 27 of the 80-odd expeditions, sharing with his men in all the discomforts and privations of desert travel and warfare.

The return to Mecca

It was now just a matter of time before the Muslims would enter Mecca. The only question was whether this would happen peacefully or by force. Muhammad was determined that there should be no more bloodshed and he wished to show his goodwill towards the Meccans and test their feelings. He decided to attempt to perform the lesser pilgrimage (that is to say a visit to the Kaaba without the full rites, in order to avoid making the full pilgrimage, due a few days later, alongside polytheist pilgrims). He counted on the Arab code of honour to ensure that the Meccans would not attack pilgrims in the sacred period.

Muhammad set out from Medina with 700 men. The Meccans, fearing an attack, barred the way of the pilgrims at Hudaybia, on the edge of the sacred territory. Here, after lengthy negotiations, an agreement was made. To save face for the Meccans, the Muslims agreed not to enter the town that year, but in the following year the Meccans would clear their way for three days. Hostilities would be suspended for ten years, and Muhammad would send back fugitives leaving Mecca without their guardian's agreement, a measure about which many Muslims complained, but which had the beneficial effect of increasing the number of Muslims remaining in Mecca.

The following year, as agreed, Muhammad made the lesser pilgrimage, for which part of the town had been evacuated. This visit greatly strengthened Muhammad's position in Mecca. The very fact that he had been able to return to his native city at all and that he had respected his agreement to the letter, showed him to be at least the equal of the leaders of Mecca. Many notable Meccans professed Islam about this time, including Khalid ibn Walid who had led the cavalry in the Battle of Uhud. Soon there was among the pagans no chief of notable military ability.

Ten months later, at the beginning of the year 630 CE, Bedouins who were allies of Mecca broke the truce by attacking others who were allied to the Muslims. The victims appealed to Muhammad for help. The Meccans, afraid of the consequences of this, sent Abu Sufyan to restore peace, but no one in Medina would negotiate with him. Muhammad was confident that Mecca would not resist if the Muslims arrived under his command. He led out most of the men of Medina, gathering Bedouin allies on the way, and arrived near Mecca with 10,000 men. Abu Sufyan came out to agree terms for surrender and was rewarded with a general amnesty. The Muslim army entered Mecca experiencing virtually no resistance.

This time there was no question of accepting the idols in and around the Kaaba. They were thrown down and destroyed. This however was the only act of destruction. Muhammad formally prohibited any looting or damage to property. Abd-Allah ibn Abi Sarh, the apostate former secretary, was condemned and then pardoned. Impressed by Muhammad's magnanimity, the rich and powerful of Quraysh queued to offer their allegiance and to submit to Islam. Their city, which had been the heart of paganism, was now to be the centre of Islam. Even Hind, Abu Sufyan's wife, who had worked for so many years against Islam and who had procured the death of Muhammad's uncle Hamza, came to Muhammad to submit and be pardoned.

Muhammad and the Christians of Arabia

Muhammad stayed only a couple of weeks in Mecca before setting out to confront a confederation of Bedouin opponents in the Battle of Hunayn. The victory of the Muslims there practically put an end to resistance in Arabia, and Muhammad was able to return to Medina confident of his ascendancy. However, even now peace was not complete. The Christian tribe of Ghassan, vassals of the Byzantine Empire, were preparing an attack. A first expedition against them, a few months before the conquest of Mecca, had led to the death of Muhammad's adopted son Zayd and his cousin Jafar, son of Abu Talib, who had recently returned from Ethiopia. Muhammad was to lead a second expedition against Ghassan, and when he was near to death he sent a third. The defensive war against Byzantium, which his followers were to pursue with such success, started in Muhammad's lifetime.

In principle, Muhammad's relations with Christians were good. Islam recognized Jesus as the greatest of all the prophets, the only one described as 'Messiah'. It was written in the Quran 3. 45:

> *The angels said: 'Mary; God gives you good news of a Word from Him,*
> *whose name shall be the Messiah, Jesus son of Mary, honoured in this*
> *world and the next, one of those nearest to God.'*

Muhammad's first contact with the Christians of Arabia had been encouraging. The Bishop of Najran, on the borders of Yemen, had led a delegation to Medina. There had been lengthy and inconclusive theological debates, in which Muhammad pressed the Christians to accept that Jesus was no more than a prophet and that the One God could not also be Three. Still, the visitors had impressed the Muslims with their simplicity and their learning. The Qur'an expressed a favourable judgement (5. 82):

> *You will indeed find that the people fiercest in enmity towards the*
> *believers are the Jews and the polytheists. You will also indeed find the*
> *closest of them in affection towards the believers are those who call*
> *themselves Christians; that is because among them are scholars and*
> *monks, and because they are not proud.*

This, however, is to be read in the light of 5. 51. Although this comes earlier in the same sura, it was revealed later, after the trouble with Ghassan had started. It reflects Muhammad's bitter experience that these monotheists too had sided against him with the pagans:

> *You who believe, do not take the Jews and Christians for friends; they*
> *are friends to each other. Whoever of you becomes their friend is one of*
> *them. God does not guide an unjust people.*

As with the Jews, the root of the problem was that Islam had a place for the followers of earlier prophets but that the Christians had no place for Islam. Muhammad accepted that the Biblical books were of divine origin, even if they had subsequently been corrupted, but the Jews and Christians did not consider the Qur'an to have any value.

Islam perfected

All through the momentous events of Muhammad's time in Medina, Qur'anic passages continued to be revealed to him. Presiding over a community that grew from hundreds to many thousand strong, Muhammad was constantly asked for advice, decisions and judgements on every sort of problem that arises when many people live together. Most of his pronouncements were given in his usual, homely colloquial Arabic and have been transmitted in the form of hadith traditions. From time to time, the answer – often after a long delay – took the form of new Qur'anic verses. There are passages relating to marriage, adultery, divorce, slavery, concubinage, inheritance, contract, theft, murder, testimony, false witness and so on.

Many Western writers on Islam have claimed that the twenty-odd Medinan suras of the Qur'an, which make up a little less than half the book, are less inspired in literary terms than the Meccan suras. This can only be properly judged in Arabic. The language of the Qur'an is so compressed, allusive and rich in overtones that translators have felt obliged to smooth out the difficulties and ambiguities. The result, particularly in the long verses of many Medinan passages, is a misleadingly bland or even turgid translation. It must not be forgotten, too, that the Qur'an was, and for Muslims still is, primarily a recitation, to be heard as well as read – and to be lived.

Western critics have also alleged that Muhammad consciously composed verses to further his own ends, but that contradicts everything we know about his character. He himself complained about a Qur'anic verse on at least one occasion, saying, 'I did not want it, but God wanted it'. The most that a sceptic can reasonably claim is that the Qur'an expresses Muhammad's unconscious.

This is not the place for a detailed study of the legislative prescriptions of the Qur'an. To Muslims they represent the will of God and not of Muhammad and so do not throw light on his thinking. However, Muhammad's actions were patterned on the Qur'an's requirements, so certain of them need to be examined here. Much in the Medinan suras is concerned with helping and protecting the social groups whose welfare had already so concerned Muhammad in Mecca – women, orphans, slaves, vagrants, the destitute. To provide the means for helping those in need, the Qur'an prescribed regular almsgiving – *zakat* – which developed into a form of income tax, but one that people should be happy to pay because it was to be used exclusively for welfare. One-fifth of war booty was to be used for the same ends.

Slaves were a particular concern. The owning of slaves continued to be permitted, as it was in Christianity, but the Qur'anic rules greatly improved their lot. The starting point was an affirmation that slaves were spiritually the complete equals of free people; indeed, a believing slave was superior to a free unbeliever (Qur'an 2. 221). A procedure was laid down for the freeing of slaves (24. 33): if a slave asked to be freed on completion of a payment in instalments, the owner could not reasonably refuse a contract and was obliged to provide suitable and legal ways for the slave to earn the necessary money. The Qur'an (24. 32) exhorts owners to arrange marriage for worthy slaves, male or female.

Concubinage was an arrangement with a female slave and ceased to be applicable when slavery was abolished. The Qur'an accepted the institution, but sought to prevent its abuse. Over and above the safeguards that applied to slaves in general, a female slave was protected by the injunction that a master was not to have sex with her without her consent, that a concubine who produced children for her master must not be sold, but must be freed if still a slave when her master died, and that a freed slave-woman should be given the option, but not the obligation, of marrying her former master. The later abuse of concubinage to establish large harems guarded by eunuchs was contrary to the spirit of Islam.

An important aspect of the Qur'anic prescriptions on slavery is that they show how completely free of racism Muhammad's Medina was. A large proportion of slaves were of African origin. By providing them with the means to become free, he ensured their integration into the community as equals. Muhammad's childhood nurse, Baraka Umm Ayman, was an African who, by his adopted Arab son Zayd, a fellow freed slave, had borne Usama, whom Muhammad treated as a virtual grandson and whom he put in charge of the last of all his military expeditions. Ibn Saad lists sixteen other people as having been Muhammad's slaves at one time or another, all of whom were given their freedom by him, except one who had died prematurely and one who was still a slave when Muhammad died.

The Qur'anic law of inheritance aims at guaranteeing fair shares for all heirs and at protecting vulnerable categories – women, minors, orphans, especially female orphans. Women had enjoyed no inheritance rights at all in pre-Islamic Arabia; on the contrary, they could themselves be part of an inheritance. Khadija had been fortunate that her husbands had left her their property. Orphaned girls had been particularly open to abuse, often becoming sex-slaves to uncles or cousins.

The aspect of the Qur'an that has attracted most Western criticism is the severe punishments for such things as murder, adultery and theft. These have been much misunderstood. As regards murder, for example, the Qur'an simply seeks to limit and as far as possible eliminate the revenge killing that was the pre-Islamic custom; it places restrictions on the categories of murderers who can be executed for particular categories of victims, and it recommends that the victims' families accept blood money instead of execution.

The punishment of stoning for adultery is not prescribed by the Qur'an, which specifies a hundred lashes (24. 2) for illicit sex – *zina'* (which includes both adultery and fornication). Whereas most societies are much harsher towards women's sexual misdemeanors, the Qur'an has no double standard for men and women. In practice, punishment was rarely administered, the offence being difficult to prove; four witnesses to the act were required – something that was rarely possible – and an accusation brought without them rendered the accuser liable to flogging. A husband could condemn his wife without witnesses by swearing five solemn oaths, but she could establish her innocence by herself swearing five oaths.

For theft, the Qur'an prescribes the cutting off of the hand (5. 38), but there are no reliable accounts of this punishment being inflicted by Muhammad. Reformist Muslims deny that 'cutting off of the hand' was to be understood literally, claiming that it was an idiom for imprisonment, just as *iqta' lisanak*, literally 'cut off your tongue', means 'hold your tongue', 'be quiet'.

The verses that prescribe these punishments are almost all followed by an escape clause, offering the offenders a way out if they repent, and recommending the victims to be merciful; it seems that the threat is more important than the execution. These verses must in any case be seen in the context of the whole Qur'an, which repeatedly emphasizes the virtues of generosity and forgiveness. Every sura except one begins with the Invocation: 'In the Name of God, the Merciful, the Forgiving'. ('Compassionate' is an inaccurate translation, meaning literally 'suffering with'; the idea of a suffering God is peculiar to Christianity).

Muhammad himself made clear what the spirit of Islam was, for he was patient, forgiving and generous. All his life, his behaviour towards people never varied. He accepted all men and women as his equals, listened to all who wished to speak with him, deprived himself to give to the needy, forgave almost all his enemies. However much later Muslim rulers may have deviated from his example, it has remained the living tradition of ordinary Muslims, and countless European visitors have experienced their tolerance and hospitality. Where this tradition has broken down, it has been because Islam has been thrown on the defensive.

In the course of the Medinan period, the Qur'an grew into the book we have today. The written text was still secondary to the recitation but its production was well in hand. Already in Mecca, Muhammad had dictated his revelations to secretaries, and copies were soon circulating, as shown by the story of the conversion of Umar. One of the early secretaries, Abd-Allah ibn Abi Sarh, gave up Islam when, on one occasion, he anticipated the words that were about to be dictated and then claimed that he could reveal the like of that which God had revealed.

Soon after arriving in Medina Muhammad took on a local man, Ubayy ibn Kaab, to continue the work. Ubayy was succeeded by Muhammad's last secretary, a young Medinan, Zayd ibn Thabit. It is reasonable to suppose that Zayd had a complete set of transcripts when Muhammad died, and that these, guarded by Muhammad's widow Hafsa, were the basis for the fair copy made by him at the request of Abu Bakr and Umar, and of the definitive, bound edition commissioned from him by Uthman.

Internal evidence too technical for inclusion here proves that the suras were put into their final form by Muhammad himself, so the only element not fixed in detail by him is their order. This was an extraordinary achievement in a society without a literary culture, and it contrasts with the decades or centuries that passed before other sacred texts were written down. For authenticity, only the letters of St Paul among Christian scriptures bear comparison, and even they – unlike the Qur'an – are full of textual problems.

For easy memorization, Muhammad summed up Islam in 'Five Pillars': Witness (the creed), Worship, Almsgiving, Fasting in Ramadan and Pilgrimage to Mecca. By the end of ten years in Medina, he had fully instituted all of these except the last. This could be put off no longer, so with his wives, many of his companions and a large part of the population of Medina, he set out at the appointed time. News had spread that the Prophet himself was leading the pilgrimage, and pilgrims came from all over Arabia to perform it with him.

Muhammad led this great assembly through the rites, and his every word and action were remembered and became the models for all future generations of pilgrims. On the ninth of the Pilgrimage month, he took up his station on Arafa, the Mount of Mercy, and preached a sermon which culminated in the final Qur'anic word of God (5. 3):

> This day those who disbelieve have despaired at your religion, so do not fear them. This day I have perfected your religion for you, completed My favour upon you and approved for you Islam as religion.

There can be no doubt that this is true: Islam was perfected in the lifetime of Muhammad, who was clearly a Muslim in the sense that we recognize today. A contemporary of his returning now would not find any important unfamiliar element of belief or practice. No other world religion is so firmly based.

Muhammad's private life

Muhammad's life in Medina was that of a public figure constantly in demand, but he protected his private life as best he could. The death of Khadija, his sole female companion for about twenty-five years, left him intensely lonely, for he had grown used to being able to share with her his every hope and fear. He could not hope ever again to find the same depth or strength of union as in his first marriage, but some feminine companionship was desirable both for his personal equilibrium and for the smooth running of his household. The year after Khadija's death, he married Sawda, a widow aged about thirty. She had been one of the first converts to Islam and she and her late husband had been among the Muslim emigrants to Ethiopia.

Before Muhammad left Mecca he became engaged to Aisha, still only a child, daughter of Abu Bakr, but he did not marry her until he was firmly established in Medina. She was his only virgin bride. Although he never admitted that he had a favourite, that is undoubtedly what she was, though even she never displaced Khadija in his affections. After his death she became an invaluable source of information about his inner thoughts.

Umar's daughter Hafsa was widowed by the Battle of Badr. She was reputed to be a difficult woman, and Umar was anxious about her future but, to his great relief, Muhammad himself offered to marry her. She was a fiery-tempered and independent-minded person, and she used to answer back to Muhammad to an extent that shocked her conservative father, but Muhammad accepted it all with good humour.

Soon after this he married a Bedouin woman from his foster mother's tribe, Zaynab bint Khuzayma, who quickly became known for her great generosity to the poor. She died a few months later, to be succeeded by Umm Salama, another veteran of Ethiopia, widow of Muhammad's first cousin Abu Salama, who had died of wounds received at Uhud. Umm Salama brought her young children to liven up the household. She was if anything even more of a feminist than Hafsa, quick to complain if something in the Qur'an seemed to be unfair to women.

Until then, Muhammad had not exceeded the limit of four wives, prescribed by Qur'an 4. 3. In his last six years he added a further five, as specially authorized by Qur'an 33. 50. The first of these was his cousin Zaynab bint Jahsh, who had been unhappily married to Muhammad's adopted son, Zayd. Muhammad refused Zayd's offer to divorce her for his sake, saying: 'Keep your wife and fear God!'. Eventually the couple divorced anyway, by mutual agreement, and the marriage was ordained by Qur'an 33. 37. The special justification for this marriage was said to be that it was necessary in order to show Muslims that adopting a person into a family neither creates parental constraints nor abolishes the ties and responsibilities of biological parenthood.

This marriage marked a wider change in Muhammad's life. From now on his home was no longer open to casual visits; people should come by invitation only, and if they were invited for a meal they should not come before it was due nor stay after it was finished. His wives were to be treated with special respect as 'Mothers of the Faithful', and should never remarry after his death (33. 53). Men from outside the family should speak to them from behind a screen or curtain. His wives were given the option of an honourable divorce if they could not accept these restrictions, but none of them took it up.

The remaining four marriages were with Juwayriya, daughter of the chief of a Bedouin tribe, the Bani Mustaliq; with Safiya, converted Jewish daughter of the infamous Huyay, chief of the Bani Nadir; with Abu Sufyan's daughter, Umm Habiba, whom Muhammad married through the good offices of the Negus when she was widowed in Ethiopia, and with Maymuna, widowed sister-in-law of Muhammad's uncle Abbas.

There was also a Coptic Christian girl, Marya, sent as a gift by the Muqawqis of Egypt, to whom Muhammad had sent an ambassador. At first a concubine, she was given her freedom when she bore him a son, Ibrahim, who died in infancy, but she did not receive the title of Mother of the Faithful, probably because she did not want it. Muhammad had married these women to give them protection and status within his family.

Europeans, long bound by the exacting prescriptions of the virgin son of the virgin mother, have painted a grotesque caricature of this history, as a pretext to indulge either in doubtfully sincere horror or in lascivious fantasy and ribald insults.

As long as Muslims were confidently in the ascendant, they accepted Muhammad's marital history without embarrassment; indeed they were proud of his success in winning the love of so many women. However, in the present century some Muslims have been affected by the Western view even to the extent of denying that his later marriages were ever consummated.

It is absurd to suggest that Muhammad married for the sake of self-indulgence. Combining the roles of Prophet, head of state, lord chief justice, guardian of the treasury and commander-in-chief, he was far too busy to spend his days idling in a harem. He personally led many of the expeditions from Medina, and was often absent for weeks on end. He was also a very abstemious man, fasting every Monday and Thursday. On other days he ate two meals, barley-bread or a little meat if these were available, with the milk of his own goats, but frequently just 'the two black things' – dates and water. As often as not, he and his family gave their food to the poor and went hungry. He was no sensualist.

All the ancient accounts agree that he had no room of his own, except an unfurnished attic over the Mosque, and that he spent his nights in his wives' rooms, staying with each in her turn. Certainly, there was the birth of his son Ibrahim to suggest this. Nevertheless it is remarkable that in the course of ten years living in Medina with nine wives, all of whom were of child-bearing age, there was no further issue. On this evidence Muhammad seems to have been highly abstemious in his conjugal relationships after he had lost his first wife, Khadija, by whom he had four daughters and a son also believed to have died in infancy. There were even no children by marriage to Aisha, universally acknowledged as his favourite in the Medinan period. Muhammad never found the type of rare emotion and intellectual bond he had enjoyed with Khadija. According to his own testimony Khadija remained irreplaceable. After all, if Muhammad was an extraordinary man, Khadija had been an exceptional woman too.

All accounts also agree in finding that Muhammad was a model husband – gentle, generous, considerate and courteous. He managed to keep nine women happy and to defuse the occasional crises of jealousy, and not one of his marriages ended in divorce. Apart from Aisha, who had the satisfaction of feeling convinced of being his favourite, his wives had all chosen as adults to marry him. They saw themselves as privileged people, closer to the Prophet than any man could ever be, and he found in them precious companions, to whom he could talk and on whom he could rely for frank opinions and wise advice.

Women in Islam

The European view of Muhammad's marriages is bound up with a distorted understanding of the position of women in Islam. Muhammad himself never treated women as inferiors. He consulted Khadija and his later wives, and his daughters once they were adult, on all aspects of the Islamic community, and they acted as advisers to the new converts. Women played an active and visible part in society. They engaged alongside men in the public observance of religious rituals and obligations and worshipped together with men in the Mosque. There are records of women going to the Mosque even at night. Women accompanied their husbands, fathers and brothers to battlefields against the enemies of Islam. They took care of the wounded and of the prisoners of war. There is no question but that the first Muslim community under Muhammad's guidance was jointly built by men and women. The Qur'an unequivocally states their complete spiritual equality (33. 35):

> *For Muslim men and women, for believing men and women, for devout men and women, for truthful men and women, for patient men and women, for humble men and women, for charitable men and women, for fasting men and women, for chaste men and women, for men and women who are constantly mindful of God – for these God has prepared forgiveness and a great reward.*

Throughout the centuries fantasies have been created by Europeans about the reward of Paradise as depicted in the Qur'an. In verses 53.41 and 76.3 one reads of Paradise as a place where there are shady and bountiful fruit trees, fountains and streams where believers may drink the water of eternal youth. It is inhabited by chaste youths – boys and girls – beautiful and forever young. The emphasis throughout is on innocence and purity as at the time of the Creation. The denizens of Paradise – virtuous believers who enter it – are both male and female. In Western accounts this Paradise has been distorted into a sensual and licentious place of gratification for men alone. Indeed some have even claimed that Muhammad deliberately invented the vision to lure men into the Faith.

As regards polygamy (more exactly polygyny), some form of it is virtually inevitable, for the simple biological reason that in any society there are normally more adult women than men – an imbalance made all the greater by war. It seems in any case that many a woman would rather share an outstanding man than be single or have a mediocre man to herself. Christian society has in practice combined a degree of involuntary female celibacy with de facto polygamy, in which many of the rich and powerful keep mistresses, who have the situation of co-wives without the legal protection.

Islam accepts the inevitability of polygamy while seeking to avoid its abuse. The Qur'an says (4. 3):

> '. . . *marry women of your choice, two, three or four, but if you fear that you will not deal fairly with them, then only one . . .*'

As few men are capable of being just to more than one wife, the implication is that polygamy should be very much the exception and monogamy the rule. Muhammad's ability to deal fairly with more than four wives was quite extraordinary and was the basis for his gentle dispensation.

The Qur'an does not prescribe inequality in marriage. There is nothing to prevent a woman from specifying in a marriage contract that the husband shall not take a second wife. Nor is a woman obliged to have her marriage arranged by a male relative. Qur'an 33. 50 specifically refers to a believing woman giving herself in marriage, as did the Prophet's wife Maymuna. These possibilities are fully realized in the Hanafi system of Sharia Law.

Unhappy marriages in Islam are easily dissolved, though care for the children is paramount. In later Islam, some legal systems made divorce too easy for men and too difficult for women, but this is not Qur'anic. A divorced or widowed wife is financially provided for as she keeps the dowry that her husband was obliged to pay when he married her (Qur'an 4. 4). The Maliki system of Sharia Law gives the fullest recognition to women's rights in divorce.

The measure that has been taken to be the symbol of women's inferior status is veiling. Special rules applied to the Mothers of the Faithful, to protect them against the intrusions of the curious and of endless petitioners, but for women in general the Qur'an says simply that they should 'draw their head-dresses over their bosoms' (24. 31) or 'pull close to themselves part of their dresses' (33. 59) when in the presence of men from outside their family. This wording is very vague and amounts to little more than a requirement to dress modestly – something that was expected of men as well.

Muhammad in the community

Muhammad was a loving father to his four daughters and had the immense pain of burying three of them as well as his baby sons. Ruqayya was married to Uthman of Abd Shams and migrated to Ethiopia with him. When she died at the time of Badr, her sister Umm Kulthum succeeded her, only to die soon after. Zaynab, though one of the first Muslims, stayed for years in Mecca, loyal to her pagan husband. She had a miscarriage after rough treatment from Meccans while migrating to Medina and died, possibly as a consequence, soon after her husband had become a Muslim and rejoined her. Only Fatima, married to Ali, survived her father but died soon after him, leaving two sons and two daughters. She became Muhammad's close confidante and the object of veneration by later generations of Muslims.

Muhammad had a deep love for children, and there are many stories that illustrate this. In his last years one of his greatest pleasures was playing with his grandchildren. He never shared the widespread Arab preference for sons; nor should any good Muslim, for the Qur'an forbids female infanticide and denounces those who are grieved when a daughter is born (16. 58–9):

When one of them is given news of a girl, his face darkens as he grieves; He hides from the people because of his 'bad' news: 'Should he keep it in spite of shame or bury it in the dust?' How evil is their judgement!

In spite of his shy and serious nature, Muhammad was a man at ease in society. He was an affectionate relative and regularly sent messages and presents even to the pagans among his aunts and uncles and cousins. He never developed the common fault of great men, namely of paying attention only to powerful people, and it was said that he always made the person he was with feel as if he or she was the most important person in the world. Countless men claimed to be his friend. Numerous enemies were won over to become friends, but there is no recorded case of a friend becoming an enemy.

Some of Muhammad's worst enemies benefited from his forgiveness. The ill treatment of Zaynab roused him to such fury that he asked for the men responsible to be burnt alive if caught. Next day he repented of his anger and declared that it was wrong to burn anyone, however wicked, 'as fire is God's way of punishment' (a doctrine that would have spared much suffering in medieval Europe!). In the event, the chief culprit became a Muslim, and Muhammad forgave him.

Muhammad's generosity of spirit did not stop at affection for people; he also had a reputation for love of animals. His camel, Qaswa, was very dear to him, and he tended and sometimes milked his own goats. He loved cats so much that he would do without his cloak rather than disturb one that was sleeping on it. He felt even for the dog – so unclean in Arab tradition – and once set a man to guard a bitch and her pups while his army passed. His respect for life extended to plants, and he forbade his warriors to cut trees. He is said to have planted 300 palm trees himself, after Uhud, to help to pay the ransom for Salman the Persian, who was the slave of one of the Bani Qurayza.

For all his social skills, Muhammad had a lifelong need for solitude to nourish his inner life. From his childhood days as a shepherd until the move to Medina, he had found this in the mountains around Mecca, where his years of prayer and meditation had culminated in the call to prophecy. In Medina it became harder and harder to escape from the ever increasing numbers of people who needed him. It was a considerable distance from the Mosque to the mountains that ringed the oasis, and there is no record of him frequenting them. It was only when on campaign that he could escape into the desert.

Muhammad's only refuge in Medina was the tiny unfurnished attic room over the Mosque. Aisha once asked him what he did alone there; he replied that, like any other man, he mended his shoes and patched his clothes, but these things must have taken second place to private prayer and meditation. Even so, an attic room was a poor substitute for mountains and deserts, with their magnificent skies and miraculously tenacious plants and animals, which figure so frequently in the Qur'an as signs of God. However, by the last years of his life, Muhammad had attained a sense of the divine so intense and constant that it illuminated even the most mundane of activities. Only this can explain the radiance of the impression that he made on all who met him.

Muhammad had face-to-face dealings with thousands of people in the course of his life. Until whole tribes of Bedouin started to convert in the last years, all who adopted Islam spoke to him at least once, to profess their allegiance. Given the admiration, respect and confidence that he inspired in all, it seems extraordinary that he should ever have been maligned.

The death of Muhammad

No mysteries surround the death of Muhammad. Two months after his return from the Farewell Pilgrimage he caught a chill praying all night in the Cemetery of Baqi, where his family and companions in Medina were buried. Returning home he complained of a headache and was soon very ill. He asked his other wives' consent for him to be nursed by Aisha in her room – the first time that he had ever made it clear that she was his favourite – and they agreed. He asked Abu Bakr to take over as imam – leader of the acts of worship.

Muhammad's condition grew rapidly worse, but then he seemed to rally and asked to be helped into the Mosque, where Abu Bakr was leading the dawn worship. The congregation of worshippers was distracted by the sight of him standing before them with his head in a cold compress, and Abu Bakr offered to let him take over, but Muhammad asked him to continue and sat beside him. At the end of the worship, Muhammad spoke loud and clear. According to Ibn Ishaq, he said, 'I have been given authority over you but I am not the best of you. If I do well, help me, and if I do ill, then put me right. Loyalty consists in Truth and treachery in Falsehood. Obey me as long as I obey God and His apostles, and if I disobey God, owe me no obedience. Arise to prayer. God has mercy on you!'[2]

With Muhammad's permission, Abu Bakr went home to the southern edge of the oasis, thinking the invalid was now out of danger. Later that day he was recalled in haste by the news that Muhammad had died in the heat of noon, his head in Aisha's lap. He hurried back and went to pay his respects to the body of his friend. Then he went into the Mosque to find Umar assuring the people that Muhammad was not really dead and that he would soon return. Abu Bakr asked Umar to stop, but he refused. So Abu Bakr started speaking 'If anyone worships Muhammad, Muhammad is dead; if anyone worships God, God is alive, immortal'. Then he quoted a verse from the Qur'an (3. 144):

Muhammad is only a messenger, and the messengers before him have passed away. If he dies or is killed, will you turn on your heels?

When the people heard this, they realized that their Prophet had truly died. It was Monday the 8th of June 632, in the Arabian calendar the 12th of First Rabi, ten Islamic years to the day from Muhammad's arrival at Medina, and the day conventionally taken to be his birthday.

Arrangements were hastily made for mourners to file past the body in Aisha's tiny room, where it lay under a mantle of Yemeni cloth; but soon people's thoughts turned to the urgent business of assuring the future. It was as if an earthquake had hit the oasis, obliterating all the familiar landmarks. All that evening groups were meeting to discuss the situation, and next day the discussions resumed. Abu Bakr and Umar and many of the older Meccan immigrants were meeting in the Mosque, while a small group of the younger ones were closeted with Ali in Fatima's home. Eventually, news reached the Mosque that a large number of the Medinan Muslims were meeting in the barn of the Bani Saida on the other side of the oasis, planning a breakaway leadership.

---

2 Ibn Ishaq, *Sirat Rasul Allah*, translated by A. Guillaume, *The Life of Muhammad*, Oxford 1978, p. 683.

Umar and Abu Bakr, with Umar's close associate Abu Ubayda, hurried to the barn to avert disaster. There was a heated debate. Finally, in exasperation, Abu Bakr invited them to choose between Umar and Abu Ubayda as leader. Umar was horrified at the idea of being above Abu Bakr, and he went down on his knees and swore allegiance to him. Everyone else followed suit, and thus was instituted the office of Caliph, the *khalifa*, 'successor'.

While all this was going on, a small group had shut themselves into Aisha's room to prepare the body for burial. She was absent, staying with another of the widows for comfort. There were Ali and Abbas, two of the sons of Abbas and a freedman of Muhammad's called Shuqran. They washed the body and shrouded it in three garments, then sent for a grave-digger, Abu Ubayda, who dug Meccan-style graves, but they could not find him. So a Medinan-style grave was dug. In the night of Tuesday to Wednesday, these five men with two Medinans buried Muhammad under the floor of Aisha's room. No great man can ever have had a more modest funeral.

Muhammad's legacy

What Muslims made of Islam after their Prophet's death will not be told here, since the concern of this book is with how Westerners have viewed Muhammad himself. Suffice it to say that he left the religion so complete that nothing of substance has had to be added to it. His closest companions created the institution of the Caliphate, and he was succeeded by Abu Bakr, who maintained the unity of Arabia, by Umar, who turned the defence against Ghassan into the conquest of Syria and Iraq, by Uthman, who issued the definitive edition of the Qur'an, and by Ali, who was the victim of a civil war brought about by the assassination of Uthman.

This war left a three-way split that has never been healed, between the majority Sunnis, who accepted a continued Hashimite Caliphate, the minority Shiites, who regarded Ali and a succession of his direct descendants as the only rightful leaders or Imams, and a tiny faction, the Kharijites, who rejected any hereditary leadership. In spite of their differences, these three groupings all profess essentially the same faith, as contained in the Qur'an and in the Five Pillars of Islam.

Later generations of Muslims created the vast body of legal thought that constitutes the Sharia, founded on the Qur'an and on the practice of Muhammad and his Companions, as reported in the Hadith literature and supplemented where necessary by analogical reasoning and the consensus of the community. There are in fact eight major versions of the Sharia – four Sunni, three Shiite and one Kharijite – leaving ample scope for discussion and development, but all derive their authority from Muhammad.

The inward spirituality of Islam developed into Sufism, which inspired a multitude of schools, many of them bridging the divide between Sunnis and Shiites. These too trace their roots back to Muhammad, who is said to have transmitted the inmost secrets of his religious experience to Ali, who in turn passed them on to be made available to every seeker.

3

Muhammad's Quest for Spirituality

> When the Spirit lovingly embraces thee
> In thy presence all images become Spirit.
>
> **Mulana Jalaleddin Rumi, thirteenth-century Persian mystic**

What were the spiritual and moral values for which Muhammad lived, fought and died? What significance, what magic did they contain to captivate generation after generation of Muslims all over the world for fourteen centuries or more, up to the present day? How could God's Message conveyed to mankind through the medium of an Arab Prophet have such resonance, such power, such timeless impact on the minds and lives of millions of believing men and women, Muslims from all walks of life and from all corners of the world, young and old, educated and uneducated, rich and poor? Men and women divided by geography, by race, by language, yet united in their reverence and devotion to Muhammad, his religion and his sacred book, the Qur'an? What were the spiritual qualities of Islam that so profoundly and permanently affected the thinking and the mode of living of such diverse peoples? And above all what was so special, so extraordinary, so unique about Muhammad that he should have been chosen by God as a supreme example of an exalted Humanity to be the vehicle of His Message and to guide man to ideals of happiness and perfection?

To answer these questions we have to establish first and foremost what spirituality means and why there is such need for it amongst all nations and all individuals. The aim of every religion including Islam is to elevate men and women above the limitations and predicament of their biological condition to higher forms of spiritual existence, giving new directions and perspectives to the meaning of earthly life. Men and women have yearned to transcend their own selves, to come closer to the source of creation, to reach a state of harmony and oneness with nature since time immemorial. The transient quality of all earthly creation, including man himself, is a source of deep-seated human anguish, promoting man to seek comfort and a sense of purpose in the spirituality of religions. To be spiritual means to believe in two spheres of consciousness: the visible and the invisible, the finite and the infinite, the human and the divine. The driving force for gaining insight into the inner realities of creation is the same in all religions. What distinguishes one religion from another is the concept, the method and the metaphors used to attain that knowledge and that most earnestly desired peace and contentment within the human soul. 'Those whose hearts are at peace in the remembrance of God', are defined by the Qur'an as having submitted their souls to Him.

In Judaism, Christianity and Islam, the three Abrahamic traditions, the spiritual concept is the same, it is just the methods and metaphors for the spiritualization process that are different. All three base their spirituality on the concept of revelation, on ethical monotheism and the rule of moral law. In Christianity, God revealed Himself through Jesus Christ, the Son of God. In Islam, God's Revelation occurred in the form of the Qur'an or the word of God. The vehicle of the divine Message in Christianity was the Virgin Mary, in Islam the Soul of Prophet Muhammad. Both the Virgin Mary and Muhammad had to be pure and untainted to be the recipient of the divine essence. Just as the Virgin Mary is believed to have been untouched at the time of her encounter with the Angel who announced the future birth of Christ, so too, Muslims believe, was Muhammad untainted by prior contact with reading and writing before the Word of God was revealed to him. This human purity, symbolized by the Virgin Birth in Christianity and by the reception of the Word of God by the unlettered Muhammad became the fountainhead of Christian and Islamic spirituality, respectively.

But why of all men did God choose Muhammad as His Messenger? The answer to this question is central to Islamic spiritual thought. Muhammad began to receive his Qur'anic Revelations at the age of forty. It was then that he was assigned by God to confirm the previous Scriptures and to renew the good tidings that the ancient prophets, Solomon, David, Abraham, Moses and Jesus had brought to mankind. The good tidings were the existence, the wisdom and the plan of a benevolent, omniscient God and creator of all things, whose realms were beyond the manifest world of human experience. There are a whole series of historical records pointing to the reasons why Muslims believe that Muhammad fulfilled all the qualities of character to carry the divine Message to the human race. These records are known as *Sunnah* or 'Traditions', which complement the Qu'ran as its commentary and interpretation. Without the Sunnah it would be difficult to understand the often disconnected and at times vague verses of the Qur'an. The Sunnah is a vast treasury of illustrations of Muhammad's temperament, his comportment, his deeds, his beliefs and his sayings, as remembered by his family, friends and disciples. The Sunnah was recorded by the early Muslim historians and was safeguarded so that following generations could assimilate and emulate Muhammad's exemplary behaviour and his vision of a well-balanced and harmonious life on earth. This was based on the union of man and God in all spheres of human reality. There is practically no aspect of life that the Sunnah does not cover, from the mundane and domestic to the social and political, from the physical and emotional to the intellectual – for every circumstance in a Muslim's day-to-day experience there is a precedent in Muhammad's own life from which inspiration and knowledge can be drawn. This can range from the hygiene of the body to behaviour towards one's wife or husband, from table manners to the mode of facing God in daily prayers. Even the most ordinary circumstance is spiritualized and has a moral and ethical significance in Islamic spirituality beyond the historical and cultural context in which it took place. The Muhammadan code of behaviour based on Muhammad's example seems so real and relevant to Muslims that even today they model their lives on him and teach their children his path to human perfection and happiness.

Spirituality permeates the daily life of every Muslim, from the most powerful to the most humble. Unlike the dualism of Christianity with its basic division between body and soul, spirit and reality, the temporal and the timeless, Islam sees the two as a unity, fused in all aspects of living. Muslims view God as constantly present, always close by, sharing every moment of day and night with them, watching and guiding them through the ups and downs of their lives. This close relationship between man and God is vividly illustrated in the following Qur'anic statement (50. 16):

We created Man. We know the promptings of his Soul and are closer to him than his jugular vein.

Islamic spirituality is conveyed through three channels. The first channel is the Word of God expressed in the Muslim sacred Scripture, the Qur'an. The second channel is Muhammad's humanism, as exemplified in his deeds recorded in the Sunnah. The third is the Soul of Muhammad through which the virtuous Muslim can reach God.

The Qur'an or the infallible Word of God

The Islamic spiritual perspective is timeless and goes back to the act of creation, but its historical manifestation begins with the passing down of the Qur'an in 610 CE. Muslims believe the Qur'an to be the Word of God revealed to Muhammad in the form of a heavenly tablet held before him by the Angel Gabriel while Muhammad was meditating in his mountain cave above the Meccan valley. The Angel urged him to read, recite and memorize the verses. Hence the name *Qur'an* which means 'Recitation'. Except in the opening verses and some few passages in which the Prophet or the Angel engage in a dialogue, the speaker throughout the Qur'an is God Himself. God speaks to Muhammad and through him to mankind in the first person plural which often changes to the first or third person singular in the course of the same verse.

The Qur'an is a storehouse of texts presented in its original version in the sequence in which it was revealed to Muhammad. The Qur'anic chapters are aphorisms on the history of man since creation – moral commandments, tales and parables, observations about the human psyche, statements about the power and greatness of God and His system of rewards and punishments. Muslim scholars argue that the absence of normal ordering and logic to these sequences is part of the divine and transcendent quality of the Qur'an.

The Qur'an preaches above all the oneness and the all-pervasive knowledge of God (2. 255):

> *There is no God but He, the living, the Eternal One. He knows what is before and behind Men. His throne is as vast as the heavens and the Earth. He is the Exalted, the Immense One.*

It also emphasizes divine mercy. God is all-powerful and all-knowing, but also kind and merciful. However, he can be stern in retribution towards those whose actions are detrimental to the harmony of Creation.

The hypocrite, the liar, the greedy, the mean, the licentious, the thief, the killer, the adulterer, the power-hungry, all are enemies of God, who face severe punishment in the life after death. But wonderful rewards await the virtuous, the God-fearing pious Muslim, who lives and acts within the framework of Qur'anic moral precepts.

In the Qur'an God represents justice and fairness. He is the supreme judge of every human movement, dealing and action on earth. The Muslim is incessantly reminded of his moral obligations towards God and towards humanity. Men and women are repeatedly challenged to improve themselves and their conduct through self-criticism and self-denunciation, through piety and generosity, through sincerity and uprightness, through eagerness in building a wholesome and organic human community. The vocation of the Qur'an is to integrate the whole of life, the entire universe and man into a sacred mould, into an eternal moral contract between God and man, making the Muslim the trustee and the servant of God on earth as exemplified by Muhammad himself.

The Qur'an as the sum total of God's Revelations to Muhammad is the foundation of Islam and the source of all Islamic thought. It is from the Qur'an and its commentary, the Sunnah, that the *Sharia*, or 'Divine Law' has been extracted. The Sharia forms the basis for all ethical and moral norms and principles which determine an Islamic society. It is the product of various interpretations of the Qur'anic texts by successive generations of Islamic jurists and theologians in the past centuries. These men sought to lay down, through analogical reasoning and consensus, a standard legal system for all Muslim societies. The Sharia can be revised, re-evaluated and adapted to modern requirements by contemporary Islamic scholars. The source of inspiration, consultation and reinterpretation remains unquestionably and forever the Qur'an itself; it is the infallible divine source from which all knowledge originates.

The Qur'an is the vast world of creation in which the Muslim lives and breathes. It reflects the reality of a Muslim from birth to death. The verses of the Qur'an are whispered into the ears of the Muslim boy or girl the minute they are born. And as soon as they begin to speak they should ideally learn how to memorize and recite the Qur'an. They should be taught how to conduct a life determined by duties towards parents, family, community and God. At school they should further their knowledge of Islam by reading and interpreting the Qur'an and by familiarizing themselves with the facts and realities of Muhammad's life and times. They should study the works of Islamic philosophers, sages and mystics. Later, their marriages are sanctified by the verses of the Qur'an and their obligations towards one another defined in a marital contract inspired by the Qur'anic Law. And no Muslim is buried without the accompaniment of chantings and recitations from the Qur'an to transport his or her body to its eternal abode.

Each Qur'anic chapter is a unique entity if studied properly. It is an impressive epic of poetry and prose, the reading of which can take the believer on a spiritual journey to the source of creation and the purpose of life. It is seen as the history of man's own soul as illustrated in the tale of ancient people and their prophets, their virtues and wrong-doings, their battles and rebellions, their loves and hatreds, their joys and sorrows. To recite the verses of the Qur'an is to become aware of one's own reality, of the opposing and mutually antagonistic forces of good and evil within oneself.

For the Muslim the Qu'ran represents the direct source of divine splendour, of the light of God, the inner beauty of existence, the unveiling of the celestial mystery. It is the source of all knowledge, physical and metaphysical. A characteristic of the Qur'an is its symbolism. Even as human beings are symbols of Creation, so all other phenomena in nature are symbolic too. It is through seeing symbols that the Muslim continues to remember God, the wonders of creation and the power and wisdom of the Creator. The Qur'anic verses are therefore called *Ayat* or 'Signs'. The Muslim is prompted to journey through this vast world of symbolism like a traveller and find analogies in the universe, in human life and in the human soul. These analogies help man to see divine unity in the multiplicity of all things. In fact the soul of a Muslim is said to be like a mosaic made up of Qur'anic formulae. Some of these formulae seem simple at first sight but have profound spiritual meaning. Most fundamental of all Qur'anic formulae is the *Shahada*, or 'Testimony'. It is the testimony of man to the unity of God and the unity of existence: *La ilaha ill Allah, Muhammad Rasul Allah* ('There is no God but God and Muhammad is the Prophet of God'). A man or a woman who testifies to this formula accepts the oneness of God and of divine mercy and recognizes Muhammad as an exalted human being who has been entrusted with the Word of God. The Shahada is therefore both concept and method of Islamic spirituality. It is concept because it symbolizes in its first part 'There is no God but God', the dissolution of the outer world in the inner world of man's soul where, the Spirit of the Creator rests. It is method because in its second part 'And Muhammad is the Prophet of God', it represents the embellished soul of man fused with the divine Spirit.

Closely connected with Shahada is the formula *Bismi 'Llahi 'r-rahmāni 'r-rahīm* ('In the Name of God, the Kind, the Merciful'). Every chapter of the Qur'an opens with this formula which, like the Shahada, is recited by the Muslim not only during prayers but many times a day on a variety of occasions. Bismi 'Llahi is uttered whenever a Muslim begins a task. It is with the Name of God that everything begins, everything is called to life, everything becomes real. The formula is repeated the moment one wakes up in the morning, it is recited before getting washed and dressed, before a meal, before leaving the house, before embarking on a journey, before writing a letter, at the opening of a meeting or a conference, before concluding a contract. Through *Bismi 'Llahi 'r-rahmāni 'r-rahīm*, uttered sincerely and from the heart, this formula allows divine joy and bliss into human life and human purposes and renders human actions acceptable in the eyes of God. It is the beginning of the Qur'an and therefore in a sense the beginning of all Creation and hence should be the starting-point of every human endeavour. The two names *al rahman* and *al rahim*, which follow the main name of God, that is *Allah*, are only two examples of God's numerous names. They are derived from the same Arabic root *rahama*, meaning 'mercy'. Yet, from the spiritual point of view they denote two different dimensions of God's mercy. *Al rahman* is regarded as the transcendental dimension of God's mercy. It is a mercy which envelopes all things. If God had been without this essential quality He would never have created the world. Man would never have been brought into being, darkness would have reigned, light and awareness would have never become manifest. *Al rahim* expresses the immanence of God's Mercy. It is like rays of light shining through man's heart, touching the innermost soul of each individual, generating a sense of relief, well-being and belonging. The two qualities combined symbolize the totality of divine goodness which draws humanity towards itself.

A third and equally important formula which plays a part in everyday speech in the life of a Muslim is *Allahu Akbar* ('God is the Greatest'). It is repeated during the call to prayer proclaimed five times a day from the minarets of mosques throughout the Islamic world. It is a way of asserting God's supreme power and man's weakness and vulnerability. The formula is a reminder that even the mightiest of men is helpless as God's mortal creature. It demonstrates human awe, human reverence towards God and human submission to God's will and to God's all-pervasive power. It nurtures humility and modesty as an essential concept of Islamic spirituality.

The final expression amongst the most common of Qur'anic formulae, frequently used in daily exchanges is *Insha Allah* and *Masha Allah* ('If God wills' and 'what God has willed'). The first points to the future and indicates man's confidence in God's will in the realization of all his hopes and dreams. A Muslim would never say for instance 'I shall see you tomorrow' without adding '*Insha Allah*'. Because he believes that only God knows what will happen between now and tomorrow. How can one be certain to keep a promise, considering the fragile and uncertain nature of human life? How could the person who promises know whether he would still be here tomorrow? '*Insha Allah*' leaves all plans and intentions, be it within the hour or in a distant future ultimately as God's decision. In the eyes of a Muslim nothing can be realized with certainty except with divine support and divine consent. No matter how well we plan an act we do not know whether we will still be alive or fit enough to carry it out. The Muslim therefore plans and acts fully conscious of the dependence of these plans and acts on the will of God, a will that transcends human will. Accordingly, whatever is achieved in this life is seen as a combination of human effort and divine blessing. The formula used at the completion of a plan or a task is *Masha Allah*, expressing man's appreciation and gratitude for God's help and benediction. This and all other Qur'anic formulae are tightly knit into the texture of Muslim daily experience and are means of constant communication with God.

The language of the Qur'an is Arabic. It is the language in which God's Word was articulated to Muhammad. It symbolizes the truth of Muhammad's religion. In Christianity, divine truth is represented by Christ himself, not by the Gospels. Greek and Latin were traditionally used as languages of the Church and were never associated with a divine source. In contrast, the Qur'an is revered as transmitted directly from God to man through Muhammad. In it the Muslim encounters the presence of God Himself who is the immediate speaker and communicator of his own message. For this reason the rites, prayers, chantings and recitations of the Qur'an must be conducted in Arabic and in no other language. The Islamic world is of course not all Arabic-speaking because of the vast empire that Islam once possessed. A Turk may philosophize about the Qur'an or Islam in Turkish, or a Persian mystic may write lyrical verses in Persian inspired by the Qur'an, but when it comes to performing prayers or reading the sacred Scripture, they all turn to Arabic as the only medium through which to reach God. This does not mean that their own native languages have remained untouched by the linguistic or spiritual influence of the Qur'an. On the contrary, the Qur'anic language has had an immense impact, both lexically and in its symbolism, on all languages of the Near and the Middle East. The formula *Insha Allah*, for instance, has never been translated into any other language and is used in its original Arabic version throughout the Muslim region.

The Qur'an is meant to be recited aloud so that everyone can hear it and be moved and stirred by it. The Qur'anic language is indeed a rich, powerful and sonorous medium of speech. It is likened to the sound of mighty oceanic waves pounding over the rocks of the earth, overwhelming and washing clean the soul of man. To the Muslim ear it is the sound of creation itself.

Muhammad's humanism

In several verses of the Qur'an there is reference to Muhammad as a human being and not as God Incarnate in the manner that Jesus is perceived by Christians. Yet, although Muhammad is not of divine essence, he is regarded as the most noble, most refined, and most polished of all human beings – a man of supreme human qualities. The Muslim sees him as an individual who participated in all dimensions of human reality with faith, courage, self-criticism, modesty and an immense sense of justice providing a model for everyone to emulate. Like the rest of humanity, he savoured life in its absolute totality and in its sweet and bitter extremes; its joys and sufferings, its failures and successes, its heights and depths, its fears and hopes. As a child he was orphaned early. At the age of thirteen he had to earn his own living. He became a merchant's apprentice. He experienced poverty and, later, wealth by marrying Khadija. He also tasted the happiness of marriage, but also the loss of his wife and children. He went through the tribulations of persecution by his own people. He was forced to engage in wars that were waged on him to save Islam. In the latter part of his life he became a statesman, a ruler, a legislator and a spiritual leader. But in all these vicissitudes and throughout his vast range of experience he displayed one overriding characteristic – namely unceasing piety and humility.

Humility therefore occupies a central position in Islamic spirituality. It embodies the awareness by man of his own meaninglessness and irrelevance in relation to the omnipotence of God. It is considered to be the first fundamental quality of enlightened humanity. Every Muslim man and woman should set humility as his or her main goal in life. It is believed that one is closer to God and to one's own nature and individuality when in a state of humility. Muslims see in humility a closeness to the origins of life and a means of attaining knowledge about the inner truth of all things. The following Qur'anic passage is one of a whole multitude of exhortations emphasizing the importance of humility. Here the old Muslim sage Luqman is admonishing his son to be virtuous and humble (31. 16–20):

> *My son, Allah will bring all things to light, be they as small as a grain of mustard seed, be they hidden inside a rock or in Heaven or Earth. Allah is Wise and All-Knowing.*

> *My son, be steadfast in prayer, enjoin justice, and forbid evil. Endure with fortitude whatever befalls you.*
> *Do not treat men with scorn, nor walk proudly on the Earth: Rather let your gait be modest and your voice low.*

> *Do you not see how Allah has subjected to you all that Heaven and Earth contain and has lavished on you both His visible and unseen favours?*

Humility encourages a sense of non-attachment to the material world and to worldly goods, Muhammad remained detached from material possessions throughout his life. He viewed possessions as robbing man of his true human identity and diverting him from his real task on earth. Possessions promote greed, and greed alienates God from man and man from God. He saw human perfection in self-denial, in charity and in modest living. Simplicity – in lifestyle, in appearance, in eating, in speech, in interpersonal relationships, in running the affairs of the state – was the hallmark of Muhammad's view of the world. It is through modesty and simplicity that man gradually becomes imbued with the fullness and profound meaning of life.

In Islam humility is not only expressed towards God, as symbolized in the many prostrations during daily prayers, but is tightly woven into the fabric of Islamic culture and society.

Humility was only one of Muhammad's virtues and ideals. Indeed each of his character traits is a spiritual model for the Muslim believer. According to traditional sources, Muhammad was kind and generous. His immediate declaration of amnesty upon his return from exile to his native Mecca as the leader of the Muslim community is often referred to as a telling example of his forgiving nature. Instead of taking revenge on his sworn enemies who had put him through the horrors of persecution, war, suffering and the loss of his loved ones, he forgave them and granted them protection and a peaceful existence. Ancient records also show that he was caring towards the poor, the needy, the ill, the orphaned, the enslaved and the widowed. They are also a testimony to Muhammad's egalitarian attitudes. Although he was of noble descent, he rejected superiority of man over man, man over woman, master over slave, or any race over another. He viewed all human beings as equal and of the same essence. Muhammad was courteous, graceful and hospitable. He was hard-working and self-disciplined. He was a good father, good husband, good friend, good relative. He was loved, admired and respected by anyone who came into contact with him. But above all he was patient and serene. None of the hardships of life had diminished his faith in the goodness of nature and the triumph of Good over Evil.

The Soul of Muhammad

Muhammad was a seeker of truth, realizing that he could not reach the inner meaning of life and grasp the relationship between man and universe, until he himself had penetrated into deeper levels of his consciousness. It was through profound spiritual longing, through years of prayer and meditation, through relentless contemplation and questioning that he had succeeded in removing the barriers between man and God and in arriving at insight and illumination. During what is known as the Night of Power God revealed Himself to Muhammad, fulfilling his greatest desire in life. Henceforth Muhammad became the universal prototype of God's love, God's blessing and God's medium of communication with mankind. Muhammad praised God for His splendour and in return received the praise of God for his humility and piety as the Servant of God – a quality which had brought him closest to the divine essence. Muhammad's Soul had not only reached the eternal, but had been dissolved into it. Through the beauty of Muhammad's Soul the Creator and the created became one inseparable unity. In mystical terms Muhammad's Soul was transformed into a mirror in which God contemplated His own work and in which lay the purpose of creation.

According to Muhammad's example the key to the unity of existence, the fusion of the temporal and timeless, the manifest and the hidden is seated deep within each individual. It is the task of the individual to search for this key within him- or herself. Muhammad had displayed how the human form was the place where two realities gather, the inner and the outer, the eternal and the temporal. He had provided a spiritual model for the fusion of these two seemingly separate entities, as his relationship to divine truth had been both immanent and transcendent, direct and indirect. Direct through prayer, meditation and concentration and indirect through living a full but virtuous life like all other men, sharing with the rest of humanity all aspects of earthly existence.

Hence, the human soul was both imperfect and perfect. So was the human body. Even the body could become perfect when its ties with the material world of multiplicity were dissolved. By purifying itself of lust and evil passions, of whatever was alien to the divine essence, it won back the Paradise that it had lost after Creation. Indeed man was made up of body, soul and spirit. The spirit was the core, the centre, the pulse and the source of creation which lay inside man's heart. The soul was man's brain and the agent of the heart. And the body was the shell that encapsulated the spirit and the soul. The degree of man's spirituality, his devotion to God and his perfection lay in the relationship between these three substances. To understand this one has to imagine a circle with its centre, diameter and circumference. In a pious, virtuous and devout servant of God the spirit is always at the centre of the circle, the soul is the diameter and the body the circumference. This is the condition of the inner man or inner woman in whom the transformation has been achieved and wisdom has been attained. In the non-spiritual man these relationships are reversed. The body forms the centre. The soul becomes the agent of the body and the spirit is thrust outside as the circumference. The path to perfection normally follows three stages – a pre-awareness stage in which the soul knows of God's existence, but is passive. A second stage is attained when the soul becomes active through its yearning for God and begins to internalize the outside world within the inner space of spiritual contemplation. At the third and highest stage the soul dissolves into the spirit and purges the body of all its impurities and worldly attachments. In this way God's presence becomes internalized and man's centre becomes divine and so the unity of spirit and being is achieved in the living individual. There is therefore no need for intercession or mediation between the individual believer and God. This potential oneness of man and God lies within reach of every Muslim who seeks to attain the highest levels of perfection manifested by Muhammad as the universal prototype.

The process in which man's soul becomes aware of the divine spirit within is called Awakening. The soul wakes to the truth of God and begins to yearn for a return to its own roots and origins, to the source of creation, where peace and unity exist. The method for approaching the centre of man's innermost being or the profoundest depths of his heart is silence, concentration, meditation and relentless invocation of God's numerous Qur'anic names of praise. This extraordinary spiritual experience is beautifully described in a tale by the thirteenth-century Persian mystic, Mulana Jalaleddin Rumi:

> One night a man was crying 'Allah'
> Till his lips grew sweet with praising Him.
> Satan said: 'O man of many words,
> Where is God's response
> To all your cries of "Allah"
> How long will you say "Allah" with your grim face?'

> The man was broken-hearted and lay down to sleep:
> In a dream he saw Khadir [an ancient mystic]
> Amidst the greenery,
> He said: 'Listen, you have ceased praising God,
> Why do you repent of calling unto Him?'
> The man replied: 'No "I am Here" comes to me in response:
> I fear that I am turned away from the Door'.

> Khadir declared: 'No, God has said: Your cry "Allah"
> Is My "I am Here",

And all your yearning, your grief and ardour,
Are My Message to you'.

Your fear and love are the thread to draw My Favour,
Beneath your every cry of "Allah."
Is many an "I am Here" from Me.'[1]

Indeed, 'thread' is a metaphor frequently used by Islamic mystics to illustrate how man's soul can pull the body from its worldly preoccupations towards divine truth. This function of the soul is well expressed by Rumi in the following poem:

Divine Wisdom created the world
So that all things
In God's knowledge should be revealed.
How can the Real, which is the Body, be at rest,
When the thread, which is the Soul, is tugging at it?[2]

Thus the present and the beyond coexist, as do Life and Death. And Islamic mysticism goes one stage further to say that death is present in every being all the time. Muhammad had said, 'I had already died before I was born'. Hence the belief that as you breathe in, you are reborn, but as you breathe out you are dying. Breathing is considered as a symbol of the transience of human existence. 'This world is but a passing moment', was a favourite phrase used frequently by Muhammad. Accordingly, for the Muslim the world is but a flash of divine illumination, revealing the unity as the multiplicity and the multiplicity as the unity, the one as the many, the many as the one, the hidden as the manifest. So, Death lies in Life and Life in Death. For the devout Muslim who reaches the hard-won state of serenity and humility amidst the turmoil of earthly existence, there is also the prospect of ultimate joy in the Hereafter, where he or she will be rewarded with the Qur'anic promise of reunification with the Source of Creation.

The Soul of Muhammad as the universal prototype for mankind inspired many schools of mystic thought. Sufism was the most popular of these, dating from at least the ninth century CE. The influence of such

---

1   A. Reynold Nicholson, *Rumi – Poet and Mystic* (Selections from his writings), translated by R. A. Nicholson, Washington D.C. 1950, p. 91
2   Ibid., p. 111.

thinking is evident in Islamic art, Islamic poetry, Islamic architecture, and above all Islamic calligraphy. Just as the reproduction of images of man are seen as hubris by Islam, calligraphy represents God's Word in the Qur'an and its use is encouraged. Verses of the Qur'an are skilfully reproduced in the mosaics of mosques, on book covers, in rugs, in miniature paintings. One of the most common motifs accompanying calligraphy is the cypress tree. The cypress symbolizes the good Muslim, tall and proud but bowing in the wind as if to God. It reflects one of Muhammad's most famous sayings, 'Humility is my Pride'.

It is difficult, then, to imagine a more different and contrary picture of Muhammad, his qualities, his vision and his spirituality than that which was to evolve in Christian Europe. For the Muslim, Muhammad, the man, Muhammad, the Prophet and the Qur'an are the guiding lights leading to a life on earth shared with God. The Christians of medieval Europe were confronted with a phenomenon that they could neither understand, nor wished to understand. With the exception of those mystical Christians who readily embraced the concept of the fusion of the temporal and the external, for mainstream Christians the duality of life and the hereafter, which are central to orthodox Christian dogma and values, obstructed any serious insight into the religious and spiritual realities of Islam and of its Prophet Muhammad. Indeed, in their eyes the coming of Jesus had rendered anyone subsequently claiming to be a prophet an impostor. The man, who for the Muslims was and is the model and prototype of goodness, was to be cast by European writers and priests into the image of the anti-Christ, into Satan. But not only was this distortion the consequence of perceiving the world through vastly different eyes, it was also a distortion that sprang from fear, the fear of a power that might conquer Europe and with it extinguish Christianity.

4

Muhammad as Mahound

Medieval Europe and the fear of Islam

When we took Alexandria he was there.
He often sat at table in the Chair
Of honour, above all nations, when in Prussia.
In Lithuania he had ridden, and Russia,
No Christian man so often, of his rank.

When in Granada, Algeciras sank
Under assault, he had been there, and in
North Africa, raiding Benamarin;
In Anatolia he had been as well
And fought when Ayas and Attalia fell,
For all along the Mediterranean Coast
He had embarked with many a noble host.
In fifteen mortal battles he had been
And jousted for our faith at Tramissene
Thrice in the lists, and always killed his man
This same distinguished knight had led the van.

Geoffrey Chaucer, Prologue to *Canterbury Tales*. 1478

Muhammad's image in medieval Europe was determined by two distinct factors – a profound revival of Christianity thanks to the Barbarian founders of the Carolingian and the Holy Roman Empires and the fear of the spread of Islam. As Europe began to move into a position of Old World Supremacy it came to identify itself more and more with its Christianity. The negative image of a menacing rival religion assisted this process of self-definition. The demonization of a prophet who claimed to be the successor to Jesus but who rejected the Christian dogma of the Trinity and the crucifixion – and whose followers were conquering one Christian land after another – was to become the very instrument of the making of Christian Europe. Psychologically and physically Islam was regarded as Christianity's worst enemy, threatening Christian identity and its very sense of superiority. The Crusades, which extended from 1095 to 1270, were only one expression of this great Christian resurgence.

To understand how Muhammad came to be cast as the 'Devil Incarnate' and the 'Anti-Christ', we must focus on the crucial historical background of the time: the scene in Europe, the Middle East and the Mediterranean between the fifth and the fifteenth centuries was marked by successive invasions of alien tribes who brought with them unceasing turmoil. In Europe it was the Barbarian invaders of the north who shattered the unity of the Roman Empire and caused its gradual decline. In the Middle East and the Mediterranean it was the Arabs of the Arab Peninsula, the Turks and the Mongols of the steppes of central Asia who transformed what remained of the Roman Empire in the east, namely the Christian Byzantine Empire.

The great Western Empire that had held sway at the dawn of the sixth century remained no more than a memory. In its place were a group of Barbarian kingdoms whose boundaries were unresolved and who were anxious to confirm their identity and allegiance to the Christian faith which they had adopted. The Ostrogoth ruler Theodoric dominated Italy and parts of Germany, the Vandals and Sueves ruled in northern Africa, Sardinia and Sicily, the Visigoths in Spain, Clovis and his Franks were in the process of conquering Gaul, and the Angles, Saxons and Jutes were beginning to settle in Britain, driving the Celts to the fringes of the Isles. 'Barbarian' was a name given to these Nordic invaders of Europe by the Romans and the Greeks. The name originally meant 'stammerer', a man outside the Greek culture. But although the Barbarian tribes had brought their own heathen traditions, ways of life and skills, they had in the main renounced the old pagan religions by embracing Christianity and becoming romanized. Ironically, it was through their efforts that a Christian culture based on a distinct Western European civilization began to emerge. In fact, they themselves became the most zealous defenders of Christian supremacy not only over paganism but over Judaism and Islam too. The man who laid the foundation of Western Christian civilization and initially restored the unity which had been lost through the Barbarian invasions was, Charlemagne, King of the Franks. He became the first Emperor of the West since the collapse of Rome in 476 CE. In 800, crowned by the Pope, he re-established what passed for the Roman tradition in the form of the Carolingian Empire, with Christianity as its religion and Latin as its language. Though the Christian territories of

Charlemagne, divided upon his death in 814 among his three sons, ultimately disintegrated, the idea of a Latin Christian Empire at the heart of Western Europe lived on. It was revived in 962 when the Saxon King Otto I was crowned Emperor by Pope John XII and the Holy Roman Empire was created.

One of Europe's most bloody, long and disastrous military and religious adventures, the Crusades, was masterminded and put into action by the Holy Roman Empire of Western Europe. They were designed to suppress the expansion of Islam into the eastern Christian lands of the long surviving Byzantine Empire. In this eastern sector Christianity continued to develop in the Greek Orthodox, Syrian Nestorian and Egyptian Coptic Churches. Indeed, as a result of the conquests by the orthodox Emperor Justinian of Africa, Italy and Spain (Italy having been reconquered from the Ostrogoths), the Byzantine Empire stretched from the Black Sea westwards and by the sixth century covered vast areas of the Middle East, the Mediterranean and Adriatic coasts, the Balkans, the whole of Italy, Sardinia, Corsica, Sicily, northern Africa and southern Spain. The nucleus of the Byzantine Empire was Constantinople founded by the Roman Emperor Constantine in 330 CE on the site of the ancient city of Byzantium, on the Bosphorus, modern-day Istanbul. Constantine had announced his conversion to the Christian faith in 312 CE and before the end of the fourth century Christianity, hitherto persecuted, had become the sole state religion of the empire. Constantine had attempted to unify the vast and heterogeneous east and make it subservient to the Church of Rome. But huge cultural differences divided the two Churches from the outset. For centuries to come innumerable conflicts and schisms were to blur their relationship. And finally, in 1054, the Church of Constantinople broke away from the Church of Rome, considering itself to be the custodian of the true orthodox faith of a Christian classical culture. As a consequence Greek remained the language of the Eastern Empire as opposed to Latin, which was the official language in Rome and the lingua franca of the rest of Europe.

From the seventh century onwards the Byzantine Empire became the object of invasions by the Arabs, the Turks and the Mongols and finally fell in 1453 when Constantinople was conquered by Ottoman Turks. In the early seventh century when Islam emerged in Arabia, both the Byzantine and its rival the Persian Empire had been in a state of gradual decline. The cost of keeping vast territorial possessions, together with wars of rivalry against each other, had finally exhausted their resources. At the time of Muhammad's death in 632 CE there was a tide of rising feeling amongst the population of both these empires. The Eastern Christians living in Byzantine territories disliked Hellenism and the Greeks who ruled them. They were also alienated from the Church of Rome which refused to recognize their version of Christianity which had evolved as a result of contact with Eastern cultures and religions. In Persia there was dissent due to the oppressive and decadent rule of the Persian kings who lived extravagantly and had scant regard for ordinary people. Moreover, the ancient faith of the Persians, Zoroastrianism, had degenerated into a feudal and exclusive religion of the court.

While the two great empires, the Byzantine and the Persian, were crumbling, the situation in neighbouring Arabia, which had been spared from falling under their sway, was quite the opposite. There, thanks to the new religion that Muhammad had given his people and to his vision and leadership, a unified and strong community had evolved. It was a community whose members were not only at peace with each other but exhilarated and euphoric about their victories over their pagan enemies within Arabia. They thought of themselves as invincible through the political and religious legacy that Muhammad had left them. It was the stimulus of a democratic and egalitarian faith which gave them the unified army and the unified command needed for external expansion, strengths unknown to the decadent Byzantine and Persian Empires. Islam had declared that all human beings were equal in the eyes of God, regardless of their social background, sex or appearance. Only through piety and service to God and community could the believers distinguish themselves. The Arab invasions of the Byzantine and Persian territories were therefore as much spiritual as material in essence and met with relatively little resistance from the populations of the two empires.

The Arabs' way into the Christian lands of Byzantium was facilitated by the readiness of the Christian population to accept the rule of Islam because of the religious liberty the Muslims accorded to Christians, upon the payment of taxes. In all Christian territories the Church survived – except in northern Africa where the Berbers had always resisted Christianity. Heretical Christians, Jews and others who had been persecuted by the Byzantines actually had their freedom restored by the Arab rulers.

The Arab conquest started only a year after Muhammad's death in 632 CE with an attack on Byzantine Syria. This was the opening to a whole series of conquests which set the scene for the rapid spread of Islam and as Islam grew stronger, the centre of the Arab-Islamic Empire moved from Mecca in the heart of Arabia first to Damascus in Syria and later to Baghdad, present-day Iraq. Between 622 and 1258 this empire stretched from Spain to North Africa, from the Red Sea to the Caspian Sea and from Turkistan to the coast of Oman.

The multinational state that the Arabs created endured for five centuries, being gradually undermined by successive invasions by Turks from the eleventh century and Mongols from the thirteenth century onwards. Both the Turks and the Mongols penetrated into Arab and remaining Byzantine territories, establishing their own dominion as a third and fourth political and military force in the region. Just as the Franks had been assimilated into Roman Christian culture and had become the very proponents of Christendom, so the Turks and Mongols embraced the religion of their conquered lands, taking over Muhammad's legacy from the Arabs and asserting the rule of Islam. The Church of Rome had tried to reach a compromise with them and convert them to Christianity, seeing them as the best vehicle for destroying the Arabs and their Islamic Empire, but had failed in its attempts. The Arab state crumbled gradually with the fall of Baghdad in 1055 and with the Arab Caliphs increasingly becoming mere puppets of their Turkish or Mongol masters and reduced to ruling Egypt and Spain alone. In Spain it was the Christian Reconquista movement which weakened Arab rule and in 1492 they were driven out of their last stronghold, Granada, leaving Spain to be rechristianized.

The holy city of Jerusalem, regarded as the centre of the universe not only by Christians, but also by Jews and Muslims, had been under Byzantine rule until the Arabs conquered it in 638 CE. Its holiness was focused on the Temple Mount, centred on a huge bare rock. For Jews, Christians and Muslims this is the foundation stone where Heaven and Earth meet. It is the rock on which Abraham is said to have been ready to sacrifice his son (Ishmael, according to the Qur'an, Ishmael's brother Isaac according to the Hebrew and Christian scriptures). It is the rock from which Muhammad is believed to have made his night journey to Heaven during one of his visions of Angel Gabriel.

In the year 1095 Pope Urban II had been approached by the Byzantine Emperor to help him repel the Muslims from Jerusalem and the remaining Christian territories of the Eastern Empire. The Pope, desirous of being the saviour of the Eastern Church, had announced that the end of the world was at hand and that it was up to the Christians to liberate their holy places. He urged pious believers to take up the Cross and to march to Jerusalem to free the Church of God. He declared that the journey could be a substitute for all the penance needed to absolve them of their sins. The response to the Pope's appeal was colossal. Crusaders from all parts of Europe flocked to take up the Cross and to embark on their deadly mission. The hordes of crusading pilgrims who invaded Anatolia and Palestine were primarily French, but there were German, English and Italian warriors amongst them too. It was an armed pilgrim force of great magnitude, including kings, priests, bishops, knights and commoners. In July 1099 they reached their goal after four years of marches and battles, having lost four out of every five men who had left Europe. On their arrival in Jerusalem they massacred not only thousands of Muslims, Arabs and Turks, but also Jews and their own fellow Christians. The latter were slain for their disobedience to the Church of Rome and their acceptance of Islamic domination. In reality, Christian and Jewish communities in the East had prospered under the Islamic law. They had been allowed freedom of worship, had been treated with tolerance and had found their taxes far lower than in the days of Byzantine rule. They had not appealed for help to the Pope. Far from it.

Almost literally the Crusaders waded up to their ankles in the blood of the infidel and the heretic, then proceeded to the Church of the Holy Sepulchre, singing in jubilation that Christ had conquered. His followers had returned to the city where he had been crucified. Before leaving, they stripped the church of all its treasures and valuable ornaments, as their self-assigned reward. The Byzantine Emperor had not expected such extreme and shocking brutality to be displayed by Christian knights and clergy. But he appeared to have had no choice but to go along with his Western liberators and watch in silence as they embarked in joyous confidence on their lethal expedition into Palestine and Syria. There, the divergence in aims among the knights became apparent. A fierce quarrel was triggered between them as to who should have a kingdom in Antioch, Edessa, Tripoli and other provinces of the Holy Land. But once the dispute was over and they had all received their share, the Latin kingdoms which they had created began to operate as a unit and as an extension of Europe. Now, pilgrims once more flocked freely to the East and with them came clergy, knights and traders, creating increased contacts between Europeans, Greeks, Arabs and Turks. Christian Europe had begun its first great expansion across the seas. Indeed the Crusades and the encounter with the world of Islam were the source of Europe's turning outward during the later Middle Ages. Born of a holy cause and fought by consecrated warriors, the Crusaders helped to create the distinction between faithful Christians and their infidel adversaries, the Muslims. This distinction was to have immense consequences for the subsequent development of Christianity and its unrelentingly hostile attitude towards Islam.

The Crusaders' state which was set up during the First Crusade was to last one hundred years. In its first phase, this state included, apart from Jerusalem, Kerak, Bethlehem, Gaza, Haifa, Acre, Montford, Tyre, Sidon, Tripoli, Tortosa, Antioch, Cilicia and Edessa. During most of the Second Crusade in 1148 the Mesopotamian warrior Saladin reconquered most of these places and became the Muslim ruler of Jerusalem. The news of his success stunned the Christian West, and three rulers – the kings of France, England and the Holy Roman Emperor – vowed to recapture the city. None succeeded, however. Richard the Lion-Heart of England came closest, and although he even suggested marrying his sister to Saladin's brother and giving the pair Jerusalem as dowry, neither his friendship nor his battles had much practical result with the Arab hero.

The Third, Fourth and Fifth Crusades were complete failures and the Crusaders never reached the Holy Land. The Sixth Crusade, led by the Emperor Frederick II in 1228, was a mockery too; Frederick went through the motion of taking Jerusalem, but established a truce with the Arabs that allowed them to resume their control. The Seventh Crusade led by Saint Louis, King of France, was even less successful; the Crusaders never came closer to the Holy Land than Egypt. When Louis decided to embark on yet another crusade, he diverted it to Tunis, ostensibly to impose Christianity on that land. By 1291 the last crusader fortress, Acre, had fallen to the Muslims and the reconquest of Jerusalem had dwindled to a long-lasting dream.

It was precisely during these centuries of bloodshed and great upheaval that Muhammad's fictitious image was moulded and became predominant in Europe.

In the learned circles of the European Middle Ages between 800 and 1400 CE a remarkable amount of information about the life of Muhammad had become known and available. Knowledge about Muhammad, while originating from genuine early Muslim sources, had been transmitted in forms that were both vague and fragmented. What was lacking in clarity was soon augmented by legend and fable. Sometimes true incidents in the life of Muhammad were changed and interwoven with fictional elements in such a way that they became divested of all historical value. On other occasions Christian scholars created their own legendary material, which was pure fabrication and had no historical foundation whatsoever. These fictive and often scornful manipulations were then recorded in monastic chronicles, polemics and dissertations and passed on from one generation to another.

Although original sources were available to medieval Latin scholars through translated excerpts from the Qur'an and Islamic biographical texts, the Bible remained the only effective intellectual reference for construing world history. These scholars interpreted the events of their time according to the clues that the Bible provided. They interpreted the rule of Islam for example as the final appearance of the Anti-Christ and they found in the Bible the evidence they needed. The Book of Daniel presented them with the apocalyptic view of what they believed was Islam:

> The fourth beast shall be the fourth kingdom upon earth, which shall be different from all kingdoms, and shall devour the whole earth and shall tread it down and break it into pieces. And the ten horns of the kingdom are the ten kings that shall arise. And another shall arise after them and he shall be different from the first, and he shall subdue three kings. And he shall speak great words against the Most High and shall wear out saints of the Most High, and think to change times and laws, and they shall be given into his hand until a time and times and the dividing of time. Daniel 7: 23–5.

In traditional medieval thought the fourth beast was the Roman Empire which followed the empires of the Assyrians, the Persians and the Greeks. The ten horns of the kingdom were the Barbarian invaders of Europe and after them came Muhammad's followers with their vast empire triumphing over the Greeks, the Franks and the Goths. They were different from the rest and changed times and laws.

The human qualities of Muhammad, which are essential to Islamic doctrine, constituted for the medieval Christian mind the conclusive argument against his prophethood. Because Muhammad was unable to work wonders he was deemed a hypocrite and an impostor, a liar on a grand scale. His claims to divine revelations were made to legitimize his own power and personal privilege, cloaking them in a religious and spiritual guise. His inspired pronouncements were regarded as delusions of a pathological nature – the term epileptic was particularly favoured. Hence, Muhammad the impostor, driven by ambition and eagerness for power, conjures up a divine mission for prophethood and proclaims a religion which is false. This view of Muhammad as the impostor gradually established itself in medieval Europe and set the cliché for centuries to come.

Islam was not merely a military threat to Christian Europe. It challenged Europeans in cultural and intellectual spheres too. Culturally northern Europe could not compete with the gracious living of the Arab conquerors of Spain and Italy. For the greater part of the Middle Ages and over most of its territories, the Christian north formed a society that was primarily agrarian, feudal, and monastic, while the strength of Islam lay in its great cities, wealthy courts, and far-flung lines of communication. Differences in lifestyle were staggering. The Arabs had introduced new types of fruit and vegetables and luxurious food and clothing to Spain and Sicily. They had cultivated poetry and music, both instrumental and vocal and they had built magnificent mosques and monuments which demonstrated high craftsmanship. Yet, compared to northern and western ideals of ecclesiastical hierarchy and sacerdotal celibacy, Islam appeared indulgent, worldly and principally egalitarian, enjoying a remarkable freedom of speculation, with no priesthood or monasteries to underpin its society. Islam had achieved power, wealth and maturity almost at one bound and had been able to retain its initial vitality in all spheres of human experience, for which there was no equivalent in medieval Europe.

In the intellectual arena there was still more reason for Europeans to feel threatened. The Islamic world was far ahead of the Christian West in medicine, mathematics and in some aspects of physics such as optics, in astronomy, chemistry, botany and other natural sciences. With the adoption of the Indian zero, the Arabs had greatly simplified arithmetical exercises and had developed new disciplines in mathematics such as algebra, analytical geometry and spherical trigonometry. Until 1600 the chief medical textbook in Europe was the *Canon of Medicine* of Avicenna, an eleventh-century Persian scientist and philosopher whose homeland had become part of the rapidly expanding Islamic Empire. The Arabs established colleges of translation in Spain and Sicily which made the wealth of knowledge in Greek, Syriac, Persian and Sanskrit writings, available in Arabic. They were in turn translated into Latin. Great halls of science with libraries and astronomical laboratories were created alongside the translation colleges to promote research. Spain and Sicily thus became two major centres for intellectual and scientific exchange between East and West, contributing significantly to the emergence of European Humanism and the Renaissance.

But how could these Bedouin men of the desert, whose civilization had begun in tribalism, achieve such high levels of sophistication and knowledge in such a short time? The answer is simple. The freshness of the new religion had enabled the Arabs to extend their faith beyond the boundaries of the Arabian peninsula into the highly civilized world of the Persians, the Greeks and the Byzantines. They had inherited the dazzling riches of Persian and Greek philosophies and had been remarkably apt in imitating the courtly manners, habits and traditions of the Persian nobility, aspects of which they introduced to southern Europe. The Europeans thus became more and more convinced of the superiority of Muslim culture, which made them envious and resentful. Consequently, Muhammad as the initiator and inspirer of this ever-growing success began to haunt them in all walks of life.

The early medieval writers knew that Muhammad had flourished at the beginning of the seventh century in Arabia when Heraclius ruled the Byzantine Empire. They knew that Muhammad's native town was Mecca, that he had grown up as an orphan with foster-parents, that his clan was not the ruling clan in Mecca, and that later he was active in the caravan trade which took him on long journeys across the desert to Christian Syria. They also knew that he had met his wealthy wife Khadija, who had employed him as her caravan leader. It was also known to Latin scholars that during such journeys Muhammad had come into contact with '*homines religiosi*' who had transmitted to the prophet-to-be notions of the monotheistic religions. Muhammad's encounter with the Christian monk Bahira was for instance equally recorded by medieval churchmen and considered as providing themes from the Old and the

New Testaments that reappear in Muhammad's Qur'anic revelations. Muhammad's relatively late call to prophethood was also a well-known fact in scholarly circles; they knew that he had experienced his revelations under immense physical and psychological pressure and that he had perceived the Angel Gabriel as the conveyor of divine messages to him. It was also known that Muhammad's explicit monotheism in the purely polytheistic Mecca had stirred up fiercely hostile opposition. Likewise, there was awareness about the central role that one supreme God, Allah, played in Muhammad's religion, that it comprised a system of punishment and reward in life after death and that God's precepts dealt with the matters of this world, too. In Latin writings therefore the Qur'an is often referred to as *Lex*, or 'Law'. Correct details were available about Muhammad's initial successes in converting his fellow Meccans to Islam and about his subsequent persecution and flight to Medina. Even the news about the incident of the Satanic Verses and the Meccan rulers' attempt to lure Muhammad into accepting worldly privileges and renouncing his religious movement, had reached Europe. That it was necessary for Muhammad to escape from Mecca and try and set up a Muslim community in Medina was another fact that Latin scholars were conscious of, as were Muhammad's various defence operations against the military attacks of his pagan enemies. Biographical details were in circulation concerning Muhammad's polygamy, his painful human death and his unpretentious burial.

There were three sources from which information about Muhammad came. The initial source was no doubt Byzantium; then Spain became the focal point for the transmission of biographical material about Muhammad, while the third source was contributed by the knights returning from their crusading expedition to the Holy Land. The information was, then, spread in Europe by non-Muslim transmitters who had experience of Islamic environment and were more or less versed in the Arabic language. Consequently these transmissions were often coloured by polemics, exaggerations and fantasies. However, the first well-founded knowledge about Muhammad and early Islam came from Byzantium and became known in the West through the works of Anastasius Bibliothecarius in the ninth century, who transcribed the eighth-century *Chronographia* of Theophanes.[1]

---

1 See *Cambridge Encyclopedia of Islam*, 1992, entry under 'Muhammad' p. 379.

Amongst oriental Christians of the early eighth century from whom much material offering a negative image of Muhammad emanated, is John of Damascus. His prejudices left a legacy of rejection and mistrust of the emergent Islam. In his *De Haeresibus Liber*[2] he claimed that Muhammad had been seduced by dubious Christian heretics and he himself had become the seducer of the 'ignorant Arabs'. He saw in Muhammad the seducer and seduced fused into one person. This view of John of Damascus prevailed for a long time in medieval Europe. Medieval concepts of Muhammad were coloured by the further assumption that his transition to prophethood had been based on deception. John of Damascus had persuaded Latin scholars to believe that Muhammad, through his cleverly contrived marriage to Khadija, had not only acquired wealth and leisure but that he had known how to disguise his epileptic attacks as phenomena accompanying visitations by the Angel Gabriel, thereby posing as the new Messenger of God. As for Muhammad's time in Medina, the medieval polemic against him sparked off by John of Damascus is marked by two characteristics – his alleged love of war and what was assumed to be his insatiable sexual appetite – both unworthy of a prophet. But rather than focusing on Muhammad's war efforts against his enemies, medieval authors concentrated pruriently on his alleged sexual life, displaying a central preoccupation which John of Damascus' writings had spread throughout Europe. Many medieval representations of Muhammad therefore give the impression from the outset that he was a man with an excessively strong sexual drive. The emphasis given to this was clearly a perverse way of giving verbal rein to the prudish Christian mind of the Middle Ages that was supremely repressed in sexual matters. By medieval standards Muhammad's polygamy in his later years was sufficient to provoke rejection and condemnation.

The prominent Biblical scholar and historian of the early Middle Ages, the Venerable Bede, was no doubt influenced by John of Damascus when he wrote his negative genealogy of Muhammad and his contemporary Saracens (from Arabic *Sharqiyin* – 'Easterners'). The Arabs had become a matter of great European concern during Bede's lifetime and before he died in 735 CE they had already reached the limit of their westward expansion, coming as far as Paris. Most of Bede's references to the Saracens and to Muhammad have been collected by C. Plummer in

---

2 Ibid., p. 379.

his edition of the *Historia Ecclesiastica*,[3] published in 1896. In his highly polemical representation of the Arabs, Bede describes Muhammad as a wild man of the desert, and likens him to his ancestor Ishmael, 'whose hand will be against every man's'. Ishmael was outside the Covenant; so were the Saracens. He describes them as rude, war-like and barbarian. Added to these unflattering origins were Muhammad's 'illiteracy' and his 'low social status', his 'ignorance' about Christian dogma, 'his unrestrained striving for power' – which helped him to become a ruler and lay behind his claims to be a prophet.

Bede's identification of Muhammad and the Saracens with war and destruction found parallels in the medieval writings of Spain, especially in those of Isidore de Seville whose writings reciprocally influenced the scholars of northern Europe. In an attempt to understand Islam, men such as Isidore, who lived in Spain and wrote in the middle of the ninth century, had turned their attention from Biblical history to Biblical prophecy and nurtured an apocalyptic interpretation centred on Muhammad and Islam. Spain was the country which naturally gave most thought to Islam, since it had become part of the Islamic-Arab Empire. But it was only until the ninth century that Spanish thoughts about Muhammad were expressed negatively. From the ninth to the fifteenth century there is in fact a long period in which Spanish opinion was varied and rational, benevolent and positive. The situation of the Christian community in Spain during these centuries was identical to that of many Christian communities throughout the Islamic world. In accordance with the teaching of the Qur'an they were given protection, they had their own bishops, priests, churches and monasteries and many of their number were in responsible positions in the service of the Emirs of Cordova. The only religious restriction was that they were not allowed any public worship, no ringing of bells, no processions, and no blasphemy against the Prophet or the Qur'an. The temper of the Christian population had become relaxed thanks to the brilliant and flourishing civilization which had emerged with the rule of Muhammad's religion. It was not only material prosperity which kept the Christians of Spain satisfied. For the first time, as we have seen, the Muslim conquerors had introduced to the West the tradition of Greek, Persian and Arab philosophical and

---

3 Ibid., p. 379. Also R. W. Southern, *Western Views of Islam in the Middle Ages*, Cambridge Massachusetts, 1962, pp. 16–19.

scientific thought which had been the formative influences in the first centuries of Islamic rule. On central theological issues, Western theologians of all shades of opinion in the mid-thirteenth century had been encouraged to re-examine traditional views in the light of Islamic philosophy, or at least to restate their traditional views in the language of these philosophers. The scholastic and philosophical influence from which Spain in particular benefited was only one aspect of a wider penetration of Islamic culture and art.

It is noteworthy that during the centuries that spanned the Arab presence in Spain, the latter was also the centre of Jewish culture. Indeed, this period is referred to by modern Jewish scholars as the Golden Age of Hebrew poetry and philosophy. Men such as Ibn Gabirol (Solomon Ben-Judah) and Yehuda Halevi felt free to fuse the heritage of Hebrew literature contained in the Bible, Talmud and other rabbinical writings with that of Qur'anic poetic imagery and Arab philosophy. It is worth remembering that Ibn Gabirol's major philosophical work, *The Fountain of Life*, had been composed by its Jewish author in Arabic and was translated into Hebrew only two hundred years later. The Judeo-Arabic school is acknowledged to have reached its zenith in the thirteenth century with the philosopher Maimonedes (Moses ben Maimom) who himself influenced a range of philosophers and traditions – Jewish, Muslim and Christian.

The study of the Arabic language, literature and especially poetry became extremely popular in ninth-century Spain and had a lasting effect in the following centuries. But it alarmed a group of Christian scholars of Spain in the years between 850 and 860 and provoked a vehement reaction among them, leading them not only to defame Muhammad and Islam in critical writings, but also to scrutinize the complacency of their fellow Christians. With their writings these early scholars laid the foundation of the Reconquista movement whose subversive activities were directed against the domination of Islam in Spain. The men who led this initial reaction were a priest, Eulogius and a layman Paul Alvarus. Eulogius was the Bishop of Toledo and died a martyr in 859. Both were inspired by the idea that the rule of Islam was a preparation for the final appearance of the Anti-Christ and they extracted what Biblical evidence they needed to incite the population. The enemies of Christendom, the Muslims, were now equated with the apocalyptic Beast. Alvarus wrote a polemical work, the *Indiculus*

Luminosus, attacking those Christians who counselled moderation and who were fascinated by the Islamic civilization. He described Islam as a demonic force and Muhammad himself as Anti-Christ. In his *Indiculus Luminosus*, Alvarus demonstrates his deep concern with the following words:

> The Christians love to read the poems and romances of the Arabs; they study the Arab theologians and philosophers, not to refute them but to form a correct and elegant Arabic. Where is the layman who now reads the Latin commentaries on the Holy Scriptures, or who studies the Gospels, prophets or apostles? Alas! All talented young Christians read and study with enthusiasm the Arab books; they gather immense libraries at great expense; they despise the Christian literature as unworthy of attention. They have forgotten their language. For every one who can write a letter in Latin to a friend, there are a thousand who can expresss themelves in Arabic with elegance, and write better poems in this language than the Arabs themselves.[4]

Alvarus's apocalyptic view of Islam was expressed in truly dramatic terms. He declared that Islam would flourish for three and half periods of 70 years each, that is for 245 years in all. Now since he was writing in 845 CE and the beginning of the Muslim Era was in 622 CE, it is evident that he saw the end of the world as very close indeed. By a curious coincidence the Emir of Cordova, Abd ar Rahman III, died in 852 and was succeeded by Mahomet I, whom Alvarus called 'the man of damnation of our time'. The congruity of his name with that of the Prophet of Islam, Muhammad, might have emboldened Alvarus to proclaim that the end of all things was even nearer than he had anticipated.

The name Mahound or sometimes Mahoun, Mahun, Mahomet, in French Mahon, in German Machmet, which was synonymous with demon, devil, idol, was invented by the writers of Christian play cycles and romances of 12th Century Europe. In these writings Muhammad does not appear as a prophet or even anti-prophet, but as a heathen idol worshipped by the Arabs.

---

4   Paul Alvarus, *Indiculus Luminosus*, PL. CXXI, pp. 555–6 quoted in R. W. Southern, *Western Views of Islam in the Middle Ages*, op. cit. p. 21.

The twelfth-century French and German romances depicted in the *chansons de geste*, in the *Chanson de Roland, Tervigant* and *Apollo* with their fusion of Greco-Roman culture and Christian religion became extremely popular. So did play cycles such as *Le Cycle de Guillaume d'Orange*, in which the resistance against the 'Saracens' in southern France is treated thematically. The romances were a form of literature celebrating a new heroic age in Europe, represented in the *Chanson de Roland* by a warrior Emperor (Charlemagne), a warrior leader (Roland) and a warrior priest (Archbishop Turpin). The common enemy were the Muslims.

In Wolfram von Eschenbach's *Willehalm* and in Ulrich von Türheim's *Rennewart* Muhammad is represented as Mahun, an idol whose image the Saracens not only worship but also take into battle. After defeat, they throw the idol to the hounds and pigs or trample on it. Like Christ or God the Father by Christians and Yaweh by Jews, Mahun is implored by the Saracens to help them, but is shown to be totally ineffective. Because he has not helped them to victory Mahun is cursed, insulted, dragged in the dust and broken into pieces. Defeat is the usual fate of the Saracens in these chansons and play cycles. The only account of a Saracen victory is when the Sowdone of Babylon takes Rome. Here Saracens are depicted burning frankincense before their gods and before Mahun, because they are polytheists, and drink the blood of beasts and feast on milk and honey.[5] Milk and honey or milk and dates were, according to early Muslim sources, Muhammad's favourite food. Thus the man who preached that there was no God but the Creator of the Universe and who renounced idolatry as the gravest of all sins, himself became an idol in the songs and play cycles of the Middle Ages in Europe. Deriving from Mahomet, a term 'mammetry' even emerged in the English language, meaning the worship of images or idolatry, a false religion.[6]

---

5 See Byron Porter Smith, *Islam in English Literature*, Beirut, 1939, p. 2.

6 A word 'mammet' meaning an idol – or a doll – became common in Middle English and by the sixteenth century we find the term 'mammitrie', sometimes spelt 'maumetry' or even presented as 'mahometry' to signify the worship of images or idols. See *The Shorter Oxford Dictionary*, 3rd edition, Oxford, 1962, p. 1220.
The Shorter Oxford Dictionary entry 'Mahound' gives the following meanings: The 'false prophet' Mohammed; a false god, an idol (also 'maumet' in Middle English), a name for the devil (also listed as an adjective) and finally 'heathen'

Another malicious fiction of this time was the account of Muhammad's death, according to which Muhammad had died of drinker's delirium, (despite the Islamic prohibition of alcohol) and that his body had been torn to pieces by dogs and pigs. These animals are known as the most unclean in Islam because of the hot climate of Arabia and the diseases they might induce. These were all motives to discredit Muhammad and to frighten the Christians of contamination through any possible contact or sympathy with Islam and its founder.

Muhammad remained one of the heathen idols in the epics of the Crusades. He features again as Mahound in Richard de Pèlerin's *La chanson d'Antioch* (*c.* 1180), *La conquête de Jérusalem* (*c.* 1180), *La chanson du chevalier au cigne* (*c.* 1200)[7] and in *Saladin* which belongs to the cycle of the Second Crusades. Muhammad continued to be depicted as an idol well into the thirteenth century in Stricker's *Karl der Grosse* (*c.* 1230) and in the old Icelandic *Karlamagnus Saga* (end of thirteenth century).

While theological polemics were confined to scholarly circles, these songs and plays were meant for a wider public. It is obvious that these coarsely counterfeited representations of Muhammad as an idol and of Islam as a polytheistic religion was to undermine a rival religion in the eyes of Christian Europe.

The transition from 'Muhammad the idol' to 'Muhammad the Devil' was not difficult. The progressively contemptuous imagery of Muhammad together with the news of the loss of the Crusaders' territory of Edessa set the scene for another of Europe's disastrous religious expeditions, the Second Crusade. In 1146 King Louis of France summoned his bishops and nobles and presented them with his scheme for recapturing Edessa. One of the most powerful clerics in Europe after the Pope, Bernard, the Abbot of Clairvaux was put in charge of the crusading sermons against the Muslims. Bernard delivered an emotive sermon outside the town of Vazelay, tearing off his own garments and cutting them into crosses for the crowd. He was extremely successful in whipping up a crusading fever not only amongst his own compatriots but across the whole of Europe. Wherever he travelled, hundreds and thousands of

---

and refers the reader to the seventeenth-century playwright Fletcher. *The Shorter Oxford Dictionary*, 3rd edition, Oxford, 1962, p. 1188.

7 See *Cambridge Encyclopedia of Islam*, 1992, entry under 'Muhammad' p. 381.

Christians gathered to assure him of their readiness to march on the Holy Land. Bernard told the crowds that the fall of Edessa had not been a setback but an opportune moment for Christians to demonstrate their love of God. And so it was that the armies north of the Rhine joined with the French under King Louis VII and set off for the East. When they reached Antioch a council was held and their advisers and tacticians gave their unanimous verdict in favour of King Louis's proposal. To weaken the Islamic Empire, Damascus was now to be attacked in place of Edessa. So, on 25 May 1148 the combined Christian armies launched their attack on Damascus. But the Muslims had mobilized their armies too, and the French and Germans suffered a crushing defeat at their hands. Back in Europe the blame fell first on the Abbot of Clairvaux who had promised them so much on behalf of God. But public opinion soon shifted from blaming the Abbot to blaming the Devil. Their defeat was the work of Muhammad, the Anti-Christ, the 'pseudo-prophet' of the Muslims.

In 1142 the Abbot of Cluny, Peter the Venerable had raised his voice against the Crusades. He advocated moderation and Christian precepts of love and compassion, arguing that violence and bloodshed were not the way to diminish the influence of Islam. The Abbot suggested the use of peaceful means in converting the Muslims to Christianity. He argued that instead of fearing contamination and refusing to familiarize fellow Christians with the tenets of Islam, it was high time to embark on a serious study of this religion. He said it was in the interest of Christendom to expose the weaknesses of the Qur'an and to encourage the Muslims to renounce Islam in favour of Christianity. He tried to enlist the support of his powerful rival, the Abbot of Clairvaux, but the latter refused to collaborate. Peter the Venerable had warned his fellow churchmen that despite the successes of the First Crusade, Islam was spreading with alarming speed while Christianity was shrinking in size and in the number of converts. He was of course speaking at a time when Europe itself was riven with heresies and rivalries at home, circumstances which did not provide an optimistic background for an objective assessment of Islam. Like his Greek predecessor, John of Damascus, Peter the Venerable considered Islam as a Christian heresy, perhaps the last and greatest of heresies and the only one that had not been answered. So the Abbot decided to commission a translation of the Qur'an into Latin at his own expense. The translator he chose was the English scholar Robert Ketton who completed the work in 1143. This translation brought a short period of more realistic appraisal of Islam, but it was the end rather than the beginning. A serious study of Islam was never to materialize, not even with the aim of converting the Muslims. Nor did the Christian message of the Abbot have any impact on the armed pilgrims who three years later set out on their infamous expedition to destroy Islam:

> I attack you, not as some of us often do by arms,
> but by words; not by force, but by reason;
> not in hatred, but in love. I love you, I write to you,
> I invite you to salvation.[8]

During the twelfth and thirteenth centuries the Christian world was divided into three camps with regard to the Crusades. There were those who fanatically supported them. There were others who called for better crusading. But there were also some who, following Peter the Venerable's argument, regarded the Crusades as futile. One of the prominent Western thinkers who belonged to the third camp was the English statesman and philosopher Roger Bacon who in the years between 1266 and 1268 achieved his long-cherished ambition of being able to address directly to the Pope his own views on what was wrong with the state of Christendom. He was writing at a time when the Seventh Crusade had been fought, resulting in the defeat of the Christians. In three major works, *Opus Maius*, *Opus Minus*, and *Opus Tertiam*[9] he expounded his ideas on the failure of Christendom and the successes of Islam. Bacon argued that the aims of Christendom had been wrong because they had been dominated by the desire for ascendancy, which had frustrated the work of conversion. The crusading wars had failed; but even if they had succeeded they would have been futile because the outcome would not have led to any significant conversions. According to Roger Bacon peaceful and logical preaching was the only way in which Christendom could be enlarged. Bacon dismissed the use of the

---

8   R. W. Southern, *Western Views of Islam in the Middle Ages*, op. cit. p. 39.
9   Roger Bacon, *Opus Maius* (edited by J. H. Bridges 3 volumes, London, 1900) – the *Opus Minus* and *Opus Tertiam* (edited by J. S. Brewer, Rolls Series, London 1859). Also see R. W. Southern, *Western Views of Islam in the Middle Ages*, op. cit. pp. 52–61.

Bible as an instrument for understanding the role of Islam and rejected the image of Muhammad as the Anti-Christ and as a preparation for the Apocalypse. For his knowledge of Islam, Bacon relied on the classical Muslim philosophers Al Kindi, Al Farabi, Averroës and Avicenna, whose works had been translated into Latin by the third quarter of the twelfth century. Unlike his contemporaries, Bacon believed that Islam was on the ascendant and had an essential role to play in history.

In 1273 a Dominican friar at Acre, William of Tripoli wrote an account of Islam for the archdecon of Liège[10] which was totally contrary to Roger Bacon's assessment. He reported that although the Muslims seemed to be wrapped up in their 'deceitful' and 'fictitious' faith, he could manifestly see that they were approaching the path of salvation and recognizing Christian truth. He claimed to have himself baptized a thousand Muslims. But the hopes of a triumphant Christianity collapsed with the fall of the last Christian bastion, Acre, in 1290. There remained no hope of any integration of the basic tenets of Islam into Christendom either. In 1323 when the Irish Franciscan Simon Semeronis travelled to Palestine as a zealous observer, he had with him a copy of the Qur'an and often quoted it, but he could not mention either Muhammad or the Muslims without opprobrious epithets – pigs, beasts, sons of Beliol, sodomites and so on. The accounts of his visit to the ruins of Acre, Tyre, Sidon and Tripoli were recorded in *Itinerarium Symeonis ab Hybernia ad Terram Sacram*.[11]

The idea of the curse of Muhammad was taken up by the English poet William Langland in his allegory of mankind, *Piers Plowman*, published in 1362. In this work we find Muhammad among the infernal powers in the lowest chambers of Hell. He is not condemned to the fires of the Inferno as the Prophet of Islam but as a renegade cardinal, who through ambition, broke away from the Church and became an apostate in Arabia by founding a new Christian sect. *Piers Plowman* is an attempt to prove the necessity of the incarnation and ministry of Christ for mankind's salvation, and his promise of ultimate victory over the forces

---

10 William of Tripoli, *Tractus de Statu Saracenorum*, printed in H. Prutz *Kulturgeschichte der Kreuzzüge*, 1883, pp. 573–98 passage quoted p. 595. Also see R. W. Southern, *Western Views of Islam in the Middle Ages*, op. cit. pp. 62–3.

11 See *Itinerarum Symeonis ab Hybernia ad Terram Sacram*, edited by Mesposito (Scriptores Latini Hiberniae), Volume IV, 1960. Also R. W. Southern, *Western Views of Islam in the Middle Ages*, op. cit. pp. 70–1.

of the Devil. In Langland's work Christian history concludes with the final appearance of the Anti-Christ. But Langland's interpretation of the Anti-Christ is profoundly different to the Anti-Christ traditionally expected to herald the end of the world. He speaks of false prophets and Anti-Christs within the Church itself. Langland develops Muhammad as a forerunner of Anti-Christ, for he was popularly understood as the Anti-Messiah of the Saracens, who systematically attempted to mislead the Christians and who according to Langland caused deceit and guile to spread.[12]

A century-and-a-half later the Scottish poet William Dunbar revived the image of Mahound or the Devil in his *Dance of the Sevin Deidly Synnis* in which Mahound is the master of ceremonies in Hell. The poet himself in a trance sees Mahound call a dance of unshriven outcasts, who are depicted with extreme and fantastic vividness.[13]

Dante Alighieri's *Divine Comedy* is the supreme work of the medieval European imagination. In it he takes the reader on a guided tour of Hell, Purgatory and Paradise, viewing the torture inflicted on the enemies of Christianity, the penance of redeemable sinners and the bliss of the saints. When Dante was writing at the close of the Middle Ages in the early 1300s in Florence, Islam still appeared as a major threat from the East. The Christian West was planning further crusading expeditions to counteract the peril which Islam presented. In 1291, some twenty years before Dante began the *Divine Comedy*, the last Crusaders' fortress, Acre, in Palestine had been reconquered by the Muslims who had driven the Crusaders from the region. The images of those wars were vivid in Dante's mind when he created the ugly portrait of Muhammad in his *Inferno*. Dante consigned Muhammad and his disciple Ali with their bodies split from head to waist, to the eighth circle of Hell. The poet portrays Muhammad as a sinner tearing apart his severed breast with his own hands, a symbolic gesture to show that he was the chief among the damned souls to have brought schism into religion. For Dante, Muhammad's crime had been to propagate a 'false religion', to deliver a divine revelation claiming to supersede Christianity, which had

---

12 William Langland, *Piers Plowman*, The Vision of William concerning Text C, edited by W. W. Skeat, EETS No. 54, 1873, Passus XXI, 1. 295, p. 384, Passus XVIII, 11. 165–7, p. 317, Passus XVIII, 11. 317–23, p. 327.

13 William Dunbar, *The Poems of William Dunbar*, edited by W. Machay-Mackenzie, Edinburgh, 1932, p. 120.

to be regarded as an impious fraud and which could only sow discord in the world.

Dante acts as the moralizing poet labelling the figures of history in accordance with these Christian beliefs. Hence the *Divine Comedy* is full of the familiar fantasies and prejudices of the Middle Ages. Certainly the depiction of Muhammad in the *Inferno*, whose motive is described as fraudulent, is an unmistakeable example of the defamatory image given to him as early as the seventh century by the Eastern Church in Byzantium.

Dante represented and represents today the culmination of medievalism. In common with his fellow countrymen, he felt immense pride in the authority of the Roman Catholic Church and the supremacy of the Pope. The Church of Rome was looked upon by the Italians as the ark of civilization. But at the same time Dante showed the first signs of the aspirations of Renaissance man. At the very beginning of the *Divine Comedy*, for instance, we find the Hebraic image of man in need of God, but also the classical image of man willing to help himself and exercise self-discipline. These two themes, the unseen God and the development of selfhood, prevail throughout Dante's work. Dante encounters four beasts on his way to the Inferno: the leopard symbolizing self-indulgence and carnality, the lion – violence and cruelty, the wolf – malice and fraud, and the greyhound – the hoped-for leader of the world.

Admirers of Dante of all ages have dwelt upon the originality shown by the poet in his conception of the architecture of Hell. But in 1926 a Professor of Arabic at the University of Madrid, Miguel Asin, published his *Islam and the Divine Comedy* in which he clearly demonstrated that Dante's imagery of his apocalyptic journey was neither original nor had any precedent in the Old or the New Testament. True, we are also reminded of the descent into Hades by Homer. But Asin argues that the structure of Hell in the *Divine Comedy* was inspired by Islamic images rather than Greek mythology. Asin analyses the Qur'anic scene of Muhammad's nocturnal journey and ascent to the spheres of the afterlife known as *Mi'raj*.[14] Upon the order of Alphonso X a translation into Spanish from various Arabic sources of the *Mi'raj* account had been undertaken between 1260 and 1264. The same text was available in Latin in *Escala de Mahoma*, which had also been translated from Arabic source materials. Asin believes that Dante must have been familiar with

---

14 Miguel Asin, *Islam and the Divine Comedy*, London 1926, pp. 3–7

these texts to be able to create similar scenes of the afterlife to those painted in the Islamic accounts. In one version of the story Muhammad is woken by the Angel Gabriel, and begins his journey on horseback, setting out for Jerusalem where he meets the resurrected prophets. With the help of a ladder guarded by angels he reaches the Hereafter and visits the Seven Heavens accompanied by Gabriel. In the eighth Heaven he meets with God and then descends to the seventh Heaven where he receives from God the Qur'an. Through the description of Gabriel and a personal view from a safe distance, Muhammad learns about the seven classes of the subterranean Hell which await sinners. Gabriel also informs him about the construction of the cosmos, about the end of the world and the Last Judgement. Then Gabriel accompanies Muhammad back to Jerusalem to the Temple Mount and Muhammad returns to Mecca on his horse. According to the same source, Muhammad later relates to his disciples his vision of Hell. Proceeding on their way Muhammad and his guide had witnessed six successive scenes of horrific torture. Men and women with lips torn asunder; others whose eyes and ears were pierced by arrows, wretched creatures in filthy clothes who reeked of latrines, and corpses in the last, abominable stages of putrefaction. These punishments, the guide explained to Muhammad, were meted out in turn to liars, those that have sinned with eyes and ears, to adulterers and to unbelievers.

Dante's *Divine Comedy* draws similarly on a visionary journey to God; a journey which takes the poet from the earth, through the circles of Hell and Purgatory to absolute Heaven. The entry to Heaven is mediated by the Virgin Mary, not named as such but called a noble lady (*Donna è gentil nel ciel*). The journey to Heaven is upwards and Dante begins this journey by climbing the hill. He can see light far above him and can thus hope for salvation. Dante's guide on this journey is the Roman poet Virgil, who held a special place in medieval belief. In his poetry he had hailed the birth of a child who should bring back the Golden Age; this was interpreted by the Church of the Middle Ages as the prophecy of Christ. Virgil leads Dante through all the phases and all the experiences of the Hereafter. These experiences are depicted as historical realities encountered by the poet. All the spirits, either historical or legendary whom Dante meets and talks with, have once lived on earth. In the circles of his Hell, Dante sees ghosts of the past who had dwelt deep in his subconscious. The voyage to Hell is downwards. Hell is a funnel sucking him in and begins in a dark forest. Dante is present all along, telling the reader what he thinks and feels and knows. The characters he meets in the *Inferno* and their motives are analysed from a specific viewpoint; that of the Christian principles of right and wrong.

Dante describes the punishment meted out to Muhammad, his companion Ali and others in the eighth circle of Hell:

> Who ever could, ev'n with unfettered words,
> tell fully of the blood and of the wounds
> which now I saw, though oft he told the tale?
> All tongues would certainly fall short of it.
>
> No cask, indeed, by loss of middle board
> or stave, is opened as was one I saw,
> split from the chin to where one breaketh wind;
> while down between his legs his entrails hung,
> his pluck appeared, and that disgusting sack,
> which maketh excrement of what is swallowed.
>
> While I on seeing him was all intent,
> he looked at me, and opening with his hands
> his breast; he said: 'See now how I am cloven!
> Behold how torn apart Mahomet is!
>
> Ali in tears moves on ahead of me,
> cloven in his face from forelock down to chin;
> and all the others, whom thou seest here
> disseminators were, when still alive,
> of strife and schism, and hence are cloven thus.
>
> There is a devil here behind, who thus
> fiercely adorns, and to the sword's edge puts
> each member of this company anew,
> when we have gone around the woeful road.[15]

Dante exerted a powerful impact on a vast readership in Europe for a long time. His English critic and commentator Wallace Fowlie considers the *Divine Comedy* as a major European work of art which is 'able to awaken in the sensibility of every generation awareness, elation, recognition, and new ways of understanding human life'.[16]

---

15 Dante Alighieri, *The Divine Comedy* (The Italian text with a translation in English blank verse and a commentary by Courtney Langdon), Oxford, 1918, Volume I, Inferno, Canto XXVIII, p. 317.

16 See Wallace Fowlie, *A Reading of Dante's Inferno*, Chicago and London, 1976, Foreword.

It hardly seems necessary to add further comment, for Wallace Fowlie's insight suggests how Dante's depiction of Muhammad in his highly acclaimed work imprinted itself on the Western mind for centuries to come.

5

The Turkish Threat

Muhammad in the Europe of the Renaissance

———

Now Casane, where's the Turkish Alcoran,
And all the heaps of superstitious books,
Found in the temples of that Mahomet
Whom I have thought a god?
They shall be burnt.

Christopher Marlowe, *Tamburlaine*. 1590

The fall of the last Emperor of Byzantium, fighting the Turkish armies that streamed into Constantinople on the morning of 29 May 1453, marked the end of a millennium of Christian domination in the east Mediterranean and Asia Minor. It was a turning point in the history of Christendom which was never to be forgiven. For centuries the Latin west and the Greek east had existed side by side, each symbolizing and upholding their own Christian traditions. The Great or East-West Schism of 1054 had marked the separation of the Eastern (Orthodox) and Western Christian Churches. To the Roman Church, which became a definitive and spiritual power at that time, Byzantium had always meant more than its territories. It had created Orthodox Christianity and had spread the Gospel and Christian values throughout the Middle East. Despite the differences between the two Churches of East and West, Europe regarded Constantinople as a classical Christian city and as an extension of its own Christian world. The gradual conquest of these Byzantine territories, which had occurred through a succession of invasions by the Arabs, Turks and Mongols from the seventh century onwards, had become a continuing source of immense anxiety for Europe. The era of the Crusades had seen Christian Europe on the offensive. Inspired by a revitalized papacy, knights had flocked to rescue Christian lands from Islamic expansion. And though in the long run the Crusader states set up in the Holy Land were to prove vulnerable to Muslim counter-attacks, leading to the eventual defeat of the Christians, the crusading spirit had remained strong amongst Europeans as late as the sixteenth century.

The Byzantine Emperor had received some military help from his Western allies to fight off the Turkish invaders of his capital city, but their support had been ineffective. Since the First Crusade in 1099 the Byzantine Emperors had relied on Latin Europe to assist them against the Muslim advances. Several times the two Churches had met in council and finally, after centuries of schism and disagreement, had joined together at the Council of Florence in 1439. But this last-hope alliance which was supposed to eradicate the power of Islam in the region had come too late. The old Eastern Empire had already been shattered by the impact of the Islamic conquests. In fact, the Empire had never fully recovered from the loss to the Arabs in the seventh and eighth centuries of its richest provinces – Syria, Egypt, Mesopotamia and then Africa and southern Spain. Between the eleventh and thirteenth centuries the Seljuk Turks and the Mongols, had, in fierce rivalry with each other, similarly weakened Byzantine rule, taking Islam even further afield. By 1300 the Ottoman Turks had emerged on the scene as the foremost Muslim power. Their conquests had practically reduced the Byzantine territories to the walls of Constantinople. This ancient seat of the Byzantine Emperors which had withstood Arab sieges in the 670s, was finally overwhelmed by the massive forces of Sultan Mehmed II in 1453.

The Turkish triumph over Constantinople was immediate – in a matter of hours the soldiers had stormed the ancient streets, marched past Constantine's statue and had taken the famous basilica of Hagia Sophia, the very nucleus of Eastern Christianity. On the evening before, the great jewelled Bibles of Byzantium had been carried in the procession to the high altar and the Imperial Mass had been conducted for the last time. Four days later, on the Friday morning, Sultan Mehmed's muezzin had cried the call to Muslim prayers from the roof of Hagia Sophia: THERE IS NO GOD BUT GOD AND MUHAMMAD IS THE PROPHET OF GOD. All the signs and symbols of Christianity had been obscured by the Sultan's masons: The mosaics that had shone with dazzling brilliance had been plastered over and the two Byzantine Emperors, Constantine and Justinian portrayed therein offering to God a model of the city of Constantinople had vanished from sight. And of the Virgin Mary who had stood lifting Christian believers into the presence of her Son and of God the Father, silhouetted against the seemingly unfathomable heights of the magnificent dome, there was no trace. And so it was that the Church of the Divine Wisdom became the Mosque of the Divine Wisdom.

With the loss of Constantinople, the last bastion of Eastern Christianity, the era of the Crusades in the Near East seemed to have come to a close. From now on Christian crusading had to be limited within Europe itself, directed against the Ottoman Turks who, from their new capital, embarked on campaigns of expansion into the remaining Christian Balkans. For prior to the conquest of Constantinople their westward drive into the eastern flanks of Europe had already won them Bulgaria and Serbia. Bosnia, Albania and Hungary were acquired afterwards. The northern boundary of the Turkish conquest in Europe was to be marked by their failed sieges of Vienna in 1529 and 1683. However, the Ottomans were able to hold on to most of their possessions in south-eastern Europe until the nineteenth century. The rise of nationalism and the emergence of the great European Powers – Britain, France, Austria and Russia – eventually reduced the Ottomans' territorial possessions and, like all great empires of history, its power started to wane. Having aligned itself with Germany in 1914, it collapsed following the Central Powers' defeat in 1918. For five hundred years the Ottoman Turks had represented Europe's most feared enemy.

In Spain, crusading against Muslims had persisted for eight centuries. There had been long interludes of peace and changes of allegiance; at times the Christians had fought alongside the Muslims against their own co-religionists. There had been intermarriages between Christians and Muslims, conversions from one religion to the other. But each side had been determined to control the entire peninsula. Finally, in 1492 Christian Spain was reunited when the Spaniards succeeded in driving the Muslims from their last stronghold, Granada.

The defeat of the Muslims in Spain marked the end of the Arab presence in Europe. With their downfall the Muslim threat to Christian Europe shifted decisively from the Arabs to the Turks. From this date onwards, Islam as a rival religion, as a cultural and military force, was to be associated with the Turks and no longer with the Arabs. And so it was that Muhammad, the Prophet of the Arabs, came to be seen as the embodiment of 'Turkish monstrosity'. In the writings of the Renaissance and the Reformation there is an obsession with the vilification of the Turks and their religion. In one volume alone of Martin Luther's collected works, 75 references to the Turks and 25 to Muhammad are to be found, all of them in the form of demonization. Because of its deep-seated fear and rejection of Islam, the West refused categorically to acknowledge the significance of the rich cultural and scientific interchange which had occurred between the Islamic and the Christian world and its crucial impact on the European Renaissance.

It was through Islamic intermediaries that western Christendom had been introduced to a large portion of the legacy of ancient Greece which had long lain undiscovered in monasteries, having been branded as pagan. Furthermore the Arabs had introduced the use of paper to Europe, which brought the possibility of printing, so vital to the diffusion of Renaissance and Reformation ideas. Spain, Italy and France thrived most from the contact with Muslim civilization, in particular imitating the outward signs of its prosperity. New refinements of Islamic architecture from which, for example, the gothic arch is derived were adopted and elegant open cloisters and formal gardens emerged. The appreciation of Italian vernacular poetry first arose in the formerly Arab Sicily, and the troubadours of late medieval France derived their name and their musical and poetic tradition from the Arabs. Medieval musical instruments, composition and interpretation were influenced by the Arab cultural legacy in Spain; the most widely played instrument of the Middle Ages, the lute, derives its name and shape from its Arab prototype, *al 'ud*.

The fall of the Arabs and the rise of the Turks in the fifteenth century coincided with a period of great intellectual and cultural upheaval in Europe. In the mid-fourteenth century the Italian poet Petrarch had inspired a new enthusiasm for the writings of ancient Greece and Rome – an enthusiasm for their style as well as their content. Following this lead, a diverse group of scholars, the Humanists, came to regard classical texts as models for public speaking, writing and perception. Initially based in northern Italy, by 1500 new ideas had begun to spread to northern Europe, where the Dutch humanist Desiderius Erasmus was the foremost scholar. Their enthusiasm for classical models led the Humanists to a new view of the world and of man's place in it. While they did not see man as superior to God, let alone as a replacement for God, man himself bore the marks of the divine. In the century to follow, Europe not only witnessed the revival of the works of Roman and Greek philosophers, artists and orators, but also the Reformation of its religious order. The Roman Catholic Church and the papacy came under unprecedented scrutiny. It was an age of rebirth or Renaissance during which man came to be seen as the moulder of his own destiny. It was the beginning of a long struggle between rediscovered and new knowledge about the world and man's place in it, and the previously uncontested founts of Christian dogma. It was not only the classical Greek and Roman heritage that was revived; the age became also the seedbed for creative writing in the secular languages of the emerging European nations. The Renaissance, which may be said to have instigated and accompanied the Reformation, would have been unthinkable without the invention of the printing machine. In 1450 just three years before the fall of Constantinople, a German aristocrat, Johann Gutenberg, developed his revolutionary idea of the type mould and thereby set in motion the first printing press at his workshop in Mainz on the Rhine in Germany. This invention was to become the very vehicle for the intellectual and religious transformation of Europe. The new printing technique spread rapidly, particularly in the urbanized regions of the Rhineland, the Netherlands and Italy. In 1475 William Caxton introduced it to England. Printing pictures as well as words meant that writers could reach a much larger audience, beyond national boundaries. The printed book became the vehicle whereby Renaissance ideas were widely communicated. When Erasmus edited the Greek New Testament, and when in letter and tracts he called for Church reform, his words, now in print reached people across the length and breadth of Europe. This anticipated the crucial role that printing was to play in the diffusion of the Reformation.

During the Middle Ages the Church, and consequently the Pope, had possessed more power than any other institution and had directed even the political affairs of Europe. The kings and the Holy Roman Emperors had all been crowned by the Pope and had been forced to pay absolute allegiance to his person and his doctrine. Indeed, in the centuries that the Byzantine Empire had been crumbling in the East, the Christian Church in the West had been growing stronger. It had consolidated a new social order and and had acquired remarkable commercial and financial riches underpinned by the establishment of a feudal rural system, dominated by feudal lords, and a Church ruled by the Roman

Catholic priesthood. The Pope had used monasteries as instruments to strengthen his control over churches throughout Europe – monasteries which had become centres of cultural and educational life in diverse Christian communities. For centuries there were few men in Europe who had learnt to read and write anywhere but within the household of a nobleman or in a monastery school. However, by the twelfth century western Europe had grown into a more populous and more complex society. The rising population throughout Europe had led to the emergence of urban settlements around monasteries, functioning as places of trade and commerce. Although western medieval cities were never large in comparison with, for instance Constantinople, which numbered about one million inhabitants (in Europe the largest cities rarely exceeded a population of one hundred thousand), they became centres for economic prosperity and an evolving European bourgeoisie. It was in as early as the twelfth century that teachers began to set up schools, still closely tied to the Church, in towns of Europe. The 'lost' learning of the ancient world which had been translated in Arab Spain into Latin became the distant basis of their scholarship. In this receptive and expansionist educational environment the earliest universities – Paris, Bologna and Oxford – were established. By 1500 more than 70 other universities had emerged, amongst them Cambridge and Heidelberg. The most popular subject was medicine, introduced by the Muslims through the works of Avicenna.

It was in the affluent Italian city-states, especially during the last half of the fifteenth century, that Renaissance ideals achieved their most vital expression. During this period Italian cities enjoyed peace and sufficient wealth to enable their rulers to patronize artists and men of letters whose works flourished splendidly. Trading cities such as Venice, Pisa, Genoa and Florence had benefited from the West's Crusading expeditions to the Holy Land between the eleventh and thirteenth centuries. Shipbuilding and the provision of transport and supplies for the Crusaders had played a significant role in generating riches at the dawn of the Italian Renaissance. However a stark difference in the mercantile city-dwellers' approach to life and in their attitudes towards the Church and state now became apparent. Although religion had remained important in the lives of Italian merchants and artisans, it did not occupy them completely. The domination of Church culture over society had lessened in these fiercely competitive financial cities. The cities, neither dependent on the feudal lords nor on the Church, had achieved the status of self-governing bodies, a model soon to be emulated in varying degrees by all western European countries.

But the emergence of modern Europe in the Renaissance, characterized above all by its scientific and technological advances, was not to dispel the fear of Islam. The new-won confidence in man as the Prometheus who stole fire from the gods did not suffice to exorcize the haunting dread of Islam, of Muhammad, of the Turk. Hostility was the hallmark of Renaissance and Reformation society's attitude towards Muhammad and his religion. Despite the new ideals of research and investigation prompted by the Humanists, no critical attempt was made to understand Muhammad's message and his teachings. The memories of the Crusades remained alive in Europe, reinforced by the ever present fear of the growing power of the Turkish Empire during the fifteenth and sixteenth centuries. The fantastic and grotesque legends about Muhammad which had been handed down from the Middle Ages were received and repeated by the writers of the Renaissance. The legendary material was either a fictional interpretation of incidents in the life of Muhammad or pure fantasized fear. Muhammad, who, for instance, had never claimed to be God or to possess any supernatural qualities, and in fact repudiated the notion of working miracles, continued to be regarded as a mythical God, a cunning magician, an astrologer or simply a trickster. Even the accounts that travellers brought back from Turkey, Egypt or Palestine did not contribute to a better knowledge of Muhammad and the Muslims. The travellers, amongst whom were European aristocrats, merchants, official envoys and ambassadors, elaborated colourfully on interesting details about the religious ceremonies of the Muslims, the call to prayer five times a day from the minarets, the Muslim system of charity and almsgiving, and the fact that the Muslims did not drink wine nor eat pork. Otherwise the medieval mythology about Muhammad remained unaltered based on nothing more than prejudice and imagination.

One legend which appeared in the Middle Ages and persisted beyond the time of the Renaissance is the story of Bahira, the heretic monk, who is alleged to have inspired Muhammad to set himself up as a prophet and who is claimed to have even written the Qur'an for Muhammad. The story originates in the Muslim tradition that Muhammad, then a boy of fourteen, was travelling with his uncle's caravan in Syria and once visited the cell of a Christian hermit by the name of Bahira. This Muslim story was elaborated by the Christians in the East into a series of legends designed to undermine Muhammad and his reception of the Qur'an by direct inspiration from God. It was claimed that the Qur'an was the work of Bahira and not Muhammad. We are for instance told in *The Travels of Sir John Mandeville* that Muhammad repeatedly frequented the cell of this monk and once he had satisfied his curiosity about Christianity and had elicited how to write the Qur'an, his men slew the hermit, using Muhammad's sword. In the meantime, Muhammad had fallen asleep from drinking wine. When he awoke, they told him that he himself had committed the crime.[1] And so it was that, according to Sir John Mandeville, wine became prohibited in the Muslim faith because of its dangerously intoxicating effects. This travel book appeared at the close of the fourteenth century and became the basis for Renaissance writings about Islam. Originally written in French, it was soon translated into English, Latin, German and other languages. During the fifteenth and sixteenth centuries it served as the guide to pilgrimage to the Holy Land.

Innumberable legends about Muhammad are to be found in the history books of the fourteenth century which the age of the Renaissance inherited. The most popular one of all was Ranulf Higden's *Polychronicon*. Higden, a Benedictine monk at St Werburg's in Chester wrote a history of the world up to the fourteenth century, which included the rise of Islam and the story of its Founder. There are several translations of Higden's history, which was written in Latin, pointing to its wide impact. A translation into English was made by John Trevisa in 1387, another by Wynkyn de Worde in 1495 and by Peter Treveris in 1527. Higden takes up the persistent legend of the dove – a medieval concoction – to prove that Muhammad used trickery to fool the people into accepting his religion. The legend claims that Muhammad trained a dove to eat grain from his ear, and then exhibited the dove to the people as the Holy Spirit who inspired him in the writing of the Qur'an. The story had of course no basis in Muslim history and furthermore there is no doctrine of the Holy Spirit in Islam. Amongst other tricks that Higden attributes to Muhammad is the legend that Muhammad trained a camel to take

---

1 *The Travels of Sir John Mandeville*, translated from the French of Jean D'outremeuse edited by P. Hamelius, 2 volumes, EETS Nos 153, 154, 1919–1923, Volume I, p. 91.

its food only from his hand. The Qur'an was hung about its neck, and when the beast approached Muhammad while he was preaching, it knelt down before him. Muhammad took the book from the camel and announced it to be a heavenly message, written by the hands of angels.[2] Higden also elaborates on the alleged sexual pleasures of the Qur'anic Paradise, provided by virgin girls. This is cited as a proof of Muhammad's wickedness and of his cunning in luring adherents to his religion. According to Higden, Muhammad has given Islam sexual licence and polygamy as its chief attraction in order to undermine the foundations of Christianity.[3]

Christian writers of the fifteenth century expressed their astonishment on how Muhammad who, in their view, was determined to crush Christianity, should speak so highly and with such reverence in his Qur'an about Jesus, and how he could so explicitly honour the Virgin Mary. Some writers were even led to believe that perhaps it was not so difficult to convert the Muslims, since they held Jesus in such high regard. However, these writers were also aware that the denial in the Qur'an of the crucifixion marked a fundamental difference between the two religions. This demonstrated that some writers were familiar with the Qur'anic texts and did not base their knowledge entirely on legends and fables. We know that an imperfect Latin translation was made of the Qur'an about the middle of the twelfth century at the instigation of Peter the Venerable. But there was no English translation available until 1649, when the translation of Du Ryer's French version was made. Lack of knowledge about the Qur'an caused European writers to attribute to the Muslim Scripture materials which it did not contain, such as the miracles of Muhammad. A vivid example of this is John Lydgate's *Fall of Princes*, written between 1430 and 1438 and printed in 1497. Lydgate, the most voluminous writer of verse of his time, tells us the story 'off Machomet the Fals Prophete', as he calls Muhammad in *Fall of Princes*. He describes Muhammad's magical powers as instrumental in bringing about his marriage with the wealthy Khadija, renamed 'Cardigan'.

---

2 Ranulf Higden, *Polychronicon Ranulphi Higden monachi Cestrensis*, edited by J. R. Lumley, 9 volumes, London 1865–86, volume VI, pp. 35–7. See also Byron Porter Smith, *Islam in English Literature*, Beirut 1939, p. 7.

3 Ranulf Higden, *Polychronicon*, op. cit. Volume VI, p. 27. Also see Porter Smith, *Islam in English Literature*, op. cit. p. 11.

According to Lydgate, Muhammad, by the use of witchcraft, flattery and spices, wins the heart of 'Cardigan' so that she considers him to be the greatest of prophets or even the Messiah. Muhammad, who acquires power and wealth through marrying 'Cardigan', then wages war on Heraclius, the Byzantine Emperor, and takes the Eastern Empire as far as Alexandria. Here, clearly, Lydgate confused the exploits of Muhammad and of his successors, as Muhammad himself made no conquests outside of his native Arabia. Lydgate also refers to the medieval story that Muhammad suffered from epilepsy. This European legend is based on statements by early Muslim historians that Muhammad was afflicted with nervous seizures when he received his revelation:

> In his excuse seide that Gabriel
> was sent to hym from the heuenli mansioun
> Be the Hooli Goost to his instruccioun:
> For the aungel shewed hym so sheene,
> To stonde upriht he myht nat susteene.[4]

Muhammad's seizures are then cited as an example of his cunning, with which he turned even his alleged physical abnormalities to his own advantage. There are various legends also about the way Muhammad died. One of the earliest is the story that Muhammad, having fallen down during an epileptic attack brought on by intoxication, was eaten by a herd of swine. This is Lydgate's version:

> Lik a glotoun deied in dronkenesse
> Bi excesse of mykil drynkyng wyn,
> Fill in a podel, deuoured among swyn.[5]

This legend was clearly invented to explain why the Muslims eat no pork and drink no wine.

The first self-aware and objective European, the first to fight against prejudice and hatred towards other nations and their beliefs was the humanist Desiderius Erasmus. He abhorred intolerance, considering it

---

4 John Lydgate, *Fall of Princes*, edited by H. Bergen, 4 volumes, EETS-ES Nos. CXXI-CXXIV, Book IX, Volume II, 87–91, p. 921. Also see Byron Porter Smith, *Islam in English Literature*, op. cit., p. 6.
5 John Lydgate, *Fall of Princes*, op. cit., Book IX, Volume II, 152–5, p. 923, Porter Smith, op. cit., p. 8

as the greatest evil encumbering our earth. He loved and respected the whole of mankind without distinction of race and creed, attaching no superiority to any nation or any religion. He saw wisdom, humaneness and morality everywhere, as forms of a universal higher humanity, not as the exclusive preserve of Christianity. Erasmus taught that there was no specifically Christian truth. In all its forms, truth was divine. For him humane reality transcended all religions; each people should be measured by the yardstick of its cultural achievements. The unremitting cultivation of learning and of reading was his only recipe for a more noble mankind. But, alas, the time for such ideas had not yet come and he influenced only a few minds. Humanism fell into relative oblivion after his death in 1536. For the multitude of people and writers the Muslim believer remained the hated enemy because he did not share their Christian view of the world.

Almost one hundred years before Erasmus was postulating peace, moderation and reflection in place of hatred, radicalism and bigotry, a heated debate about the treatment of Islam had arisen among four European bishops. These were John of Segovia, a Spaniard, Nicholas of Cusa, a German, Jean Germain, a Frenchman and Aenas Silvius, an Italian, who became Pope in 1458. All of them had played their part in bringing about the union of the Greek and Latin Churches at the fall of Constantinople. Only the problem of Islam remained a major challenge to the bishops' peace of mind. It was the Spaniard, John of Segovia, who decided to seek a solution to the disunity between Islam and Christianity. He believed that earlier writers had been troubled by too many inessential problems such as the 'morals' of Muhammad, and the tenor of his personal life and the refutation of his claim to be a prophet. But the most important question was to see whether the Qur'an itself contained a truly divine message. An accurate translation was therefore the very first requirement. In John of Segovia's plan to have the Qur'an properly translated so that a critical study could be made, the first signs of the Renaissance could be discerned. But his translation, which was produced with the assistance of a Muslim Spaniard, disappeared mysteriously after his death in 1458, probably suppressed by his fellow clergy. Only his commentary to the translation has been preserved in the Vatican, pointing mainly to the difficulties of rendering the Qur'anic texts from the Arabic.

John of Segovia was of the opinion that war could never solve the clash between Christendom and Islam. War was contrary to the essence of Christianity. It was therefore only by peaceful means that Christendom could win, because only then was it true to itself and to the Gospels. So he excluded the possibility of reconquest, looking for a new kind of communication. He suggested a *conferentia* – to which representatives of the Turks would be invited and who would describe at first hand the ideas and practices of Islam.

John of Segovia wrote at length about his plans to his German colleague, Bishop Nicholas of Cusa, in whom he found a most sympathetic supporter. Nicholas was in philosophy a Platonist and in attitude pacifist and moderate, committed to the idea of unity. He took John of Segovia's letter seriously and welcomed the proposal of a conference in order to reconcile Islam with Christianity. He carefully studied John of Segovia's translation of the Qur'an and wrote his own commentary, the *Cribratio Alchoran*. In this 'sieving' of the Muslim scripture, Nicholas of Cusa found three strands. Firstly, a basic Nestorian Christianity, secondly 'anti-Christian sentiments' fuelled by the 'Jewish advisers of Muhammad', and thirdly 'corruption of the New Testament' introduced by 'Jewish correctors' after Muhammad's death. These were, according to Nicholas of Cusa, issues that separated Islam and Christendom and which should be put to debate at the conference. But such a conference was never to materialize and the whole inspiration vanished with John of Segovia's death.

In 1455, three years before his death and two years after the fall of Constantinople, John of Segovia wrote to his French friend Jean Germain, the Bishop of Châlon. Unlike Nicholas of Cusa, Jean Germain's proposal to counter the Islamic peril was not to investigate afresh the tenets of the Qur'an and the message that it contained, but to return to the more warlike and spirited virtues of Christianity, as depicted in the epics of the early Crusades. He wanted to revive the heroic deeds of the Christians through chivalry and discipline and through the suppression of heresy and error. Jean Germain was therefore not at all pleased to receive John of Segovia's conciliatory letter, condemning the futility of war and urging the need to find a peaceful solution to the challenge of Islam. His answer to John of Segovia's letter, which has been preserved in the Vatican, was explicit: The Turks were continuing their advances and Europe's fate lay in the balance until they were defeated. The Holy War, he asserted, had long been consecrated by the decisions of Popes and the practice of kings. The Roman Church had given its rewards to those who took part in it. It was supported by the Old Testament and by a long line of Christian heroes and martyrs. A new Crusade was in the course of preparation and nothing must be done to weaken the military purpose of western Europe.

The last recipient of John of Segovia's letter was Aenas Silvius, the Pope himself. It was written in the last month of John of Segovia's life. He was fatally ill and could scarcely hold the pen. But it was important to him as a humanist to appeal to another kindred mind. No doubt some of the points of his letter were of interest to Aenas Silvius whose humanistic disposition favoured the idea of critical analysis and debate. But the letter did not appeal to him as a politician. He never replied to the dying author of the letter. Instead, he addressed an official declaration to the Conqueror of Constantinople, Sultan Mehmed II, which for its magnificent rhetoric, eloquence and vigour became an exemplary document of the Renaissance. It is recorded in Toffanin's 1953 edition under the title *Pio II Lettera a Maometto II*. The letter begins with a glorified account of the strength of the kingdoms of western Christendom:

> You are not so ignorant of our affairs that you do not know the power of the Christian people – of Spain so steadfast, Gaul so warlike, Germany so populous, Britain so strong, Poland so daring, Hungary so active, and Italy so rich, high-spirited and experienced in the art of war.[6]

Aenas Silvius urged the Turkish Sultan not to suppose from his latest military successes that he could hope to overcome the nations of Europe. The letter continues thus:

> There are many points of agreement between Christians and Muslims; One God, the Creator of the World, a belief in the necessity for faith, a future life of rewards and punishment, the immortality of soul and the common use of the Old Testament as a basis. All this is shared grounds. We only differ about the nature of God.[7]

The Pope then criticized the Muslims for their charges made against the Christians for having corrupted the Bible:

---

6 G. Toffanin, PIO II, *Lettera a Maometto II*, 1953 edition, p. 110. Also see R. W. Southern, *Western Views of Islam in the Middle Ages*, Beirut, 1961, p. 100.
7 Ibid.

Are the old texts of the Old Testament likely to be more corrupt than those newer texts known to Muhammad and his followers?[8]

But the most intriguing part of the letter is the Pope's invitation to the Sultan to embrace Christianity and put an end to centuries of heresy and hostility:

> It is a small thing, however, that can make you the greatest and most powerful and most famous man of your time. You ask what it is. It is not difficult to find. Nor have you far to seek. it is to be found all over the world – a little water with which you may be baptised, and turn to the Christian sacraments and believe the gospel. Do this, and there is no prince in the world who will exceed you in glory, or equal you in power. We will call you Emperor of the Greeks and of the East. The land which you now occupy by force you will then hold by right, and all Christians will reverence you and make you their judge. It is impossible for you to succeed while you follow the Muslim law. But only turn to Christianity and you will be the greatest man of your time by universal consent.[9]

The Pope closed his letter by emphasizing the self-confidence of the West which it owed to the superiority of its Classical and Christian heritage – in contrast to Islam.

The three bishops and the Pope failed to get to grips with Islam, no matter how hard they tried. The Pope's letter had no effect on the Turkish Sultan. Islamic power continued to grow in the Mediterranean. By 1542 the Turks had overrun Hungary and were advancing deep into Europe. The King of France decided to ally himself with the Turks. It seemed that the whole Austrian Empire might succumb at any moment.

During this time there emerged a large body of writings dealing with the contemporary Muslim nations and especially the Turkish Empire. Several plays were staged representing the bloodthirstiness of the Turks and the intrigues, murder and brutalities within their palaces. It was this extraordinary yearning for the depiction of the Turks as villains that led Richard Knolle to write his famous *Generall History of the Turkes* published around 1600. He believed that Muhammad's own history belonged to a dead past. The history of the Muslims as exemplified by the conduct of the Turks was much more accurate than even the Qur'an

---

8 Ibid.
9 Ibid.

itself, claimed Knolle. The Qur'an was imperfect and full of visions and fables, he argued. Thus in his interpretation of history 'the wickedness of the Turks' fatefully became synonymous with the 'wickedness of Islam' and the 'wickedness of Muhammad'.

Around the same time as Richard Knolle was writing his 'Definitive History of the Turks and of Islam', Christopher Marlowe, an iconoclastic twenty-three year old who had studied at Cambridge University, was composing his *Tamburlaine*. He wrote it between 1587 and 1588 in blank verse. It was published in 1590. Marlowe took a historical figure, the notorious Mongol conqueror Tamburlaine, as his protagonist, who had mercilessly ravaged the Turks and their lands in the thirteenth century. Marlowe's purpose in writing this play was first and foremost to glorify and celebrate the Mongol triumph over the Turks. He also wanted to show his own vision of Renaissance Man in the Mongol warrior's colossal and unbridled character and image. *Tamburlaine* is said to have exercised a powerful influence on Machiavelli who took it as an endorsement of the new approach to history that saw in great individuals the creators of the future. Indeed, Tamburlaine, with his manly physical strength, his powerful will, his rhetorical gifts, his prowess as a warrior and his ruthless nature, mirrored on a gigantic scale the new-won confidence of man in the universe. By constantly challenging God to prove Himself and His existence, Tamburlaine transmitted the core message of Marlowe's play. Tamburlaine's revolt was not only against God, but also against Muhammad and his religion.

This is the scene where Tamburlaine orders his soldiers to burn the Qur'an before his eyes as a token of his great victory over the Turks:

Now, Casane, where's the Turkish Alcoran,
And all the heaps of superstitious books
Found in the temples of that Mahomet
Whom I have thought a god? They shall be burnt!

In vain, I see, men worship Mahomet:
My sword hath sent millions of Turks to hell,
Slew all his priests, his kinsmen, and his friends,
And yet I live untouched by Mahomet.
There is a God full of revenging wrath,
From whom the thunder and the lightening breaks,
Whose scourge I am, and him will I obey.
So Casane, fling them in the fire!

[they burn the books]

Now, Mahomet, if thou have any power,
Come down thyself and work a miracle;
Thou are not worthy to be worshipped
That suffers flames of fire to burn the writ
Wherein the sum of thy religion rests.

Why sendest thou not a furious whirlwind down,
To blow thy Alcoran up to thy throne
Where men report thou sittest by God himself –
Or vengeance on the head of Tamburlaine
That shakes his sword against thy majesty
And spurns the abstracts of thy foolish laws?

Well, soldiers, Mahomet remains in hell;
He cannot hear the voice of Tamburlaine.
Seek out another godhead to adore,
The God that sits in heaven, if any god,
For he is God alone, and none but he.[10]

For all Tamburlaine's posturing, the underlying pull of the Christian doctrine is here clearly evident. In reality Tamburlaine had been a Buddhist. Marlowe appears to let him seem to be a Christian, casting himself in the role of God's avenger on the infidel Turk.

Having burnt the Muslim scriptures, Tamburlaine orders his generals to have all Turks and Persians slain or drowned in Asphaltis lake.

But perhaps nowhere in European literature is the Turkish or rather the Islamic menace which terrified the Christian world more bluntly and more excruciatingly illustrated than in François Rabelais' famous epic, *Pantagruel*. Rabelais, a French humanist, satirist and monk, was above all a physician, who studied medicine at the Sorbonne university in Paris. Later he practised and lectured on medicine at Lyons, at that time a great centre for medical scholarship. Considering that the canon of the Muslim scholar Avicenna on medicine had, until the end of the seventeenth century, been the major work taught at European universities, it is unlikely that Rabelais did not study this vital source of medical knowlege. However, if Avicenna provided Rabelais with background research materials for his medical degree, he certainly failed to alter his

---

10 Christopher Marlowe, *Tamburlaine The Great*, edited by J. S. Cunningham, London, 1981, Act V, pp. 303–4.

view of Islam. In his epic of the deeds and sayings of the hero Pantagruel there is a long passage on the captivity of a Christian friend in Turkey and the brutality he had suffered at the hand of the Turks. Rabelais' gruesome depiction of the Christian's torture while in Turkish captivity was created despite the evidence in contemporary travel books that the Muslims whether Arab, Turk or Persian treated their guests with the greatest hospitality no matter what their religion.

Rabelais' scene opens with Pantagruel asking his friend and his disciple Panurge to tell him the tale of his captivity in Turkey and how he had managed to escape from Muslim terror. Panurge is savouring the delicious wine that Pantagruel has offered him and laments 'the miserable Turks' who, because of the prohibition by their religion, cannot drink this marvellous elixir, as Christians do. 'Even if Muhammad's Qur'an were to contain no other evil rules than this one, I would still not submit myself to its laws', says Panurge.

The story that Panurge recounts is unbearably gruesome. Ignorant, perhaps, of the fact that Islam forbids the use of fire as punishment, and that the custom of burning heretics was an exclusively Christian prerogative, he describes in detail how the 'lascivious Turks' had tied him up; put him on skewers like a rabbit, wrapped in larding bacon and started roasting him alive over a roaring fire, merely because he was a Christian.

> Master, in the name of the Lord, Panurge said, not a word shall be a lie. Those lascivious Turks put me on a skewer, larded me up like a rabbit ready for roasting me alive. And as they were roasting me, I commended myself to the grace of God, remembering the good St. Laurence and always trusting in God that he would deliver me from this torment which did indeed occur in the strangest of ways. For just as I was commending myself to God in good faith, crying out: 'Lord God, help me! Lord God, save me! Lord God, spare me this torment to which these treacherous dogs are submitting me in order to adhere to their law!' the turnspit fell asleep by the will of God.[11]

Taking advantage of the opportunity, Panurge who is half-roasted, picks up a twig with his teeth from the edge of the fire and throws it

---

11 *Pantagruel* (Edition critique sur le texte original), Verdun L. Saulnier, Genève et Paris, 1959, pp. 76–81. (Passage translated by N. B. R. Reeves)

into a bundle of kindling wood piled up by the fireplace. A fire starts and soon reaches different parts of the room, waking Panurge's captor who, in horror, screams for help. The owners of the house storm in and without enquiring about the cause of the fire stab their servant to death for his negligence. The thongs that had tied Panurge's hand and foot have burnt away in the fire. He manages to get himself off the skewers and escapes. On the road he encounters people who pity him and pour buckets of water over him to cool down his burns. As Panurge walks away in agony he can see the whole house and its contents conflagrate and collapse. The fire soon becomes uncontrollable, growing in size and devouring one building after another, tearing in all directions. Soon the entire city is plunged into devastating flames. Panurge, standing on a hillock on the outskirts of the city watches the dramatic scene with an immense sense of joy and triumph. But as he is quietly savouring the pleasures of having inflicted such deadly harm upon his hated enemies, he sees a horde of maddened dogs, who have run away from the city fires, bounding towards him. The dogs had sniffed the odours of his freshly roasted flesh, as he puts it, and were heading towards him to tear him apart. But as they set out to attack him, Panurge pulled off the larding bacon that his cruel captors had tied all around him to roast him, and throwing them before the hungry dogs he ran away. The story ends with Panurge's return to France from his devastating Turkish nightmare.

Rabelais' *Pantagruel* was published in 1550 almost precisely one hundred years after the fall of Constantinople. The city that Panurge sets in flame is no doubt none other than Constantinople and in a satirical reversal of fate this humble Christian Frenchman single-handedly wreaks revenge on the city's conquerors, causing it to burn to the ground.

The scars of losing Constantinople to the Muslim Turks never healed in Europe. The crusading spirit persisted. A deep desire to recapture this classical Christian city remained alive.

It was revived by William Shakespeare when he wrote *Henry V* between the years 1598 and 1600. In this play, Henry, King of England is courting Princess Katherine, the daughter of King of France. He wants to make her the Queen of England. Their marriage is to seal the peace between England and France. The wooing scene is blunt and, although Henry denies possessing any eloquence or any courtly rhetoric, being a soldier, he embodies nevertheless the very essence of the Renaissance age. He is confident, forceful and above all a hard negotiator. He does not comply with the over-fastidious etiquette of the French court and tells Katherine that he, as the King of England, is the maker of law, not its follower. Henry's desire to unite the crowns of England and France is expressed in direct and unveiled terms. Their offspring, assumed to be male, is to be conceived between Saint Denis, and Saint George's day and is envisaged as a leader of Christendom who will relieve Europe of the Turkish menace:

> *Henry* Shall not thou and I, between Saint Denis and Saint George,
> Compound a boy, half French, half English, that shall go to
> Constantinople and take the Turk by the beard?[12]

Of course the idea is an anachronism on Shakespeare's part, since Constantinople did not fall to the Turks until 1453, while these events date from 1420. But they tell a clear tale. Even in Shakespeare's day the loss of Constantinople was lamented and the crusading mentality lived on in folk memory.

During the two hundred years of the Renaissance the flame of tolerance and understanding towards Muhammad and Islam had flickered only on a few occasions, lit by the Humanists who had taken a genuine interest in discovering more about the Qur'an instead of condemning it unread. But the flame was rapidly dowsed. The noble ideals of truth through knowledge and humanity proved no match for the Age's vision of man rivalling the gods. The powerful Renaissance notion of human beings defying all odds fused with lingering medieval superstitions and prejudice towards Islam. Thus, one proof of 'man's grandeur' came to be defiance of the Turks. Of course the threat to European Christianity from the expanding Turkish Empire was real, but this only reinforced the Renaissance dream of reborn man as reborn European man.

As the Church reformed itself in the late Renaissance, contempt and hatred for Islam and its founder were to be turned into a sinister backdrop against which Protestants could identify themselves. Martin Luther was the larger-than-life German priest who was not only to spark off the continental Reformation, but to fan the flames of vituperation directed against Muhammad. The Anti-Christ and the Satan of the Middle Ages were once more resurrected. The enemies of reformed

---

12 William Shakespeare, *King Henry V*, The Arden Shakespeare, edited by T. W. Craik, London, 1995, p. 359, line 205.

Christianity were declared to be, on the one hand, the internal enemy, the Pope, and, on the other, the external enemy, Muhammad, exemplified in the Turks.

6

Muhammad as an Anti-Christ

The fate of Muhammad and Islam in the Reformation

Therefore let him who can be angry with the Pope, execrate him, and curse him. For he has done more harm to the Kingdom of Christ and the Church than Muhammad. The Turk kills the body and plunders and lays waste the property of Christians, but the Pope stresses his Qur'an far more cruelly, in order that Christ may be denied. Both, of course, are the enemies of the Church and the Devil's own slaves, because both reject the Gospel.

Martin Luther: *Lectures on Genesis chapters 45–50.* 1545

The two leading men in Europe who split the fabric of Christendom and initiated the Reformation of the Roman Catholic Church and the establishment of Protestantism were the Dutch humanist Desiderius Erasmus and the German Roman Catholic monk, Martin Luther. Their names were frequently coupled and their portraits appeared side by side in the opening decades of the sixteenth century, when Europe was facing its most explosive religious conflict from within. Yet, God could not have produced two more different men than Erasmus and Luther, fundamental opposites in physique, character, conduct of life, manners and capacity of mind. Luther, some twenty years younger than Erasmus, was stout, thick-set, full-blooded with robust health, an exuberant personality and a forceful will. Erasmus, by contrast was physically delicate, sensitive and serene, a thin and sickly looking man with a pale complexion and a fragile body. While Erasmus, though brought up in poverty-stricken obscurity, was refined in his manners and habits, Luther, who had enjoyed a privileged upbringing, was coarse, tumultuous and rough. When Luther spoke, it was as if the church was filled with the rumble of thunder. By temperament and conviction a man of the people, his speech rushed forth like a torrent. Erasmus preferred to address himself to an educational audience, expressing his views and concerns through books, letters and tracts. He had a soft and gentle voice which he never raised. Instead he carefully trimmed and polished his sentences, sharpening his words to the finest of points. Luther's language was often violent and he did not refrain from fulminating against the Pope, Muhammad, the Turks and the Jews. Erasmus was a man of a conciliatory disposition who had a strong dislike of extremes. When a papal ban was pronounced on Luther as an excommunicated heretic at the Diet of Worms in 1521 – a response to his nailing his famous Theses to the door of the castle church in Wittenberg in denial of the supremacy of the Pope, Erasmus refused to intervene, either for or against Luther. He urged moderation on both sides and disclaimed sympathy with Luther. At a later stage, in his *Tract on Free Will*, Erasmus entered into real controversy with Luther. As a humanist, Erasmus did not dream of a rebellion against the ecclesiastical system, but of a *re-florescentia*, a re-flourishing of religion, of a renewal of the Christian ideal by a return to its Nazarene purity. On these latter points, Erasmus and Luther agreed. Just as the Renaissance had brought fresh vigour into the arts and sciences by the study of works of classical antiquity, so Erasmus hoped that the Church might be reformed by ridding it of fanaticism and superstition, going back to the teachings of the Gospels and the words of Christ. Erasmus worked at the practical realization of his vision by making a new translation of the Gospels from Greek into Latin, published in 1516, thus perhaps paving the way for Luther's rendering of the Bible into the German vernacular five years later.

Innumerable times Erasmus and Luther uttered the same ideas, but whereas Erasmus exercised a stimulating effect and great influence upon intellectuals, Luther's oratory animated the masses, becoming popular through slogans and hymns, racing across Germany and into other parts of Europe. Naturally when two such antagonistic temperaments work towards the same goal they are bound to clash. Their aims were broadly speaking the same, but their methods were different. Erasmus' scholarly phraseology, his classical eloquence, his smooth-tongued diplomacy and above all his call for unity were seen as unrealistic by his plain-spoken rival. And it is obvious who won the battle! Tolerance towards all mani-festations of reverence for God, not just acceptance of others' perceptions of truth, but a genuine interest in their discoveries and insights could appeal to individual thinkers. But the call for radical change, the elimination of evil, of immorality and of all that did not match one's own view, could enthuse the crowds. While the religion of Muhammad as expressed in his Scripture, the Qur'an, could fascinate the humanist, to the Christian reformer it was anathema, yet another distortion of God's truth. Perhaps it was natural, then, that the Pope and Muhammad should find themselves together in the pillory, at the receiving end of Luther's hurled invectives.

It was not as if the desire for reform was new. There had been unrest and dissatisfaction within the Church since the late fourteenth century. High-minded clergymen throughout Europe bemoaned the abuses perpetrated by successive Popes, their authoritarianism and the worldly direction the Church had assumed. The Pope was seen to live in exaggerated luxury, oblivious to the spiritual needs of the faithful, while the Church and its monasteries had acquired so much wealth as to arouse fierce criticism. Complaints centred mainly on three points: the Church's secular, political involvement as an Italian territorial power, severe financial demands imposed upon believers before they could be absolved from their sins and from eternal damnation, and the neglect of the parishes. The enforcement of clerical celibacy had led in many instances to clerical concubinage, and protests about clerical incontinence were heard in every country of Europe; the Papacy itself was among the most notorious offenders.

The dispute was on the doctrinal level, too. Those religious doctrines and practices not firmly founded in Scripture, such as monastic orders and the worship of Mary and the saints were now regarded by the sceptics as abuses of the Gospel. Furthermore, the special status of the clergy and the benefices heaped on them was questioned. Many of the lower clergy were uneducated and the ignorance of the people was blamed in part on their incompetence in guiding Christians to the path of spiritual and moral awareness. Erasmus, himself coming from a theological background, was conscious of the evils within the Church of his time. He had been educated in the humanist tradition by the Brethren of the Common Life. Upon the death of his father, his guardians had persuaded him to enter a monastery, but the lack of freedom to pursue his studies led Erasmus to leave it in 1495, and at the age of twenty-five he embarked on a scholarly career. Over the ensuing years he wrote the learned works that won him a reputation as one of Europe's most influential intellects. *The Praise of Folly* which he wrote in 1509, when he was a guest in the London home of Sir Thomas More, one of the pioneers of the English Counter-Reformation, was a bitter satire directed against monasticism, theologians and Church dignitaries. There is no mention of Muhammad or Islam in this work. Erasmus was much more concerned to correct morals, curb ambition and greed and stimulate piety within Christianity itself, not only through ridicule, but by the dissemination and encouragement of worthwhile learning. He insisted that the essence of Christianity was not to be found in outward observance, in pilgrimage, in crusading, in worship of saints and their relics or in psalm-singing, but in man's faith within himself and in his compassion for others.

Erasmus' evangelical humanism was not confined to the Netherlands but had exponents throughout Europe. In England there was John Colet, the Dean of St Paul's, who also postulated inwardness and piety. His Oxford lectures became popular and attracted Erasmus amongst his hearers. Another influential pioneer of the English Reformation was William Lily, the headmaster of St Paul's School who, with the rest of the English reformists, joined Erasmus' circle seeking to reform medieval Christendom. In France Jacques Lefèvre stressed the same ideals to his countrymen, and in Italy there were the ardent reforming churchmen and noblemen who represented the new humanism, amongst them Cardinal Giovanni Morone, Pietro Carnessecchi, the papal secretary himself, and the Spanish humanist Juan de Valdes who lived in exile in Naples as a consequence of the Inquisition.

But the reform that was to convulse Christendom and subvert the old religious order of Europe came from Germany and more precisely from the University of Wittenberg, where the Roman Catholic priest Martin Luther taught and preached his explosive ideas concerning the contrast between Christ – the poor and humble – and the Anti-Christ – the Pope, luxurious, indulgent and lofty. His revolutionary tracts were rapidly sold all over Germany; copies circulated in England, France, Switzerland, Holland and even Spain and Rome. Luther soon became a famous European figure for having rejected Papal supremacy and calling for the return to the simplicity of the early Christian Church. The decisive factor that enabled this dissemination of militant and inflammatory ideas was printing. Without that one cannot imagine the speed with which Luther's doctrines, in particular, managed to reach not just other priests and intellectuals but soon ordinary people too. His stormy views on Muhammad and Islam were simultaneously transmitted to the rest of reformist Europe, forming an integral part of the Protestant dogma, if not its very raison d'être. But no doubt a lasting and profound effect on people's new perception of their faith was ensured by Luther's German translation of the Old and New Testaments of 1534, which literally brought home the truths of the Christian scriptures directly to the congregations, breaking the monopoly of exclusive access to God's Word by the Latin-reading clergy. In England William Tyndale had already published the New Testament in English in 1525, precisely with the intention of providing this access. An admirer of Erasmus, he had fled from the wrath of the English Cardinal Thomas Wolsey to Germany, but was finally seized in 1536, strangled and burnt at the stake at Louvain in the Netherlands. He had also visited Luther on numerous occasions.

Luther's protest was not directed against the amorality and worldliness of individual popes, but rather against the Papacy as an institution. Anti-Christ was not one person against Christ, but doctrine against doctrine, church against church, faith against faith. Luther believed that in its false doctrine, the Papacy taught the Anti-Christ's deceit; hence the followers of Anti-Christ were members of the false church. The apocalyptic expectations, characteristic of the medieval Anti-Christ tradition thus continued into the Reformation. Protestants in different parts of Europe identified the Papacy with the Anti-Christ, claiming prophetic justification for their break from Rome. During the Crusades and long afterwards Muhammad and the 'Saracens' had been cast as Anti-Christs and as representatives of the forces of Satan on earth. Pope Innocent III had associated them with the seven-headed Beast of Apocalypse 13, calling for yet another Crusade in 1213. So Christians had continued to identify Muhammad and the 'Saracens' with Anti-Christ well into the late Middle Ages, whereupon the Turks were in their turn to become the personification of the Devil.

The Anti-Christ myth goes back to the beginnings of Christianity. For many centuries before the Reformation and for some hundred and fifty years afterwards the Anti-Christ seemed an intensely real and an extremely important focal point for the conceptualization of Christianity. Thomas Beard, Oliver Cromwell's schoolmaster and author of a best-seller in his day, said in the preface to his book of 1625, *Antichrist, the*

Pope of Rome, that 'Next unto our Lord and Saviour Jesus Christ, there is nothing so necessary as the true and solid knowledge of anti-Christ'.[1]

This may sound strange. But one must bear in mind that despite the emergence of the Renaissance and the shift of focus on man rather than God, the Bible had continued to be the main source of inspiration for the majority of Europeans. It was believed to contain divine truth on all matters; to be the guide to action in all spheres of life. That is why the medieval church had frowned on translation and study of the Bible by laymen. As the Reformation and printing had changed all that, Bible commentators began to find many more passages in the Old and New Testaments describing the characteristics of the Anti-Christ's kingdom. Those who, in the revolutionary crises of the sixteenth and seventeenth centuries, felt it their vocation to hasten this historic process, naturally wanted to know who the Anti-Christ was and whose downfall was at hand. Was it the Pope? The bishops? The Roman Catholic Church generally? Or was it Muhammad? The Turks? The Jews? Or was it simply a term of abuse hurled at anybody one disliked? Indeed, many used the symbolism of the Anti-Christ with no conscious purpose in mind. They drew on allegorical habits of mind inherited from the past, reinforced by the availability for all of the Bible in the vernacular.

For Luther the true Anti-Christ was decidedly the Pope. In his pamphlet *De Anti-Christo*, translated into English in 1529, Luther referred to the Pope in his *Table Talk* as 'the right Antichrist' and held that 'the conviction that the Pope is Antichrist is a life and death matter for the Church'.[2] Similarly, Jean Calvin, the French Reformist, saw his mission as abolition of the Anti-Christ. All the late-Renaissance heretics similarly regarded the Pope as the Anti-Christ. Indeed William Tyndale had attacked the Pope as 'the very Antichrist'.[3]

In England since the very beginnings of the Reformation in the first half of the sixteenth century, invidious comparisons had been made between Christendom and Islam, although the 'the tyranny of the Turks' was declared as more endurable than 'the tyranny of the Popes'. In the eyes of the English Protestants the Pope and Muhammad were both evil, but the Pope was several degrees more evil than Muhammad. While

1 Thomas Beard, *Antichrist the Pope of Rome*, London, 1625, Preface.
2 *Dr. Martin Luther's Divine Discourses*, translated by Captain Henry Bell, London 1652, pp. 299, 312, 325–6.
3 William Tyndale, *Doctrinal Treatises*, Parker Society, London, 1848, pp. 185–6.

Muhammad was the enemy without, the Pope was the enemy within and hence more dangerous. Bishop John Bale, author of several religious plays and numerous polemical works in favour of the cause of the Reformation wrote *King John II* around the year 1550, the first English historical play to be written. In it a comparison between the Islamic and the Catholic peril was made by the protagonist Veryte who expresses his dislike of Catholicism in the following passage:

> *Veryte* As I sayde afore, I aborre to shewe your doynges. The Turks
> I dare saye, are a thousande tyme better than you.[4]

In his exposition of the Book of Revelations which is incorporated in the modern edition of his collected works, Bale identifies the Pope with Gog and Muhammad with Magog and predicts a common catastrophe will overwhelm these two 'enemies of the Christian faith':

> When these enemies Gog and Magog shall be at the highest in
> their vengeable enterprises against the elect city . . . the fire that is
> kindled in the wrath of God shall burn unto the bottom of hell and
> consume up these terrible termagants.[5]

But the first person to have compared the vices in the Church with the dangers of Islam was the fourteenth-century Oxford scholar John Wycliff. In all his later writings and especially from about 1378 to 1384 he has something to say about Islam. In his polemical work *De Christo et Suo Adversario Anti-Christo* the main characteristics of Islam are described as being also the main characteristics of the western Church. These were, according to Wycliff, pride, cupidity, the desire for power, the lust for possession and the preference of human ingenuity to divine spirituality. Wycliff argued that these features in the western Church were the main cause both of the divisions within Christendom and of the division of the west from Nestorian and other eastern Churches. 'We Western Mahomets,[6] was his favourite slogan, referring to the abuses of the

---

4 *Select Works of John Bale*, edited by Henry Christmas, Cambridge, 1849, *King John II*, 2256–7, p. 114.
5 *Select Works of John Bale*,. op. cit., p. 575.
6 John Wycliff, *Dialogus*, Wycliff Society Publications, London, 1382, p. 91, quoted by R. W. Southern in *Western Views of Islam in the Middle Ages*, Cambridge Massachusetts, 1962, p. 79.

Church. The sins of the Church were, in Wycliff's appraisal, the cause of the rise of Islam, which only began with the growth of pride and greed within the Christian Church. And just as the worldliness of the Church produced the religion of worldliness in Islam, so Islam would wither away with the reversal of this tendency and the return of Christianity to its pure and innocent origins.

Referring to Islam in his other work *De Veritate Sacrae Scripturae*, Wycliff stressed that 'this anti-religion will grow until the clergy returned to the poverty of Jesus Christ'.[7] Even preaching and argument directed against Islam should be subordinate to the reform of the Church from within, he urged. Islam, he said, was only curable by curing the diseases of Christendom. It was clearly in this tradition that Luther wrote, but with far more devastating effect.

In 1542 when religious tension was reaching its pinnacle in Europe, with Catholics and Protestants at each others' throats, the Turks had overrun Hungary, the first great European kingdom to suffer external attack since the Barbarian invasion over a thousand years earlier. This was the continuation of Turkish expansion into Europe's eastern frontiers, a huge disaster for an already divided and troubled Continent.

It was at this critical time that the aging Luther made a translation, in his eloquent German, of one of the great anti-Islamic works of the thirteenth century, Montecroce's *Confutatio Alchoran*.[8]

In his preface to the above translation Luther gave powerful expression to one well-established medieval concept, that of despair about the possibility of any religious or intellectual solution that would meet the challenge of Islam. Luther agreed with Montecroce that Muslims could not be converted, 'their hearts were hardened, they mocked and ridiculed the articles of our Faith and they thought Christians were fools to believe in such impossible things'[9]

Luther wrote to strengthen the faith of those Christians who might find themselves wondering whether there was more salvation in Islam than in Christianity. He was profoundly fearful that Christendom might be engulfed by Islam. The success of the Turks and the Saracens over so many hundreds of years, he claimed, did not show that they enjoyed

---

7 John Wycliff, *De Veritate Sacrae Scripturae*, Wycliff Society, London 1378, pp. 266–7, quoted by R. W. Southern, op. cit., p. 80.
8 R. W. Southern, op. cit, p. 105.
9 Ibid.

God's favour; they were only fulfilling the prophecy that the blood of Christ must be shed from the beginning of the world to the end. Luther urged his fellow Protestants to be patient until the Muslims had exhausted themselves, as men on whom the wrath of God had fallen. 'Let us stay in God's grace and observe His word and sacraments'.[10]

Luther's immense anxiety about the possibility of Christians wanting to become Muslims remained with him throughout his life. In his *Selected Psalms* dating from 1530, he expressed his fears thus, urging Christians to watch out unceasingly so that they do not succumb to the temptations of the Devil:

> Whoever is interested may learn a lesson from my example, which I shall now confess. A few times – when I did not bear this principal teaching in mind – the Devil caught up with me and plagued me with Scripture passages until heaven and earth became too small for me. Then all the words and laws of man were right, and not an error was to be found in the whole papacy. In short, the only one who had ever erred was Luther. All my best works, teachings, sermons and books had to be condemned. The abominable Muhammad almost became my prophet, and both Turks and Jews were on the way to pure sainthood.
> Therefore, dear brother, be not proud or sure and certain that you know Christ well. You hear what I confess to you, admitting what the Devil was able to do against Luther, who is supposed to be a doctor in this art, who has preached, composed, written, said, sung, and read so much in these matters. So take my advice, and do not celebrate too soon. Watch out that your skill does not desert you. Be concerned, be humble, and pray that you may grow in this art and be protected against the crafty Devil.[11]

In the end it was the Turks who assured the status of Islam as a worldwide religion. During the years of revolutionary religious struggle which split the Protestants from the Catholics, the Turks were trying their political fortune in expanding the boundaries of their Empire. They conquered Egypt in 1517. They attacked Vienna in 1529 and again in 1683, but were driven out, having already suffered naval defeat in the Mediterranean at Lepanto in 1571. The Otttoman Turks did

---

10 Ibid., p. 106.
11 *Martin Luther's Works* translated by Jaroslav Pelikan, Saint Louis, 1958–1967, *Selected Psalms III*, 1530, Volume 14, pp. 37–8.

what they could to promote the spread of Islam. When Christian Spain and Portugal embarked on great voyages of discovery, building up the first large colonial empires by European powers, they found that Muslim venturers had already carried Islam to Africa and to south-east Asia.

However, for Luther the real Anti-Christ remained as before, the Pope rather than Muhammad or the Turks. He labelled Muhammad 'the Son of the Devil, second in wickedness to the Pope'.

Luther taught that Anti-Christ had existed not only outside the Church, but within the Church itself. He illustrated the record of conflict between the 'true, spiritual, hidden Church' and the 'false, fleshly, institutional Church' as promoted by the Pope. Inspired by Luther, the Protestants developed a consistent pattern of condemnation of the Catholic doctrine and the papacy and interpreted the Reformation as fulfilling an apocalyptic role. The reforms in Germany, England and northern Europe were presented as the wounding of the Beast's head – normally portrayed in images of the Pope. But this does not mean that Islam seemed less ominous or that the great contempt for the Pope mitigated the hatred of the Turks. On the contrary, Luther was paranoid about the Muslims and their faith.

Throughout his collected works a deep and agonized odium for the Pope, for Muhammad, for Turks and for Jews is to be found in lengthy arguments to prove that they are the true enemies of Christ. In the exposition of the 14th, 15th and 16th chapters of the *Gospel of St John*, which Luther presented in sermons delivered between the years 1537 and 1538, he obdurately insists on drawing parallels between Islam and Catholicism:

> Thus the Turks, to begin with, introduced something novel and refused to remain with the simple Gospel. 'Oh', exclaimed Muhammad, 'Christ has ascended into heaven; I must have an angel through whom God communicates with me! Then he proceeded to create a new Bible – that is, his Qur'an – and would not accept Baptism – The Pope, together with his priests and monks, has been doing the same thing. They have surrendered Christ and the words about faith, ignored the Bible, and claimed that God sits enthroned up in heaven like a terrible Judge.[12]

---

12 *Martin Luther's Works*, op. cit, *Sermons delivered in the years 1537–1538*, Volume 14, *Martin Luther's exposition of the 14th, 15th and 16th chapters of the Gospel of St John*, p. 69.

From Luther's own statements it transpires that he had not even read the Qur'an until 1542, when a translation came to hand. Until then his knowledge had been based on speculations by Italian authors and not on a study of the Islamic Scripture. But even after having read the Qur'an, he rejected it as profoundly anti-Christian and anti-Biblical. Luther mocked Muhammad for having believed in one supreme God alone, refusing to recognize the divine in Christ. He accused him of false prophethood and identified him alongside the Pope as having received his promptings not from God, but from the Devil, as this excerpt from his *Sermons on St John's Gospel* illustrates:

> But if a new doctrine – such as Muhammad's was – were to be introduced, it should be confirmed with signs and miracles, as is commended in Deut. 18. 22. To be sure, the papacy and its monasticism were confirmed in this manner, but by the Devil. This agrees with St Paul's prediction about the Anti-Christ in Thess. 2. 11, where he says that God would 'send upon them a strong delusion' and preachers who would come with signs and wonders, which are, in fact, the Devil's lies.[13]

And in his *First Lectures on Psalms 1–75* the Muslims' triumph and prosperity are attributed to Muhammad's legacy of 'cunning and deceit':

> Everything that Christ wanted will prosper (even though it looks like the opposite to fools), because His church perseveres against all attacks of enemies. Muhammad prospered. 'By his cunning he makes deceit prosper under his hand', as Daniel 8. 25 says.[14]

Luther's apocalyptic views of Christ and Anti-Christ found dramatic expression in his *Selected Psalms*. In the interpretation of the Apocalypse, he proved that despite his reforms he was still basically a medieval churchman. Here is his vision of the annihilation of the Anti-Christ through the final appearance of Christ:

> The Roman Empire opposed itself to Christ with all its power and attempted to eradicate His name. Christians were martyred and murdered – without number. But what did the Romans accomplish,

---

13 Ibid., p. 368
14 *Luther's Works*, op. cit. Volume 10, *Martin Luther's First Lectures on the Psalms I, Psalms 1–75.*

except that they all exhausted themselves against Christ and were compelled to put their heads into the earth under his feet? And since they would not stop their raging and persecution of Christ, God struck back at them. Their kingdom, power, and might were torn apart. As penalty for the contempt and persecution of the Gospel, God has similarly allowed other great kingdoms, but especially the beautiful lands of Greece and Asia Minor, to be miserably and shamefully devastated and destroyed by the Saracens and Turks. To sum up, He has always been forced to have a row with enemies great and small, who wickedly opposed Him, until they were crushed and Christendom was revenged and survived them.

On the basis of this, we can be prophets and prophesy with certainty to the present enemies and persecutors of the Gospel – both the Turk with his Muhammadan sects and factions and the Pope with his Anti-Christian ones, who intend to cast down this Lord with His throne – that they will achieve nothing at all. Their heads must also lie under the feet of this Christ. Somewhere He will also find a power against them by which He will overthrow them, just as He has found such means before. He can certainly punish His enemies through other enemies. The Jews through the Romans, the Romans through the Goths. He will find someone to ruin both the Turks and the Pope with his tyrants. Or else reaching down from heaven, He will finish them off Himself and strike them down with the Last Day, so that all at once they lie in a heap under His feet, just as the Scriptures tell of Anti-Christ that he is to be destroyed without human hands, through the final and glorious appearance and coming of Christ.[15]

Although Luther had not read the Qur'an at the time of his *Lectures on the Song of Solomon* in 1526, he knew well that Muhammad had denied the divinity of Jesus and his crucifixion and that he had presented him as a prophet in the lineage of Abraham. During these lectures Luther's anger was vividly displayed in his court-room defence of the Holy Trinity:

Now, if you believe and understand that Christ is very God and very man, as Scripture teaches us, then see to it that you do not separate the person of Christ nor intermingle the two natures or the divine and the human essence into one essence, but that you differentiate between the natures and preserve the one Person. For

---

15 *Luther's Works*, op. cit. Volume 13 *Martin Luther's Selected Psalms*, pp. 270 f.

many wiseacres have come to grief on this point, for they have insisted either on uniting deity and humanity into one nature or on dividing them into two persons, as Nestorius and Euches and their like did. The Jews and Turks presume to be extraordinarily clever, exceedingly clever and look down upon us Christians as great dolts. If Christ is God, they say, how can he die like a man, for God is immortal? If He is man, how can He be God's Son, for God has no wife? Here the saying is pertinent: Money implies honour, said the frog, and sat down on a penny.

Here these wise, yes, wise, wiser, wisest people, the Turks and the Jews teach us that God cannot die and that He has no wife. How could we stupid Christians ever acquire such profound wisdom if these great and supreme teachers did not instruct and enlighten us silly ducks and geese of the fact that God has no life and that He cannot die?[16]

Here Luther's anti-Jewish sentiments are conjoined with his contempt for Islam. In his indignation he descends into vitriolic and obscene imagery:

Reason, Jew and Muhammad shout at us Christians: 'How can that be understood as speaking of God? How can God be a servant? How can He be a wretched sinner? 0 God, what non-sensical, stupid and monstrous people we Christians are before such exalted, wise and holy people who worship no creature but only the one God! Reason admittedly does not find that in its Bible, that is, in its chimney flue, its dreamland. Nor do the Jews find this in their Bible, that is, in the Talmud, under the sow's tail, where they study their Schamhaperes. Neither does Muhammad find it in his Bible, that is, in his bed of harlotry; for that is where he did most of his studying. Thus this contemptible, filthy fellow boasts that God, that is, the Devil, had endowed him with so much physical strength that he could bed with as many as forty women and yet remain unsatisfied. Indeed his choice book, the Qur'an smells and savours of his studies in that Bible, the carnality of harlots. He looked for and found the spirit of his prophecy in the rigid spot, that is in the Mons Veneris. And it is surely not surprising that he who pores over such books knows nothing of God, or Messiah. Thus they do not know what they are saying and what they are doing. Thanks and praise be to God in all eternity that we Christians

---

16 *Luther's Works*, op. cit. Volume 15, *Martin Luther's Notes on Ecclesiastes, Lectures. on the Song of Solomon, Treatise on the last words of David*, pp. 340 f.

know the Messiah is God's one eternal Son whom He set into the world to take our sins upon Himself.[17]

Luther's constant appeal to his fellow Christians was to disregard what Muhammad had said about Christianity and to remain steadfast in their allegiance to Christ. This was of course symptomatic of a religion which still felt vulnerable:

> All right, let these miserable fools go their way and think themselves clever until they are surfeited with it. But you cling firmly to the Christian faith, taught us by Scripture that Jesus Christ is true God and God's Son, and also true man, David's and Mary's son and yet not two sons, two men, two persons, but one Son, one Person of and in two distinct natures, deity and humanity.[18]

> As for you, be content with the God incarnate. Then you will remain in peace and safety, and you will know God. Cast off speculations about divine glory, as the Pope and Muhammad speculate. You stay with Christ crucified, whom Paul and others preach.[19]

As a Protestant and a Reformer of the Catholic faith, Luther clearly opposed any sanctification of the Virgin Mary. The following passage, extracted from *Sermons on the Gospel of St John,* demonstrates once again Luther's characteristically coarse and offensive language whenever he spoke about Muhammad or Islam. It is also a clear illustration of his profound bitterness that the Muslims should exalt Muhammad over and above Jesus:

> The Turks do not believe in Christ. Muhammad, with his Turkish faith, raved and ranted against Christ. To be sure, he conceded that Christ was born of a virgin; but the Turks claim that such a thing is no rarity among them – well this may happen and be true among them, but with us those virgins who bear children become women. A virgin who gives birth to a child cannot remain a virgin. We do not want them to spread it in our homes; otherwise our daughters would all become whores. I do not believe that a virgin who has a child remains a virgin. Among us this is incredible. Those who have

---

17 Ibid.
18 Ibid.
19 *Luther's Works,* op. cit., Volume 17, *Martin Luther's Lectures on Isaiah,* 1527–1530, p. 331.

the audacity to claim that it is true are stupid asses. Furthermore the Turks say that Christ was indeed an excellent prophet and a great man. They exalt Him above David, Isaiah, and all other prophets. They must admit that Christ was the Word of the Father, and yet they claim that Christ was not so great as their Muhammad.[20]

That the Muslims could not be converted and that their loyalty to Muhammad was so unshakeable remained the bane of Luther's life.

For Luther, faith meant Christianity alone, a religion based on historical fact, resting upon something truly done by God at a given time – the Incarnation and Redemption – and done once and for all. This unique event had become known to man solely through Christian scriptures. The Roman Catholic Church had however distorted these scriptures and had been preaching a false religion for centuries. Luther saw his vocation in taking the Christian faith back to its true origins. Although he remained a medieval Christian in many ways, his reforms within the Church went far beyond anything medieval. In the Middle Ages it was held that only priests, monks and nuns held vocations. Only they had been called by God to dedicate themselves to his service. But in Luther's teachings every occupation was a calling since all Christians were priests. This, according to the nineteenth-century German sociologist Max Weber, was to be the driving force behind Western capitalism and Western welfare and prosperity. Another great departure from Catholic teaching and practice was Luther's abolition of monasticism and clerical celibacy. A further revolutionary measure which was to shake the very foundations of Catholicism was his reduction of the sacraments from seven to two: baptism and the eucharist. The others, he stressed, were not instituted by Jesus. Marriage, he said, was basically a civil matter and should receive no more than a blessing from the Church. But it was through the abolition of the sacrament of penance that Luther presented a new picture of God and Jesus. The medieval Church had required man to seek to purge himself of sinful inclinations by acts of self-denial such as going on a pilgrimage or contributing money towards a good cause. The Roman Church addressed itself to sinners in the sacrament of penance, offering absolution to all who obeyed its commands. Luther on the other hand concluded that God's favour is not a prize to be won,

---

20 *Luther's Works*, op. cit., Volume 22, *Martin Luther's Sermons on the Gospel of St John*, 1526, p. 17.

but a gift. Only when individuals stop trying to achieve God's favour by their own abilities and accomplishments can they understand the grace of God. God makes persons righteous in His eyes, not through moral goodness or faithfulness to duty, but because of His love for creation. God's love, Luther held, was given to the world in the life, death and resurrection of Christ. In other words, this was Luther's message of justification by faith in God's grace – without the need of the priest's intercession on behalf of the sinner.

'Dangerous heretics' like Luther who were perceived as a threat to the power of the Church, were tortured and burnt at the stake in those turbulent years. That Luther remained unscathed is testimony to the enormous support he received not only from the universities where his ideas had gained considerable currency, but also from a distinguished protector, Frederick the Wise of Saxony. The Holy Roman Emperor, Charles V, had aligned himself with the Pope, placing Luther under the ban of the Empire. In 1522 Frederick secretly subverted the Emperor's intentions by hiding Luther for a year in his castle at Warburg. Luther took advantage of this enforced withdrawal to undertake his famous translation of the Bible into German. At the end of that year his translation along with other tracts and pamphlets were rolling off the press and circulating throughout Germany. From now on nothing could stop the spread of Lutheran revolutionary religion.

In 1525 the monks and nuns who in consequence began leaving their monasteries and convents in large numbers, were, Luther said, free to marry. In the same year the whole community of a nunnery had escaped in a cart used to transport empty barrels and had come to Wittenberg. 'A wagon load of vestal virgins has come to town', a contemporary declared. 'God give them husbands lest worse befall'. Luther tried to find them homes and jobs. One, Katherina von Bora, intimated that she would consider Luther as a husband, if asked. And so it was that 'to please her father and displease the Pope', as Luther put it, he married her, thereby establishing the archetype of the Protestant family parsonage. In fact, according to some accounts Luther even favoured polygamy for men, seeing no contradiction with it in the Bible and noting that the patriarchs of the Old Testaments had all been polygamous. Indeed during the Reformation, the topics of marriage, divorce and polygamy were fervently propagated as the antithesis to the doctrine of celibacy and monogamy represented by the Church of Rome. Yet, Muhammad's marriages, also in the tradition of Biblical times, were condemned as licence.

In England, the Reformation, as we know, had not started with a quarrel with Rome primarily over morality or finances, but mainly over the matter of a royal marriage. As a sacrament of the Church, marriage was subject to ecclesiastical jurisdiction, but royal marriages were affairs of the state, emphatically so, because kings were expected to ensure the succession by producing progeny. England required a male heir to King Henry VIII, but after six years of marriage to his first wife, Queen Catherine of Aragon, only one child had survived – and a girl at that, the Princess Mary. Henry took his case before Pope Clemens VII. The Pope refused divorce on doctrinal grounds but also because he did not wish to offend Catherine's uncle, the Holy Roman Emperor, Charles V. So, Henry declared himself supreme Head of the Church in England, which then granted him an annulment.

In the century following Luther's schism Western Europe underwent vast changes, for the religious and secular events of the era were inextricably entwined. The success of the Reformation increased the pressure for the Catholics themselves to undertake reforms from within. But the Council of Trent which met between the years 1551 and 1563 to determine the extent to which changes should occur, decided in the end to reinstate traditional doctrine regarding the sacraments, the Bible and papal supremacy. Only few concessions were made to Protestant criticism. In Spain, Italy and the rest of Catholic Europe the Inquisition investigated suspected heretics, passing offenders to the secular authorities for punishment. Not only Protestants, but also Muslims and Jews were subjected to the laws of the Inquisition. In Spain, by the extensive and horrifying methods used by the well-established Spanish Inquisition, the devout Queen of Spain, Isabella and the ascetic monk Cardinal Ximènez had already achieved total uniformity in religion, expelling all the Jewish and Muslim population from their country at the close of the fifteenth century. The Protestants were not any more compassionate towards their rivals. They embarked on their own purges, eliminating those who contradicted them in their new view of the world. Protestants even killed their co-religionists for slight doctrinal differences. But ultimately politics and war were largely determined by the efforts of Protestantism and Catholicism to gain the ascendency in Europe. The religious tensions that had built up during the sixteenth century finally erupted in a long and devastating war which lasted thirty years and which was concluded in 1648 with the Treaty of Westphalia. It embroiled all Europe. Catholics and different shades of Protestants fought against each other in a Europe that had been increasingly weakened by economic and social disruption, military distruction, famine and consequent disease.

The Treaty of Westphalia marked the close of the Reformation and was to lead to the emergence of the modern secular states. The religious divisions of Europe as they are today were the outcome of the Reformation and the Thirty Years War. The reduction in the power of the churches opened the way to the rise of a new ruling class in Europe. In Europe's modern nation states it was not the old order of knights and aristocrats who had once led the Crusades, but the new trading and professional urban gentry who began to dominate the scene.

In spite of the fact that most European monarchs had by the year 1600 sent ambassadors to the court of the Turkish Sultans in Constantinople, acknowledging their status and their rule, the myth of the Anti-Christ and its identification with the Turks and Islam continued to haunt Europe. From Portugal to Spain, from Germany to England, from France to Holland the dread of Islam remained widespread during the seventeenth century. It was still so powerful that the Mayor of Amsterdam and later ambassasor to Paris and London, Coenraad von Beuningen, became convinced that the coming of Christ's kingdom on earth was at hand. One night he got up and raged through the streets of Amsterdam, banging on doors to raise the alarm.[21] There were various other individuals who felt a personal call to travel up and down the Dutch provinces, for example, preaching repentance and the coming of God's kingdom as the power of Islam had continued to gather with the expansion of the Turkish Empire. In 1672 Sir Johannes Rothe, an English aristocrat and Dutch Fifth Monarchist, who had been sent as a child by his father to school in Amsterdam and had stayed on to settle there, proclaimed in a pamphlet that Daniel's Fourth Monarchy was shortly to be replaced by the Fifth. The Kingdom of Rome would be torn to pieces by 'the Emperor of the Mahometans'. The King of France would punish the Emperor for his sins and the Turks would then accept Jesus as their Lord.[22]

---

21   Christopher Hill, *The World Turned Upside Down*, London, 1986, p. 310.
22   Christopher Hill, op. cit., pp. 310–11.

The apocalypse had even attracted mathematicians at the beginnning of the seventeenth century. They were concerned with dating Biblical history and Biblical prophecy. John Napier is said to have especially valued his invention of logarithms because it speeded up his calculations of the number of the Beast of the Apocalypse. He had identified the Anti-Christ with the Pope and the Turks, and had predicted the Day of Judgement to be the year 1688.[23] Another astrologer, Master Thomas Brightman, equally believed that the seventeenth century was to see the climax of Christian history. In *The Revelation of St John*, published in 1644, he wrote, 'We wait every day, while the Anti-Christ of Rome and the Turk shall be utterly destroyed'.[24] His expectation was that Rome would fall in around 1650 and the Turks would be overthrown by 1686.

By the year 1600 the Protestant heresy that the Pope was the real Anti-Christ had also been officially accepted by the Church of England. However the topic became a major political controversy at the end of King James' reign, when Richard Montagu declared that the Pope was an Anti-Christ, but not the Anti-Christ. The Turks, rather than the Pope were the supreme Anti-Christ.[25] Indeed, for the English revolutionary poet, John Milton, the theme of the Anti-Christ constituted a major intellectual challenge. In *The Tenure* and in *Eikonoklastes*, he declared it to be the duty of the English revolutionaries 'first to overcome those European kings who receive their power not from God but from the Beast'[26] and that he would be delighted 'to see the English army and navy liberate Greece from the Turks'.[27] In *Of Reformation*, Milton announced that Christ would come shortly and judge these kingdoms and put an end to all earthly tyrannies. As with Milton, one of the most important aspects of the Anti-Christ tradition in Europe remained the view that Anti-Christ was always the holder of political power who persecutes

---

23 This prophecy had been quoted in a sermon preached to the House of Commons in 1641. See Nathaneal Homes, *The New World*, 1641, p. 37, quoted by Christopher Hill, *The Antichrist in Seventeenth-Century England*, London 1969, pp. 25–6.

24 Thomas Brightman *The Revelation of St John*, 4th edition, 1644, pp. 109–57, 378–81, 520, 566, 612–746, 966–7, 1077, quoted by Christopher Hill in *The Antichrist in Seventeenth Century England*, op. cit., p. 26.

25 Richard Montagu, *A New Gagg for an Old Goose*, 1624, pp. 73–5 quoted by Christopher Hill, op. cit., p. 35.

26 Christopher Hill, *The World Turned Upside Down*, op. cit. ('Milton's Christian Doctrine'), p. 283.

27 Ibid.

God's people and who opposes the teachings of Christ. It was on this understanding of the Anti-Christ that the continental Reformation and the Thirty Years War had been fought – and it was in the same spirit that the English Civil War of 1640 broke out. It was also in this particular light that the Turks were viewed as oriental tyrants and simultaneously as the embodiment of the Anti-Christ. Milton's epic and covert political enquiry *Paradise Lost*, published in 1667, rests for example on the dualism between Heaven and Hell. Here Satan is the King of Hell just as Christ is the King of Heaven and it can be no coincidence that in Book X, verse 445, Satan is depicted as ascending a throne similar to that of a Turkish Sultan, surrounded by evil councillors, constituting a Divan, a Turkish Council of State.[28] Satan's power also symbolizes what Milton saw as the uncontrolled drive of the English Puritan revolutionaries. Yet, this is a complex poem, for Milton had himself been a revolutionary, and in this sense the epic can be read as a profound exercise in soul-searching. But if anything was to represent the negative excesses of revolution it still had to be the Turks!

The Reformation, both on mainland Europe and in England, had drastically and permanently curbed the power of the Roman Church in the north of the continent. The doctrine of the Anti-Christ had served its purpose in the war of words. If the Papacy was not completely destroyed it was contained. The defeat of the Turks outside Vienna in 1683 was likewise to mark their final containment outside central Europe. In the coming decades the nation states of Europe, Spain, Portugal, England and Holland were to follow the example of France under Louis XIV, the Sun King, and emerge as the dominant and rival secular powers in post-Reformation Europe. Their interests were turning outwards to the East and West Indies, and to the New World, north and south, to which their increasingly sophisticated ships were taking them. The great monarchs of the seventeenth century had already patronized men of letters and the arts, to their own greater glory. It was in this climate that the Age of Reason could be born; and the medieval heritage of the Anti-Christ as a source of fear and of invective against the Pope and Muhammad grew weaker and anachronistic. Would a fresh and more balanced look at Islam and Muhammad now be possible in Europe?

---

28 For an analysis of Milton's Paradise Lost, see Christopher Hill, *The World Turned Upside Down*, op. cit. (The Great Poems), p. 364 f.

7

Humanist or Fanatic?

The Enlightenment divided

But when a camel dealer stirs up rebellion, claims to have conversed with Gabriel, and to have received this incomprehensible book, in which every page does violence to sober reason, when he murders men and abducts women in order to force them to believe in this book, such conduct can be defended by no man unless he is born a Turk, or unless superstition has choked all of the light of nature in him.

Voltaire, Preface to *Mahomet ou le Fanatisme*. 1742

Europe, during the first half of the eighteenth century, was thought by the French to be, without question, the centre of the universe and France the centre of Europe. For fifty years from 1660, France basked in the glory of being the most dominant power in Europe and Louis XIV in his sumptuous palace at Versailles was feared and revered as the ultimate autocrat and the symbol of a triumphant France. To mark this central position Louis called himself *Le Roi Soleil*, the Sun King. His army, he believed, was invincible. It had conquered much of mainland Europe, including Bavaria and the Rhineland and parts of Italy. In 1700, following the death of the heirless Charles II of Spain, Louis secured an alliance with Spain, the other great Catholic and rival power, by accepting on behalf of his grandson, the Duc of Anjou, the Spanish throne and its empire. Protestantism in France had been practically extinguished through Louis' unscrupulous persecutions and the Calvinist Huguenots had fled to Germany, the Low Countries and England. The Church of France, although adamant about its independence, had remained wedded to the Church of Rome. Louis believed that kings reigned by divine right, receiving their power from God. This belief was summarized in the famous words attributed to him: *L'état c'est moi*! ('I *am* the state'!). Never since the days of the Roman Emperors had the rule of a single man been accepted with such acquiescence, never had the principles of monarchy and the divine right of kings seemed more secure and never again was any sovereign to create around his person and his palace a legend of equal majesty and splendour. The opulence and glitter of the court, the monumental design of the Palace of Versailles and its magnificent gardens were imitated throughout Europe, especially among the innumerable petty states and courts of the German lands.

Night after night the flicker of ten thousand or more candles would be reflected in the mirrors of salons and galleries, throwing a dazzling radiance on tapestried or marbled walls, on painted ceilings, upon crowds of courtiers dressed in silk and velvet, upon the rubies and diamonds looped in their high head-dresses, upon blue liveries and white wigs. From the garden terraces outside would come the sound of stringed and wind instruments mingling with the splash of fountains and cascades. The Sun King would be making an appearance. The heels of the guardsmen would be clattering upon the marbled floors of the royal ante-rooms and the master of ceremonies would announce the arrival of the Sovereign, upon which the nervous courtiers would range themselves carefully along the aisles, and as they bowed to their waists and their wives or mistresses curtsied the King would acknowledge with a perfunctory nod, marking his undisputed and self-evident authority.

Between the end of the Thirty Years War in 1648 and the French Revolution in 1789 the most typical form of government in Europe was absolute monarchy. Louis XIV, who ruled France for seventy-two years from 1643, had set the example as the archetypal European monarch. In this style of government kings were unhindered by the need to refer to representative assemblies, and instead developed ways of controlling their states more firmly. Louis' absolutist measures, his tax system and his standing army were copied across the whole of Europe together with his style of personal rule.

Louis' identification of himself with the state was most evident in his foreign policy. He saw his personal reputation, or *gloire*, as inseparable from that of France. Between 1667 and 1713 he fought a series of increasingly large-scale and expensive wars in an effort to assert his own prestige and dynastic rights and to strengthen France's frontiers at home and in its colonies abroad. French colonization had begun in a number of West Indian islands and in Canada early in the seventeenth century and in Louisiana and the Mississippi basin at the end of seventeenth century. In 1664 the French East India Company was founded to compete with the flourishing Dutch and English East India companies. The ambitions of the French were not to cease with the death of Louis in 1715, but continued with their capture of Madras from the British in the 1740s. In the early eighteenth century the French had established factories in Bengal on the east coast of India and had thus grown into a natural trading and colonial rival to England. The conflict came to a head during the Seven Years War from 1756 to 1763, when France, diverted by her war with Prussia, was defeated by England in Canada and the Ohio Valley. At the same time the English Commander Robert Clive drove the French out of southern India. But despite the defeats in the colonies and the loss of territories through wars of rivalry in Europe itself, the French cultural and intellectual influence remained dominant throughout the eighteenth century and Versailles continued to be an enduring symbol of the graces and the arts. No European could claim to be a man of letters unless he possessed a thorough knowledge of the language, literature and art of France. During the eighteenth century the whole of educated Europe thought French.

Europe's attention was no longer focused on the Turkish threat which had been so feared in the previous two centuries. Instead, it was the riches and territories of overseas which fascinated and engaged the French, the English, the Dutch, the Portuguese and the Spaniards. The military defeat of the Turks outside Vienna in 1683 had been a decisive turning-point. Their power in Europe had been contained and the Turks had instead concentrated on their ambitions in the Middle East. Islam and Muhammad had become a source of provocation for the mind rather than a source of military confrontation. The thinkers and writers of the Age of Reason and the Enlightenment were to use the sometime rival religion and its Prophet as examples and comparators in their tracts on the state of European affairs, beliefs and thinking. What had represented a deadly menace, prompting invective and defamation, became sometimes exotic, though in most cases a still despised analogy for absolutism, corruption and abuse of human rights in Europe itself. Indeed, religion generally was losing its power over thinkers' minds as a direct consequence of the insights gained through the science of Newton and the earlier pioneering astronomers, Copernicus, Brahe, Kepler and Galileo. The Catholic Church's fundamental dogma that the sun revolved around the earth had proved decisively wrong, undermining its claim to final knowledge of things on Heaven and Earth and allowing philosophers to concentrate on the nature of man rather than his relationship with and dependence upon God.

The rationalist school inspired by Descartes (1596–1650) was of the view that nature and the universe were accessible to human reason. Indeed for Leibniz (1646–1716), reason interpenetrated the whole of the universe since human consciousness, the divine consciousness of the Creator and the consciousness of all living things were essentially linked and similar in essence. Thus, it was perfectly possible for a rationalist to place man on centre stage and to believe even in the virtual omniscience of the human mind without denying the existence of a divine force that had set in motion the wonderful machinery of nature, obeying so precisely the Creator's laws that their movements and changes could be measured and predicted. In all this, the role of the Church and its priests became increasingly irrelevant, obscurantist, and a hindrance to human understanding and co-operation.

The seventeenth-century Age of Reason heralded the eighteenth-century Age of Enlightenment, which built on its achievements and beliefs. Indeed the very term enlightenment meant the illumination of ignorance and lies, which together were seen as the source of all evil. The Devil was no longer an external force, or an Anti-Christ, but an internal one, within man himself, and could be exorcized by the proper use of reason. The supreme German philosopher Immanuel Kant (1724–1804), had said, 'Habe den Mut, dich deines eigenen Verstandes zu bedienen'[1] ('Have the courage to use your own powers of reason') and had defined the Enlightenment in the following terms, 'Die Aufklärung ist der Ausgang des Menschen aus seiner eigenen selbstverschuldeten Unmündigkeit'.[2] ('Enlightenment is man's departure from a state of self-incurred tutelage').

In France it was in the salons of Paris that the new conceptions of reason and of free thought were moulded, sifted and disseminated. French thinkers gathering in the Parisian salons led the intellectual world of Europe – scientific discussions, technological advances, liberal

---

1 Immanuel Kant, 'Beantwortung der Frage was ist Aufklärung?' in *Was ist Aufklärung*, Kant, Erhard, Hamann, Herder, Lessing, Mendelssohn, Riem, Schiller, Wieland. Thesen und Definitionen, edited by Erhard Bahr, Stuttgart, 1975, p. 9

2 Ibid.

ideas were all the subject of lively debate. There was a feeling that knowledge was advancing apace and that there was nothing in the world that could not be scrutinized and held up to the light. And this was in part to be the downfall of the French monarchy whose absolutism was no more spared examination than the realms of botany, mechanics, physics and mathematics.

In the privacy of the salons there was a relative freedom of speech. But the printed word was strictly censured and criticism of the regime was out of the question. And so it was that Montesquieu's *Lettres Persanes* (*Persian Letters*) of 1721, a critique of absolutism and religious intolerance at the court of Versailles, was dressed in oriental garb and had to appear in print anonymously in Amsterdam.

Montesquieu's influential epistolary novel and his subsequent monumental exploration of all forms of social and political governance in *L'Esprit des Lois* (*The Spirit of the Laws*) were to pave the way for the gigantic undertaking of the *Encyclopédie* of Diderot and D'Alembert, the unbridled satire of Voltaire and, later in the century, Rousseau's critique of civilization as he had experienced it in the Sun King's capital and thus of all Europe that had sought to imitate it.

Montesquieu's story in *Lettre Persanes*[3] is set partly in a Persian harem and partly in the regency salons of Paris. The exuberance that followed the death of Louis XIV is felt on all its pages. The sudden lifting of the monarch's oppressive policies gave France a chaotic government. Compared to the immediate past, the regency seemed easy going and its atmosphere more favourable to questioning minds. But the censorship of publications continued. Religious tolerance was not even contemplated and Protestants remained in exile. Montesquieu was both pleased and worried by the disarray around him. Despotism and intolerance, but also chaos and lawlessness were his perpetual nightmare. It was thus that in *Lettres Persanes* the French court and French society were not spared his ironic, caustic and mockingly irreverent pen.

In 1721 his Dutch publisher applied for tacit permission to distribute the novel in France, but the censors neither granted nor denied the request, which meant that it could be smuggled into France without much danger. However it did not appear in the catalogue of French

---

3   *Oeuvres complètes de Montesquieu*, (2 volumes), Tome Premier et Tome Second, *Lettres Persanes*, Paris 1949.

booksellers until some ten years later. The *Persian Letters* sold like hot cakes not only in France but across the whole of Europe. For eight years a new edition came out annually and there were countless imitations.

Montesquieu's novel consists of letters exchanged mainly between two Persian visitors to Europe and France and their friends, servants and wives at home. The use of foreigners in novels had become fashionable and a common literary device for making fun of one's own time and place. In these letters the author shows how, under the gaze of two astonished foreigners, every belief and custom wilts and loses its validity. They also reveal how the visitors were gradually transformed by the experience of an alien way of life. The French reader saw himself as he appeared to a Persian, while the latter was changed by being abroad. The novel mercilessly ridiculed the most cherished illusions of the French and readers were struck by the audacity of the opinions that the novelist had put into the mouth of his Persian visitors.

Through the setting of a Persian harem, filled with innumerable women and an army of eunuchs and run by a despotic master, Montesquieu obliquely explores the dark side of monastic and court life in France. The parallel absolute power and absolute servitude, legitimized by religion, enabled him to question why such an enormous number of people were willing to obey one man.

The harem's rigid hierarchy, the reign of fear beneath the opulent surface, the puppet-like insignificance of the individual and the system of punishment for transgressions against the code are mirror images of the Versailles court. The immense popularity of the novel suggests that he had accurately captured the system and atmosphere of look-alike courts across Europe.

But in accordance with the aspirations of the time, Uzbek the owner of the harem (the names used are not Persian but Turkish!) is an enlightened despot who is eager to pursue knowledge. When we first meet him he is an orthodox Muslim. His religious practices are made to resemble Catholic rituals. In one of his first letters he tells his friend that he stayed one whole day at the holy city of Qum, paying tribute and devotion to the tomb of the Virgin who gave birth to twelve Imams. But religion does not cloud Uzbek's mind entirely. He writes in another letter that he wanted to go abroad to seek enlightenment beyond the borders of his own country. In another letter he admits that telling the truth at the court of the Persian King had made him numerous enemies. He says that he has to withdraw from the court to dedicate himself to the study of the sciences for which he has developed a keen interest. His life seems to be in danger as a result, and therefore he must leave.

Uzbek is not the only Persian visitor to Paris. He is accompanied by an older friend, Rica, who does not have a harem back home. This accounts for his cheerfulness. He is light-hearted, adaptable, good humoured and enjoys every new experience. Uzbek, however, is an unhappy man with great worries and cares, owing to the troublesome events that keep recurring in his harem. Uzbek expects nothing but total obedience and chastity from his wives and eunuchs. In one letter he rejoices that he will be the only uncastrated male whom his daughter will have seen before being sent off to her husband's harem. Extreme corporal punishments are afflicted by the eunuchs on disobedient or frivolous wives who do not abide by the strict rules of their captivity. The contradiction between Uzbek's theoretical knowledge and personal conduct becomes increasingly evident – it is the distance between rational thinking and irrational behaviour. He is an intelligent and reflective man who engages in deep philosophical and moral discussions, condemning arrogance and tyranny. But it never occurs to him that he also has much to answer for in his treatment of his wives. He is able to criticize not only the French, but his own countrymen, but he never questions his own attitudes and actions. Indeed he never doubts that his oppressed wives adore him and are perfectly happy in his harem, even though he receives reports of constant trouble and unrest among them. It is only the reader who is regularly reminded that although Uzbek is a thinking man, he is also infatuated with himself and a cruel tyrant. This dichotomy of personality and attitude is well-illustrated in Uzbek's reaction when he learns from a friend that a young woman has undergone a marriage of convenience only to be rejected after the wedding ceremony by the bridegroom since he claimed she was not a virgin. It emerges however that his true motive was dissatisfaction with the size of the dowry and the appearance of his bride. Even as Uzbek deplores this capricious behaviour towards the young woman and her dishonoured family and condemns the laxity of the law which allows such behaviour, he wishes his friend a happier fate for his daughter within the confines of a future husband's harem, 'where alone her glorious beauty can be realized'!

Evidently Montesquieu wanted to show the vulnerability of rational man to the irrationality of inherited credulity. Although we see Uzbek as completely capable of rising above his normal condition of atavistic indoctrination and observing a foreign culture's reality clearly and rationally, he utterly fails to gain critical distance from his own, and is often torn between reason and unreason. Montesquieu's target was to portray the 'rational beings' of eighteenth-century France, how restricted was their view of themselves and unacceptable the treatment and status of women. However, he had no compunction in using a Persian, or in fact Turkish analogy, as the butt of his satire. Nevertheless, there is a striking difference between the playful treatment of oriental and Islamic images in *Lettres Persanes* and the biting attacks of the former centuries. Yet Montesquieu had not set out to re-evaluate Islam. He was simply using it for his own satirical ends to change French society.

In the first decades of the eighteenth century the many provincial academies established by the royal charter during Louis XIV's reign continued to flourish alongside the salons. Indeed, Montesquieu himself was the director of one such académie in Bordeaux. These academies promoted and encouraged the sciences and arts by inviting papers and encouraging readings of literary and scientific works. Montesquieu often read extracts of his own works on such occasions. But this does not mean that there was complete freedom of expression and that the academicians were allowed to air their views about the court and social or religious issues. In fact, many leading members of the academies were compelled to flee the country and their membership was annulled as a result of censorship. One area, however, in which they were free to say what they like was Islam and its Prophet!

It was far from true that the image of Muhammad and Islam had become benevolent, neutral or had even vanished from discussion. On the contrary, the distinguished members of the French academies continued to subject Islam to vehement attacks, but they tended to concentrate their attention on the person of Muhammad rather than on the nature of his religion.

For example the Abbé de Vertot, a member of the Académie des Belles Lettres, wrote a dissertation 'Sur l'Auteur de l'Alcoran' ('On the Author of the Qur'an') which he read before the Academy on 14 November 1724, three years after the publication of Montesquieu's *Lettres Persanes*. It was full of clichés that came to be associated with Muhammad from the Middle Ages, that is, that he preached Islam by the sword, favoured loose morals and that his book was lacking in divine inspiration and originality. These clichés reached a wider readership in a popular magazine of the time, the *Mercure de France*, in December of that year. From Vertot the reader learnt that Muhammad had dealings with people who were even more ignorant than he was. The dissertation stressed Muhammad's 'clandestine' use of retreat to a solitary place for prayers. Here, according to Vertot, he secretly studied the contents of the Old and the New Testaments, drawing from them what might suit his project of founding a religion.

In Vertot's view, Muhammad was the most skilful and dangerous impostor to have appeared in Asia. It was his marriage to a rich widow, he claimed, that fostered Muhammad's ambition for glory. But glory without domination was not sufficient for him. To achieve his aim, the best method seemed to be the setting up of a new religion, 'machine dont bien des imposteurs avant lui s'etoient déjà servis'[4] ('a technique which many impostors before him had used'). To Vertot, Muhammad's revelations were nothing but epileptic fits which the clever impostor passed off as ecstatic trances. Vertot's accounts were clearly based on hostile medieval images of Muhammad, presented to the French public as if they were new discoveries of the Age of Enlightenment.

An attitude to Muhammad different from that of the Abbé de Vertot was displayed in *La Vie de Mahomet* (*The Life of Mahomet*) by the Comte de Boulainvilliers, published in 1728. Instead of taking the establishment line and vilifying Muhammad and his religion the Count praised Islam, seeing in it a natural religion, simple and reasonable in contrast to the artificiality and irrationality of Christianity. He described Muhammad as an enlightened and wise lawgiver whose sincerity was reflected in the simplicity and straightforwardness of his religion. There are two erroneous Christian opinions, says Boulainvilliers, the first is that the religion of Muhammad should be rejected on the grounds of common sense, whereas there could not be 'a more plausible system than his, more agreeable to the light of reason'.[5] The second opinion is that Muhammad was a coarse and barbarous person. The Count insists

---

4 Abbé de Vertot (1655–1735), *Dissertation sur l'auteur de l'Alcoran*, 1724, quoted in 'Images of Islam in some French writings of the first half of the Eighteenth Century', *British Journal for Eighteenth-Century Studies*, 14/ii (Autumn 1991, p. 191).
5 Henri comte de Boulainvilliers, *The Life of Mahomet*, anonymous translator, London 1731, p. 75 f.

that Muhammad was neither coarse nor barbarous, but was a man of great finesse and possessed all the arts of resolution, intrepidity and vision that Alexander or Caesar had been capable of in similar circumstances. *La Vie de Mahomet*, of which a translation in English appeared in 1731, is written with fair accuracy, for the historical background comes from Islamic sources. As a deist, the Count believed that the solitude of the desert kept the Arabs free from the superstitions common to the rest of the world and 'preserved among them the natural notion of the true God'. Boulainvilliers defends the laws and customs of the Muslims and considers them as wise and intelligible: circumcision is necessary for hygiene and health; hogs spread disease in hot countries. Frequent bathing (before prayers) is also important in hot climates. Pilgrimage illustrates the value of keeping up an old tradition. But this new, brave appraisal of Muhammad's character and of Islam itself had no lasting effect on mainstream thought and did not alter Muhammad's image in France and the rest of Europe.

In 1733 the Abbé de Saint-Pierre published his *Discours contre le Mahométisme*.[6] He was a former member of the Académie Française, having been admitted to the Académie in 1695, but expelled from it in 1718 for his criticism of Louis XIV. Saint-Pierre preached the doctrine of the elimination of prejudice and ignorance through which, he believed, humanity could attain happiness. In his discourse, the Abbé argued that only those readers who know nothing about the ignorance of the Muslims of Asia, Africa and Europe could find in the rise of Islam a remarkable event. The causes of the rise were so natural that it was morally impossible for Islam not to have been established under the circumstances. Muhammad, he claimed, was a fanatic of initially good faith and would never have succeeded in converting his wife, relatives and neighbours to believe in the truth and reality of his visions if he had begun as an impostor. Muhammad was accordingly the first to be deceived and that made him more disposed to deceive others. The Abbé further argued that Muhammad had recognized his errors afterwards but refrained from enlightening his followers. From his fanatical beginnings he went on to become an impostor, learning how to exploit the errors

---

6 Abbé de Saint Pierre, (1658–1743), *Discours contre le Mahométisme*, 1733, quoted in 'Images of Islam in some French writings of the first Half of the Eighteenth Century', op. cit., p. 193.

into which he had made the believers fall. Two factors which Saint-Pierre emphasizes in his attempt to explain the rise of Islam are climate and imagination. His theory is based on the assumption that as the climate of Arabia is particularly hot, the imagination of the Arabs is consequently more fertile. Imagination in hot countries, he says, amounts to fanaticism. The persuasive Muhammad made use of this natural advantage in depicting the delights of an eternal Paradise and the woes of Hell, and no men were more predisposed to believe in him than the ignorant Arabs. But according to the Abbé the wild visions and fanaticism of hot countries can reach the more rational people of cold countries through contagion, provided the latter are ignorant too. Basically, the Abbé blamed the sun for the emergence of Europe's hated religion, Islam.

It often happened in the eighteenth century that someone who was little known to the literary world could nevertheless have a great impact in projecting certain images of Islam. One such person was Jean Antoine Guer, a Parisian barrister who in 1747 published his *Moeurs et usages des Turcs, leur religion, leur Gouvernement civil, militaire et politique*. Guer provided Voltaire with some useful documentation for episodes in his *l'Essai sur les Moeurs des Nations*. It is in Volume I of Guer's two-volume work that the reader will find an elaborate account of Islam.[7] The negative tone is set right from the outset where attention is focused on Muhammad himself. He is made to appear as an ambitious opportunist who, by corrupting religion and making it pander to the basic instincts of his followers, caused it to gain ground rapidly. When his eloquence failed, Guer argues, he used force to win over adherents to his cause, and the progress made by Islam in the times of his successors was entirely due to force of arms. To this medieval and well-established view of Muhammad, Guer adds a personal note. He compares Muhammad with Cromwell – a comparison which was to be taken up by Voltaire later in the *Remarques pour servir le Supplément à l'Essai sur les Moeurs*, published in 1763. While Voltaire finds Muhammad as fanatical as Cromwell, but greater than he, Guer finds him less enlightened than the 'English usurper', his mind less cultivated, his politics less subtle, his eloquence

---

7 Jean Antoine Guer (1713–64), *Moeurs et usages des Turcs, leur religion, leur Gouvernement civil, militaire et politique*, 1747, Volume I, quoted in 'Images of Islam in some French writings of the First Half of the Eighteenth Century', op. cit., p. 196.

less flexible and his designs less profound. But what established a common trait between the 'two impostors' was the concealed hypocrisy which raised them to high levels of power. Yet the most original point of comparison between the two figures is the role played by their respective wives who were both vital to their husbands' success. Like Khadija, who proclaimed Muhammad's revelations and dedicated herself to his new religion, Cromwell's wife worked ceaselessly to show her husband's devotion to the public cause. Both helped to promote their husbands' missions by winning them friends and followers. However, Guer contradicts himself in chapter II by claiming that according to Islam, Muslim women have no souls and do not go to Paradise. There is no such Islamic text to support this view of course. The Qur'an teaches in fact in Suras 10 and 33 that men and women who have followed the precepts of Islam will have their rich reward in Paradise and that husbands and wives enter together. Despite this Qur'anic teaching the myth about the exclusion of wives from Paradise came to exert a strange fascination on European thinkers for centuries and is still alive today. Guer claims that Muhammad the impostor, who was so eloquent about what should constitute men's happiness in the next world, kept quiet about women's happiness in the life after death. Thus the myth was propagated that the Islamic Heaven was only made for men, and was populated by voluptuous virgins or Houris who tended to the deceased males' every wish, while their former wives could never enter this sensual after-world.

Guer's opinion that Muhammad had a great appetite for women and that he encouraged men to follow his example became fashionable. Diderot, the prominent editor and author of the *Encyclopédie*, claimed that Muhammad was the greatest friend of women and the greatest enemy of reason who ever lived. It was not only Muhammad's religion which Diderot criticized, but all revealed religions and above all Christianity. 'The first step towards philosophy is incredulity.' These were the last words which Diderot's daughter heard him speak the night before he died in July 1784 at the age of seventy. They echoed what Diderot had believed and written throughout his life. They marked a central continuity in his thinking. Diderot studied theology, but soon turned against the religion of his upbringing, becoming alternately a sceptic, a deist and an atheist. But despite growing disillusionment, the Catholic Church still occupied a commanding position in Diderot's France. Even though there were signs of the beginnings of de-Christianization in certain aspects of social life, the clergy were still quite powerful, churches and religious orders were dominant everywhere, and the orthodox faith was given the backing of the secular power of the kings. In particular, the Church largely controlled the education system and had an important say in the restriction of publications.

Diderot's personal target in his various attacks on religion was that which was closest to him and most affected him, namely Roman Catholicism. However, it was difficult for him to attack the state religion of his country in a work such as the *Encyclopédie*. Like Montesquieu and, as we shall see, Voltaire, he therefore mounted a veiled criticism, lambasting Islam which was allowed to stand as an example of revealed religions. So, once again we see how a European thinker whose real intention was to scrutinize his own religion and society had no moral compunction or censorship difficulties in using. another religion, Islam, as a substitute. The main thrust of Diderot's critique was to label Islam as superstitious and fanatical, labels which were to become easily repeated clichés.

The *Encyclopédie* was published between 1751 and 1765. It was initiated by Diderot and his friend D'Alembert who together compiled and edited the articles written by many hands. The insistence was on the value of experiment in different fields of knowledge. Diderot particularly attached great importance to the description of technological processes on the one hand and the exposition of the new philosophical thinking about the nature of the universe and man's place in it on the other. These were the ideals of the *Encyclopédie* and its great claim to usefulness and its contribution to general learning. In a leading article entitled 'Encyclopédie', Diderot declared that 'the aim of an encyclopedia is to gather the knowledge which is scattered over the surface of the earth and to expose the general systems of knowledge to those with whom we live'. D'Alembert called the *Encyclopédie* 'a vista across the whole universe', seen as a single truth in which knowledge could be understood as both vast and yet ordered as in an avenue stretching into the distance. D'Alembert's description was another use of an image derived from the Versailles gardens with their geometric patterns, long avenues and carefully structured perspectives. Arranged alphabetically, the *Encyclopédie* claimed to be ordered according to the dictates of reason, covering all branches of knowledge, as Diderot implied in the title, *Dictionnaire Raisonné des Sciences, des Arts et des Métiers* (*Dictionary of Sciences, Arts and Trades based on the principles of Reason*).

The entry under 'Mahomet' provides a short biography, but is a curious mixture of praise and censure. Some passages are identical to Voltaire's treatment of Muhammad in his *l'Essai sur les Moeurs* of 1756. On the one hand the article stresses Muhammad's courage, tenacity and sobriety and compares these with those of Alexander the Great. On the other hand he is reduced to a lecher with remarkable sexual stamina and lust for women:

> The passion that his hot-blooded temperament demanded of him and that brought him so many wives and concubines, weakened neither his courage, nor his diligence, nor his health. The evidence for this portrait is to be found in his deeds.[8]

The article goes on to describe Muhammad's strategy of deception and pretence:

> Once he understood the character of his fellow citizens, their ignorance, their credulity and their tendency to fanaticism, he saw that he could pose as a prophet, he feigned revelations, he spoke of them, and began by convincing the members of his household, which was the most difficult task.[9]

The reader of the article also learnt that Muhammad allowed men to take more than one wife and in fact favoured a whole harem of women, which the author admits was an established custom in the Orient. However, the article effectively recognizes what it presents as men's deep-seated universal moral feeling that it is right for them to have more than one woman. Here we see an ambivalence in Diderot, in which he both draws attention to Muhammad's polygamous life, so contrary to the Christian insistence on monogamy, while suggesting that Muhammad was acting and legislating in accordance with the true nature of the human male:

---

8 Diderot et D'Alembert, *Encylopédie ou Dictionnaire Raisonné des Arts et des Métiers*, (Supplément), Amsterdam, 1969, entry: Mahomet and Abdallah. (Translations by N. B. R. Reeves.)

9 Ibid.

He permitted men to have any number of wives, a practice through-out the Orient since time immemorial. In no way did he alter the morals that deep down have always characterized men and which no legislator has ever succeeded in corrupting.[10]

Diderot was also inspired by another early French Enlightenment thinker, Pierre Bayle, who had already struck the note of religious scepticism at the opening of the eighteenth century and had initiated the concept of the sovereignty of Reason. Bayle had published a massive dictionary entitled *Dictionnaire Historique et Critique* in 1697, of which an English translation appeared in 1709. Bayle's article on Muhammad was yet another statement about his alleged sexual obsession. But at the same time the article contained a remarkable contradiction. It claimed that, Khadija, being either deceived, or feigning to be so, went about, and told from house to house that her husband was a prophet, and by that means endeavoured to procure him followers. But in the summary at the end Bayle states, 'He was not supported by the intrigues of women, nor did he at all engage the fair sex in his interests. Perhaps he feared the Persian women, because he intended to establish a Code full of severity toward the women'.[11] Bayle intimates in a footnote that the women of Persia were so beautiful that Muhammad did not invade that country because he dared not trust himself there!

There were of course no objections at all to the entries in Bayle's dictionary and Diderot's encyclopedia on Muhammad and Islam. On the contrary, the French clergy must have been delighted to see that they had taken the establishment line of stamping Muhammad as unimportant enunciator of a rival religion. But they reacted most fiercely to the articles that subjected the Christian dogma to scepticism. Although conventional deference was paid in the *Encyclopédie* to orthodox opinion, it was obvious that on the whole physics was preferred to metaphysics and science to abstract beliefs. The *Encyclopédie* had indeed aroused a vivid interest in, and excited awareness of, human potentiality. The Church of France became alarmed by the popularity of this work and determined on drastic action. It was quick to recognize a great enemy. The first action

---

10 Ibid.
11 Pierre Bayle, *Dictionnaire Historique et Critique*, 1697, Volume IV, Article: 'Mahomet', pp. 27 f.

of the Church was to denounce the Abbé de Prades who had contributed some harmless articles on Christian theology. He was deprived of his licence to preach and was obliged to flee the country and take refuge in Berlin. The Bishop of Auxerre then publicly attacked Diderot and Montesquieu, an ardent contributor to the *Encyclopédie*, on the grounds that their articles were subversive. The final blow was the decree of the King's Council on 7 February 1752, forbidding the sale of the second volume of the *Encyclopédie*. The order was not enforced, but Diderot himself was imprisoned several times. Despite these difficulties the *Encyclopédie* was sold and read throughout Europe in its original and in pirated editions. Its influence upon the thinking world was enormous, as were its interpretations of Muhammad and his religion.

But the supreme intellectual influence on eighteenth-century Europe was without doubt Voltaire. He was the very embodiment of the epoch. His lifelong motto 'Écrasez l'Infâme! became a lasting legacy, a motto with which he seems to have meant, in a blanket term of dismissal, 'Destroy everything that is disreputable, dishonest, based on lies, wicked and cruel'. He would have included every form of religious fanaticism or what he called 'enthusiasme' as 'l'Infâme', whether Catholic, Protestant or Islamic. Voltaire described atheism as 'the vice of the wise' and superstition as 'the vice of the fool'. Under his rebellious influence men of letters across the whole of Europe began to question all established institutions and conventions, including revealed religions. Voltaire was a brilliant speaker and his satirical works mounted against the establishment made him welcome from an early age in the salons of Paris. On 16 May 1717, at the age of twenty-two, he was sent to prison at the Bastille under a *lettre de cachet* or royal order. He was charged with being the author of an anti-royal epigram which had in fact been written by someone else. The injustice of this sentence filled him with a lasting hatred of the court and of arbitrary arrest and imprisonment. So disgusted was he by this episode that he decided to change his name from Arouet to Voltaire. In the first half of the eighteenth century the word *roi* or 'King' was not pronounced in upper-class circles as rhyming with *Loi*, but was pronounced *Rouet*. This assonance between his own name and that of the French monarch irritated him and he therefore invented for himself the part anagram and pseudonym Voltaire, under which he immediately became famous. Before he had reached the age of thirty he was already acclaimed as a literary genius and the whole of Parisian society lay at his feet.

Voltaire's most popular work, and the work which he himself regarded as his best was, extraordinarily by modern judgement, *Mahomet ou le Fanatisme* (*Mahomet or Fanaticism*), a tragedy on which he began working in 1738 and which was performed amid a political and religious furore in Lille in 1741 and in Paris in 1742. Voltaire dedicated it to his friend King Frederick the Great of Prussia and secondly to Pope Benedict XIV. The Pope expressed his delight by saying that he read the work 'con sommo piacere' ('with greatest pleasure') and praised it as 'una bellissima tragedia!' ('a very fine tragedy').

Initially banned by the censor after a formal complaint by the Turkish ambassador, it returned to the stage after popular outcry. What were the reasons for this astounding success? Was it that the theatre-going public in Paris were enthused by the attacks in the play on what was presented as superstitious, fanatical and cruel? Was this, then, a genuine display of the fruits of the Enlightenment? Was it, on the contrary, a display of the age-old hatred and contempt for Islam? Or was it that, once again, Islam was serving as an analogy for Christianity and the real source of its popularity was a growing scepticism towards the tenets of faith underpinning the Catholic Church? If the latter, Pope Benedict had clearly not discerned it.

With complete unconcern for historical truth Voltaire grossly caricatured Muhammad as a bloodthirsty, power-obsessed warrior and conqueror who ravages and plunders, conspires and intrigues and destroys his best friends for the sake of his insatiable ambition and sexual appetite. Setting authenticity aside, Voltaire picked a few characters out of Muhammad's life to concoct his plot, characters whom we have already encountered earlier in this book in Muhammad's biography. Abu Sufyan, Muhammad's pagan arch-enemy and the leader of Mecca, becomes Sheikh Zopire (Zubayr), whose wife, brother, son and daughter in the play have either been killed or abducted by Muhammad. Umar, Muhammad's close friend and adviser, becomes an accomplice to his murderous plans. Zayd ibn Haritha, Muhammad's adoptive son, is the character called Séide, Séide's sister, Palmire, given to him by Muhammad as an incestuous lover and a promised reward for the murder of Zopire, appears to be compounded of Umm Habiba, Abu Sufyan's daughter, and Zeynab bint Jahsh, Muhammad's cousin and at one time Zayd's wife, both of whom Muhammad married. Muhammad is presented by Voltaire as having no moral scruples whatsoever when striving for power and domination, a man who even promotes incest to reach his goal.

In his letter on 20 December 1740 to Frederick the Great, Voltaire, who considered him as a peace-loving and enlightened monarch, has this to say about the play:

> It concerns a young man born virtuous, who, seduced by fanaticism, murders an old man who loves him, a young man who, thinking to serve God, unknowingly becomes a parricide; it concerns an impostor who orders this murder, and who promises the murderer an incest for reward.[12]

But this was not all, because in Voltaire's tragedy Mahomet has a more definite and horrifying purpose. The second act, which apparently Jean Jacques Rousseau admired most, contains passages which reveal Voltaire's intentions in writing the play. It embodies almost all the central features of the assault on Muhammad's personality that had begun in the early Middle Ages. The play culminates in this dialogue between Muhammad and the leader of Mecca:

Mahomet   Come closer, and as the heavens wish to unite us,
           Look upon Mahomet without fear, speak and do
           not blush!

Zopire   I blush for you alone, for you whose artifice
           Has dragged your country to the very precipice;
           For you, whose hand is sowing heinous crimes
           And nurtures war amidst the peace.
           Your name alone amongst us divides our families,
           Our spouses, parents, mothers and their daughters;
           And the truce for you is but another means
           To encroach upon my heart, plunging deep your
           knife. Civil discord follows upon your every step:
           With your outrageous mix of audacity and lies,
           Your tyrant o'er your land, can it be in this place
           You wish to sue for peace and announce to me a
           God?

Mahomet   See who Mahomet is. We are alone; now listen:
           I am ambitious; all men are, we cannot doubt; But
           never has a king, a pontiff, a chieftain or a citizen,

---

12 Voltaire's letter of 20 December 1740 to Frederick the Great recorded in *Voltaire*, Théodore Besterman, London, 1969, p. 253.

Conceived a project as great as mine.
Every people upon the earth has had its turn to
shine
Through laws, through arts, above all through war.
The time of Araby has come at last.
This generous people, too long known,
Has let its glory be entombed within its deserts;
Now the days marked out for victory are at hand.
Look upon a devastated universe from North to
South, Persia bleeding still, its throne shaken to the
ground.
The Indies enslaved, and cowed, Egypt bowed,
The splendour of Constantinople's walls eclipsed;
Look upon the Empire of the Romans in fragments,
This great body torn, its scattered limbs
All slack, flung aside without honour and devoid -
Upon this debris of a world let us raise Arabia.
We need a new God for this unseeing universe.
In Egypt Osiris, in Asia Zoroaster, on the Cretan
Isle Minos, in Italy Numa
They gave with ease their insufficient laws
To peoples with no principles, no cult, no kings.
After a thousand years I come to change these rude laws
I bring more noble judgement to whole nations;
I abolish the false gods; and my pure cult, springing
from my greatness is the first step.
Do not reproach me with deceiving my native land; I
am destroying its weakness and its idolatry.
Beneath one king, beneath one God,
I come to reunite it,
And to make it renowned it must be made to serve.

Zopire   So these are your designs! Yours is the audacity
That seeks to change by whim the earth's whole
face?
Your desire, by spreading carnage and fear, to force
all men to think like you?
You ravage the world, yet claim to teach it?
Oh, if the world has been seduced by error,
If the night of lies has led us astray,
With what terrible torches do you wish to bring
light?
With what right do you swing the censer and upset
the Empire?

Mahomet   It is the right possessed of a mind, vast and firm in
its designs,
O'er the rude spirit of vulgar humanity.[13]

What was the true purpose behind this attack? Voltaire himself stated that he wished he had made the tragedy even more powerful and Mahomet even more violent. This suggests that he wished to write a tragedy to exceed anything produced in Shakespearean England, bursting the classical conventions that had bound Racine and Corneille so tightly a hundred years before. Could it even have been an attack on blood-thirstier chapters in Christian history? The text hardly supports that view, although as a deist Voltaire scrutinized the greed, cruelty and superstition of the clerics and their followers. We are therefore forced to the conclusion that it served a double purpose – to produce a high melodrama such as Paris had never seen before and to highlight the need for Enlightenment ideals to replace the nefarious practices of the powerful. For the Parisian theatregoers Islam was not an immediate reality, but they could recognize in Mahomet's unscrupulousness the amorality and intrigue that had characterized the corrupt court of Louis. Certainly Voltaire did not feel the conventional respect shown to the court by virtue of its privileged status. In 1726 he had clashed in a salon with a chevalier and, when told he was in no position to criticize those socially higher than himself, had challenged his accuser to a duel, claiming that a man of letters was equal to a chevalier. It was this incident that had led to his six months imprisonment in the Bastille followed by a three-year banishment to England. So we cannot doubt that in painting the viciousness that characterizes his Mahomet he drew on his personal knowledge of the French court, which defied all that the Enlightenment was coming to stand for. Ironically, historical truth was not a priority in this critical endeavour. But we have no reason to suppose that Voltaire had any deep-seated personal motive for his travesty of early Islamic history. It was a target that did not affect him emotionally and was therefore easy for him to pillory with a clear conscience. Whatever Voltaire's ultimate purpose in writing *Mahomet ou le Fanatisme*, his grossly distorted portrayal of Muhammad rekindled age-old prejudices and hatred, achieving in

---

13 Voltaire *Mahomet ou le Fanatisme*, précédé d'un extrait du Traité sur la Tolérance, Le Temps Singulier, Collection "L'Immortel", Paris 1979, pp. 53–7, Translation by N.B.R. Reeves.

effect the opposite of what might have been hoped for in the Age of Enlightenment, namely tolerance.

That Muhammad was not Voltaire's primary target is suggested by his far more balanced portrait in his later historical work of 1756, *L'Essai sur les Mœurs des Nations*, where he praises Muhammad as a genius for his impact on world history. But the accusation that he was a deceiver and an impostor remains and here Voltaire was building on the biased biographical sources that he will also have used for the tragedy. Vertot's *Dissertation sur l'auteur de l'Alcoran* and Saint-Pierre's *Discours contre le Mahométisme* had certainly impressed Voltaire and had stimulated him to write his own version. He had opposed le Comte de Boulainvilliers in 1730, who had defended Muhammad and Islam and who had provided the Western world for the first time with a new and enlightening biography in *La Vie de Mahomet*. Voltaire argued that he would have accepted Boulainvilliers' apologia had Muhammad been a politician. But he could not possibly accept that a true prophet could act in that manner, allowing the spiritual to mingle with the temporal. This was of course a covert Christian view derived from Jesus' clear distinction between the realms of the spiritual and temporal, demonstrating that despite his anti-Christian views, Voltaire had remained Christian in his innermost feelings. Indeed, on his estate at Ferney he had pulled down the village church since it obscured his view, but he obtained permission from the bishop to build a new one in its place. On Easter Sundays he even attended mass in this church and insisted on preaching a sermon from its pulpit. On his deathbed in 1778 he agreed to receive the sacraments and was buried according to the rites of the Catholic faith.

Another highly acclaimed work on Islam in eighteenth-century Europe was the famous tract by Humphrey Prideaux, Dean of Norwich *The True Nature of Imposture, Fully Displayed in the Life of Mahomet*, published in 1697. Voltaire had read Prideaux's violent attack on Muhammad during his exile in England. According to Prideaux there are six characteristics of imposture: it panders to a carnal interest, wicked men are its authors, it contains falsehood, it is propagated by fraud, its nature cannot be long concealed when entrusted to many conspirators, and it can be established only by force. Prideaux declared that Muhammad qualified on all these counts and that his religion was promulgated as deliberate imposture. This was the argument that had been the basis of his thesis:

What it was that put Mahomet upon his imposture, the foregoing History of his life sufficiently shows. It was his Ambition and his lust. To have the sovereignty over his country, to gratify his ambition and as many women as he pleased to satiate his lust, was what he aimed at, and to gain himself a party for the composing of this, was the grand Design of that new Religion which he invented. and the whole End and Reason of his imposing it on those deluded hereinto.[14]

As this quotation from the highly influential Prideaux suggests, the picture painted of Islam in the English Enlightenment was black. It was one of a completely evil system, deserving only of universal condemnation.

Voltaire had praised England as a free country without the prejudices and absolutism of France. In his *Letters Concerning the English* of which a pirated edition was issued in Paris in 1734 and which was publicly burnt on the king's orders, he had suggested that the democratic institutions of England were preferable in practice and likely to last longer than the monolithic autocracy of France. He had also appreciated the religious toleration which, as compared to his own country, was widespread and generally accepted in England. In fact in England discrimination between the various churches of the Christian faith was still strongly felt. Catholics and dissenters were not allowed to hold public office, though they were not prevented from worshipping and following their denomination religion, as Voltaire had observed. Intermarriage was strongly discouraged. England's governmental institutions were, however, more advanced than France. The country had already gone through two revolutions. The first, following the Civil War fought between the monarchists and their Puritan opponents from 1642 to 1649, had culminated in the beheading in 1649 of Charles I, the Stuart King who, like Louis XIV, had claimed a divine right to rule. The second, revolution of 1688 had followed the restoration of the monarchy in 1660 when Charles II's successor, his brother James II, a Roman Catholic, had tried to reassert kingly powers of law suspension against the wishes of the English Parliament. He had been deposed from the throne and escaped to France after the Dutchman, Prince William of Orange, a cousin of King James who was married to James' Protestant daughter Mary, had landed with an army upon the invitation of Parliament. These events had led to

---

14 Humphrey Prideaux, *The True Nature of Imposture Fully Displayed in the Life of Mahomet*, 8th edition, London 1723, pp. 132 f.

the establishment of a constitutional monarchy. Although the vast majority of people had no say in the election of the members of the House of Commons, it was an unparalleled example of early parliamentary democracy, to be surpassed only by the Proclamation of Independence by the former British colonies in America and their Bill of Rights. Both developments were to be of fateful influence on thinkers in absolutist France. But England's relative liberalism in the eighteenth century only partially extended to judgements on Islam. Indeed, Prideaux's influence remained dominant.

The chorus of denunciation continued with numerous authors making Prideaux's opinion of Muhammad their own. One such author was Joseph Pitts, a traveller in Arabia who published his memoirs in 1731 entitled *A Faithful Account of the Religion and Manners of the Mahometans*. In his descriptions of the spirit of Islam, Pitts called Muhammad 'a vile and debauched impostor' and the Muslims 'blind and idolatrous creatures'. Here are a few lines by Pitts on his experience of Mecca, Muhammad's birthplace:

> The Zeal of those poor blind Mahometans is a lesson to negligent Christians. Even shopkeepers and artisans can repeat the Qur'an without book from beginning to end. I could not choose but admire to see those poor Creatures so extraordinarily devout and affectionate when they were about their superstitions, and with what Awe and Trembling they were possessed, in so much, that I could scarce forbear shedding of Tears, to see their Zeal, tho' blind and idolatrous.[15]

But not all the accounts of travellers to the Middle East during the eighteenth century were negative. Islam had started to make an impression on groups of European adventurers, diplomats, Catholic and Protestant missionaries and scholars of Islam. The latter showed a better understanding of the Muslim traditions and the Muslims they met than ordinary travellers. But they too, had their own reservations about Muhammad himself.

Two major works which made important contributions to the discussion of Islam were by two English scholars of Arabic: Simon

---

15 Joseph Pitts, *A Faithful Account of the Religion and Manners of the Mahometans*, London, 1731, p. xvii.

Ockley, the author of *The History of the Saracens* and George Sale, the translator of the Qur'an. Ockley's *History* was published between 1708 and 1718 and Sale's translation of the Qur'an appeared in 1734. Both works became classics and were long regarded as standard English sources of knowledge about Islam and Muhammad. Both authors claimed to have tried to be fair in their treatment of Islam and in their judgements of Muhammad, as well as in avoiding stereotypes. Indeed they are considered to be the first apologists of Muhammad who wrote about him in the spirit of the Enlightenment. But even they could not completely detach themselves from their native prejudices.

Ockley in fact begins his history with the words, 'Mahomet, the great impostor', using these two expressions throughout as interchangeable terms. Nevertheless he expresses admiration for the heroic deeds of the Muslim conquerors and praises their sense of justice. He points out that the Arabs in contrast to other conquerors treated the conquered peoples with fairness and consideration. He recounts the story of the submission of Jerusalem to Muhammad's successor Umar in 638 CE and states that the Muslim conquerors strictly obeyed the instructions of their commander not to kill any children, women or old people. He then describes Umar's courtesy towards the Christian community:

> Umar was making a tour of the city with the Patriarch who was acting as his guide, and they were in the Church of the Holy Sepulchre when the hour of prayer came. Refusing the invitation of the Patriarch to pray in the Church, Umar performed his devotions in the open air, on the steps of a church nearby. In explanation of his action he said to the Patriarch: 'You know that I promised you that none of your churches should be taken away from you,' but that you should possess them quietly yourselves. Now if I had prayed in any one of these churches the Muslims would infallibly have taken it away from you'.[16]

Ockley's high esteem for Arab chivalrous conduct found further expression in the introduction to his translation in 1717 of proverbs attributed to Ali, Muhammad's son-in-law, whom the Muslims celebrate as a symbol of justice and generosity of mind. The work appeared under

---

16 Simon Ockley, *History of the Saracens*, 3rd edition, 2 volumes, Cambridge 1757, Volume I, p. 22.

the title *Sentences of Ali*. In it Ockley highlights Ali's wisdom and points out that the West had always been enlightened by the wisdom of the Muslim East:

> The Little smattering of Knowledge which we have is entirely derived from the East. They first communicated to the Greeks, (a vain conceited People) from whom the Romans had theirs. And after Barbarity had spread itself over the Western World, the Arabians, by their Conquests, restored it again in Europe.[17]

George Sale was another sympathetic Arabist. His interest in Arabic began when he entered the Inner Temple, one of the Four Inns of Court in London, as a law student in 1720. The Society for the Promotion of Christian Knowledge, whose offices were in the Temple, was then making a translation of the New Testament into Arabic, employing a Syrian of Damascus and a Greek of Aleppo for that purpose. Sale studied Arabic with them and, in 1726, became corrector of the Arabic text for the Society. He then embarked on translating the Qur'an. Sale prefixed to his translation a 'Preliminary Discourse' containing episodes of Arab history, a biography of Muhammad and an exposition of the laws, rites and ceremonies of Islam. Sale's attempt to produce a translation of the Qur'an in English (the Latin translation of 1691 by the Italian monk Louis Marracci served as a basis) caused an uproar of protest. He was accused of being a half Muslim and found himself bombarded by hostile comments. In his defence Sale issued the following telling statement in the 'Preliminary Discourse':

> I have not in speaking of Muhammad and his Qur'an, allowed myself to use those opprobrious appellations, and unmannerly expressions, which seem to be the strongest arguments of several who have written against them. On the contrary, 1 have thought myself obliged to treat both with common decency, and even to approve such particulars as seemed to me to deserve such approbation: for how criminal soever Muhammad may have been in imposing a false religion on mankind, the praises due to his real virtues ought not to be denied him.[18]

---

17 Ibid, Volume II, p. 329 f.
18 George Sale, *The Koran or Alcoran of Mohammed*, London, Warne, n.d., p. X.

The mere admission that Muhammad had any virtues, real or assumed, was too bold a step to take for any English writer who did not hide under the cloak of anonymity. Sale was condemned for putting Islam on a level with Christianity and had to keep a low profile thereafter due to the social rejection of his work. In the second section of his 'Preliminary Discourse', Sale discusses the character and life of Muhammad. The purpose of Muhammad, he says, was to destroy idolatry and, by weeding out the corruptions which the Jews and Christians had introduced into their religions, bring religion back to its original purity, 'which consisted chiefly in the worship of one only God'. But in self-defence, Sale declared once more:

> Whether this was the effect of enthusiasm [the word so much dreaded in the eighteenth century through Voltaire's influence as synonymous with fanaticism] or only a design to raise himself to the supreme government of his country, I will not pretend to determine. The latter is the general opinion of the Christian writers, who agree that ambition and the desire of satisfying his sensuality, were the motives of his undertaking. It may be so; yet his first views, perhaps, were not so interested. His original design of bringing the pagan Arabs to the knowledge of the true God, was certainly noble, and highly to be commended, for I cannot possibly subscribe to the assertion of a late learned writer [Prideaux!] that he made that nation exchange their idolatry for another religion altogether as bad. Mohammad was no doubt fully satisfied in his conscience of the truth of his grand point, the unity of God . . . All his other doctrines and institutions being rather accidental and unavoidable, than premeditated and designed.[19]

Sale was certainly a remarkably courageous man even to utter such cautious words in approval of Muhammad. Similar writings were so dangerous to their authors that they were circulated in manuscript form and anonymously. Fortunately copies are still extant at the British Library and today it is possible with a few exceptions to establish who wrote them. The earliest work by an English apologist which remained in manuscript until recent years is *An Account of the Rise and Progress of Mahometanism, and a Vindication of Mahomet and his Religion from the*

---

19 Ibid, *Preliminary Discourse in the Koran*, p. 28. The Preliminary Discourse is divided into eight sections. In Section 2, Sale deals with the life and character of Muhammad.

Calumnies of the Christians. Charles Hornby of the Pipe Office found the manuscript in 1705 and attributed it to Henry Stubbe (born 1631). There are three copies of Stubbe's manuscript at the British Library. Stubbe was Second Keeper of the Bodleian Library at Oxford. He was dismissed for writing a 'pestilent book' which according to the *Dictionary of National Biography* must have been his book on Islam. Stubbe portrays Muhammad 'as a great law-giver', as 'the wisest legislator that ever was'.[20] He even praises the military prowess of Muhammad's successors and their zeal for their religion. He disagrees with those Christian writers who accuse Muhammad of having promised a sensual Paradise to his followers. If the biblical description of Heaven as a cubical city may be interpreted allegorically, he argues, the Muslims have the same right to interpret their own Heaven as they wished. As for polygamy, Stubbe points to the Christian traditions and wonders why people in the West are not shocked by the marriage customs of biblical patriarchs?

In the year after the publication of Sale's *The Koran* another anonymous essay appeared. It was entitled *Reflections on Mahometism and the Conduct of Mohammed*. After several pages of vindication as to why this essay had to be written and a reassurance to the reader that in essence Islam was an ally to Protestant Christianity, the author states:

> The Title of the Essay may tempt the Reader to think I am going to preach up Mahometism against Christianity; but I solemnly protest, my Design is quite the contrary; for though I do intend in general to vindicate Mohammed and his Religion from some of the Falsehoods charged on both, and, as well as I can, to represent them in a more desirable Light than the Custom has hitherto been; I do it purely for the sake of Truth, and to exalt the majesty of the Christian Religion.[21]

'The violent prejudices against Mohammed', says the anonymous author, 'proceed from Ignorance, or something worse'

> The English clergy are pretty much infected with this groundless Malevolence towards Mohammed. This procedure is Knight errantry, and no better than fighting with imaginary Monsters. There is

---

20 Henry Stubbe, *An account of the Rise and Progress of Mahometism*, edited by Hafiz Mahmud Khan Shairani, London, 1911, p. 150.
21 *Reflections on Mahometism*, an anonymous essay published in 1735, quoted in Byron Porter Smith's *Islam in English Literature*, Beirut, 1939, pp. 73–5.

nothing so enormous in Mahometism as has been falsely represented. I shall here attempt to show, that Mahometism may have been ordained for the good of Christianity, to withstand the Corruption of it in Days past, and to increase and enlarge it in Days to come.[22]

Stubbe proceeded to condemn Prideaux for his highly damaging misrepresentation of Mohammad's character. 'The laws of Islam are in no way an indulgence of sensual appetite', the author emphasizes. 'Marriage in Islam is strictly regulated and fornication and adultery punished. Gambling and wine-drinking are prohibited, while the religious practices of fasts, prayers, almsgiving and pilgrimages are encouraged'. But the most striking feature of the *Reflections* is its attack on Christian attitudes towards Islam:

> The Christians and Mahometans have always been at most cruel Variance with each other, in which we can not but tax ourselves with having been the Aggressors; for they have at all times been ready to make large Concessions in Honour of our divine Lawgiver and Religion; while we have been quite outrageous against them and their Prophet, allowing no one Point in favour of them, but condemning them as the accursed of god, from whom they cannot possibly hope for Mercy. The Eastern Churches are protected by the Muslims and allowed to exercise their religious rites, but in Europe, the Roman Catholics, to whom we may, perhaps, add some zealously mistaken Protestants, would as soon suffer Death, almost, as permit any Sect of them the free Exercise of their Religion under our Wing.[23]

Another Englishman to make his sympathetic voice heard about Islam was the statesman Viscount Henry Bolingbroke whom Voltaire visited on several occasions during his exile in England but who does not seem to have had any luck in influencing his negative views of Muhammad. In Letter IV of his *Letters on the Study and Use of History*, published in 1735, Bolingbroke accused the Christian world of having purposefully and systematically distorted history in all ages:

> The charge of corrupting history, in the cause of religion has been always committed to the most famous champions of the church.

---

22 Ibid.
23 Henry Bolingbroke, *Letters on the Study and Use of History*, 2 volumes, London 1752, Volume I, letter IV, pp. 128–9.

What accusations of idolatry and superstition have not been brought, and aggravated against the Mahometans? Those wretched Christians who returned from those wars, so improperly called the holy wars, rumoured these stories about the West: And you may find, in some of the old chroniclers and romance writers, as well as poets, the Saracens called Paynims; though surely they were much further off from any suspicion of polytheism, than those who called them by that name. Many such instances may be collected from Marracci's refutation of the Koran, and Relandus has published a very valuable treatise on purpose to justify the Mahometans.[24]

Adrian Reland, to whom Viscount Bolingbroke refers, was Professor of Oriental Languages at the University of Utrecht in the Netherlands. Utterly free of prejudice, Reland spoke frankly and scornfully of those who, through hatred of Islam, had continued to hold and transmit the old legends and fables about Muhammad and his religion. In his preface to *Four Treatises Concerning the Doctrine, Discipline, and Worship of the Mahometans*, published anonymously in London in 1712, Reland quotes the advice he has heard given to many students not to waste time on the study of Arabic 'because it is not worthwhile (say many) to undergo so much Trouble and Fatigue, only to consult the Dreams and Ravings of a Fanatic'. Reland himself repudiates this view and counterbalances it with his own:

> But really the Mahometans are not so mad as we think them. I have always been of the Mind, that that Religion, which has largely spread itself over Asia, Africa and even Europe, commands itself to Men by a great Appearance of Truth.[25]

But the most profound and lasting testimony to the tolerance and understanding that some Enlightenment thinkers were able to show towards Islam was the German play *Nathan der Weise* (*Nathan the Wise*) by Gotthold lphraim Lessing, published in 1780. Lessing was one of the most eloquent proponents of the German Enlightenment. Philosopher, critic and dramatist, he had studied theology and came to adopt a deist-humanistic viewpoint in which the three great religions that shaped

---

24 Byron Porter Smith, *Islam in English Literature*, Beirut, 1939, p. 78.
25 Adrian Reland, *Four Treatises Concerning the Doctrine, Discipline and Worship of the Mahometans*, anonymous translator, London, 1712, p. 12.

Europe, Judaism, Christianity and Islam, were worthy of equal respect and thoughtful consideration. He was concerned with the validity of claims made by any religion to the possession of ultimate truth on the basis of revelation and miracles. His primary target had been Christianity, which brought upon him the wrath of the clergy. His final response to their bigoted protestations was the drama *Nathan der Weise*, in which he suggests that the three monotheistic religions are essentially similar and that the acid test of possessing truth based on revelation has to be in the behaviour of their adherents. Thus Lessing placed humanity above the claims of organized religions and orthodoxy.

The play is set in Jerusalem of 1187, two years before the Third Crusade, when the Arab Warrior Saladin reconquered the Holy City from the Christian zealots who had established a Latin Kingdom there. Saladin who features in the play, is celebrated in the annals of both East and West as a just and enlightened ruler whose tolerance towards all religions had become legendary. He had immediately declared a truce and in contrast to the Crusaders who had taken Jerusalem eighty-eight years earlier had not allowed a single building to be looted or a person to be harmed. The terms were that a ransom should be paid of 10 dinars for every man, 5 dinars for every woman and 1 for every child, the sum of which was then given to the poor. The inhabitants of Jerusalem were deeply moved by Saladin's generosity and his humane behaviour, especially when they realized that they could continue to practise their faith. Saladin's advisers had urged him to demolish the Church of the Holy Sepulchre but he had refused to do so and had instead let the Church be closed for three days and then reopened it to pilgrims again – for a fee. During his rule the holy places remained open to the worshippers of all religions. It is precisely for this exemplary tolerance that Lessing chose Saladin as one of his key characters. The protagonist however is the Jewish merchant, Nathan, known as Nathan the Wise, because of his balanced powers of judgement.

Nathan has lost his wife and seven sons in the persecution of Jews by the Knights of the Cross. His tragic fate has not, however, filled him with hatred but with knowledge and understanding (*Erkenntnis*). Remarkably, he has overcome his anguish and has maintained his love of mankind (*Menschenliebe*) – which he displays by adopting an orphaned Christian girl as his daughter. Her name is Recha and Nathan employs a Christian governess to look after her and to raise her in the Christian faith. But as Nathan's daughter she is seen as a Jewess by the outside world. One day when Nathan is away on a business journey to Jordan, a fire breaks out in his house and Recha is rescued by a young Christian knight. On his return Nathan, who is deeply grateful for having regained his beloved daughter, wants to reward her saviour. Recha and her governess Daja, as devout Christians, believe that a miracle had occurred and that Recha's life had been saved by an angel. Nathan however tries to persuade them that good human beings can also accomplish good deeds and that we do not need to believe in miracles and guardian angels when we can help each other. After a long search they succeed in finding the Christian knight to whom they all feel indebted. The dialogue between Nathan and the knight under the palm trees of Nathan's gardens is one of the most famous scenes in the history of German drama. The dialogue is sparked off by the knight's refusal to enter a Jew's house, in accordance with the rules of his order. Thereupon Nathan asks him why then he had rescued a Jewish child? Was it not because she was a human being? And the goodness he displayed derived surely from his own humanity rather than from his religion? Nathan insists that all human beings are human before they are adherents to a particular religion. He already feels that in the knight he has recognized a kindred spirit.

In the meantime Nathan visits the ruler of Jerusalem, Sultan Saladin, who, on the pretence of wishing to borrow money from him to run the affairs of state, has invited Nathan to his palace. His true intention however is to engage this renowned thinker in debate on the relative merits of the three monotheistic religions, Judaism, Christianity and Islam. To illustrate his standpoint Nathan tells the Sultan the Parable of the Three Rings, which forms the heart of the play's message:

A man possessed a ring which had the power of making anyone who owned it beloved of God and of humankind. According to family tradition, the ring had always been passed on from father to favourite son. But the last owner had had three sons. All three were equally dear to him. So, he had two other rings made to match the one he already owned. In the end the three rings looked so alike that he himself could not tell which one was the original and which were the copies. After his death, each of the three sons claimed to possess the original ring. They took their feud before a court of law, but even the judge was unable to tell the difference between the rings. So he advised them thus:

Let each one emulate your father's love,
Without all partiality and free of prejudice!
Let each one compete to show the world
The power of the stone within his ring.
Help this power with kindness,
With heartfelt tolerance, with good deeds,
Help it with deepest devotion to God![26]

The three rings evidently represent Judaism, Christianity and Islam. It emerges, as the dramatic action continues, that the Christian knight himself had been saved from execution by decree of Saladin, who was against religious retribution. Moreover, the final proof of Nathan's declaration of the primacy of humanity is shown in the discovery at the end that the knight is in fact Saladin's nephew – the son of his long-lost brother – and that the Christian orphan Recha is his sister and thus Saladin's niece. But Recha still recognizes in Nathan her adoptive Jewish father and elects to stay with him. It is through the demonstration of humanity by Nathan towards Recha, through the knight's refusal to bear resentment against his persecutors by instinctively rescuing Recha and through Saladin's benign sense of justice towards the knight that the plot itself illustrates the truth of the parable: that goodness is shown through man's actions and not his professed religion, and that human communality is greater than external differences. Nathan's own words addressed to the knight after he had refused his invitation to enter his house are more eloquent than any interpretation:

We must, we must be friends!
Scorn my people to your heart's content,
We have neither of us chosen our people.
Are we our people? What does people mean?
Are Christian and Jew, Christian and Jew before they are human?
Oh, had I only found in you another
For whom it was enough to be called a human![27]

Just two years after Lessing's *Nathan der Weise*, Mozart presented the world with one of the most attractive of all his operas, *The Abduction*

---

26 Gotthold Iphraim Lessing, *Nathan der Weise*, edited by Peter Demetz, Frankfurt 1966, III.7 p. 67. (Translation by N. B. R. Reeves)
27 Ibid. II. 5, p. 47. (Translation by N. B. R. Reeves)

from the Seraglio. The work begins with a conventionally stereotyped view of the Turkish court, which Mozart presents with tongue-in-cheek exaggeration. After many vicissitudes, the two captive Western lovers, Constanze and Belmonte are magnanimously pardoned and freed by the Pasha, who himself becomes the symbol of Enlightenment.

But alas Lessing and Mozart were drowned out by the vociferous opposition to tolerance from the many extremist clerics. Already in 1703, D. D. Neretter had set the tone in Germany by calling Muhammad a 'Heuchler' (hypocrite), a 'geiler' (lecher) and 'niedriger Mensch' (base person) in the introduction to his translation of the Qur'an, one of the first to appear in the German language. And for Kant, Muhammad was the worst type of the 'Fanatiker' (fanatic), 'Visionär' (visionary) and 'Schwärmer' (enthusiast). It was precisely thanks to this extreme enthusiasm or fanaticism that in Kant's view Muhammad had been able to rise to power or, to quote the philosopher's own words, place himself 'auf den Fürstenthron', 'upon the princely throne'. Against this background of condemnation it is hardly surprising that Voltaire's *Mahomet ou le Fanatisme* was repeatedly translated into German, of which Goethe's translation in 1800 was the last. An English translation had appeared in 1770 by J. Miller.

While the Enlightenment was deeply divided in its attitude and approach to Muhammad, its insistence on human rights, its hatred of arbitrary rule and the suppression of freedom had irrevocably gained in resonance. Indeed, Muhammad had served as the innocent whipping boy for the Enlightenment's covert but unflagging attacks on the abuse of power and moral corruption of Louis and his court. Muhammad and his religion had, unlike in the preceding seventeenth century, not been the true target, since they were no longer felt to be an immediate threat. The religion, on the contrary, that the Enlightenment thinkers wished to satirize was their own. However effective their direct and indirect illumination of Christianity, especially Catholicism, may have been, they failed to illuminate Islam. But that had rarely been their intention!

Yet, the Enlightenment had truly struck a mortal blow upon its real enemies. Political change was on the way. In England the ground had been well prepared. Two revolutions had occurred there before the seventeenth century was even out. Germany, unlike England and France, was politically highly fragmented. It has been said, with slight exaggeration, that there were as many German princely states as there were days of the year. And many of these petty states were modelled on French absolutist rule, both in denial of freedom of speech and in the mannerisms of court. But the foundations of modern Germany were already being laid by Frederick the Great of Prussia. While the power of Prussia was growing through the efficiency of the army and the civil service that Frederick and his successors built up, Frederick was also, and significantly, being admired by the French thinkers of the Enlightenment, and above all by Voltaire. A French speaker (German was not used at court), a patron of the arts, a tolerably good composer and musician, Frederick brought to his court many of the great men of letters and arts of his time. Voltaire was the greatest of these. In Frederick, Voltaire and others saw an exemplary realization of benevolent monarchy in a modern state. By today's standards Frederick was still an absolutist ruler. Not so in eighteenth-century terms!

In France events were to turn out differently. As Voltaire was personally to experience, after the death of Louis XIV, the Sun King, the power of the French monarchy had began to slip. At the age of 23, Voltaire had witnessed in 1715 Louis' funeral. The decadence of the subsequent regency (for Louis XV succeeded to the throne at the age of five) aroused the scorn of his pen, and Louis' consequent long reign of nearly sixty years was characterized by frivolity, indulgence at court, and neglect by the monarch of the affairs of state. The expense of the Seven Years War, the loss of colonies in America to the English, the alliance of other great European powers, including Prussia, against France all led to a weakening of the latter's power. By the time Louis XVI succeeded to his father's throne in 1774 the French court had lost much respect and prestige. French intervention against the English in the American War of Independence from 1777 to 1783 was exceedingly costly. A trade recession and the failure of the harvest in 1788 put intolerable pressure on the impoverished rural population and on the numerous working-class inhabitants of France's great metropolis, Paris. The constraints imposed by over a century of unbroken absolutism on the freethinking of the country's intellectuals, the salons and the academies, flying in the face of what the Enlightenment stood for, had reached breaking-point. This was to prove a deadly mix of volatile elements.

On 14 July 1789, a Paris mob stormed the Bastille, the royal fortress and prison, in search of arms to protect themselves against royal troops. The hated Bastille was where Voltaire, Diderot and many other

Enlighteners of the age had served months of imprisonment for their anti-establishment views on the monarchy and on Christianity. A wave of revolts broke out across the country, royal authority collapsed and the National Assembly eventually promulgated the Declaration of the Rights of Man and a constitution which severely limited the powers of monarchy.

But the invasion in 1792 by Austria and Prussia to halt the Revolution not only failed – it provoked the accusation that Louis had plotted against the National Assembly. He and his Queen, Marie Antoinette, were beheaded on 21 January 1793. The Divine Right of the French monarch to rule had come to a bloody end, as it had in England one hundred and forty-four years before. France was a republic.

Two years earlier, in 1791, Voltaire's coffin had been fetched from a distant village burial-place and borne in state through the streets of Paris to a new resting-place in the Pantheon. On Voltaire's coffin had been inscribed the words 'Il nous a enseigné à être libre' (He taught us to be free).

The outcome of the French Enlightenment proved, then, to be drastic indeed. The glory of the court of Versailles had been extinguished. A new era in the history of France and of Europe had been born. But the birth was bloodstained. Freedom had been bought at a high cost in human lives and in a different manner from that hoped for and expected by the thinkers. And just as violence had characterized the emergence of the republic, so the man who was acclaimed as its father, Voltaire, had wittingly or unwittingly nourished the age-old tradition of suspicion and contempt for Islam and for Muhammad. The world of *Nathan the Wise* had receded.

8

Hero or Impostor?

Muhammad in the age of hero worship

But of a Great Man especially, of him I will venture to assert that it is incredible he should have been other than true. It seems to me the primary foundation of him, and of all that can lie in him, is this. No Mirabeau, Napoleon, Burns, Cromwell, no man adequate to do anything, but is first of all in right earnest about it; what 1 call a sincere man. I should say sincerity, a deep, great, genuine sincerity, is the first characteristic of all men in any way heroic.

Thomas Carlyle, *Lecture on The Hero as Prophet. Mahomet: Islam.*
8 May 1840

As the nineteenth century was born, a new earthly god came to power, Napoleon Bonaparte. Celebrated and remembered for decades as a hero, he assumed in people's imagination (though not in Britain) divine proportions. The great German poet and romantic satirist, Heinrich Heine, remembered the French general in *Ideen. Das Buch Le Grand* of 1824 arriving in Düsseldorf as if he were Jesus entering Jerusalem on Palm Sunday, mounted on a horse not a donkey, but riding to an ultimate defeat that would eventually spell immortality. A new age was breaking, which, driven by the events of the French Revolution, driven by the technological fruits of the Age of Reason – that is the Industrial Revolution – fostered a sense of European supremacy over all other continents. The worship of man on earth was to triumph. Napoleon, this brilliant young Corsican general, became the archetypal hero, the secular god of the new century.

It was Napoleon who turned the invasions of revolutionary France into resounding victories. France in the 1790s stormed forward to triumphant conquests over Austria, Prussia, Poland, Holland, Belgium,

Switzerland and Italy. Since the French Revolution too much history had happened in too short a time. Between 1789 and 1791 the political and social institutions that had characterized France for the previous century and more had been overthrown. By 1792 France had become a republic and between 1793 and 1794 had experienced a revolutionary dictatorship led by Robespierre. Thereafter a reaction had set in, culminating in Robespierre's execution and in a military coup which brought Napoleon to power.

The French Revolution was the most important event in the history of modern Europe, comparable in its vast consequences to Luther's Reformation of the sixteenth century. It released dynamic and explosive forces throughout Europe. The forces of continuity and change clashed. The former included the monarchy, the Church and the landowning aristocracy, the latter nationalism and the quest for democracy. Napoleon and the dominant classes of revolutionary France believed that they were conducting a revolution on behalf of all mankind and welcomed to their ranks men of any other nation whom they regarded as sharing their aspirations. Napoleon's success in Europe was mainly founded on a vast reservoir of conscripts of all nationalities and on his popularity not only with his troops but also with Europe's intellectuals, especially those of Germany, Italy and Spain. Many liberal-thinking men of these nations enthusiastically responded to his universal view of the revolution – at least until the excesses of the French armies and Napoleon's own despotism disillusioned them. Germany's most prominent man of letters Wolfgang von Goethe, now fifty-nine years old, attended the festivities at Erfurt in 1808 which were a tribute to Napoleon's victory over Germany. Goethe was decorated and honoured by Napoleon and he reiterated his admiration for the Emperor in return. Beethoven at first dedicated his 1800 Eroica Symphony to Napoleon, but on hearing that the latter had assumed the title of Emperor, he angrily tore the dedication out. And Heine saw the divine both in Goethe and in Napoleon, assessing them in his *Romantische Schule* of 1835 as personalities whose divine stature was reflected even in their outward appearance:

> Indeed you found that correspondence between personality and genius that you expect of exceptional men, entirely present in Goethe. His external appearance was as impressive as the words that lived in his writings – his stature was harmonious, clear, joyful,

noble. His eyes were serene like those of a God – qualities shared by Napoleon's eyes also. That's why I am convinced that he was a God.[1]

Napoleon was driven by a sense of mission, supported by his military genius. His empire was based on invasion and war and the destruction of old political systems. In 1803 he proclaimed himself Emperor of France and of its territories in Europe, and proceeded to assemble an army to invade England. A year later the Franco-Spanish fleet was defeated at Trafalgar by Napoleon's most determined enemy, the British. This however did not deter him from placing his brother on the throne of Spain in 1808, and four years later he invaded Russia. Napoleon's expansive military ventures stimulated the formation of several coalitions between Britain and other European powers, Austria, Prussia and Russia. This eventually led to Napoleon's defeat in 1813 at Leipzig, whereupon he was exiled to Elba. His attempted return to power in 1815 ended in the Battle of Waterloo and in his final defeat. He was forced to abdicate and was again exiled, this time to the Island of St Helena in the South Atlantic, where he died in 1821. Power in France was restored to Louis XVIII, the brother of Louis XVI and it was agreed that France should be given the frontiers it had in 1792, before the revolutionary wars began.

Seven years after Napoleon's defeat at Waterloo, the German philosopher and major intellectual force behind the regeneration of Prussia, Wilhelm Friedrich Hegel, was in the process of delivering his renowned lectures on the *Philosophy of World History*. He was setting the scene not only for German nationalism, but also for the hero worship and imperialism of nineteenth-century Europe. He was paradoxically also laying the foundation of Karl Marx's theory of historical materialism. The lectures were given at the University of Berlin, in the very city that Napoleon had occupied following his victory at Jena. In his grand philosophical scheme Hegel claimed that the world of the finite, our world, is governed by a transcendental force beyond the confines of space and time. This force was the force of pure reason, divine reason or *Vernunft*. At the other end of universal reality was the world of the finite

---

1 Heinrich Heine, *Sämtliche Werke*, herausgegeben von (edited by) Ernst Elster, Leipzig und Wien (Vienna) 1890, Band V (Volume V), *Romantische Schule*, pp. 264–5. (Quotation translated by N. B. R. Reeves)

– the human world – which existed in historical time. The *Weltgeist* or the universal spirit (*Vernunft* in action so to speak) was seeking to unite itself in a future, permanent fusion with the world of the finite. In order to achieve this great plan which is played out in history, the *Weltgeist* intervened in human affairs, Hegel argued, to push human societies forward towards ever greater realization of freedom. This ultimate fusion of *Weltgeist* and *Welt* – the universal spirit and the human world, could only occur when human societies completely embodied the idea and realization of freedom. For Hegel the vehicle for this historical achievement was the nation state and the framework for this freedom had to be a constitution founded on the rule of law. Hegel's grandiose philosophical design was to form a basis, on the continent of Europe at least, for justifying the emergence of nation states. And they became the single greatest driving force in nineteenth-century European politics. Hegel's theory of history also provided a justification for imperialism, as 'superior' and 'progressive' nation states came to assert themselves over both the ancient civilizations and the tribal societies of the rest of the world.

According to Hegel the historical progress towards realizing freedom on earth entailed conflict and bloodshed. Every step forward could only occur through the defeat of the status quo while the fate of the victorious new element was itself to become a new status quo and so be defeated in its turn by more progressive forces. The agents of change who instigated this process of conflict were world historical figures of colossal stature such as Julius Caesar, Alexander and Napoleon. For Hegel they were great heroic figures but also tragic, because in the end they died for their cause, having been used by the *Weltgeist* for its higher purpose. The influence of Napoleon's fate at Waterloo and his exile on St Helena on Hegel's thinking can hardly be underestimated.

This was how Hegel characterized the great heroic figures of history and their missions in his *Philosophy of World History*:

> They knew how to obtain satisfaction and to accomplish their end, which is the universal end. With so great an end before them, they boldly resolved to challenge all the beliefs of their fellows. Thus it was not happiness that they chose, but exertion, conflict and labour in the service of their end. And even when they reached their goal, peaceful enjoyment and happiness were not their lot. Their actions are their entire being, and their whole nature and character are determined by their ruling passion. When their end is

attained, they fall aside like empty husks. They may have undergone great difficulties in order to accomplish their purpose, but as soon as they have done so, they die early like Alexander, are murdered like Caesar, or deported like Napoleon.[2]

It was in the same light that Hegel saw Muhammad as a world historical character who through his genius changed two continents, Asia and Africa, in the direction of progress. Hegel justified the wars of conquest conducted by Muhammad's successors as a historically determined necessity, when a higher spiritual principle asserts itself over less advanced elements of human history:

> But in world history, a higher right comes into play. In fact, this is even recognised in reality in those situations where civilised nations come into contact with barbarian hordes. And in wars of religion, one of the parties involved will invariably claim to be defending a sacred principle in relation to which the rights of other nations are secondary and of lesser validity. This was true of the Mohammedans in former times, and in theory even today. The Christians likewise, in making war on heathen nations with a view to converting them, have claimed that their religion invests them with superior rights.[3]

But Muhammad's religion, in Hegel's eyes, did not attain the fusion of the infinite with the finite, as in the figure of Jesus as God Incarnate. Only in the western European Christian world had the Spirit's recognition of itself and its profundity been realized. Hegel emphasized the superiority of Christianity over other religions of the world – a view which most conveniently gave licence to Europe's growing colonial aspirations to dominate the non-Christian cultures of the East. It became a fixed idea of the nineteenth century, especially amongst politicians, diplomats, administrators and of course Catholic and Protestant missionaries, that Christianity had led to progress and prosperity – as Luther had also ironically prophesied. And indeed, since Luther's time Islam had gradually sunk into poverty and underdevelopment, after centuries of power, wealth and empire.

---

2 C. W. F. Hegel, *Lectures on the Philosophy of World History*, translated by H. B. Nisbet, Cambridge, 1975, p. 85.

3 Ibid., p. 65.

Hegel was not the first writer to highlight heroism and the importance of man's genius in human history. The ground for his theories had been prepared by the late eighteenth-century German literary movement, known colourfully as *Sturm und Drang* or Storm and Stress. The prominent leaders of this movement had been Johann Gottfried Herder and the young Goethe who came to dominate the German literary scene for the next half century. The *Sturm und Drang* period had seen the revival of Baroque drama and an imitation of Shakespeare and Marlowe with their larger-than-life heroes. Caesar, Socrates, Muhammad, they were all seen as significant sources of self-expression in this period when sensibility and the primacy of human genius and creative imagination were the dominant themes.

Goethe's celebration of Muhammad and his religion had found expression in his dramatic fragment, *Mahomet*, of 1772 of which his poem 'Mahomets Gesang' ('Mahomet's Song') was a part. In it Goethe's notion of genius and the value of inspiration, both poetic and prophetic, are joyfully displayed. Goethe celebrates the pure, infinite, self-generating energy of the spirit within, embodied in the figure of Muhammad and his prophecy. In the poem Muhammad is compared with a boundless river, constantly growing in size and bearing mankind to its eternal abode. There is no conflict in 'Mahomets Gesang' between the spirit turning from its home in the infinite to the finite and to worldly forms, seeking companionship, life and civilization. In the traditional Christian-European view Muhammad's rule over the early Muslim community in Medina had been regarded as serving his worldly ambitions or doing the Devil's work. Goethe turned this 'vice' into a 'virtue' by celebrating the spirit which in 'Mahomets Gesang' descends into the world and offers ecstatic love of God. The river is a symbol of immense activity and movement. It is restless, inexhaustible and dynamic, echoing the energy of man's longing and enthusiasm and attracting the admiration and devotion of converts. In the end only the vast ocean can be its adequate home, only infinity the final abode for the all-embracing spirit. *L'enthousiasme* or *Schwärmerei* which Voltaire, Diderot and Kant had abhorred in religions such as Islam and which they branded as unhealthy and insane was now admired by Goethe and his contemporaries as enthusiasm of a positive kind. Unlike those rationalist Enlightenment thinkers who regarded Muhammad with horror, Goethe embraced him as a fountainhead of liberating inspiration. 'Mahomets Gesang' opens with these lines:

> Behold the rocky spring
> As joyful and as bright
> As a radiant star!
> Above the clouds
> Good Spirits
> Nourished his youth
> Between crag and thicket.
>
> Young and vigorous
> He dances from the cloud
> Down to the marble rocks,
> Gambolling back
> Towards the Heavens
>
> Darting between the peaks
> He chases glistening pebbles
> And with an early leader's stride
> He carries with him
> His brotherly springs.[4]

The river progresses through valleys and plains, taking with it kindred streams with the promise of reaching an ocean of eternity:

> Streams join gently in
> As friends.
> Now he enters
> The plain, shining like silver,
> And the plain shines with him,
> And the rivers of the plain
> And the streams from the hills
> Call joyously to him: Brother,
> Brother, take your brothers too,
> On to your ancient Father,
> To the eternal Ocean,
> Awaiting us
> With outspread arms.
> Arms that open, alas, in vain

---

4 *Goethes Werke*, Hamburger Ausgabe, edited by Erich Trunz, 7th impression, 1964, Volume I, pp. 42–4 'Mahomets Gesang', passage quoted p. 42. (Quotations translated by N. B. R. Reeves)

To embrace his longing children;
For we are swallowed in the bleak desert
By greedy sand.[5]

As the river grows and ever more tributaries join, it leaves the mountains, the valleys and the desert to reach the cities of civilization that come to bear its name:

Come all of you!
And now in glory, onwards he flows
A whole race bearing on high their prince,
And in processional triumph
He gives lands their names and
Cities grow beneath his foot.[6]

Goethe concludes his 'Mahomet's Song' with the following stanza:

And so he bears his brothers,
His treasures, his children
On to his awaiting Creator,
And in a torrent of joy,
On to His very heart.[7]

In the original dramatic fragment *Mahomet*, it is Muhammad's daughter Fatima, his son-in-law Ali and his adopted son Zayd (Beyd in the fragment) who watch the river or the prophetic spirit take over and embrace them. Goethe's verses are in fact recited by these first converts to Muhammad's religion and indicate at one and the same time both the triumphant advances of Islam from Muhammad's lonely mountain cave to its adoption throughout the Arab Empire – and the spiritual progress of the believers who are borne along by the faith towards an infinite afterlife.

Goethe's 'Mahomets Gesang' had been written as early as 1772, some twenty years before the rise of Napoleon and nearly sixty years before Hegel's theories on the role of world historical figures were published. Goethe had praised Muhammad as an extraordinary man who left in his Qur'an a legacy that would last an eternity.

---

5 Ibid., p. 43.
6 Ibid., p. 44.
7 Ibid., p. 44.

Goethe was not alone in recognizing the element of genius in Muhammad. In the early years of the nineteenth century another great admirer of Napoleon, Karoline von Günderode was writing a play and a poem, presenting Muhammad as a remarkable figure of colossal proportions. Her poem entitled, '*Mahomets Traum in der Wüste*' ('Mahomet's Dream in the Desert'), was published in 1804. Günderode was a nun who spent her life separated from ordinary life. But this did not preclude her from the hero-worship which had started to establish itself with the German *Sturm und Drang* of the 1770s and was to become a major feature of nineteenth-century sensibilities. As for many, it was Napoleon who aroused this admiration, and even in her German nunnery Günderode looked up to this distant figure with adoration. In '*Mahomets Traum in der Wüste*' ('Mahomet's Dream in the Desert') Muhammad is a Napoleonic character whose grand ambition to conquer the world and to change all its existing laws, is idealized.

It is a powerful poem which links images of Muhammad's experience of divine revelation in the desert with aspects of Jesus' prayers in the Garden of Gethsemane before his crucifixion, and with notions of the ancient Persian religion of Zarathustra or Zoroaster in its depiction of the four elements: Earth, Water, Air and Fire. Muhammad the *Seher* or visionary is tormented by his longing to gain insight into the secrets of life and his own future. He wants to meditate, to listen to his own heart and to conjure up the spirit of the Creator that he believes to lie within. But the more he looks, the more he listens, the more his own plight and eventual downfall – his *Untergang* – become apparent. His dream soon turns into a nightmare. A world of chaos and damnation unfolds before his eyes. His intervention has disturbed the harmony of the elements. They turn wild and violent. The earth begins to quake, the sea turns upside down and roaring flames of fire engulf cliffs and rocks, devouring all that was created on earth, leaving nothing but an overwhelming smell of sulphur in the air. Deeply shaken, Muhammad awakes, filled with a sense of confusion and horror. It is as if he has risen from the torment of a terrifying, godless death. But suddenly he hears a voice descending from the stars. It is the voice of the Creator who announces that Muhammad had indeed stirred up world history by wanting to penetrate into the realms of divine reality. What he saw, God confirms, was human history in its making. The war of the elements had triggered off an unceasing rain which was to cleanse the earth of all its impurities, leaving behind nothing but light. This light was to remain forever, beaming upward towards its eternal source. Thereupon the darkness of the night is replaced by floods of dazzling morning light which inundate Muhammad's soul. 'From now on', he exclaims, 'nothing shall stand in my way. May the Light be my future guiding star so that my deeds may become immortal.'[8]

But Günderode's Muhammad is no mere ascetic recluse nor mystic seeking illumination and divine perfection to attain absolute knowledge. Her Muhammad is primarily concerned with his own destiny and his own ambitions. His desire (like that of Napoleon) is to conquer the world so that his own laws may reign over it and bring justice:

> May the power of God
> Tear open the night
> Of Fate, before my very eyes!
> Let me see the future!
> Will my flags fly in triumph?
> Will my law rule the world?[9]

In 1840, some thirty-seven years after Günderode's 'Mahomet's Dream in the Desert' had been published, Thomas Carlyle, the great Victorian man of letters, a Scotsman by birth, was deeply absorbed in writing his famous London lectures *On Heroes, Hero-Worship and the Heroic in History*. As the reviews show, they caused a great stir when they were published a year later. Editions followed in 1842, 1846 and 1853. They then became a part of the edition of Carlyle's collected works, the first appearing between 1856 and 1868. But Carlyle's lectures on heroes have been reprinted many times since, both separately and in further collected editions. In fact, few literary figures in the nineteenth century generated as much response in the public and in the press and over such a long period of time as Carlyle. By 1840 he commanded the attention of most literary journals of his day, especially after the publication of his book *History of the French Revolution* in 1837 in which the concept

---

8 Karoline von Günderode, *Der Schatten eines Traumes*, Gedichte, Prosa, Briefe, Zeugnisse von Zeitgenossen (poems, prose, testimonies by contemporaries) und mit einem Essay von Christa Wolf (with an essay by Christa Wolf), Darmstadt und Neuwied, 1979, p. 79.
9 Ibid., pp. 78–9. (Quotation translated by N. B. R. Reeves.)

of the hero had first been advanced. Responses to his lecture series on hero-worship ranged from denunciation and blame to partial acceptance, from fulsome praise to violent attack.

Fascinated all his life by the relationship between spiritual and secular power, Carlyle believed that historical figures like Muhammad, Luther, Cromwell and Napoleon had succeeded as leaders of their fellows because they had been inspired by God and because they incorporated in conscious and unconscious form the central spiritual truth. The hero was primarily the man of vision, the seer. The hero saw through material phenomena and interpreted reality for the multitude – in so doing he made history. The sincerity of the hero was the corollary of the truth of his vision. Carlyle saw an element of divinity in each man, allowing him to recognize the supreme form of divine inspiration that manifested itself in great historical characters and in the originality of their works. By drawing his heroic figures, or his 'original men', from disparate cultures he was able to delineate the underlying forces of personality and nature whose basis he believed to be the unconscious and the divine.

Carlyle's views had evolved in the course of his studies of theology, mathematics and German literature, particularly the works of Goethe, Schiller and Hegel. He had established himself as a leading transmitter of German literature to the British public by writing his *Life of Schiller* and by translating Goethe's *Wilhelm Meisters Lehrjahre* (*Wilhelm Meister's Apprenticeship*) into English. He had also studied the Qur'an and the teachings of Islam. Goethe's vision of the spiritual structure of the universe illumined by the divine force within genius had especially and profoundly affected him. Carlyle postulated the same transcendental theory that the material universe was the symbol or manifestation of the spiritual world of reality – which corresponded to the Qur'anic interpretation of God's creation. Throughout his life Carlyle admired and idolized Goethe as his mentor. Goethe of course was one of the first European thinkers to be fascinated by Islamic mysticism. Indeed, in his depiction of Muhammad as a great historical hero, Carlyle followed in Goethe's steps, recognizing Muhammad's genius, his spiritual and heroic stature, his achievements and his overwhelming and lasting impact on man's ideas and beliefs. It took Carlyle a long time to identify his historical heroes. He had to measure the length of the hero's shadow as it stretched across the ages, the continuance of the institutions on which the hero was the founder. Muhammad immediately qualified for his purpose, in view of the success and permanence of Islam, which Carlyle confirms in his introductory words to his second lecture, 'The Hero as Prophet':

> The word this man spoke has been the life guidance now of hundred and eighty millions of men these twelve hundred years. A greater number of God's creatures believe in Mahomet's word at this hour than in any other word whatever.[10]

Carlyle's first lecture had been on Odin, the chief deity of Norse mythology. He depicted Odin as the teacher and lord of the Norse people's body and soul, a pagan hero of immeasurable worth. It was through him that the Norse people became conscious of themselves and the world around them. Odin breathed life into Scandinavian existence, making its people articulate and giving meaning to their lives. He gave Norsemen an assurance of their identity and destiny. Odin is presented by Carlyle as a figure of exceptional talent and vision who distinguished himself amongst his people by accomplishing truly heroic tasks. Carlyle recounts how this legendary figure, whom he depicts as a heroic prince inhabiting a region along the Black Sea, led his people, restricted for land, out of their native lands and settled them in parts of northern Europe through military conquests. Odin invented letters of the alphabet and poetry, and came to be worshipped in Scandinavia as a national hero and as a divinity. In a similar way, explained Carlyle, Muhammad had been chosen by God to become the leader of his fellow Arabs, uniting them into a nation and giving them a sense of direction and vocation in life. Carlyle's second lecture looked closely at Muhammad and his mission, his impact on history and his significance in consolidating the notion of monotheism and the unity of God. This lecture was an attempt to tell British Christendom that divine inspiration and individual genius transcended cultural boundaries and was therefore not exclusive to Christianity.

The third lecture focused on the hero as poet. In Dante and Shakespeare, the author suggested, were role models for the modern artist whom he proclaimed to be the new vehicle of the divine force in the universe. In his fourth lecture, Carlyle discussed the importance of

---

10 Thomas Carlyle, *On Heroes, Hero-Worship and the Heroic in History*, London, 1888, p. 41.

the priest as a hero, taking Luther as his example. Carlyle argued that Luther had proved, through the sheer force of his character, that the reforming spirit of Protestantism could touch the spiritual core of unconscious powers within modern European man – a core that needed only to be addressed in a bold voice like Luther's to be awakened. The fifth lecture portrayed the man of letters as hero. Here Carlyle felt his own mission embodied in writers such as Rousseau, Johnson and Burns, who, in his view, brought new and liberating ideas into the world. In his concluding lecture, the sixth, Carlyle, articulated his central theme of hero-worship and the praise of the heroic, concentrating on the role played by Napoleon and Cromwell in shaping European history.

It was the first time in the entire register of European writing from the early Middle Ages to the day that Muhammad was being daringly and openly placed alongside great men of universal history, men who had been immortalized through their ideas and actions. It was at three o'clock in the afternoon of Friday 8 May 1840 that Carlyle gave his lecture on Mahomet and Islam in a lecture room in Portman Square in London. From the crude days of paganism among the Nordic people, he said, he now wanted to take his listeners to a very different epoch of religion, among a very different people: 'Mahometanism' among the Arabs. The hero, the audience was told, was now regarded not as a God among his fellow men, but as one who was God-inspired, as a Prophet. It heralded the second phase of hero-worship in the history of mankind. The most precious gift that Heaven could give the earth, he declared, was a man of genius, a man like Mahomet, sent down from above with God's message to us. He dismissed the popular European view that Mahomet's religion was a combination of charlatanism and stupidity, as a mere figment of Europe's imagination that had no foundation in truth. He went on to argue that for centuries countless men and women had been taking Mahomet as the guiding star of their lives. Islam had inspired these men and women to pray, to fast, to give to the poor, to make the pilgrimage to Mecca. Could it be possible, he asked, that so many million creatures, created by God, had lived and died for something which Europe regarded as a tragic deception? 'What are we to think of this world, if charlatans really had such power over the minds of human beings?' Carlyle blamed the persistence of the distorted image of Mahomet on the godless theories of the Age of Reason, indicative, as he described it, of mental paralysis and the spiritual death of Europe. In contrast, he attested to Mahomet's uprightness and sincerity. He called Mahomet an 'original man', a genius, a messenger who brought us news of the infinite and the unknown. 'We might call him a poet or prophet,' he said, 'for we feel that the words which he spoke were not the words of an ordinary man. They had their immediate source in the inner reality of things and Mahomet had lived in constant fellowship with that reality.' But the following passage from 'The Hero as Prophet' shows that even an emancipated and courageous apologist like Carlyle living in mid-nineteenth-century Victorian England had to be exceedingly cautious not to be branded a traitor and a convert to Muhammad's religion, when trying to break the ancient and well-established clichés:

> We have chosen Mahomet not as the most eminent Prophet; but as the one we are freest to speak of. He is by no means the truest of Prophets; but I do esteem him a true one. Farther, as there is no danger of our becoming, any of us, Mahometans, I mean to say all the good of him I justly can . . . Our current hypothesis about Mahomet, that he was a scheming Impostor, a Falsehood incarnate, that his religion is a mere mass of quackery and fatuity, begins really to be now untenable to any one. The lies which well-meaning zeal has heaped round this man are disgraceful to ourselves only.[11]

Carlyle went on to present a biographical sketch of Muhammad and of different episodes of his life and his ministry, based on authentic Muslim sources. From an early age, Carlyle told his listeners, Mahomet had been regarded in Arabia as a serious and sincere character, amiable, cordial, companionable, generous, thoughtful and humble – 'a man of truth and fidelity, true in what he did, true in what he spoke, true in what he thought. This deep-hearted Son of the Desert', said Carlyle, 'was rather taciturn in speech, silent when there was nothing to be said, but pertinent, wise, sincere, when he spoke, always throwing light on the matter in hand. Through his life we find him to have been regarded as an altogether solid, brotherly, genuine man'.

Then the listeners were taken on a mental journey to the Arabian Peninsula of Muhammad's times. Carlyle urged them to judge Mahomet in his proper environment and the proper historical context in which he operated. The desert scene was skilfully drawn before their eyes, its fierceness during the day when the sun blazes down mercilessly, its

---

11 Thomas Carlyle, *On Heroes*, op. cit., p. 40.

tranquil green oases, its deep, vast skies at night when the magical world of stars seem to be so close and so real. Such a country was fit for a deep-hearted, spiritual race, Carlyle argued. Muhammad's birthplace, Mecca, was described and its history related. It is the sacred place of worship for Muslims throughout the world, the listeners learnt, the eyes of innumerable praying men and women are turned towards it, five times today, and all days. 'It is one of the noblest centres in the habitation of man', declared Carlyle. Then the audience was taken across the deserts of Arabia, first to the period when Muhammad accompanied his merchant uncle on his trading expeditions to Syria, then to the time when he was married to the wealthy Khadija and travelled on her behalf to the fairs of Asia Minor until his divine inspiration began to make him conscious of his real vocation in life.

The long, serene years of Muhammad's married life with Khadija were recounted in order to refute the charge that he was ruled by ambition and lust. 'He seems', Carlyle told the audience, 'to have lived in a most affectionate, peaceable, wholesome way with his wedded benefactress, loving her truly, and her alone.' Carlyle spoke of Muhammad's spirituality and the humble and exemplary life he had led. As an orphan boy, as an adolescent, as a young man, as a man in middle age Muhammad's conduct had been immaculate, marked by fidelity, adroitness, devotion and selflessness in relation to friends and relatives, wife and children, and towards the Meccan community. Carlyle asked how this embodiment of good, of innocence, of purity, of humanity was suddenly turned into a bloodthirsty, ambitious man who permitted sexual licence, violence and immorality and who set out to propagate his religion by the sword? No Muslim biographer, the speaker pointed out, attested to this. These are mere vituperations of the Western world, attributing to Muhammad such irregularities of behaviour, supposed to date from after his fifty-fifth birthday, when the good Khadija died. Until then Muhammad's ambition had been to live an honest life. The audience was reminded that there was no inconsistency in Muhammad's conduct from the very beginning to the very end. They were told that all his life Muhammad had fought against violence, licence, despotism, ambition and injustice. He had introduced civil and moral laws precisely to abolish savagery and to replace lawlessness with order and civilization. His Book, the Qur'an, contrary to popular belief in Europe, did not postulate immorality, but in fact a highly restricted and orderly way of life, in accordance with the will of God. Mahomet's religion, Carlyle explained, 'was not an easy one with its rigorous fasts, lavations, strict, complex formulae, prayers five times a day, almsgiving and abstinence from wine'. It was not true either that the Muslims were roused to heroic deeds by the promise of pleasure and sensual recompense in a voluptuous Paradise that their Prophet had designed for them. It was not the taste of licence that led his followers to embrace Islam, but its passionate spirituality, its immediacy and freshness. The highest joys of Paradise were not to indulge in food and drinks and the pleasures of the flesh, but the experience of the purest presence of the Highest which transcends all other human joys. This was the verdict of the Qur'an, the ultimate blessing and reward that Muhammad had promised the devout. It was the flame of divine longing that he had kindled in their innermost hearts, which had gained him such a rapid following, not licence and obscenity. It was his honesty and his integrity that had impressed the people around him. His converts had not been spellbound by his sword, but by his word, powerful, absolute, pure and original, emanating directly from the heart of nature, from our Creator Himself. Not ambition, but the search for ultimate truth had driven Mahomet on: 'What is life? What is death? What am I to believe? What am I to do?' Carlyle tried to display Muhammad's desire to gain insight into the inner realities of the world. 'The grim rocks of Mount Hira, of Mount Sinai', he said, 'the stern sandy solitudes answered not. The great Heaven rolling silent overhead, with its blue glancing stars answered not'. So came Muhammad's illumination, his discovery that the meaning of life was Islam, submission to the will of God. 'Submission to the will of God was inevitable', Carlyle insisted, 'for God was the one and only reality that could exist. We and all things are but a shadow of Him, a transitory garment veiling the Eternal Splendour.' Goethe had said, 'If the word Islam means submission to God, do we not all live and die in *Islam*?'[12] 'Yes', replied Carlyle, 'all of us that have any moral life, we all live so. It has ever been held the highest wisdom for man,' he said, 'not merely to submit to Necessity – but to know and believe well that the stern thing which Necessity had ordered was the wisest, the best, the thing wanted there. This is the soul of Islam', the listeners were told, 'it is properly the soul of Christianity. Islam means in its way denial of Self, Annihilation of Self. This is the highest wisdom that Heaven has revealed to our Earth.'

---

12 Ibid., p. 52.

'Mahomet can work no miracles', the speaker confessed, 'he often answers impatiently, "I can work no miracles!, I am a Public Preacher, appointed to preach this doctrine to all creatures . . . Look over the world", he said, "is it not miraculous, the work of God? Wholly a sign to you, if your eyes were open!" '[13]

Then followed the episode of Muhammad's persecution and years of hardship and immense suffering, leading to his departure from Mecca to Medina where he was welcomed by a group of new converts. Naturally, Carlyle went on, Muhammad gave offence to the Quraysh, his own mighty tribe and keepers of the Kaaba, their most sacred shrine and their ancestral idols. 'Who is this that pretends to be wiser than we all? That rebukes us all, as mere fools and worshippers of Wood?' Abu Thaleb, the good uncle spoke with him, Carlyle explained. 'Could he not be silent – believe it all for himself, and not trouble others, anger the chiefmen, endanger himself and them all?' Muhammad answered: 'No!' 'There was something in this truth he had got which was of Nature herself; equal in rank to Sun, or Moon . . . He went on speaking to who would listen to him; publishing his doctrine among the pilgrims as they came to Mecca; gaining adherents in this place and that.'

Carlyle told the story of the dismal fate that awaited Muhammad after the disclosure that he was determined to preach his religion. How he was compelled to hide in caverns, homeless and in constant peril, move in disguise hither and there. But Muhammad was not deterred by persecution. He went on speaking to the pilgrims to Mecca 'by the way of preaching and persuasion alone'. He told them about his doctrine of the unity of God. The rulers of Mecca laid plots and swore oaths against him, they swore to put him to death, forcing him to leave his home town and engage in defensive wars. Carlyle reminded his audience that Christianity had used the sword on numerous occasions in history – not only as a defensive weapon, but for reasons of conversion and expansion. He praised Muhammad for his freedom from ostentatious pride and ambition and admitted that he saw a great deal of similarity and affinity between Muhammad and Jesus, particularly in their sense of justice, their modesty and their capacity for self-criticism. He related a story, stemming from Muhammad's last visit to the mosque in Medina, the city of his exile, two days before he died. After prayer, Muhammad asked

---

13 Ibid., p. 62.

the Muslims present in the mosque to try to remember whether 'he owed any man? Better be in shame now, said he, than at the Day of Judgement'. 'Traits of this kind,' Carlyle argued, 'show us the genuine man, the brother of us all, brought visible through twelve centuries – the veritable Son of our common Mother':

> On the whole, we will repeat that this Religion of Mahomet's is a kind of Christianity; has a genuine element of what is spiritually highest looking through it not to be hidden by all its imperfection.[14]

'Much has been said and written about Mahomet's sensuality,' Carlyle said reproachfully. This was not true at all. On the contrary, Mahomet was an ascetic who disapproved of indulgence of all kind:

> Mahomet himself, after all that can be said about him, was not a sensual man. We shall err widely if we consider this man as a common voluptuary, intent mainly on base enjoyments, – nay on enjoyments of any kind. His household was of the frugalist, his common diet barley bread and water: sometimes for months there was not a fire once lighted on his hearth.
> They record with just pride that he would mend his own shoes, patch his own cloak. A poor, hard-toiling, ill-provided man; careless of what vulgar men toil for. Not a bad man, I should say; something better in him than hunger of any sort . . . Let him be called what you like! No emperor with his tiaras was obeyed as this man in a cloak of his own clouting, during three and twenty years of rough actual trial. I find something of a veritable Hero necessary for that, of itself.[15]

Undoubtedly Carlyle, this brave and bold Scotsman, attempted to lay aside all the prejudices against Muhammad and Islam and to share with sympathetic imagination the experiences of Muslim believers and to see in Muhammad the essential man, the man of vision and sincerity who had been obscured for centuries through hostile misrepresentation. 'Let us try to understand what he meant with the world!' was Carlyle's exhortation to his contemporaries. Although most critics did not accept his interpretation of Muhammad's character, not many of them openly championed the old theory of conscious imposture. Interestingly however,

---

14 Ibid., p. 70.
15 Ibid., p. 65.

a large number of reviews were anonymous. One such review in *The Christian Remembrancer*, dating from 1842 was even reluctant to mention Muhammad by name. The author recognizes no greatness in men who are not professed Christians, who do not belong to 'the brotherhood of redeemed and regenerate men, the brotherhood into which baptism admits us, which the Eucharist cements'.[16] He therefore censures Carlyle for seeing any divine element in paganism or Islam, because there is only one true religion, an original revelation made to the sons of man, and that is Christianity. He alerts Carlyle's readers to be on their guard against his preaching and the possible dangers of his judgements.

Indeed, Carlyle's unorthodox religious stance, his belief in transcendental reality, his reliance upon intuition instead of reason and particularly his concept of the universal hero had provoked many reviewers to take it upon themselves to expose what they declared to be his infidelity to Christianity. His championing of heroes was above all condemned by many British churchmen who felt that Britain needed 'gentle heroes', men of the Christian spirit, and not Muhammads, Cromwells, Luthers and Napoleons, figures that Carlyle had set before the public. One of the most hostile critiques appeared in *The Catholic Dublin Review* of September 1846. The author, George Crolly, priest and professor at St Patrick's College, argued that Carlyle's heroes were bigoted, intolerant and belligerent, more in keeping with the Old Testament than the New. He condemned Carlyle for having selected the wrong heroes in history: 'Mr Carlyle,' he wrote, 'need not fear that the species shall not become extinct so long as hatred of Truth, hypocrisy and avarice reign in the heart of men'.[17] Another person who voiced his strong disapproval of Carlyle's views was the Reverend George Gilfillan, a Scottish dissenter. His criticisms appeared in *The Eclectic Review* of December 1851. Gilfillan claimed that Carlyle had broken with all established religious beliefs and that he had poured out hatred and contempt on the clergy and on the Church by inference and insinuation about 'traditions' and 'incredibilities' of Christianity.[18] Carlyle's religious verdicts had driven some reviewers

---

16 *The Christian Remembrancer*, London, 1842, Volume III, p. 349.
17 *Thomas Carlyle. The Critical Heritage*, edited by Jules Paul Seigel, London, 1971, Reviewing in the Periodical Press, p. 7. (*The Catholic Dublin Review*, September 1846, XXI, pp. 68–9).
18 *Thomas Carlyle. The Critical Heritage*, op. cit., p. 7. (*The Eclectic Review*, December 1851, CIV, 719)

to regard him as a heretic, a dangerous moral influence, particularly on the young. One anonymous reviewer in a leading article in *The Congregationalist British Quarterly Review* of August 1849 cautions his readers that 'Carlyle was by no means a safe author to put into the hands of young men who do not bring some power of independent thinking to what they read.'[19]

The accusation that Carlyle was guilty of idolatry and of advocating dangerous religious doctrines like that of Islam can be seen more clearly in another article published in *The High Church Christian Remembrancer* of 1843, written by William Thomson, later the Archbishop of York, who relentlessly attacked a second edition of *Heroes and Hero-Worship*. Thomson acknowledged that the purpose of his paper was merely to show that 'the whole philosophy of this writer is defective and unsatisfactory'. All Carlyle's heroes were dismissed by Thomson, particularly 'Mahomet, the impostor', who was perhaps 'guided more by dyspeptic visions than by communings with the real and credible'[20] Another reviewer, George McCrie, blamed Carlyle in *The Religion of Our Literature* of 1875 for not distinguishing between truth and error: 'It is plain', he writes, 'that Carlyle holds the distinction between Truth and Error as of little importance. The earnestness of Luther and of Dante, of Mahomet and of Oliver Cromwell, of Odin and of John Knox, is all one in his eyes'.[21] But while an anonymous critic who voiced his opinion in volume IX of *The American Review* in 1849 could not divest himself of his belief that Muhammad was an impostor and a religious fanatic, he admitted nevertheless that his life was heroic:

> Mahomet was a reformer, an imitator of higher labours of Moses and Christ. He gave a new direction to the world's affairs, we grant, and put an end to many idolatrous mummeries. Mr Carlyle esteems him a truly great man, and thinks he made the world better. We shall not now stop to controvert this opinion.[22]

---

19 *The Congregationalist British Quarterly Review*, August 1849, X.34): Herodotus Smith (Francis Espinasse) attributes this essay to George H. Lewes (*Espinasse's literary recollections*), London, 1893, pp. 366–89.
20 *Thomas Carlyle, The Critical Heritage*, op. cit., p. 15.
21 *George McCrie, The Religion of our Literature*, London 1875, p. 65.
22 *The American Review*, New York, 1849, Volume IX, p. 343.

But despite the numerous powerful responses to Carlyle's outspoken doctrines and his defence of Muhammad and Islam, there were also a large number of Victorian Englishmen and women who admired him as a new prophet, shaping and giving direction to religious thought, shaking up rigid and obsolete beliefs and clichés, promoting ideas of tolerance. But it took almost fifty years for anyone to dare to praise him openly and confidently in public. One such admirer was George Dawson of the Church of the Saviour in Birmingham, whose *Biographical lectures on the Genius and Works of Thomas Carlyle* published in 1887 was the most sympathetic tribute. He first gave his lectures, in Manchester in January 1846 and repeated them in Sheffield, Liverpool and other northern towns. And more importantly for us, Dawson's reinforcement of Carlyle's views on Muhammad were instrumental in prompting a new appraisal of Islam and its founder in England and across the rest of Europe, encouraging serious research into the teachings of Islam and the Qur'an. Dawson believed that men should be judged not by today's standards, but by the standards of their own times:

> The absurdity of many of the usual judgements passed upon men is, that they are tried by a standard which they never had; sentenced by a law to which they were never amenable; executed for not obeying a precept which they never heard. Carlyle shows in respect to Mahomet that he had a true and an earnest heart; that because he did not teach Christianity, it does not follow that he taught an unmitigated lie; that because he had not our book to reverence, it does not follow that the book he gave out had nothing reverenceable in it.[23]

Dawson praised Carlyle for his courage to have singlehandedly and without assistance engaged in such an arduous undertaking to reverse the sentence of the ages upon some of those men he honoured with the title of heroes. Dawson's defence of Muhammad was not less imposing than Carlyle's and made him into one of the few apologists of Muhammad in Europe at that time. Here is Dawson's discussion of Carlyle's appraisal of Muhammad:

---

23 George Dawson, *Biographical Lectures*, edited by George St. Claire, London, 1887, Quotations pp. 383–9.

He takes the Prophet Mahomet, whom we were taught in our school-days to regard as an impostor, and the greatest hypocrite the world ever had – a mean liar and deceiver. To reverse this decision, Carlyle has not laboured in vain. The accepted version of this man's character is mercilessly shown to be false, Carlyle proving him to have been a truthful, earnest, deep hearted son of the desert, who achieved what he did by virtue of this earnestness, by virtue of his adherence to the truth of things, and to those sublime visions which visited his spirit . . . It cannot be believed that so many millions of our fellow creatures have passed through this life under the guidance of such an unmitigated lie, as the life and writings of Mahomet are usually believed to be.[24]

Dawson agrees fully with Carlyle that Muhammad had brought nobler thinking to his people and to the world:

Mahomet taught some great neglected truths, revived faith in some forgotten verities, and surely did teach to his people a higher rule of life, and a nobler aspiration of the soul, than they had had before.[25]

Through his various illustrations, the author showed how Carlyle had bravely held up the character of Muhammad as the sincere and earnest child of the desert against the traditional traits of deception and imposture attributed to him by the Christian West.

While Carlyle saw the shapers of history to be the exceptionally gifted individuals, chosen by God to guide their people to a better and more meaningful destiny, for his German contemporary, the philosopher Karl Marx, the shapers of history were economic forces embodied in social classes with different economic interests. Unlike Carlyle who believed in the transcendental significance of religions, whether Christianity or Islam, for Marx religions were gigantic confidence tricks elaborated over centuries to keep power structures intact and potential revolutionary classes in their place. He called all religions the 'opium of the people'; they were sets of ideas and behavioural patterns that served nothing but the interests of ruling classes. In Marx's theory change was determined by class rather than by individuals and classes were merely driven by economic forces. Carlyle, in contrast, saw genius in men as

24 Ibid.
25 Ibid.

God's gift and the realization of their ideas as the realization of God's plan. The history of mankind was therefore the history of these great heroic men sent into the world to bring change and progress.

Both Carlyle and Marx were writing in an epoch in Europe which was increasingly governed by the forces of science and industrialization which had led to enormous psychological, social and religious tensions. Europe at that time was divided between orthodox religiosity, free spirituality, materialism and atheism. The scientific discoveries of previous centuries had resulted in the disaffection of many intellectuals. Some, like Carlyle, Hegel or Goethe, saw no contradiction between divine knowledge and man's scientific achievements. According to Hegel God Himself had planned the progress of man. He was not therefore dismissive of the portentous insights into the measurability and predictability of planetary movements which had caused Newton's discovery of the laws of gravity. For Hegel, and after him Marx, there were analogous laws determining human history, but unlike Marx, Hegel saw the great individuals that history had produced as part and parcel of the same natural laws which were the work of the *Weltgeist* or 'World Spirit'. For orthodox churchmen however the cosmologies of Copernicus, Newton and Galileo strongly contradicted those of the Bible and were pure blasphemy.

At the same time as the discovery was being made that there were natural laws governing the physical world, engineers in Europe were beginning to build machines that were more effective and productive than human labour or horsepower. Power-driven looms, steam engines, improved processes for smelting iron, all contributed to the emergence of the Industrial Revolution, initially in England by the late eighteenth century. But other European nations followed close behind. Industrialization was radically to alter the face of European society and turn Europe into the most powerful continent in the world. Within decades the cottage weaving and spinning industries were wiped out and replaced by mechanized production. Simultaneous improvements in agricultural machinery led to mass migrations to burgeoning cities, a movement that was exacerbated by the continuing enclosure of subsistence farming lands and the disappearance of the remnants of feudal security. A new class was emerging.

Marx, in his early days as a journalist in the Rhineland had been outraged by the impoverishment of the winegrowers. Friedrich Engels whom he had met in the 1840s – in the years during which Carlyle's thesis was being debated in the English press – was himself the son of a textile manufacturer. He had seen the appalling and effectively uncontrolled living conditions of the new working classes in Britain's northern industrial cities. From a mixture of Hegelian belief in laws determining historical developments, Engel's observation and sense of moral outrage and Marx's own reading of classical economics and history, there developed the theory of historical materialism. And historical materialism was to form the theoretical basis for the ideology of communism and Russia's Bolshevic Revolution of 1917.

These strands, the secularism of modern thought, the improbability of religious dogma, the constraining function of orthodox morality and the belief in the potential greatness of the individual, all re-emerge in the works of the late nineteenth-century German thinker Friedrich Nietzsche, whose philosophy became one of the main sources of twentieth-century Western thought. His striking and radical ideas such as the declaration that 'God is Dead!' or that the world was the product of the will to power and nothing else beside, was used as the basis for a pre-fascist ideology which was to sweep across Europe and particularly through Germany at the time and in the aftermath of the First World War.

Nietzsche, who had been born on 15 October 1844, four years after the publication of Carlyle's book on heroes, derived his own concept of hero-worship and the heroic in history from his readings of Carlyle. Prior to developing his notorious idea of the *Übermensch* or 'Superman', Nietzsche had seen the heroic in historical figures such as Muhammad, Napoleon, Julius Caesar and Alexander the Great in the form of a liberating mental disorder. He ascribed to Muhammad and the others epilepsy, which in the case of Muhammad stemmed from the old stereotype. But the epilepsy that Nietzsche had in mind was a mental disorder to be celebrated because it enabled men such as Muhammad to free themselves from existing conventions and to introduce new thinking and new laws to the world. The self-realization of men such as Muhammad was a purely earthly manifestation which had nothing to do with transcendental spirituality or divine inspiration. Nietzsche's heroes were, unlike Carlyle's, not guided by a supernatural force; it was their will to power that turned them into heroes and leaders of men. For God was dead and man himself had the potential of reaching divine heights through strength, belief in himself, the earth, the here and now. Belief in

God, Nietzsche argued, had resulted in an impoverishment of men's lives and their ability to act and think for themselves. Belief in Heaven had reduced the value and dignity of physical existence. Religiously determined morality was a straitjacket that crippled individuality and self-realization. Religions such as Judaism, Christianity and Islam, which guided men through life with the promise of a reward and punishment system in the afterlife, were demeaning men to the level of lowly, primitive and weak creatures, unable to control their own destiny. Nietzsche blamed Christianity for having passed on to Islam the concepts of Heaven and Hell. While he celebrated Muhammad as a hero, he rejected the Qur'anic doctrine of a powerful God sitting in Heaven and reigning over and guiding his subjects on earth, a God on whose will everything depended. Such a doctrine, Nietzsche declared, suppressed individuality and the creativity of man, nurturing a master–slave morality and degrading men to a position of dependency – as children were dependent upon adults.

The seeds for Nietzsche's idea of the *Übermensch* as the individual who reaches out and beyond the constraints of religion and social convention to find his own path and salvation had already been sown by Carlyle. But from the beginning of the century, with the emergence of a larger-than-life character such as Napoleon, the romantic creed of individualism and notion of the superman had been in the air. This was to culminate in Nietzsche's most famous work *Also Sprach Zarathustra* (*Thus Spake Zarathustra*), published in 1884. Nietzsche himself declared this work as being the sum total of his philosophy. He chose this ancient Persian Prophet, Zarathustra or Zoroaster, as the spokesman for his philosophy, because, as Nietzsche personally stated, he was the first religious thinker to introduce to the world the dogma of fixed good and evil and their opposition to each other, leading to the establishment of moral codes. It fell to Zarathustra therefore, Nietzsche argued, to be the first to abolish these fixed and suffocating moralities, which he called *Geist der Schwere* or the 'spirit of heaviness'. Indeed in north-east Persia in the sixth century BCE, a religious reformer named Zarathustra had preached the first religion of salvation that man has known. According to Zarathustra, life meant a choice between *Ahura Mazda* (the good spirit) or *Ahriman* (the evil spirit). A person's destiny after death (Heaven or Hell) was determined by his or her choice. Zoroastrian dualism, seeing the world as a constant struggle between the forces of good and evil, may have influenced Greek and early Jewish thought. In its poetic rhapsodic style of presentation, its recurrent parables and its imagery, Nietzsche's *Also Sprach Zarathustra* seems to have been inspired by the Qur'an rather than the Gospels of which it has been said the work is an intended parody. Nietzsche had claimed that his *Zarathustra* was extended to exalt all other Holy Scriptures in its use of language, including Luther's Bible. Furthermore, the figure of Zarathustra emerging from his lonely mountain cave to teach his doctrine to end all doctrines resembles less Christ than Muhammad, who similarly descended from a cave on Mount Hira to the Meccan valley to proclaim his divine revelations. But it is plain that Nietzsche's Zarathustra is essentially anti-religious in his message and the Qur'anic model is therefore only an ironic vehicle to declare that God was dead. A further irony that will not have escaped Nietzsche is that it was precisely Muhammad's religion, Islam, which had pushed Zoroastrianism to the fringes of Middle Eastern societies. On his descent from his solitary mountain retreat towards the settlements of human communities, Nietzsche's Zarathustra encounters a religious recluse, a holy man, in the forest, who has withdrawn from life amongst his fellows to dedicate himself entirely to the praise and worship of God. It is only God that he has loved all these years and not human beings.

And what does the saint do in the forest? asked Zarathustra.

The saint answered: I make songs and sing them and when I make songs, 1 laugh, weep, and mutter: thus I praise God. With singing, weeping, laughing and muttering I praise the God, who is my God. But what do you bring us as a gift?

When Zarathustra heard these words, he saluted the saint and said: What should I have to give you! But let me go quickly, that I may take nothing from you! And thus they parted from one another, the old man and Zarathustra, laughing as two boys laugh.

But when Zarathustra was alone, he spoke thus to his heart: Could it be possible! This old saint has not yet heard in his forest that *God is dead!*[26]

---

26 Friedrich Nietzsche, *Thus Spake Zarathustra, Book for Everyone and No one*, translated with an introduction by R J. Hollingdale, Harmondsworth, 1974, p. 41.

Even more shattering than Carlyle's theory of the heroic in history, Marx's historical materialism and Nietzsche's concept of a godless universe, was the science of the nineteenth century. Both the newly discovered geological evidence and the theory of biological evolution conflicted with the accounts of the Creation in the Book of Genesis and in the Qur'an. These scientific discoveries had led to great excitement. The scientists now claimed that the story of creation could not be science but inspired mythology. This conclusion had already been reached by many when, in 1859, Charles Darwin's *On the Origin of Species* provided a further demonstration of the inaccuracy of the Biblical or the Qur'anic accounts, by showing that the species did not originate each in a separate act of creation. Much more disconcerting was the claim elaborated in Darwin's *Descent of Man* published in 1871 that Adam was not fashioned by God but of the earth, and was descended from a progenitor not remote in nature from the ape. The guiding principle in this evolutionary process had been the struggle for existence, resulting in the survival of the fittest – those that were capable of coping with their environment and able to eliminate rivals. Nietzsche had absorbed the most general implications of Darwinism. He saw man's development as part of the whole development of living things. In this sense the theory of evolution was one of his major starting points. However, he came to believe that it was ultimately an exploitative drive for self-aggrandisement, rather than the struggle for existence, which directed the evolutionary process, that is, the will to power rather than the mere will to life.

If God was dead, as Nietzsche had proclaimed, what then was truth? What was the meaning of life and death? Zarathustra had an answer to these questions: The superman is the meaning of earth, he declared. Truth was accordingly a concept belonging to the human mind and will, and apart from the human mind and will there was no truth. Zarathustra taught that your own truth shall be the truth and, the sole origin of the truth on earth. At this level, truth was not something that could be proved or disproved, it was something which you yourself determined upon. It was not something waiting to be discovered, some-thing to which you submitted. It was something you created yourself. It was the expression of the individuality of your being which ventured to assert itself. Truth, said Zarathustra, is man's will to power. This was the purpose, joy and justification of life, the feeling that one's power increased, that resistance was overcome, – it was then that the superman, having overcome all the threats to life, experienced an ever greater degree of happiness. He who attained that joy of overcoming the dark sides of existence would affirm life and love it however much pain it contained. Only the superman was so well disposed towards his own life as to want it to recur again and again for ever. Thus Nietzsche developed his theory of the 'eternal recurrence of the permanently same' in order to complete the life-affirming joys of his superman. Whatever the Christian or the Muslim says of God, Nietzsche's Zarathustra, this prophet of the modern age, says of his superman: Thine is the Kingdom of Earth, and the power, and the glory, for ever and ever.

Nietzsche heralded, then, an age in Europe in which religion was to diminish in its power over large masses of the population, in which secularization of thought was to advance and the materialism born of industrialization was to be accompanied by conquests brought about by rampant imperialism. Through the writings of Hegel, Goethe and Carlyle, Muhammad had been established within the new tradition of hero-worship as one the great spiritual men of history. But at the same time the European powers, in the wake of Napoleon's early Middle Eastern conquests were expanding their empires and protectorates into the Islamic orient and another element in the old legacy of stereotypes about Islam and its Prophet was asserting itself: Islam as the religion of sensuality and licence. Carlyle's pioneering reappraisal of Muhammad's personality and character, which had broken with centuries of uncritically transmitted clichés, was to be swamped by images of an altogether different nature.

9

Fantasies of Sensuality and Cruelty

Muhammad and Islam in nineteenth-century
European imagination

———

The Moon of Mahomet
Arose, and it shall set:
While blazoned as on Heaven's immortal noon
The cross leads generations on.

Percy Bysshe Shelley, *The Revolt of Islam.* **1817**

Napoleon's grand design for conquering the world had not been confined to his victories over Europe. One of his first military expeditions had been in the Islamic Orient. In 1798 his battleship, *The Orient,* with an armada of frigates and transport vessels, had appeared off the coast of Egypt in the east Mediterranean Sea. Alexandria had been swiftly occupied and three weeks later Napoleon had entered Cairo despite the losses that his fleet had suffered at the Battle of the Nile at the hands of the British. He had won victory over Lower and Upper Egypt. Napoleon's ambition after his Egyptian conquest had been to march through Syria, conquer Jersualem and return to Europe via Constantinople, the seat of the Turkish Sultan, who still ruled over a vast empire, including Egypt. Bonaparte had said to one of his close advisers, Général Murat, that his Eastern Campaign would decide the fate of the world. Whether Napoleon meant to revive the old crusading sentiments of Europe, wishing to reconquer the Holy Lands from the hands of the Infidel or to cut off the British from India and their other Eastern possessions, is not quite clear. It seems most likely however that his intention was to achieve both these aims. The massacre of thousands of Turks at Jaffa must have certainly brought back the memory of the arrival of the crusading knights and clergy some seven hundred years before. Napoleon's advances naturally alarmed the British, too, who rapidly embarked on forming a coalition against France, a coalition which included Turkey and Russia. However, the Turkish governor of Acre successfully resisted a two-month siege by the French armies, compelling them, as a plague had also broken out, to withdraw to their base in Alexandria.

The French painter Jean Antoine Gros has captured Napoleon's invasion of Jaffa and the outbreak of the plague in a painting entitled *Les Pestiférés à Jaffa* (*The Pesthouses at Jaffa*), now in the Louvre in Paris. Gros' interpretation of the events gives no hint of the controversy surrounding Napoleon's benevolence and his role as the moral and spiritual leader of the French people. The General is depicted as a caring and concerned visitor to the hospital, showing compassion and kindness to the plague-stricken men of Jaffa. British accounts of the event, however, point to the brutal slaughter of Turkish prisoners and to Napoleon's ruthless abandonment of plague-ridden soldiers and their families.

Soon after his defeat at Jaffa, in August 1799, Napoleon, over-whelmed by his great reverses of fortune, sailed from Alexandria, carefully watched by the British fleet, reaching France in October. And by 1802 the entire French force had been evacuated from Egypt, having fallen under renewed and continous pressure from the Egyptian army and the British navy. Napoleon had been defeated and compelled to leave the Islamic land that he had dreamed of possessing. But with his military campaigns in Egypt, Syria and Palestine he had instigated a turning-point not only in the history of those territories, but in the history of the entire Islamic Orient. At the same time he had opened a new chapter in the history of European colonialism. He had triggered a long-lasting conflict between France and Britain in a region hitherto untouched by their territorial aspirations. He had linked the fortunes of the Christian West and the Islamic East in a way not experienced since the end of the Middle Ages.

Napoleon's Eastern campagins engendered a great deal of enthusiasm for Napoleonic themes amongst French artists, especially during the second half of the nineteenth century. The declaration of the Second Empire in 1852 under Napoleon's nephew, Louis Napoleon, stirred renewed interest in the First Empire. Many French painters, including Yvon Doré and de Neuville, provided important large-scale records of great French military battles in Egypt and Palestine for the walls of the Galeries des Batailles and Versailles. The same fascination is also to be found in Jean Léon Gérôme's various portraits of Napoleon in Egypt, which are imbued with a profound sense of nostalgia. Gérôme's 1863 portrait entitled *Général Bonaparte au Caire*, now at the Art Museum at Princeton University, conveys the same feeling. Napoleon is depicted standing in his famous uniform against the backdrop of some ancient Egyptian tombs in the eastern cemetery of Cairo. The young general's glance is directed away from the spectator and his hat casts a shadow over his face, expressing a sense of premonition and sadness at the imminent loss of this ancient city.

Before the Napoleonic wars, the Mediterranean had been regarded as the highly feared frontier between Europe and Islam except for the deep encroachment of Turkish power into the Balkans over which Europe particularly agonized. For centuries the bulwarks of Christendom against Islam had been held in the south-west by Spain after the expulsion of the Arab Moors from Granada in 1495, and in the south-east by Austria against the Turks, who had been pushed back from Vienna in 1683. These defensive points seemed of little significance now that the Turkish Sultan's power had been waning for more than a century and that his diverse subjects living in different parts of his gigantic empire no longer paid absolute allegiance to the central rule from Constantinople. Moreover, with the expansion of Russia and Austria during the eighteenth century, Turkish supremacy had been severely curtailed, providing a favourable situation which Napoleon sought to exploit.

In the first decade of the nineteenth century the Ottoman Sultan still ruled, or at least demonstrated a pretence of ruling Greece, Crete, Cyprus, the greater part of the Balkans, as far as the lower reaches of the Danube, Asia Minor, Iraq, Syria, Lebanon, Palestine, the whole coast of North Africa, Egypt, Libya, Tunisia and Algeria, but also the Arab Peninsula, including the holy city of Mecca. Millions of the Sultan's subjects in eastern Europe, Asia and north Africa were Christians of different denominations – Greek or Russian Orthodox, Armenian, Nestorian, Coptic, Maronite, Jacobite or Roman Catholic. There were also millions of Jews and Muslims who lived side-by-side with the Christian population of this vast dynastic empire which comprised a great mixture of races, languages and religious convictions held together by subservience to a ruling class which was Turkish and therefore Muslim. Certainly Ottoman rule had been arbitrary but the Turks did not maltreat the Jews or the Christians. In fact, there were no racial or religious tensions between Jews, Christians and Muslims in the empire.

Some Slavs had adopted Islam, some Arabs and Turks Christianity, and inter-marriage, although not common, had occurred. The governors of the principalities were however recruited for the most part from among the Turks, Albanians and Ciracassians who were Muslim. During the seventeenth century this ruling elite, especially those whose territories were separated from Constantinople by huge geographical distances, had achieved a certain degree of autonomy. But they still recognized the Turkish Sultan's formal sovereignty. During the eighteenth century, Austria, Hungary and Russia had taken the lead in recovering large areas of Hungary and the northern shores of the Black Sea. At the beginning of the nineteenth century when Napoleon's armies had marched into Egypt, Syria and Palestine, the popular view in Europe of the Muslim Turkish Ottoman Empire was the same as it had been for centuries – one of an infidel race misruling the territories east and south of the Mediterranean, the *Mare Nostrum* which was believed to have been appropriated from Christendom by Islam.

It was precisely in this light that the emergent nationalist struggle and the desire for self-determination and independence amongst the diverse peoples of the Turkish Empire were keenly supported and hailed by the European powers and by public opinion throughout the continent of Europe. The Greeks set the example with their successful revolts in the 1820s, taking advantage of the backing they were granted by Russia, Britain and France, to break away from Turkish rule. A whole decade of armed battle and bloodshed finally led to their independence in 1830. This was regarded as a great triumph and became the basis for the recognition of Serbia, Moldavia and Wallachia as autonomous principalities within the Turkish Empire. It was above all Russia that was instrumental in shaking and loosening the structures of Turkish power in eastern Europe. But Austria also played a crucial role. In 1856 Serbia's special rights were re-affirmed by the European powers, by which time it was raising the issue of southern Slav unification. Throughout Europe jubilant celebrations were taking place in solidarity with the peoples of the Balkans, Greek independence being particularly emphasized. In the meantime, the Russians were fuelling anti-Turkish sentiments in Albania and Bulgaria, using these as weapons against their Turkish rival.

Egypt, too, became independent under Mehmet Ali and with the help of the British during this period of great upheaval. The process of dissolution of the Turkish Empire was further hastened by the French conquest of Algeria commencing in 1830 and coinciding with the celebrations of Greek independence. Arabia had also been inspired by the turbulent events in the Balkans and in Egypt. The inhabitants of the birthplace of Muhammad and Islam, which had been obscured for several centuries through the shift of power to Constantinople and Turkish rule, rose up in protest. A group of Arabs of Wahabi stock besieged the holy city of Mecca and the Islamic sanctuary of the Kaaba, where Muhammad had once preached and fought for the survival of his nascent religion. The Arabs had regarded the decline of Islam's power as a consequence of the alienation of the Turks from the origins of Islam and of Muhammad's ideals. They believed they could restore true Islamic values, at least in the country where Islam had been conceived. This resulted in frequent crises, war and bloodshed during the remainder of the nineteenth century, not only between the Arabs and the Turks, but also between the Egyptians and the Arabs who both claimed to be the real custodians of Muhammad's legacy.

As the Turkish grip grew weaker, Europe's desire for expansion and domination increased. The ideological bases for European imperialism differed somewhat between the two major colonial powers, France and Britain. France was proud of its republican ideals and constitution and of its belief in political modernity and progressiveness. Britain's idealism was less secularist in nature and was couched in terms of the diffusion of Christianity and missionary aspirations. Muslims were regarded as pagans who had to be converted to the true religion. The British saw the weakening of the Sultan's power over his subjects as an opportunity to convert the local Muslim populations to Christianity. But to their surprise this was the only region in the world that did not respond to their missionary efforts. The Muslims were too devout, too pious and too firmly grounded in their beliefs to give up their religious convictions for any other faith. In the late eighteenth and early nineteenth centuries a greater number of Protestant missionary societies than ever before had been founded to carry the Gospel to non-Christian peoples of the world. The same evangelical revival had occurred in the Roman Catholic Church. But in their missionary endeavour, the Protestants were in the lead in the nineteenth century. Many British government officials engaged in missionary work, and missionaries themselves were willing to enter government service; some were such excellent diplomats that their career even led to postings as ambassadors.

Regardless of their ideological differences and their justification for expansion, both France and Britain were unanimous in believing in their own cultural superiority over the nations they intended to conquer or rule over. Napoleon's call to the Egyptians during his occupation of Egypt to submit to the ideals of the French Revolution was a vivid example of France's conviction that the rest of the world should emulate its ideals of freedom and democracy. His campaigns were ostensibly intended to free the Islamic Orient from Ottoman oppression. In the case of Britain, on the other hand, now that Islam was no longer at the zenith of its power, a sense of religious superiority was given further impetus by the desire also to protect the long-standing and ancient Christian communities which the Turkish rulers had tolerated for several centuries. Britain and to a certain degree France saw it as their responsibility to guard these communities acorss the whole of the declining Ottoman Empire. The sense of unique cultural and political superiority that Napoleon had instilled in his compatriots continued to inspire later colonial generations, who claimed that one of the most important motives for extending France's territorial possessions was *une mission civilisatrice*. But clearly for both powers the main and fundamental justification for expansion was the economic imperative. The rationalization of motives was largely a humanistic or religious cloak. Missionaries and colonial administrators accompanied their country's flags not only in seeking to introduce whatever they deemed to be good in their own culture, but also in seeking to serve the economic and political interests of their native lands. The growth of industrial capitalism in Europe had not only encouraged Europeans to wield greater political influence abroad, but had necessitated reliable and cheap access to raw materials. The regions of the Ottoman Empire represented new markets for the products of the burgeoning engineering and textile industries both as captive export markets and as sources of raw materials. This lay at the very heart of the strategy of both France and Britain when promulgating secular and Christian ideals. Unquestionably, they also brought medicine, sanitation, infrastructure and technology. They also imported Western cultural values which at times uprooted or disrupted ancient cultural patterns and religious beliefs, leading to confusion and identity crises.

Alphonse de Lamartine, one of France's major poets of the early Romantic Movement, until 1830 a diplomat by profession and a political orator thereafter, predicted and defined colonial rule over the remnants of the Islamic Empire in an account of his travels, *Un Voyage en Orient*, published in 1835. Lamartine spent part of 1832 and 1833 in Syria, Palestine and the Lebanon. After describing the decline of Turkish power and the disaffection of many nations which had constituted the vast Turkish Empire he comes to the conclusion that 'l'Empire Ottoman n'existe aujourd'hui que de nom'[1] (It is only in name that the Ottoman Empire exists today). Constantinople, once the world's most beautiful, most affluent and most animated city, is depicted as the capital of 'un peuple en décadence'.[2]

Lamartine's suggestion to the European powers is to adopt 'une politique prévoyante' (a more far-sighted political strategy), 'une politique d'humanité' (humanistic politics) 'et non pas d'aveugle et stupide égoisme'.[3] (and not a political strategy based on blind and stupid egoism). He utterly disapproves of a military confrontation between France, England, Russia and Austria in their struggle to fill the power vacuum in the region. Aggression would only lead to anarchy and destruction, bringing misery not only to the peoples of the Orient, but also to those of Europe itself. Russia, he writes, is striving to gain control over the lands around the Black Sea and Constantinople. Austria's ambition is to possess that half of Turkey's territories which extend into the Balkans. Britain is keen to hold on to Egypt as a naval base for its colonial route to India across the Red Sea. Greece and part of the Balkans have acquired complete or partial independence. France aspires to rule over Syria and Lebanon. A war, signals Lamartine, would destroy all these dreams and deprive the Europeans of an important mission which history has bestowed on them, namely: 'de protéger la race humaine par le patronage de l'Europe, pour qu'elle y multiplie, y grandisse, et que la civilisation s'y répande.'[4] (to protect the human race under its patronage, so that it multiplies, expands and spreads civilization far and wide).

Lamartine's proposal to the European powers is to wait until a revolution erupts, which he regards as imminent and which would bring down the Sultan and put an end to his rule. Meanwhile, a European

---

1 *Oeuvres de Alphonse de Lamartine*, Tome IV (Volume IV), *Souvenirs, Impressions, Pensées, Paysages pendant un Voyage en Orient*, Paris 1832–1833, p. 356.
2 Ibid., p. 351.
3 Ibid., p. 355.
4 Ibid., p. 357.

congress should make the necessary and legal provisions for the future. The future means partitioning the territories which will have become free, with well-defined boundaries for each protectorate and the rights and sovereignty of each European power laid down. The nations which will fall under their protection, Lamartine suggests, should be classified according to religion, tribal customs and traditions and cultural characteristics. Existing local laws should not be abolished, but recognized and preserved. Only the legislative or colonial council administering the protectorate will be subjected to the laws of the motherland.

As a diplomat and a political spokesman Lamartine was able to influence the minds of European decision-makers and of the ruling classes. He urged them, when the time was ripe, to free those nations of the East from their 'oppressive and barbaric governments'. Lamartine sums up his vision of an Islamic world under European domination with the following words:

> It is merely an armed and civilising tutelage which each Power extends over her own Protectorate as the guarantor of its existence and its national make-up under the flag of a stronger nationhood. She will protect it from invasions, dismemberments, disintegration and anarchy; she will furnish it with peaceful means to develop its own commerce and its own industry.[5]

What Lamartine failed however to see was that no true nationhood could emerge or exist under foreign rule. Nation, nationality, nationhood, nationalism are all emotive concepts that bind peoples of the same cultural, historical, racial and linguistic background and are by definition and nature opposed to foreign influence or domination. But a version of Lamartine's vision did indeed come to pass, though in large part not until the First World War. The irony was that in the creation of these protectorates the boundaries drawn did effectively cause dismemberment. It also caused hostility and racial and religious tension not only amongst the indigenous peoples themselves, but also towards the colonial powers. Old forgotten hatreds between Jews, Muslims and Christians were brought to the surface. They turned the Near and Middle East into a tinderbox which finally ignited in the 1950s. Perhaps what was most

---

5 Ibid, p. 359. (Translation by N.B.R. Reeves)

remarkable was the long stretch of time that this process took, well over a hundred years since Lamartine had first published his thoughts.

European expansion into the Islamic Orient happened in various forms according to the historical, geographical and institutional circumstances of each region. In the case of Algeria for instance it took the form of straightforward military occupation and annexation as a French province, a process however which took several decades to conclude as local resistance repeatedly flared. In Egypt the initial invasion by Napoleon was followed by a technological and economic dependency on both France and Britain in the early decades of the century, which ended in complete military, political and administrative control of the country by Britain by 1914. The countries of the Levant, Palestine, Lebanon and Trans-Jordania, however, were increasingly influenced by the French and British political and economic impact and eventually became their protectorates after the First World War. Likewise, after a bitter struggle in the closing years of the war, Iraq passed from Turkish rule to British mandate, following the final collapse of the Ottoman Empire in 1918. The Arabs of the Peninsula were encouraged in their initial aspirations for independence from the Turks by the efforts of the legendary British army officer, T. E. Lawrence. Their ambition was to restore an Arab nation founded on a purer form of Islam than that represented by their decadent Ottoman rulers. The uprising in Mecca in 1916 which was indirectly supported by the British, started a long struggle that continued through and after the First World War. The Turks were finally expelled in 1925. The Wahabi tribe under the leadership of Ibn Saud wrested power from all rivals, including the sheriff of Mecca, and declared himself King of Saudi Arabia in 1923. The British ensured their domination by signing treaties with the Arab Emirates along the Gulf that gave them control of military and foreign affairs.

Although France and Britain were the dominant colonializing forces in the Islamic lands, other European countries were also involved because they supplied technological and administrative skills and expertise. Germany was a prominent example. For instance in the mid-nineteenth century Prussian military experts were commissioned to train the Turkish army to European standards of discipline and weaponry. The great munition firms Krupp and Mauser maintained important branches in Constantinople. Later, more ambitious projects such as the Berlin–Baghdad Railway were predominantly German in their engineering and funding. These connections laid the foundation for Turkey's increasing dependency on the technical and financial aid that the Germans were able to provide. Reforms and improvements to the infrastructures throughout the Muslim world drew foreign advisers and necessitated European loans. Italy, for its part, took the colonial route by seizing Libya.

No matter in what form or under what name European domination asserted itself in the Islamic world, one thing is certain: The unity of Islam was shattered – a unity of civilization which had been kept alive for several centuries by the Arab and the Turkish Empires despite the diverse environment and cultures in which it had flourished. Furthermore, the region had in the past two centuries fallen far behind Europe economically, sinking ever deeper into poverty and backwardness. The Islamic nations had not been exposed to any of the religious, philosophical, social and political movements that had shaped modern Europe: the Reformation, the Enlightenment, Rationalism and the discoveries of science, the Industrial Revolution and of course the French Revolution – from which the ideas of liberalism, nationalism and democracy had sprung. The reversal of fortunes could not have been more striking, if we were to compare Europe's nineteenth-century encroachment into the Islamic Orient with the conquest of Spain by Muhammad's successors eleven hundred years earlier. The Arabs had brought wealth and sophistication, philosophical and scientific knowledge to an underdeveloped, rural Europe which had sought to emulate them. Now Europe had gained enough self-confidence and technological power to embark on a *mission civilisatrice,* a mission to civilize the Muslims. Islam was no longer the religion of the powerful, the affluent, nor was it a cultural, political or military rival to Christian Europe. It had become the religion of the weak, the poor, the dependent. The dreaded Anti-Christ personified in the figure of the Arab and later the Turk, haunting the continent of Europe since the early Middle ages now seemed to be 'the sick man of Europe' lying on his deathbed.

Instead, Europe was in a position where it could afford to be charmed by the exoticism of a weaker culture now opened for its citizens to observe, to visit and to fantasize about. The age-old feeling that Islam represented a fearful threat to the West had vanished, to be replaced by a deep sense of longing for the unknown and exotic world of the Orient: the Holy Land, the remote landscapes of the desert, the caravans, the Bedouins, the bustling life of oriental market places, depicted in stories and fables. The Orient, as European visitors and observers understood it, had for the majority, not yet expanded to include India and the Far East. It was still largely the East of the ancient Mediterranean. Not just Palestine was regarded as the Holy Land, but the whole of the Near East, North Africa, Turkey, Asia Minor, Mesopotamia, Arabia, Syria and Lebanon. This was the home of the patriarchs and the prophets and of ancient Biblical and Islamic sites. Orientalism based on Jewish, early Christian and above all Islamic themes and subject-matter became a significant force in the literature and art of the West. The penetration of the fading Turkish Empire by an expansionist Europe had opened the gates of the Orient to waves of European travellers, traders, chroniclers, geologists, historians, administrators, diplomats, writers, poets and artists. They became fascinated by the striking difference between the dress, lifestyle, climate, architecture, literature and of course the religion of the peoples they encountered, and their own. The Western encounter with the Islamic world manifested itself in a variety of ways: the scholarly study of ancient Eastern civilizations and contemporary cultures, a wave of publications on Islam and on Muhammad, descriptions by enthusiastic or hostile travellers as well as extensive attempts by European poets and painters to evoke this exotic, colourful and seemingly sensual, passionate and cruel world.

Many European visitors responded with awe and respect and often envy to the practices of the devout Muslims. The image of an Arab or a Turk at prayer appealed to many, though far more to the Roman Catholic French than the Protestant English. Those who looked longingly to Islam as a pre-scientific, pure and unchanged religion, displayed a yearning for earlier times when religion in Europe had been a matter of faith before scientific rationalism had shaken it. This, they felt was a debasement of the spirit brought about by Western civilization. Sir John Carne, a prominent traveller, describes his first gripping experience of Islam one early morning in the town of Foua on the Nile in his *Letters from the East*, published in London in 1826. He writes:

> More than one good Moslem, who had just risen from his bed had taken his seat without the door, and with the Koran in his hand, was reading the Prophet's splendid promises, or teaching his child his prayers. Even in this town there were twelve mosques; and the muezzin, from the top of the minaret had begun to call to prayers.

This cry, in so still a country as Egypt, and heard at the dawn or at night from a distance, has an effect the most beautiful and solemn that can be conceived. Often on the Nile in Upper Egypt, when the silence of the desert has been around, that cry has come from afar: 'There is but one God – God alone is great and eternal and Mohammad is his Prophet', like the voice of an undying being calling from the upper air.[6]

In his *Voyage en Orient*, Lamartine, while condemning the fatalism of Islam, had also been full of praise for Islam's sincerity of worship, its tolerance and administration of justice.

Before becoming a leading scholar of Islam, Henri de Castries served during the 1870s as an officer in the colonial cavalry in Algeria. His feelings on seeing the Muslim troops under his command engaged in communal prayer were expressed in his reflections *L'Islam, Impressions et Études* of 1896:

I heard the invocation 'Allah Akbar!' ring out loud and clear. God is Supreme! that simple concept of divinity took on a meaning in my soul beyond anything theology or metaphysics had taught me. I was struck down by an inexpressible malaise, a mixture of shame and anger. I felt that, in this moment of prayer, these Arab cavalrymen, so subordinate just a short time ago, were asserting their superiority over me. how I wished I could have cried out to them that I too believe, that I too knew how to worship God.[7]

Parallel to such positive images there was a range of hostile opinion too. The Scottish painter David Roberts who had visited Egypt, the Sinai desert, Syria, Palestine and the Lebanon between the years 1838 and 1839, reproduced his visual experiences as lithographs when he returned to Europe. But the quotation shows how much he disliked the Muslims and their way of life

Splendid cities once teeming with a busy population and embellished with temples and edifices, the wonder of the world, now deserted and lonely, or reduced by mismanagement and the barbarism of the Muslim creed to a state as savage as wild animals by which they

---

6 John Carne, *Letters from the East*, London, 1826, p. 75.
7 Henri de Castries, *L'Islam: Impressions et Études*, Paris, 1896, p. 4.

are surrounded. Often have I gazed on them till my heart actually sickened within me.[8]

But Lady Duff Gordon's *Letters* written during her five-year sojourn in Egypt between 1863 and 1869 were to prove the partiality of David Roberts' statement. In these *Letters* there is repeated reference to the excellence, the industry and the nobility of the Egyptians.[9]

Blatant cruelty, passive submission and implacable fatalism were characteristics which most European painters depicted in their works as being a speciality of Muslim culture. In an age before photography, paintings played an immensely more powerful part in cultural life than today. They fulfilled the role of illustration and of documentation. These images, which were largely the product of the Europeans' heightened imagination, coloured many Western perceptions of the Islamic Near and Middle East. Many painters such as Gérôme, Fromentin, Benjamin-Constant and Delacroix provide images of the Islamic Orient utterly devoid of compassion and humanity.

The critical assessment of the life of Muslims had started as early as 1808 with Robert Southey's translation from the Spanish of *Cronicá del Cid* (*Chronicle of the Cid*). The *Chronicle* recounts Spanish national traditions of the struggle against the Arab conquest and domination of Spain from the eighth to the fifteenth century. The Cid is the Spanish equivalent of King Arthur or Roland, less mythical, but no less revered. The *Chronicle of the Cid* is the earliest and best of the heroic prose of Spain, a romance of history, celebrating the achievements of Cid, the *campeador* or champion of his countrymen against the Muslim rulers of Spain. In his introduction to the translation, Southey, who wrote an immense amount both of verse and prose and was highly esteemed by Coleridge and Byron, gives his opinion of Muhammad. Southey believes that one of the greatest errors of the Prophet of Islam was to encourage his followers to marry so many women. Muhammad himself is described as a man who gave free reign to lust and indulgence:

Muhammad attempted nothing like a fabric of society, he took abuses as he found them. Other founders of religions have not

---

8 J. Ballentine, *The Life of David Roberts*, London, 1866, pp. 104–5.
9 Lady Duff Gordon, *letters from Egypt*, London, 1865, 1983 edition, pp. 59–79.

hesitated to crucify the lusts of the flesh, but Muhammad attempted no such conquest over human nature, he did not feel himself strong enough to conquer.[10]

Southey attributed the decline both of the Arab and the Turkish Empires to the institution of polygamy and seclusion of women in harems. Of course neither of these accusations applied to Muhammad. He had neither sanctioned the lusts of the flesh, nor the locking away of women in harems.

Indeed the enduring and dominant picture of oriental life and culture in the poetry and paintings of much of the century is centred around sensuality and male polygamy. The harem, associated closely with what considered to be Muhammad's idea of heaven populated with beautiful female angels or *houris*, came to be seen as an earthly paradise, longed for by European poets, writers and artists.

The Turkish Sultan's Grand Seraglio in Constantinople with its oriental splendour and its secret world behind the arches of the Imperial Gate captured the imagination of many Europeans. The Seraglio, which means enclosure, comprised the Sultan's palace, his harem where his wives and children, mother, sisters and female relatives lived, and the living quarters of his courtiers. But the Seraglio was not merely the Sultan's residence, it was also the seat of the Turkish government. This was a hidden world of golden domes and pointed minarets, glittering mosaics, exquisite tiles, artificial lakes and lush gardens with the mingled scents of herbs and fruit trees and roses and the scores of tinkling fountains. This was the earthly paradise which became the focus of Europe's most fanciful flights of the imagination. In 1853 with his publication of a book entitled *Constantinople* which was printed in Paris, a perceptive commentator of the Orient, Théophile Gautier, admitted to the discrepancy between his own preconceptions of a Muslim husband's relationship with his wives and the dignified reality he happened to discover by talking to Muslims:

> If one becomes aware of the dignity and even the chastity which exists between a Muslim and his wives, one would renounce all this voluptuous mirage which our writers of the eighteenth century

---

10 *The Spanish Ballads*, translated by J. G. Lockhart, and *The Chronicle of the Cid*, translated by Robert Southey, London, n.d., pp. 188–9.

have created, the idea of these harems described by the author of Lettres persanes.[11]

Undoubtedly Montesquieu with his images of a Muslim potentate's harem had a great deal to answer for. But at least he had also endeavoured to display the sadness and boredom endured by the so-called odalisques living in a harem. While he sketched a restricted life devoid of love and male companionship in the confines of a kind of female boarding-school, the writers, poets and artists of the nineteenth century picture a supernatural, erotically charged institution filled with perfumed odalisques resting on silken cushions waiting to please their master. In reality, except for one or two lucky ones, life in a Sultan's harem meant subordination to a highly regimented and hierarchical system ruled by the mothers and sisters of the Sultans. Only a selected few slept with the Sultan. *Odalik* is a Turkish word which means the female inhabitant of a harem and which became odalisque in French and other European languages. It is neither an Islamic nor a Qur'anic term. The number of Sultan's wives was only a symbolic projection of his wealth and worldly power. In the mid-sixteenth century for instance, when no court in Europe could equal the splendour and wealth of the Sultan's Seraglio in Constantinople, when Turkey was the most powerful military rival to the West, Sultan Suleiman's harem consisted of three hundred odalisques, living in its bewildering assortment of rooms and chambers. But the Sultan fell in love with a newly captured Russian slave who bore him a son. This woman who was given the title of Sultana brought so much happiness and joy to the Sultan's life that he never desired any other woman except her and remained faithful to her until she died. But the Seraglio as a whole, which so fired European imagination, had nothing to do with Muhammad's teachings and original Islam. What the European reader or spectator encountered in orientalist literature and art was exaggerated reproductions of the Turkish Sultanate. A Sultan's harem was not in fact a licence for debauched living. Nor was the harem a common institution in Islamic societies, but a custom which only Sultans and the governors of the Turkish Empire could afford.

---

11 Th. Gautier, *Constantinople*, Paris, 1853, pp. 164–5. (Translation by N. B. R. Reeves)

In England it was the immensely popular romantic poet Lord Byron who established the myth of Islam as a highly sensual religion, designed for men. Houris, odalisques and concubines repeatedly feature in his verse. Byron, who was to exert great influence on the Romantic Movement throughout Europe, left England in July 1800 to spend two years in the Near East. Athens was his principal place of residence but he stayed a short while in Albania and several months in Constantinople. His portrait painted by Thomas Phillips in 1835 based on earlier portraits, now in the London Portrait Gallery, shows him in the costume and turban of an Albanian tribesman, reflecting the oriental settings of his poems and his own image as a romantic adventurer. On his return from the East, Byron published his observations in the first two Cantos of *Childe Harold's Pilgrimage* with which he rose to fame. The narrative poems, *The Giaour* and *The Turkish Tales* which followed made him the unrivalled popular poet of the day.

In the first canto of *Childe Harold*, written in 1812, he points out the resemblance of the Spanish girls he encounters on his way to the Orient with the 'Houris of Muhammad's Paradise':

Match me those Houris, whom ye scarce allow
To taste the gale lest love should ride the wind,
With Spain's dark-glancing daughters – deign to know,
There your wise Prophet's paradise we find,
His black-eyed maids of Heaven, angelically kind.[12]

And in *The Giaour*, published the following year, the emphasis remains on the sensuality of Muhammad's paradise and its promises for men:

But Soul beam'd forth in every spark
That darted from beneath the lid,
bright as the jewel of Giamschid.
Yea, Soul, and should our prophet say
That form was nought but breathing clay,

By All! I would answer nay;
Though on Al-Sirat's arch I stood,

---

12 Lord Byron, *Selected Poems*, edited by Susan J. Wolfson and Peter J. Manning, Harmondsworth, 1996, *Childe Harold*, First Canto, Verse LIX, p. 82.

Which totters o'er the fiery flood
With Paradise within my view
And all his Houris beckoning through.[13]

In the *Bride of Abydos* dedicated to Robert Southey and published in 1813, Byron pictures a Muslim Paradise exclusive to men, but denied to mortal women:

And oft her Koran conn'd apart;
And oft in youthful reverie
She dream'd what Paradise might be:
Where woman's parted soul shall go
Her prophet had disdain'd to show.[14]

Here again we are faced with a gap between myth and reality. The Qur'an promises life after death in Paradise both for believing men and women who have served God and who have been modest, pious, charitable and sincere.

Byron's *Siege of Corinth* of 1816 once again contains a passage on the rewards of Muslim warriors in Paradise. 'Alp', the renegade Christian, serves conscientiously amongst the Muslim soldiers, but without their hope of the sensual pleasures of the Muslim afterlife:

He stood alone amongst the host;
Not his the loud fantastic boast
To plant the crescent o'er the cross,
To risk a life with little loss,
Secure in paradise to be
By Houris loved immortally.[15]

A fuller elaboration of the theme recurs in *Don Juan* written between 1818 and 1823 which deals for most part with polygamy on earth and with amorous provisions in life after death. In one passage Byron suggests that the houris have the power to select their mortal consorts, and this accounts for the fact that so many handsome young men are slain in the battle:

---

13 Ibid., *The Giaour*, p. 182, line 483.
14 Ibid., p. 228, *The Bride of Abydos*, Second Canto, Verse VII.
15 Ibid., p. 368, *Siege of Corinth*, Verse XII.

The eldest was a true and tameless Tartar,
As great a scorner of the Nazarene
As ever Mahomet pick'd out for a martyr,
Who only saw the black-eyed girls in green,
Who make the beds of those who won't take quarter
On earth, in Paradise, and when once seen,
Those Houris, like all other pretty creatures,
Do just whate'er they please by dint of features.
And what they pleased to do with the young Khan
In heaven I know not, nor pretend to guess;
But doubtless they prefer a fine young man
To tough old heroes, and can do no less;
And that's the cause no doubt why, if we scan
A field of battle's ghastly wilderness,
For one rough, weather-beaten veteran body,
You'll find ten thousand handsome coxcombs bloody.[16]

In Germany, Goethe who had first been fascinated by Muhammad as a genius in the 1770s, turned his attention to the Islamic world again some forty years later. It was now a different kind of oriental tradition which seized his imagination. Now Goethe thought he had found in Muhammad's religion a dimension of sensuality and a celebration of the earthly which was missing in Christianity. Goethe's paradoxical admiration for Islam and Islamic mysticism was expressed in a major work entitled *Der West-östlicher Divan* published in 1819.

Goethe's travels never took him further south or east than Italy. His mentor on his mental journey to the Islamic Orient was the fourteenth-century Persian (Iranian) mystic Mohammad Shamsuddin Hafez. Hafez, whose name means 'Memorizer' (referring to someone who could recite the whole collection of verses of the Qur'an by heart), was himself a rebel against orthodox Islam of his time. He saw salvation, in distinction to Muhammad's teachings, not only in ascetic devotion and service to God and community, but in taking solace in wine, women and song as antidotes to the transience of life. In this way Hafez believed that his tormented soul could attain unity with God and the concealed truth. Muhammad on the other hand had strictly prohibited wine and other alcoholic beverages as intoxicants and detrimental to sober judgement

---

16 Lord Byron, *Don Juan*, edited by T. G. Steffan and W. W. Pratt, Harmondsworth, 1966, pp. 344–5, Canto VIII, Verse 114.

and reasonable behaviour. But wine, which is forbidden and despised on earth, flows in the fountains of Paradise as described in the Qur'an and is served to the faithful in cups by immortal youth. The wine, however, is pure and free of intoxicants; it will rejuvenate, quench thirst and regenerate well-being without debilitating the body and mind of the drinker.

Hafez's five hundred or more lyrical poems had been translated into German by the noted Orientalist Josef von Hammer-Purgstall in 1812 under the title *Der Diwan von Hafis*. Goethe celebrated Hafez in his own *Divan* as a libertine hedonist who sought union with God through erotic love, wine and song, a God who provided an earthly salvation for mortal men. The opening lines of the *Divan* contain all that Goethe perceived as the Islamic Orient:

> North and West and South fragment,
> Thrones collapse, and Empires quake,
> Flee then and savour
> In the pure Orient, the air of patriarchs
> While, loving, drinking, singing,
> Khizer's verdant spring shall make young again.[17]

Hafez, however, had built on the tradition which sought direct personal experience of God. This tradition, known as Sufism or Islamic Mysticism, had existed for hundreds of years before Hafez. It had originally grown out of reactions to the worldliness of Muhammad's own successors, the later Caliphs. These reactions were on the part of devout ascetics who emphasized the Qur'an's stern warnings about Judgement Day. Piety and the forsaking of worldly pleasures, as Muhammad had taught, were hallmarks of these early Sufis. Their name is said to derive from the Arabic word 'Suf' or wool, referring to the coarse woollen garments some of them wore to demonstrate their rejection of worldly comfort. From these beginnings various Sufi brotherhoods developed, one of which was the sect of Mevlani dervishes borrowing their name from their master, The Persian Thirteenth century mystic, Mulana Jalaluddin Rumi. The term Dervish became virtually synonymous with Sufi. These fraternities devoted themselves entirely to the mystical life, whereby the soul journeys through a series of stages, ultimately entering into an ecstatic dialogue

---

17 *Goethes Werke*, Hamburger Ausgabe, edited by Erich Trunz, 7th impression, 1964, Volume II, p. 7. (Translation by N. B. R. Reeves)

with God. Western visitors to the Islamic Orient in the first decades of the nineteenth century became fascinated by the intense emotionalism of these Dervishes, who, through their whirling dances attained a state of ecstatic communion with God. Lamartine and Flaubert attended such ceremonies during their visits to Cairo, and Gérôme recorded the dance of these mystics in his painting *The Whirling Dervishes* of 1895. Sufism, not only in the cult of Dervishes, but in various other form had inspired generations of unorthodox Muslims from all corners of the Islamic world. But its most outstanding manifestations in the Arts were in Persian poetry, represented by poets such as Rudaki, Saadi, Rumi, Jami, Omar Khayyam and the most radical of them all, Hafez. Each of these poets had developed his individualistic way to attain divine love without subscribing to conventional religious practices and rituals. Hafez, for instance, believed that he had come closer to divine truth by drinking wine than praying in a mosque of his time, which he lamented had moved away from the spirit of Muhammad. The following verses written by this rebellious mystic poet are quintessential to his vision of life and explain his fascination for Goethe and his other European admirers:

> The splendour of youth again
> Has come to the garden
> The fragrance of the rose carries
> A sweet message to the nightingale
> So drink in joy, Hafez!
> And balance on the brink.
> But do not twist as others have
> The sacred Word of God
> in a hypocritical snare of lies.[18]

And in another verse entitled 'The Veil', Hafez expresses his vision of divine reality:

> Last night I saw the angels
> Rapping at the tavern door.

---

18 *Hafez. Dance of Life*, A modern discovery of his greatest poems, translated by Michael Boylan, selected by Mohammad and Najmieh Batmanglij, Mage Publishers, Washington DC, 1988, *Paean of a Dreg-Drinker*, p. 28.

The clay of Adam
in a bowl they kneaded and shaped.

The visitors from that secret realm of purity
Sat me down
On a dusty road
And poured me out a drink.

The veil of Wisdom's beauty – uniquely by Hafez
had been drawn – and through his songs
The bride of poetry's flowing locks
lovingly he has groomed.[19]

It is seemingly in the spirit of Hafez, his muse, that the figure of the poet
in Goethe's *Divan* gives himself up to the youthful joys of intoxication,
celebrating life on earth in a state of drunkenness. The depth of Hafez's
experience and his quest for reunion with God are completely missing.
Goethe approaches the question of God, afterlife, the system of punishment and reward with ironic distance and at times with cynicism. In
a poem collected under the title *Das Schenkenbuch* (*The Book of the
Cupbearer*) there occurs an argument between the drunken poet and a
beautiful female cupbearer in a tavern. The poet insists that she should
pour more wine into his vessel, but she refuses, expressing her reservation:

Poet	Cupbearer, come here! Another goblet!
Cupbearer	Lord, you have drunk enough.
	They call you the wild imbiber!
Poet	Did you ever see me drop?
Cupbearer	Mahomet forbids it.
Poet	My Beloved!
	Let me tell you something that no one else shall
	hear.
Cupbearer	If you wish to speak
	I do not need to ask so much.
Poet	Listen! We Muslims
	Are meant to bow and stay sober
	He, in his holy ecstasy
	Wished alone to be transported.[20]

---

19 Ibid., *The Veil*, p. 48.
20 *Goethes Werke*, op. cit., *Schenkenbuch*, pp. 89–99, passage quoted 95–6.
    (Translations by N. B. R. Reeves.)

The cupbearer is disarmed and offers the inebriated poet fresh almonds so that he can better savour the taste of the intoxicating wine. Beside the sweetness of wine and almonds the poet is also promised the kiss and embrace of his beautiful cupbearer:

Cupbearer   Here enjoy fresh almonds
And the wine will taste again

Then upon the terrace
I shall plunge you in fresh breezes;
And as I look you in the eyes
You may kiss the bearer of your cup

Behold! The world is no dark cavern,
But rich in fledglings and in nests,
In scent and oils of roses,
The nightingale, she too sings like yesteryear.[21]

In Goethe's *Divan* the traditional Western misconception of the Islamic Paradise reaches its height. It is a place where free rein can be given to a man's erotic fantasies, a place populated with voluptuous young girls and blessed with unceasing fountains of intoxicating and delectable wines. In a verse, under the collected title of *Buch des Paradieses* (*Book of Paradise*), Goethe confesses that the most treasured corner of his heart is occupied by the picture of Paradise promised by Muhammad in his Qur'an:

Upon my lap, close to my heart I hold
The essence of Heaven – I wish to know no more;
And I believe in Paradise with passion
For I would kiss her so tenderly in all eternity.[22]

Goethe's imaginary entry into the 'Islamic Paradise' is illustrated in a poetic exchange between the poet and a Houri, or a female angel. In the following verse the poet asks the Houri who opens the gates of Paradise to him and offers herself as a passionate lover, whether she has ever visited our earth:

---

21 Ibid., p. 94.
22 Goethes Werke, op. cit., *Buch des Paradieses*, pp. 107–20, passage quoted, p. 107.

> Your love, your kiss entrance me!
> Secrets I may not know;
> But tell me, have you encountered
> Earthly days?[23]

The Houri replies:

> We never descend to you below;
> But when you come to rest with us,
> We have quite enough to do.[24]

Then the Houri tells the poet how Muhammad has explicitly instructed them to use all their selfless female love to please the male visitors to Heaven in the way they wanted:

> Then we had him in our midst!
> Grave yet kind as is the custom of all Prophets,
> We speedily received his commandments
> But we were greatly discontented.
> For to achieve his purposes
> We were to take the lead
> As you men think, so were we to think,
> We were to be like your lovers.
>
> Our self-love came to vanish
> The girls began to doubt,
> But we thought, in eternal life
> You have no choice but to submit.[25]

Another influential German intellect to be fascinated by what he thought was 'Islam, the world of Muhammad and his Qur'anic promises', was the romantic satirist, critic and lyrical poet Heinrich Heine, born in 1797 and hence Goethe's junior by 48 years. A Jew by birth, he left Germany in 1830 to live in Paris where he spent the rest of his life. He wrote both in German and French and most of his prose works exist in both languages. His writings had therefore a much wider circulation than those of any other German author of his time. A close look at

---

23. Ibid., p. 112.
24. Ibid., p. 113.
25. Ibid., p. 113.

Heine's works unveils the deep impression that Goethean images had left on him. In a letter addressed to his friend Christian Sethe in April 1822, three years after the publication of Goethe's *Divan*, Heine expresses his yearning to visit Muhammad's native land, Arabia:

> As soon as my health is restored I shall leave Germany, I shall go to Arabia, I shall lead a pastoral life, live among camels who aren't students, I shall write Arab verse . . . Christian, if only you knew how my soul longs for peace and yet is further torn apart by the day.[26]

A year later at the end of 1823 Heine read Boysen's translation of the Qur'an and, like Goethe, all he seems to have learnt from it is an imaginary eroticism and sensuality which he decides to emulate. In a letter to Moses Moser dated 9 January 1824 he writes:

> I am, thank God, cured of this annoying [sexually transmitted] skin rash. I caught it from Boysen's translation of the Qur'an. I had to believe this Mahomet. There is no limit to my bestiality.[27]

Heine praised the Islamic Orient for its alleged openness to sensual pleasures and repudiated the Christian Occident as a dull, puritanical world that promotes a deep and permanent sense of guilt and sin. Like Goethe, Heine never visited the Islamic Orient of his dreams. But in *Die Romantische Schule* (*The Romantic School*), published in 1836, he praises Goethe for having captured the Orient's way of thinking and feeling:

> In it are the scents and ardour of a harem filled with odalisques in love, their eyes like gazelles', black and painted, their arms lustfully white. It makes the reader ... horribly desirous ... The magic of this book is beyond description: It is a heartfelt greeting and salute [Selam] presented to the Orient by the Occident, and there are some crazy flowers in it; sensual red roses, hydrangeas white like girls' bare breasts, jolly snapdragons, foxgloves like human fingers, twisted crocus blooms and in the midst, hidden and listening, quiet German violets. But this Salute means that the Occident has grown tired of its chilly, spindly spiritualism and wishes to be refreshed by the healthy bodily world of the Orient. When Goethe had declared

---

26 Heinrich Heine, *Briefe*, edited by Friedrich Hirth, Mainz, 1950, Volume I, p. 38. (Translations by N. B. R. Reeves)
27 Ibid., p. 135.

his discomfort with the abstract and spiritual in *Faust* and his desire for real pleasures, he threw himself and his mind into the arms, as it were, of Sensualism by writing the *West-östlicher Divan*.[28]

Heine's Islamic Orient is either a place of tranquillity, beauty and erotic love or a place of savage masculine cruelty. Both notions are celebrated by him as emphatic assertions of the domination of the senses. The Persian rose and nightingale motif, epitomizing the suffering of lovers, which Heine borrowed from Goethe's *Divan*, continue to express erotic love throughout his work. In his early romantic tragedy *Almansor*, set in Christian Spain after the fall of the Muslim Kingdom of Granada, the hero, Almansor, declares his love to his beloved Zuleima through song and poetry, emulating the legendary adoration of the rose by the nightingale. In Persian poetry, the rose is lamented at the same time for its beauty and grace and as the beloved whose unattainability is symbolized by her wounding thorns. The nightingale is the passionate lover who longs to be united with the rose, but his attempts to embrace her through his intoxicating songs of praise only lead to more suffering as the rose's thorns cut ever deeper into his wounds. Heine's young hero, Almansor, who had fled the Spain of the Catholic Kings and Inquisitors, has now returned to his homeland to look for his beloved Zuleima. She, in the meantime, has been converted to Christianity, baptized Dona Clara and is about to marry Don Enrique. Zuleima still loves Almansor, but her Christian conscience tells her she belongs to Don Enrique. Almansor contemplates taking his own life, if Zuleima refuses to be reunited with him. But he meets a group of partisans from the Muslim resistance to Christian rule. They promise to help him abduct Zuleima before she is wedded to Don Enrique. On Zuleima's wedding day, they storm in, remove Zuleima, who loses consciousness, and hand her over to Almansor, who has been wounded by Don Enrique. There follows a scene where both Almansor and Zuleima are standing on a high cliff above a gorge after Zuleima has regained consciousness. She believes that she has died and is now in Paradise, lying in the arms of her lover:

> I am in heaven and best of all
> Almansor is with me and here in Heaven

28 Heinrich Heine, *Sämtliche Werke*, edited by Ernst Elster, Leipzig und Wien, 1890, Volume V, *Romantische Schule*, pp. 262–3.

You need no deceptive arts
And freely I can declare, I love you,
I love you, I love you Almansor![29]

Almansor reassures her that this is no illusion and that indeed they are in Paradise. The rose and the nightingale had been telling him through all these years of separation that one day they would be physically at one. The Qur'an, he confesses, had been promising this during his relentless nightly readings:

I knew it all along, you loved me still
More than you yourself. The Nightingale has
Whispered it, the Rose has laid it upon the scented air,
A breeze has wafted it upon my ear
And every night I read it clear
In the Blue Book with Golden Letters.[30]

Zuleima replies that she is now completely convinced that Muhammad had been truthful in his description of Paradise and its delights:

No! No! The man of piety has told no lie
It is so wonderful in this lovely heavenly realm!
Enclose me in your dear arms,
And cradle me upon your soft lap,
And let me, immersed in ecstasy
Rest a thousand years in this Heaven in the Sky![31]

In his letter of 21 January 1824 to Moses Moser, Heine declares that no poet has ever surpassed Muhammad, 'that great author of the Qur'an', the reading of which has emblazoned upon his soul an everlasting mark:

I must admit that you, great Prophet of Mecca, are the
greatest Poet and your Qur'an, though I only know it in
Boysen's translation, will not easily escape my memory.[32]

29 Heinrich Heine, *Sämtliche Werke*, op. cit. Volume II, *Almansor*, p. 309. (Translations by N. B. R. Reeves)
30 Ibid.
31 Ibid.
32 Heinrich Heine, *Briefe*, op. cit, 1950, Volume I, p. 136. (Translations by N. B. R. Reeves)

The story of Almansor concludes with Almansor and Zuleima throwing themselves off the cliff, plunging to their deaths in a suicide pact that Zuleima believes to be a flight to the inner recesses of Muhammad's Paradise.

Heine's poem 'Ali Bei' collected under *Romanzen* (*Romances*), which he published in 1839, possesses all the ingredients which the Age of Colonialism liked to see assembled in Islam.

Ali Bei is a warrior hero, he is religious, he is sensual and he is cruel. He lives in the Era of the Expansion of Islam in eighth-century Spain:

> Ali Bei, that hero of the Faith,
> Lies happy in the arms of maidens,
> A foretaste of the Paradise to come
> Is granted him by Allah on Earth.
>
> Odalisques as fair as Houris,
> And lithe and willowy as gazelles
> One toying with his bearded curls
> Another smoothing his forehead's frown.
>
> While a third strikes up the lute,
> And sings and dances, laughingly
> Kissing him upon the heart where smoulder
> The flames of all those ecstasies.[33]

But as Ali Bei is being pampered by his concubines in complete oblivion, he is disturbed by the sudden sound of trumpets and the rattling of swords. There is a tumult outside and Ali Bei hears the call to arms:

> But suddenly, outside, the blare
> Of trumpets and the rattle of swords.
> A cry to arms and shots of arquebus,
> Lord, the Franks are close upon us![34]

Ali Bei instantly leaves his harem, mounts his horse, galloping to the battlefield:

---

33 Heinrich Heine, *Sämtliche Werke*, op. cit, Volume I, p. 278. (Translations by N. B. R. Reeves)
34 Ibid., p. 278.

And the hero leaps upon his battle-steed,
Hurtles to the fight, yet to him it seems
As were he in a trance, lying
Still in his maidens' embrace.[35]

And:

As he severs Frankish heads
Toppling them by the dozen,
He smiles like a man in love,
Ah, a smile so gentle and tender.[36]

In France it was Victor Hugo who with the publication of his epic poem *Les Orientales* in 1829 created an extravagant vision of a sensual and brutal Orient. In a poem entitled 'Le Poète au Calife' ('From the Poet to the Caliph') for instance, Hugo conjures up scenes in a Sultan's Seraglio and the forbidden chambers of his harem:

Your harem is so great, your gardens are so beautiful.
Your wives have eyes as bright as torches,
That pierce their veils for you alone.
When you, imperial star, shine before the peoples
Filled with fear, your three hundred sons
Surround you, sparkling like a procession across the night sky.

Your forehead bears a crest, encircled by your turban of green
You can espy frolicking in their bath, half open
Beneath the window through which you lean
The women of Madras, sweeter than perfume,
And the maids of Aleppo, wearing upon their lovely brown breast
Necklaces of white pearls.
Your broad, naked sword seems to grow within your hand.
In battle it is seen ceaselessly shining.
Encountering no turban that can break it,
Until the place where the fray is dark with confusion
And great elephants, their towers clashing,
Seize up horses in their trunks.[37]

---

35 Ibid. (Translations by N. B. R. Reeves)
36 Ibid.
37 *Oeuvres Complètes de Victor Hugo*, Poesie II, Paris, 1880. *le Poète au Calife*, p. 498. (Translations by N. B. R. Reeves)

In another poem, *Les Têtes du Sérail*, a terrifying and gruesome picture of Constantinople at night is presented with its centrepiece, the Seraglio, where the Sultan is celebrating the suppression of an uprising in Greece by his soldiers:

> To the harem ... that night it quivered joyously
> To the sound of gay drums, upon carpets of silk
> The Sultan's wives danced beneath its sacred dome,
> And, like a king bedecked with festive jewels,
> Superb, it revealed itself to the children of the Prophet,
> Adorned with the heads of six thousand men!
>
> Pale, their eyes all dead, maned with black hair,
> These heads set out upon the battlements
> Crowned terraces of roses and of jasmine in full bloom;
> As sad as a friend, a consoler like one such,
> The moon, that star of the dead, spread across their bloodied pallor
> The pallor of its own sweet light.[38]

But one mutilated head begins to talk. It is the poet's own voice, the voice of a Greek soldier whose desire had been to free the Greek islands from the 'yoke of Islam':

> Farewell, proud homeland, Hydra, O Sparta new!
> Through songs your young liberty declares itself!
> Ships' masts veil your walls, city of seafarers.
> Farewell. I love your isle where grows our hope,
> Your lawns carress'd by the ocean
> Your rocks smitten by lightning and devour'd by waves.
>
> ...
>
> Victory! friends . . . O heavens, a bomb bursting
> Upon my swift skiff breaks its fragile bridge ...
> It splits, it turns, it is open to the bitter waves!
> In vain my lips cry out, stifled by the waters!
> Farewell! I go to my shroud of green seaweed,
> My bed of sand in the depths of the seas.[39]

---

38 Ibid., *Têtes du Sérail*, II, p. 41. (Translations by N. B. R. Reeves)
39 Ibid., *La Première Voix*, III, p. 42. (Translations by N. B. R. Reeves)

The poet realizes that his voice is not emanating out of a watery grave from the depths of the sea, where he thought he had been disposed of but to his amazement from the inner chambers of the Sultan's Seraglio:

But no! I wake at last … But what mystery!
What frightful dream! my arm is missing for my scimitar
What is this so close to me, this dark horror?
What do I hear from afar. Choirs … are these the voices of women?
Songs murmured by dead souls?
Concerts! am I in Heaven? Blood! It is the harem.[40]

Hugo was inspired by Byron's translation of a famous Greek war song written by Riga, who perished in the attempt to liberate Greece from Turkish domination. The song that features in Byron's *Childe Harold's Pilgrimage* shows how close the Greek independence wars were to people's hearts in Europe and how much they despised the rule of Islam:

Son of the Greeks, arise!
The glorious hour's gone forth
And, worthy of such ties,
Display who gave us birth.

Sons of Greeks! let us go
In arms against the foe,
Till their hated blood shall flow
In a river past our feet.

Then manfully despising
The Turkish tyrant's yoke,
Let your country see you rising,
And all her chains are broke,
Brave shades of chiefs and sages,
Behold the coming strife!
Helenes of past ages,
Oh, start again to life!
At the sound of my trumpet, braking
Your sleep, oh, join with me!
And the seven hill'd city seeking,
Fight, conquer, till we're free.[41]

---

40 Ibid.
41 Lord Byron, *Childe Harold's Pilgrimage*, 2nd edition, London, 1812, pp. 223– 4.

The Greek cause had captured the imagination of another important literary figure in England as early as 1817. In the same epic style of long narrative poem and sonorous verses as in Byron and Hugo, Percy Bysshe Shelley's *The Revolt of Islam* tells us about the wanderings and warlike exploits of two Greek youths, Laon and Cythna. It is a love story and the story of an idealised revolution which is supposed to create Heaven on earth. It should have really been called 'The Revolt Against Islam'. Shelley, like Byron and Hugo, was epic-minded. So was the century in which they lived and wrote. Out of the storm and turmoil of the French Revolution had emerged a conviction that Europe, in spite of all the sorrows and setback that the Napoleonic Wars had brought, was advancing towards a divinely appointed goal. The mystics and poets were best able to discern and express this reality. And the epic or poetic-prophetic poetry was the best possible medium for conveying the good news. The good news was that Europe had taken the lead to emancipate the rest of the world from tyranny and licence.

The story in *The Revolt of Islam*[42] is this. The poet, rising from visions of despair occasioned by the slow progress of the emancipation of mankind, as in the case of Greek struggle against Turkish despotism, goes to meditate by the seashore. Suddenly he sees in the air the extraordinary spectacle of a combat between a serpent and an eagle. The serpent is defeated and falls into the sea and is received into the bosom of a beautiful woman who sits lamenting upon the shore. She and the poet meet and she invites the poet to go somewhere across the sea in a boat with her and the serpent. He consents, more in fear for her than for himself and in the course of the voyage she tells him that the serpent and the eagle are the powers of Good and Evil, who engage in combat with each other at intervals and that the serpent or the power of Good, has again been defeated. The serpent all this while lies still, recovering from the effects of the combat, when at last the voyagers come to a magnificent Greek temple beyond the realms of the vast sea. A magical and obscure event then takes place. The woman and the serpent disappear. But a cloud opens asunder and two bright and beautiful figures emerge as if out of Greek mythology. They are the hero and heroine of the story, Laon and Cythna. Laon relates that he has been an ardent and

---

42 *The Complete Poetical Works of Shelley*, edited by Thomas Hutchinson, Oxford, 1904, *The Revolt of Islam*, a poem in twelve cantos.

revolutionary youth who grew up in modern Greece with great admiration for the beauties of his country and a great horror for the superstitions and oppressions with which his people were afflicted. A beautiful female orphan under the care of his parents shares these feelings with him. It is Cythna. A mutual and strong love has been the consequence of their views. They believed that through love and gentle conduct they could liberate their country from violence until Cythna is torn away from Laon by slaves of the Grand Turk's Seraglio. Laon himself in his endeavour to rescue her had been captured and locked in a prison in a rock. But he had been delivered from the dungeon by an old man and had been told that the people of Constantinople had been awakened to his ideas and that there was a maiden going about inciting them. It was Cythna who, after having been made a victim of the tyrant's lust and imprisoned in his harem, had been freed by the mob. Laon takes leave of the old man and journeys to Constantinople, or the Golden City, where he finds people in revolt while chaos, famine and havoc reign over the Turkish capital. Women and babies who have been slaughtered lie around confusedly.

He finally finds Cythna who tells him of her ordeal. Meanwhile, the tyrant, his wives and slaves are living in terror inside the Seraglio. In fear, they invoke their God and Prophet. In the end an Islamic priest advises the tyrant to send out for Laon and Cythna who have fomented revolt and to have them assassinated. The lovers are found and brought to the Sultan's Seraglio where they are burnt at the stake. Shelley's story concludes with the lovers' souls sailing on a wonderful sea to a heavenly destination where the spirit of Good resides, leaving hope for the disappearance of the 'Evil Empire'.

But perhaps nowhere in European art is the portrayal of Islam and the Orient more outrageous, more violent, more obscene than in Victor Eugène Delacroix's painting *The Death of Sardanapalus* of 1844.[43] In this powerful evocation of the Orient, Delacroix drew upon the Greek War of Independence, a collection of Persian miniatures that his friend Jules Robert Auguste had brought back from the Orient, and the

---

43 Victor Eugène Delacroix, *La Mort de Sardanaple* (Salon 1827; J. 125), now in the Louvre, Paris. Another later and smaller variant, *The Death of Sardanapalus* (1844), 74 x 93 cm can be seen at Henry Mclhenny Collection, Philadelphia.
Also see *The Orientalists: Delacroix to Matisse, European Painters in North Africa and the Near East*, edited by Mary Anne Stevens, London, 1984, p. 125.

images provided by Byron and Victor Hugo. It is flamboyantly allusive to *Childe Harold's Pilgrimage* and *Les Orientales*. But it was Byron's direct influence that prompted the painting, namely his dramatic poem *Sardanapalus* written in 1821. This poem was based on an ancient legend dating from the fourth century BCE which Delacroix intertwined with the subject-matter he was attracted by, namely the Greek War against the Turks. The painting depicts the slaughter of Sardanapalus and his retinue by a Muslim ruler. The scenes painted on the canvas are concoctions of a wild, imagined view of the Islamic Orient as the dominion of unbridled lust and violence. The setting is the sleeping chambers of a turbaned Muslim potentate, who is shown lying indolently on his opulent bed, draped with silks and satins. With his elbow on a raised cushion and his hand under his head, he is able to watch a dream-like orgy of sexual ecstasy, rape and murderous combat unfold before his eyes. Elusive female nudes mingle mystically with a horde of male warriors dressed in Islamic garb. The evocation is one of intense psychic, supernatural experience symbolizing once again the amalgam of mysticism and violent sensuality that tells us more about the fevered imagination of nineteenth-century Europe than of the Islamic Orient as it actually was.

For the rest of the century the illusion of an erotic Orient was given further impetus in the continuing fascination of Western visitors and painters with the women of the Islamic East. In fact Orientalism and Exoticism became synonymous with the portrayal of female lives behind the veil. These unobtainable women with their secret existence, excited the Western visitor to seek access, if only in his imagination, to the forbidden quarters of the harem and the bath. The most popular manifestations of this fascination are to be found in a sequence of bathers and odalisques created by Jean-Auguste Ingres throughout his career as a painter. Ingres' representation of the Orient with its female nudes and magical, exotic colours and textures shaped the expectations of artists and the public for decades to come. His famous *Le Bain Turc*[44]

---

44 Jean-Auguste Dominique Ingres, *Le Bain Turc*, 1862, Musée du Louvre, Paris. This painting was executed for Prince Napoleon. The theme of the odalisque follows a distinct pattern of development within Ingres' oeuvre. See *Beigneuse*, 1807, Musée Bonnat, Bayonne, *Dormeuse*, 1808, painted for Queen Caroline of Naples, *La Grande harem*, 1828, Musée du Louvre, Paris and *L'Odalisque et l'Esclave*, 1842, Walters Art Gallery, Baltimore. Also see *The Orientalists*, op. cit., p. 17 and p. 194.

of 1862 showing a multitude of voluptuous nudes, lying, sitting, standing or leaning on one another against a backdrop of a luxurious bathing place, conveys the powerful allure of an imagined oriental sensuality and provocative beauty to an audience that only a painting can reach. And in an era when travel to the Orient was still reserved for a privileged few, Ingres' paintings could perhaps satisfy Europe's great hunger for exotic experiences.

The tone for the century's yearning for sensuality had been set in modern European scholarship itself by the much-acclaimed work of the noted historian Edward Gibbon, The *Decline and Fall of the Roman Empire*, published in 1788. In it there is a biography of Muhammad in which the Prophet is depicted as an impostor, a deceiver and a sensualist. But his alleged sensualism is praised as an enhancement of human life which is lacking in Christianity. What awaits the pious Muslim in the Hereafter, Gibbon declares, is a luxuriant Paradise of ultimate sexual pleasures set in the mild, sweet coolness of lush gardens in which fabulously beautiful and willing Houris provide men with an unending fare of sexual delights. But in spite of his admiration for the 'Islamic paradise', and in spite of the fact that he had set out to examine Muhammad's life from an analytical point of view, using authentic Islamic sources, Gibbon was unable to assess Muhammad other than through conscious comparison with Jesus:

> From enthusiasm to imposture, the step is perilous and slippery; The daemon of Socrates affords memorable instance, how a wise man may deceive himself, how a good man may deceive others, how the conscience may slumber in a mixed and middle state between self-illusion and voluntary fraud. Charity may believe that original motives of Mahomet were those of pure and genuine benevolence; but a human missionary is incapable of cherishing the obstinate unbelievers who reject his claims, despise his arguments and persecute his life.[45]

Even William Muir's four-volume biography, *The Life of Mahomet*, published in 1858 failed to banish the image of Muhammad as a sensualist:

---

45 Edward Gibbon, *Decline and Fall of the Roman Empire*, Frederick Warne, London, 1872, chapter I – Description of Arabia and its inhabitants – Birth, character and doctrines of Mahomet, p. 515.

But the scene changes at Medina. There temporal power, aggrandisement and self-gratification mingled rapidly with the grand object of the Prophet's life, and they were sought and attained by just the same instrumentality. Messages from heaven were freely brought down to justify political conduct . . . Nay even personal indulgences were not only excused but encouraged by the divine approval or command. A special licence was produced, allowing the Prophet many wives.[46]

Muir elaborated on those Qur'anic verses that allowed Muhammad and his followers to marry the widows of war or those early female converts, persecuted by the Meccan rulers and deserted by their relatives. He completely distorts the Qur'anic recommendations on how to shelter and protect these women within Muslim families.

The vain conceit, that he was the Favourite of Heaven, once admitted into the heart of Mahomet (and cherished there, as the Christian may surmise, by some special Satanic suggestion), will, I think, be found the key to those strange Revelations which secured for the Prophet peculiar privileges, especially in his conjugal relations. In the self-complacency of these fatal and impious pretensions, he brought himself to believe that no immunity or indulgence would be withheld from him, but that every wish and desire of his heart would be gratified, and that even by the direct interposition of the Almighty![47]

Muir lamented that Muhammad did not become a Christian in his early stages of 'religious naivity' to avoid the 'sinful life', which awaited him in Medina:

We cannot doubt that, in the sincerity of his early search after truth, he might readily have embraced and faithfully adhered to the faith of our Lord Jesus.[48]

Another English-speaking biographer, Washington Irving, in spite of his initial attempt to be fair in his judgements, cannot help but give free

---

46 Sir William Muir, *The Life of Mohammad*, Edinburgh, 1912, Chapter 37 (The Person and character of Mohammad), p. 520.
47 Sir William Muir, *The Life of Mohammad*, Osnabrück, 1988, Volume III, p. 299.
48 Sir William Muir, *The Life of Mohammad*, Edinburgh, 1912, Chapter 2 (From the youth of Mohammed to his fortieth year), p. 21.

reign to his fertile imagination about Muhammad's alleged sexual appetite and the lust which, according to the biographer, he promoted amongst his male followers. In *The Life of Mahomet*, published in London in 1851, Irving provides a quasi-pornographic picture of the Islamic Paradise:

> Above all, the faithful will be blessed with female society to the full extent even of Oriental imaginings. Beside the wives he had on earth, who will rejoin him in all their pristine charms, he will be attended by the Houris, so called for their large black eyes, resplendent beings, free from every human defect or frailty, perpetually retaining their youth and beauty and renewing their virginity. Seventy-two of these are allotted to every believer.[49]

Irving's fantasies ran wild. He conjured up young, athletic Muslims rising from the grave and being received by beautiful girls in Muhammad's Paradise where they were expected to perform their unequalled virility:

> That the true believer may be fully competent to the enjoyments of this blissful region, he will rise from the grave in the prime manhood, at the age of thirty, of the stature of Adam, which was thirty cubits; with all his faculties improved to preternatural perfection, with the abilities of a hundred men, and with desires and appetites quickened rather than sated by enjoyment.[50]

However, in 1861 Alois Sprenger acknowledged in his *Leben und Lehre des Mohammad*, published in Berlin, that Islam was one of the greatest phenomena that man had known. He categorically rejected the Christian standpoint that Muhammad was a man of the flesh, devoid of all morality. He explained how much the continent of Europe has benefited from the contribution of knowledge by the early Muslims in science, medicine, mathematics, astronomy, optics, physics and philosophy. He defended Islam against all false allegations, portraying Muhammad as a product of Arab history and society:

> The results of my investigations have brought me to the conviction that Islam was not conceived by the will of the blood, nor the will of the flesh, nor by the will of a man, but by the necessities of the

---

49 Irving Washington, *The Life of Mahomet*, London, 1851, pp. 289–90.
50 Ibid., p. 290.

age. I have tried to demonstrate that Muhammad was neither a Hero in Carlyle's sense nor an instrument of the devil.[51]

In 1918 a German translation from a Swedish work written by Tor Andrae appeared under the title *Die Person Mohammeds*.[52] (*The Personality of Muhammad*). Andrae portrayed Muhammad as a truthful religious and social reformer who annihilated the Age of Ignorance in Arabia and who offered new perspectives and new modes of thinking to his people. Driven by God's commandments which inspired him, he felt himself commissioned to put into action the social and intellectual change that he believed his society was starved of and yearned after. Like Sprenger, Andrae viewed Muhammad in the context of his time and age without prejudice.

In 1905 D. S. Margolioth published a biography which was also initially intended to redeem Muhammad from the labels stuck on him by European writers of previous centuries. He took up the sensitive issue of Muhammad's marriages which had given rise to so much criticism in Europe: Margolioth's research had convinced him that these marriages had not been concluded for any material or sexual gains:

> Muhammad's numerous marriages after Khadija's death have been attributed by many European writers to gross passion, but they would seem to have been mainly dictated by motives of a less coarse kind. Several of his alliances were political in character. The prophet being anxious to bind his chief followers more and more closely to himself. This was doubtless his object of marrying the daughters of Abu Bakr and Omar; while a political motive of a different sort is to be found in his alliances with the daughters of political opponents or fallen enemies.[53]

But for all his goodwill even this biographer is forced to contradict himself, unable to resist slipping back to the traditional Western view,

51 Alois Sprenger, *Das Leben und die Lehre des Mohammad*, Berlin, 1861, Vorrede (Preface), pp. X–XI. (Translation by N. B. R. Reeves)
52 Tor Andrae, *Die Person Muhammads in Lehre und Glauben seiner Gemeinde*, Stockholm, 1918. Also see the English translation: *Muhammad: The Man and His Faith*, translated by Theophil Menzel, New York, 1935.
53 D. S. Margolioth, *Mohammed and the Rise of Islam*, London, 1905, (history of the Meccan Period), pp. 176–7.

seeing Muhammad ultimately as a schemer and a man who merely pretended to be happy in his monogamous marriage with Khadija. In reality he was waiting for her to die, in order to indulge in polygamy and licence:

> In Khadija's lifetime, as has been seen, Mohammed could not follow the dictates of either of the motives that have been alleged. Viewed in the light of his subsequent conduct, his behaviour prior to her death illustrates in a striking way his extraordinary self-control and determination to wait for the favourable moment before putting any plan into execution.[54]

But nothing displays more scurrilously how the sense of threat once posed by Islam in the West had declined by the mid-nineteenth century into a casual dismissal (or, in some cases, fervent admiration) of Muhammad as a man of the flesh than the English satirist William Thackerays's *Journey from Cornhill to Grand Cairo* published in 1846. True, Islam was still seen as a religion of cruelty and irrationality. Yet the dominant image remained that of sensual indulgence seen by Thackeray as a decadence that extended also to Muhammad's very religion – for Muhammad's heaven is now devoid of all promises. Even the Houris of the Islamic Paradise have grown old, melancholic, bored and purposeless. Thackeray proclaims the end of Islam:

> Old Mahometanism is lingering about, just ready to drop. Think of the poor dear Houris in Paradise, how sad they must look as the arrivals of the Faithful become less and less frequent every day. I can fancy the fountains of eternal wine are beginning to run rather dry. Of nights you may see the Houris sitting sadly darning their faded muslins: Ali, Omar and Imaums are reconciled and have gloomy consultations and the Chief of Faithful himself . . . sits alone in a tumbledown kiosk, thinking moodily of the destiny that is impending over him, and of the day when his gardens of bliss shall be as vacant as the bankrupt Olympus.[55]

---

54 Ibid., p. 177.
55 William Makepeace Thackeray, *Notes of a Journey from Cornhill to Grand Cairo*, London, 1846, p. 183.

10

The Return of the Crusades and Jihads
Islam at the end of the Ottoman Empire

———

The best Jihad is to say a Word of Truth to a Wrongdoer.

A saying by Muhammad, seventh century CE

During the nineteenth century France and Britain had contributed to the gradual carving up of the declining Ottoman Empire and had done little towards its salvation. They had pursued a joint policy of keeping the Turkish Sultan in a twilight status, while his Empire slowly disintegrated. On the one hand they wanted the head of the Ottoman Empire to survive as a figurehead and bulwark against Russian expansion into the Eastern Mediterranean. On the other, they had little compunction about detaching most of his outer principalities when it served their interests. Their relationship with the Sultan had therefore been ambivalent. They helped him for instance in the Crimean War in 1853 against Russian encroachment, but allowed him to be defeated and to sign a humiliating treaty at San Stefano in 1877. They backed Russia in its aspirations to win freedom for all the Slav peoples under Turkish rule. Therefore it was not surprising that when the First World War broke out, the Sultan sided with Austro-Hungary and Germany against Britain, France and Russia, despite the fact that the Austrians had annexed Bosnia and Herzegovina in 1908. And perhaps if Germany and Austria had won the war, the Sultan might have been granted a few more years of power. But instead, victorious France and Britain not only retained their colonial possessions in North Africa, but also France became the protecting power in Syria and the Lebanon, while Britain acquired the same role in Palestine, Trans-Jordan and Iraq. The Ottoman Empire was definitively abolished and in November 1922 the British battleship, *Malaya*, took the last Ottoman Sultan to his exile in San Remo.

The fragmentation and colonialization after the war of the shattered Islamic world, especially greater Syria, was both for the Christian West and the Islamic East a poignant reminder of the medieval Crusades and Holy Wars. The Crusaders had reappeared in the guise of French and British colonialists, and resistance to their encroachment was seen as a religious duty, a Jihad against infidel conquerors of Islamic lands. The Crusaders had created the Kingdom of Jerusalem through bloodshed and the elimination of the Muslim population. The colonialists had fought the First World War against the Muslim Sultan, had defeated him and had subjected his territories to British or French colonial or mandatory rule. They brutally suppressed all threats to their supremacy and were determined to introduce their own cultural concepts and modes of living. But unlike the colonialists who had taken control of practically the whole of the Muslim East, the Christian knights had never possessed more than a coastal strip. Facing them had lain a whole series of Syrian emirates, occupying the hinterland. In 1187 the Muslim legendary warrior, Saladin had launched a decisive attack on the Crusader Kingdom and had defeated the King of Jerusalem. The Crusaders had been driven out and Saladin had become the Ruler of the Holy City. From that date onwards Jerusalem had remained in Arab hands for several centuries, falling ultimately under Ottoman Turkish domination. In December 1917, some 800 years after the Crusaders' defeat at the hand of the Muslims, Jerusalem fell to General Edmund Allenby and the British Expeditionary Army. It was to stay under uneasy British control during the entire mandatory period until 1948.

On his arrival in Jerusalem General Allenby made a historic remark which indicated that the long-standing animosity between Christendom and Islam was not over and that the crusading mentality was still alive. Speaking in public, he announced that the Crusades were now finally completed. And three years later, in 1920, when French troops occupied Damascus, their commander marched up to Saladin's tomb in the Great Mosque and cried: 'Nous revenons Saladin!' (We are back Saladin!).

The deep-seated contempt for Islam had long displayed itself amongst the French colonialists as a sense of vindictiveness towards the Muslim populations of the former Ottoman Empire. The brutality with which the Algerians had been treated by the French settlers and rulers from 1830 onwards seems to have been a conscious act of reprisal for centuries of fear and resentment of Islamic cultural, political and military domination and peril. Their reprisal was not at all unlike that of the Crusaders. The only difference was that the Crusaders had shed Muslim blood in the name of Christianity, while the colonialists brutally repressed the Algerians and confiscated their land in the name of the French 'mission civilisatrice'. In the eyes of the French, Islam was the symbol of fanaticism, tyranny and backwardness. The French had of course a long and well-established tradition of literary crusading against Islam – the crusade of the pen had replaced the medieval crusade of the sword. The most effective and popular of the literary crusades had been conducted by their revered literary figures, Montesquieu, Voltaire and Hugo. Ugly images of brutality and cruelty, associated with Islam since the medieval Crusades, had been revived in their highly acclaimed works *Lettres Persanes*, *Mahomet ou le Fanatisme*, and *Les Orientales*, badly damaging the reputation of Islam. The British viewed Muhammad's religion and those who adhered to it more ambivalently, reflected in the long-standing conflict between Islamophiles and Islamophobes in the India Office and Foreign Office. Europe's crusades of the pen had also left their imprints on Britain's popular imagination. Byron's and Shelley's romanticized portrayals of Islamic sensuality, violence and cruelty were only the most recent and perhaps the mildest expressions of how Islam had been received in Britain. So it was not at all surprising that the first British Consul in Cairo, Lord Cromer, declared in his two-volume work on *Modern Egypt*, published in 1908, that Islam was archaic and not in a position to reform itself and that the Arabs and all those nations who followed Muhammad's religion were incapable of regenerating their own societies. They were described as simplistic and childish, irrational and devoid of initiative. And although in earlier times Arabs had acquired a high degree of sophistication in their science of dialectics, their descendants were singularly deficient in logical thinking. Cromer argued that the cultural climate which nurtured Muslim reasoning was diametrically opposed to that of a European, which encouraged probing and scientific reasoning, producing statements devoid of ambiguity. And because the Muslim East looked at things so differently, it had lagged behind the West and had to be brought under Western tutelage in order to learn how to conduct its own affairs. The type of despotic oriental rule, predating Islam and based on the power of monarchy, nobility and military hierarchy which prevailed in Ottoman territories and was contrary to Muhammad's concept of a democratic Islamic society, was *de facto* associated with him and his religion. In reality, centuries before the West had developed its ideals of freedom, democracy, equality and social justice, symbolized by the French Revolution and the Marxist theories of the nineteenth century, Muhammad had postulated the concept of a democratic and egalitarian society in which everyone was regarded as equal before God as proclaimed in the Qur'an. Muhammad had established a model Muslim community in Medina where rulers and ruled had been at one with each other and where wealth had been fairly shared between them. His leadership had been spiritual and moral. With the expansion of Islam as a world power after his death, his remarkably progressive precepts had been gradually swamped by forms of traditional oriental rule, giving rise to divisions between wealth and poverty, between the rulers and the ruled. This, and not Islam, had largely characterized the Turkish Sultanate.

But now that the tide had turned in favour of the West and Christianity after nearly a millennium of Islamic ascendency, Islam was viewed as an inferior creed responsible for the decadence and despotism of the Islamic Orient. A new and turbulent phase in the long struggle between Islam and Western world had commenced, a second era of Crusades and Jihads. Islam was no longer the proud, conquering religion of Muhammad. It was now helplessly confronted with the all-pervasive display of Western superiority deriving from advances not only in technology and industry, but through the European experience of democracy and constitutional rule. A belief that Europe deserved morally to dominate also stemmed from concessions made in previous decades by the Sultanate to European merchants trading in Islamic territories. By the middle of nineteenth century there had already been flourishing European business communities in many parts of the Ottoman Empire which enjoyed privileges granted them by the increasingly weakened Sultan. These commercial and legal privileges, known as Capitulations, had eventually paved the way for the establishment and consolidation of Western colonial rule in the region.

Capitulations were privileges that exempted the Europeans not only from paying taxes, imposed otherwise on Muslim subjects of the Sultan, but also from being tried in Muslim courts should they infringe local laws. The Sultan had given the Europeans the right to be tried in their own consulates, which had been able to offer similar concessions to the indigenous Christians and Jews who worked for them. Later, these

Capitulation rights were taken to the rest of the Muslim lands which became British or French mandates, protectorates or colonies, granting the colonialists absolute freedom to live and act as they pleased without the fear of being pursued by the Islamic law.

It was not only the Europeans' insensitive and unbridled conduct clashing, as it often did, with Islamic ethical values and traditions, that began to alienate and infuriate the Muslims and thereby sowed the seeds for discontent and anti-Western sentiments. It was also the vast disappointment, especially amongst the Arabs, at the outcome of the Anglo-French victory over the Turkish Sultan in the First World War. Most of the Arab nations had been encouraged to fight alongside Britain and France against the Ottoman Empire and had been promised national independence should the latter be defeated. But once victory had been completed, the Arabs had realized that Britain and France were reneguing on their promises. The Allies showed little interest in creating national governments which derived their authority from the free initiative of the indigenous population. Doubts had been raised towards the end of the First World War, when peace negotiations between the Allies regarding the future of the Islamic territories had begun to take an unfavourable form for the Muslims. In August 1918, the British Foreign Secretary, Balfour, had written a memorandum on the position of Syria, Palestine and Iraq, stressing that in these lands the population had no choice other than to accept a British or French controlled administration.

Muslim protest had been expressed in the spring of that year in an open enquiry made by seven prominent Arabs living in Cairo who had urged Britain to clarify its policy in the region. The British government's reply, which came to be known as the Declaration to the Seven, was given vast publicity, circulating throughout the Muslim territories. In it Britain declared its desire that the Islamic peoples 'oppressed by the Turks' should obtain their freedom and independence. This statement was further reinforced by an Anglo-French Declaration on 7 November 1918 in which the creation of national, independent governments was once again promised. In reality however, events took precisely the course anticipated by Balfour. Britain and France established themselves as colonial powers and as masters of the East, imposing their own will on how the Near and the Middle East, the territories that had once symbolized triumphant Islam, should be governed. They decided on frontier demarcation, on the political status of every state that had been created or that already existed and of course they took control of all Middle Eastern natural resources, especially mineral oil.

Resistance to colonialism was seen as a fierce prerogative from the outset. Popular uprisings and unrest began to sweep across the whole region, suppressed by the colonial armies. In March 1920 the Central Syrian Congress passed a resolution proclaiming the independence of Syria, including Palestine and Lebanon. At the same time the leaders of Iraq declared their country's independence. Britain and France reacted swiftly, declaring that they did not acknowledge either resolutions and calling an urgent meeting of the Supreme Council of the League of Nations on 25 April. On 5 May the League of Nations announced that Syria had to be partitioned and was under the control of the two victorious powers. The Muslims appealed to Ibn Saud of Arabia, urging him to launch a military attack on French positions near the Lebanese border. Saud, who himself was desperately trying to free Arabia from British domination, began to mobilize his Wahabi warriors to confront the French. This provoked the French to inflict the first bombardment of civilians in history, on the population of Damascus. France went on to invade Damascus, Aleppo and the Bekka Valley, regions that the Crusaders had once conquered, driving the Muslims back. Saud's young Wahabi forces, backed by Syrian troops and the population of Damascus, bravely attempted resistance, but were not able to retain their position in the face of French tanks and bomber planes. Unlike the bombardment of Guernica by Germany during the Spanish Civil War some fifteen years later, there was no international outcry against the French bombing of Syrian civilians. Syria was defeated and the French flag was raised as a sign of victory over the lands of the Infidel. The British refrained from intervening. Winston Churchill, then Secretary of State for the Colonies, had argued that Britain had such strong ties with France that it was unable to do anything to help the Arabs in the matter.

And so it was that the partition that had officially been approved by the League of Nations in July 1922 became effective in September 1923, leaving the Arabs with a deep sense of humiliation, helplessness and anger. Muslims felt badly betrayed by the West that had treated them as partners when it had needed them and was now crushing them as inferior nations and forcing upon them its own rules and laws. Thus long before the Second World War, before the Holocaust and before the creation by the European powers and by Zionists of the Jewish State of Israel, a sense of pan-Islamic, anti-Western solidarity had begun to establish itself. It was to turn the region into a tinderbox of wars and bloodshed for years to come.

The basis for the eventual creation of Israel had been laid down on 2 November 1917, seven months prior to the Paris Peace Conference. It had been formulated in a letter written by the Earl of Balfour to Lord Rothschild, a leading British Jew, whose family had sponsored the Jews of Palestine since the nineteenth century. This letter, which came to be known as the the Balfour Declaration, envisaged a new national homeland for Jews living in different parts of the world. Balfour declared that the British government was in favour of the establishment of such a territory for the Jewish people in Palestine. His aim was to help the Jews of Europe to return to the land that had been promised them in ancient Scriptures and from which they had been deprived for centuries. Balfour's sympathy with the Jews and his concept of creating a national home for them in Palestine was far removed from the realities of that territory during the First World War. The number of Jews living there at that time was 60,000, out of a total population of 750,000 Muslims, predominantly Arabs. In his 1918 memorandum on Syria and Palestine Balfour declared:

> The four Great Powers are committed to Zionism and Zionism, be it right or wrong, good or bad, is rooted in age long tradition, in present needs, future hopes, of far profounder import than the desires and prejudices of the 700,000 Arabs who now inhabit that ancient land.[1]

Balfour was writing during a critical period of conflicting territorial claims made by both the Jews and the Arabs of Palestine, which had become a British mandate. It was not only the Palestinian Arabs who were fearful of British plans regarding the Jews, Palestine had also become a source of anxiety for all Muslims in the region. They urged Ibn Saud to intervene on their behalf and to veto any decisions by the powers in Europe which would favour Jewish rights at the expense of the Muslims. In June 1918 Saud came to London to meet the Zionist leader Chaim Weizman. Discussion continued throughout that year

---

1 *The Ottoman Empire and its Successors*, Peter Mansfield, London, 1973, p. 47.

and an agreement was eventually signed the following January. Saud found himself in an extremely weak position, as his own country ran the risk of becoming a mandate too, a development which he wanted to prevent at all cost. However, he had been reassured both by Britain and Weizman that the Zionists did not aim to establish a Jewish state in Palestine and that the agreement was merely to allow Jewish immigration into the Holy Land for humanitarian reasons. It had been agreed that Palestine should remain an Arab state and that civil and religious rights of both the Muslims and the Jews be safeguarded.

The Balfour Declaration was pro-Jewish in essence and encouraged the Zionist leaders of Jerusalem, as it had been feared by Muslim circles, to look forward to a practically complete dispossession of Palestinian Muslims who formed the majority of the population.

The first Jewish–Muslim territorial and ideological conflict since the advent of Islam in seventh-century Arabia was in the making. Muhammad had wanted to befriend the Jews of Medina and had seen himself as a Semitic Prophet in the Abrahamic tradition, but the Jews had not accepted him and had sided with Muhammad's pagan enemies to destroy him. The feud had resulted in the expulsion of most of the Jews from Medina where the first Muslim community had been created by Muhammad and his companions. But, once Islam had become established, and during the entire period of the Islamic Empire, Arabs, Turks, Jews and Christians had lived peacefully side by side for successive centuries. There had not been any religious tensions between them. The Crusaders had come from Europe to crush Islam and had not been welcomed by the Jews and the Christians of the East. In fact, Jewish and Christian communities had been flattened alongside those of the Muslims, once the hordes of Christian knights had poured into the Holy Land. Their swords had shown no more mercy towards Jews and Christians, who had been regarded as collaborators of the infidel enemy. Islam had always championed the cause of the oppressed. This had been an essential component of Muhammad's conception of Islam, namely to protect the oppressed against all oppressors. This had been the reason why the Jews of Damascus, of Spain, as well as of Constantinople, the Balkans and Central Europe had helped the Muslims in their conquest of these lands. The Jews of later centuries themselves had been convinced that Islam's championing of justice was genuine and that they could benefit and prosper with its help.

The modern conflict between Muslims and Jews was triggered by Western colonial dictates and by Zionism. It radicalized Islam and divorced it once again, as in the Medieval Ages from its mother-faiths, Judaism and Christianity. Islam had been forced into isolation, provoking anti-European feelings amongst its followers. The Balfour Declaration had reinforced the Jewish people's awareness of its ancient claim, rooted in the religious history of Israel and the destruction of its state by the Romans in CE 70. The Muslims declared that Palestine was historically their country too and were not inclined to give up their homeland and that of their ancestors. They argued that they too were descended from the Jews and Christians of pre-Islamic Palestine, and from the Arab children of Abraham who settled there in the seventh century, and that Jerusalem was a sacred symbol, as one of three holiest cities after Mecca and Medina. Upon their arrival in Jerusalem about CE 635 the Muslims had immediately set about refurbishing its chief holy place, the neglected Temple Mount or Noble Sanctuary. They had then built the splendid Mosque known as the Dome of Rock on the site selected by Umar. For the Jews too, Jerusalem was of great religious and emotional importance. It was where David, King of Israel, had built his capital and his son Solomon had erected the Holy Temple. Saladin, the twelfth-century conqueror of Jerusalem, the bloodthirsty ruler of Western myth, was in fact renowned for his tolerance. He had restored the holy places to their original use, turning them into places of worship for Muslims, Christians and Jews alike. The Ottoman Turks who in their turn inherited the city in 1517 continued their predecessors' support of the holy shrines, maintaining their accessibility to all three religions.

In the period between the two world wars and in response to Hitler's persecution, without which there would never have been enough immigrants to create Israel, large-scale Jewish resettlement in Palestine began to occur. Soon Palestine became dominated by thousands of Jewish settlers who poured into the Promised Land in search of national and religious cohesion. In 1948, weakened by the war, Britain abandoned its Mandate and the UN voted to partition Palestine between Jews and Arabs. As a result hundreds of thousands of Palestinians were driven out of their homes and settled in refugee camps outside Israel's frontiers.

The consequences of the creation of Israel were dramatic. They were dramatic for the Jews, as they began to thrive and prosper with the speedy assistance of aid from the United States and other Western allies and Zionist organizations. Dramatic it was for the Palestinian Muslims too, as they plunged into ever deeper misery, poverty and suffering in the years to come, ignored, with the exception of a few charitable organizations, by the rest of the world. Nobody was interested in the fate of 750,000 people who had once numbered the majority of Palestine's indigenous population and had now become dispossessed. About 150,000 managed, by chance or by choice, to stay in their homes within lands controlled by Israel. The rest became homeless. For economic and political reasons, Arab countries absorbed only a fraction of them. Most Palestinians themselves refused assimilation because they hoped to go back to their own homes. With the passage of time the bitter reality of their condition began to sink in. Israel's 1967 pre-emptive strike on Jordan, Egypt and Syria and its occupation of the Sinai, the Gaza Strip, the Golan Heights and the West Bank with East Jerusalem, banished all hopes for the Palestinians of ever returning to their homeland. They began to see themselves as helpless victims of the West, to whom nothing could symbolize Western imperialism more starkly than the display (and use) of military power by Israel.

It was not only the homeless Palestinians who were outraged; the sensitivities of the entire Muslim world had been inflamed. The sense of injustice among Muslim nations of the Middle East became focused on the question of Palestine and the fate of Israel's immediate Arab neighbours whose frontiers were now exposed to Israeli expansionist attacks. None of the Muslim states which had struggled in the interwar period to acquire independence from Britain or France, recognized Israel's status. This did not prevent the United Nations from acknowledging the new Jewish state as independent in 1949. This recognition, and the subsequent sustained aid on a large-scale, especially from America, equipped the Jews with the confidence to absorb the atrocities of the Nazi Holocaust and to emerge as a powerful Western-style state in the midst of an economically poor and morally distressed Arab world.

It was the start of an explosive era. If the European colonialists had felt themselves the latter day Crusaders, the aggrieved Muslims were now driven into further radicalism and the revival of the idea of Jihad (which means literally 'striving') or Holy War. They were attaching themselves to a tradition which had established itself from the onset of European impact.

The first Palestinian organization to use the word Jihad was Usrat al Jihad (Family of the Holy War). It was founded in 1948 soon after the creation of Israel and during the first territorial war which was fought by Israel and the neighbouring Arab allies, supporting their fellow Palestinian Muslims. The organization became established in the Jordanian-occupied West Bank, a region which was to be conquered by Israel in the 1967 war. The main Palestinian Jihad organization, the Islamic Jihad Movement, emerged in the Israeli-occupied territory of Gaza. The PLO, the Palestinian Liberation Organization was also founded around the same time. Both these anti-Western, anti-Israeli organizations became the militant and subversive voices of the deeply humiliated Muslim world. But while they shared their belief in armed struggle and use of violence as the only alternative to Israel's aggression, their idealistic, moral political motives were different. The PLO drew its inspiration largely from Marxism and the ideals of the Bolshevik Revolution in Russia; the Jihad Movement, on the other hand, looked to Muhammad and early Islam for inspiration, promoting Islamic idealism as the only credible and culturally and ideologically convincing alternative to those Western secularist schools of thought which had penetrated the Islamic East. The young supporters of Jihad emphasized their Islamic identity and Islamic traditional beliefs by comparing the injustice done to Muslims by the West to the persecution, war, trials and tribulations suffered by Muhammad and his companions at the hand of their pagan Meccan enemies. Their ideological mentors were Egyptians and called themselves the Muslim Brotherhood. They had been active as an anti-colonialist movement since 1928.

Jihad, as the Holy War, returned to our century as a result of the plight of Islam in its new encounter with a powerful and expansionist Europe. In its core Qur'anic context, Jihad has not primarily a military connotation. First and foremost it refers to the struggle to better one's moral behaviour and to resist all evil. Beyond that it speaks of efforts to improve the moral standing of the Islamic community through the pursuit of knowledge and education, through piety and through service to God. Sometimes, it embodies a missionary effort by a Muslim to convert unbelievers to Islam by peaceful means. These meanings are regarded in the Qur'an as the 'Greater Jihad' which is spiritual and moral in essence and is the religious duty of every Muslim. However, when nascent Islam was threatened from without by Muhammad's polytheist enemies, the term was also used to denote the effort to resist the armies of the Meccan tribes whose numbers far exceeded those of the Muslims.

This is known as the 'little Jihad' and though military in aspiration, it indicates a resort to arms only under special circumstances for purely defensive purposes. But it is precisely this aspect of Jihad that has been exploited in this century and especially in recent years by radical Islam in its perception of what Jihad means and what justifies it. Of course, in the eyes of militant and belligerent Muslims who see the West as an aggressive force that has encroached upon their territory, dominated their political life and betrayed their hopes through the creation of an alien state, Israel, the equivalent of an external and lethal enemy does exist. Thus Jihad is seen by them as an entirely legitimate concept and the resort to arms as a divinely mandated duty.

The most influential figures in this century to inspire successive generations of radical Muslims across the Muslim world and to promote the concept of Jihad were the two Egyptian ideologues and activists, Hassan Al Banna and Sayyid Qutb. Al Banna was the charismatic leader and founder of al-Ikhwan al Muslimin or Muslim Brotherhood from 1928 and Qutb became its main theoretician in 1948. Al Banna had already mobilized Islam as a revolutionary force when Qutb joined the organization after the Second World War. Through his prolific militant Islamic writing and his ardent activism, Qutb was soon catapulted into a position of leadership in the Brotherhood. Amongst his activist writings, which condemned the West as a dangerous enemy of Islam and offered Islamic alternatives to Western perspectives, were *This Religion of Islam, Islam, The Religion of the Future* and *Signposts on the Road*, published in the two decades following the creation of Israel. Qutb was the same age as Al Banna. They were both born in 1906. But unlike Al Banna, Qutb had been initially attracted by the West and Western ideas and had only become profoundly disillusioned in 1948. Western complicity after the establishment of Israel and his own visit to America had convinced him of the West's strong anti-Islamic bias. Al Banna's radicalism had started much earlier, at the age of thirteen, when he had fought in the 1919 Egyptian revolt against British hegemony. He had declared that defending one's country against imperialist Britain was a religious obligation, or a Jihad. The aborted revolt and British occupation of Al Banna's provincial hometown near Cairo had reinforced his sense of contempt for the foreign domination of his country. After completing his studies in 1927 in Cairo, Al Banna accepted a post as a schoolteacher in Ismailiyya, a town which had been at the heart of the British-occupied

Suez Zone. There, he had been able to experience the Western religious, cultural and political challenge to traditional Egyptian society. Qutb had experienced similar manifestations of the confrontation between Islam and Western modes of thinking and behaving. But Al Banna came from a scholarly religious family. His father, Sheikh Abd Al Rahman, taught at the highly respected religious Al Azhar University. From an early age Al Banna had been exposed to the militant Islamic writings of the turn of the century and had been able to develop his own theories of what constitutes an Islamic society and how it could be saved from the impact of the West.

Al Banna and Qutb identified and discussed many of the Muslim concerns which have continued to trouble Islam to the present day. The central question was this: was Islam able to respond to the needs of modern society? Were Islamic laws compatible with the social, political and legal systems that industrial societies required? Could the Islamic view of state and society compete with that of Western secularism?

Al Banna and Qutb started from a conviction that Islam was completely self-sufficient in all those areas. They argued that Islam had accommodated politics and law within religion from its very beginnings. Islam's comprehensive laws provided for social, as well as political and legal aspects of society. Moreover, Islam was not a rigid or dogmatic religion that did not allow change. Muhammad, they declared, had realized God's Will not by creating a society in which submission to God was a passive acceptance of fate, or a set of dogmas and rituals. It was rather a submission to the divine command to strive and actively to realise God's progressive Will in history. Islam was in their view not against evolution and modernity, but in fact promoted a spiritual and intellectual obligation for improvement and progress. Qutb's writings carefully analysed what he believed to be the disease of Muslims who struggled to accommodate alien models, attempting to replicate them in their own societies, while they had perfect models if they looked to Muhammad and Islam.

Although both Al Banna and Qutb idealized the early Muslim community created by Muhammad and the rule of his four immediate companions and successors, the first four Caliphs, Abu Bakr, Umar, Uthman and Ali, in practice their followers sought models not in the seventh century, but in the law books that had emerged in the centuries after Muhammad. Indeed, it was in the strict Sharia Law written by

Islamic jurists of the expanding Islamic Empire that the Brotherhood looked for a rationale to combat Western influences. They claimed that the Sharia was God's only Law for the framework of state and society and civil matters.

According to the Brothers, only through the introduction of the Sharia could a government or a society be made Islamic. Therefore the implementation of this divine law became the primary goal of the movement alongside its political commitment to the concept of Jihad.

The Brotherhood's interpretation of the Sharia was this: the only sovereign ruler of the Universe, the only legislator, was God, and God's Will had been expressed in the Sharia Law, which provided the blueprint for the constitution of state and society. The temporal ruler received his authority and power from God. He had to ensure that society was strictly governed by the Sharia. The ruler had to be a Muslim, male, virtuous and knowledgeable in Islamic jurisprudence. Total obedience was owed to the Muslim ruler who governed according to the dictates of the Sharia. A covenant between him and the ruled, realized through a consultative assembly, crystallized the unity that God had envisaged. Moreover, the concept of family was at the heart of Muslim society. The leader of the family was the man because, the Brothers believed, he was endowed with superior mental ability and emotional stability. This was the reason, they claimed, that the Qur'an had made the man responsible for the welfare of women and children. Women's primary sphere of activity was home and family. And although education was important for women, the emphasis had to be on those areas that best prepared Muslim women for their roles as wives and mothers. Coeducation was rejected. Veiling and segregation were essential to preserve women's dignity and chastity, on which the morals of society depended. Western secularism undermined morality and weakened the fabric of society and family.

For many Muslims the Brotherhood's critique both of the West and of those Muslim societies which were adopting Western models under British or French colonial or mandatory pressures rang true. They seemed like a ray of hope in a Muslim world gripped by disillusionment and cynicism. Those Muslims who had initially admired the West for its progress and liberalism were waking up to new perspectives. The disastrous defeat of the Arabs in Palestine, the establishment of Israel, the continued struggle of Muslims with massive unemployment and poverty in the decades following the Second World War, moved many former protagonists of Western culture to reassess their views. But the Brotherhood had already radically shifted from its initial aim to return to the values of original Islam and the model that Muhammad himself had provided.

If the Muslim faithful were to restore Islamic ascendency and self-determination, they should return to their own laws and above all they should not downplay the concept of Jihad against those whose intention was to destroy Islam. The individual moral discipline which the Qur'an promoted as true Jihad should become secondary to the Muslims' primary obligation to rid their cultures of the destructive influences of the West. Al Banna and Qutb reminded the Muslims that the Qur'an mandated the waging of war where God's enemies prevented Islamic governance. Muhammad himself, they declared, had resorted to arms when Islam had been attacked from without. They called for an Islamic Revolution which would restore justice to a society in which the Law of God would reign and in which there would be no sign of Western irreligiosity and godlessness.

Al Banna's explosive words in 1928 when he founded the Muslim Brotherhood had set the tone for revolutionary Islam not only in Egypt but across the entire Muslim world. Al Banna had said:

> My Brothers you are not a benevolent society, nor a political nor a local organisation having limited purposes. Rather, you are a new soul in the heart of this nation to give it life by means of the Qur'an; you are a new light which shines to destroy the darkness of materialism through knowing God; and you are the strong voice which rises to recall the message of Muhammad, the religion that contains within it government, and has as one of its obligations freedom. If you are told that you are political, answer that Islam admits no such distinction. If you are accused of being revolutionaries, say we are voices for right and for peace in which we dearly believe and of which we are proud. If you rise against us or stand in the path of our message, then we are permitted by God to defend ourselves against your injustice.[2]

Al Banna's movement initially appealed to students, schoolteachers and young university lecturers, but from the 1950s onwards it began

---

2 *Islam in Revolution*, R. Hrair Dekmejian, New York, 1985, p. 81.

to attract a large membership from the new middle classes: engineers, scientists, civil servants and even military officers. However, the successive generations of Islamic activists who came to be regarded by the West and their own governments as 'fundamentalists' were not fundamentalists in a real sense. They did not envisage a return to the original Islam advocated by Muhammad, but to the strict implementation of norms which had established themselves as Islamic laws in later Arab and Ottoman Empires.

The original conception of Islamic renewal had been markedly different. It had emerged from the pioneering work of Jamal Al Din Afqhani who had lived in the previous century. The motives behind it had been the same. It was Islam's defensive weapon against control by the West as a superior power to Muslim societies. Born in 1839, Afghani had first revived Islamic self-consciousness in his own country, Afghanistan. His radical speeches and writings had made him numerous enemies, compelling him to leave Afghanistan and settle in Cairo in 1871. But even in Egypt he had aroused opposition because of his subversive anti-British views. Egypt had fallen under British control after the failure of Napoleon's expedition into that country in 1799. Ever since, Egypt had become exposed to Western technology and science and Western style social and institutional reforms. During his eight years' stay in Cairo Al Afghani had been able to witness how Egyptian society was being Europeanized and how it was sinking into ever deeper financial debt and dependency on Britain. His criticisms had unsettled the British, who ensured that he was expelled from Egypt. In 1879 the new Egyptian ruler, Tawfik Pasha who was brought to power by the British, gave orders for his expulsion. Al Afghani went to Paris, where he embarked upon a period of active international propaganda with the object of arousing Muslims in all corners of the Islamic world to fight against Western imperialism. With the assistance of his Egyptian disciple, Mohammad Abduh, he founded the Arabic weekly *Al Urwah al Wuthqa*, in French *Le Lion Indissoluble*. It was to symbolize the indissoluble political bond which they had set out to engender among Muslims. They criticized Muslim intellectuals, who, in their desperate search for liberation and independence from colonialism, were opting for Western ideologies such as constitutionalism and parliamentarism, which were destined to make them even more dependent on the West. Why imitate an alien cultural model whose aspiration was to shape the whole world into its own ideological mould? Muslims had their own perfect model for democratic and popularist rule, they declared. Muhammad's example of the first Muslim community had been based on complete rejection of absolutism. Instead of blind imitation of rigid laws which had alienated Islam from its true origins, Muslims had to embark on a fresh interpretation of the Qur'an and of Muhammad's traditions in search of ideal models of state and society.

Abduh subsequently founded the journal *Al-Manar*, which became a widely read source of ideas for the renewal of Islam. He called upon Muslims to return to their Islamic roots and revive Muhammad's glorious era. This would give them the self-esteem and the strength they needed to fight against the Western destruction of their culture. But at the same time he warned that Islam had been alienated from its true origins through the ever stricter and more dogmatic laws which now governed Muslim life. These laws, he explained, although inspired by the Qur'an, had been written by men serving the rulers of great Arab or Ottoman empires. They had been conceived in response to specific historical and social situations over the ages. The Qur'an had to be made workable through interpretations and adjustments, matching the realities that faced a multitude of peoples of varied cultural backgrounds. So too the depictions of Muhammad's life and deeds had been modified to suit the ambitions of the rulers of conquered territories. Most laws and practices which were called Islamic had little if any relationship to Muhammad's original thought. A return to authentic, pure Islam would not only rescue Islam as a religion, but save Muslim societies from backwardness and exploitation by the West.

So, the model that these first Islamic revivalists presented was substantially different from the ideal society that the Muslim Brothers were to champion during the twentieth century. Abduh argued that the ideological foundation of Muhammad's exemplary community had lain in the doctrine of *Towhid* or the Unity of God and Human Life. The Muslims had been declared equal before God and their obedience had been to God alone and not to any temporal rulers. Every Muslim had been assigned as the Viceregent or Caliph of God on earth and as a free but moral individual who created a harmonious life devoid of oppression and tyranny. The word Caliph had accordingly been misused throughout the ages because in its original Qur'anic context its function has not been restricted to a ruler.

Abduh argued that in the seventh century Muhammad had created a system of consultation during his leadership in Medina which could very well be equated with Western parliamentarism. He had set up an institution called Ahl al Shura (Consultative Council), a system which compelled him to consult his companions and the representatives of the community. The mosque had not only been a place of worship, but a place where people met Muhammad to discuss and debate legal, political social and religious issues. Moreover, Abduh stressed, Muhammad's system of religious tax or *Zakat*, imposed on all Muslims for the general welfare of the community, could only be used for charitable purposes and nothing else, which also prevented any ruler from abusing public funds. Both Afghani and Abduh strongly advocated the emancipation of women, which Muhammad had championed and which had been obscured by later laws. Muhammad, they argued, had not deprived women of education, social interaction or participation in public life. The Qur'an had not made any distinction between men and women when it had declared that all Muslims were equal in the eyes of God. During Muhammad's lifetime women had been free to travel within and outside Arabia; they had been able to move freely in society, to choose their own husbands without intermediary and had prayed together with their men in the mosque. There had been no segregation in early Muslim communities. Moreover, Muhammad had introduced laws to protect women against the prejudices and constraints of pre-Islamic society. Thanks to the rights granted to women by the Qur'an they had been in control of their own lives. A genuine return to original Islamic values would therefore liberate women from the restrictions forced upon them by the religious laws of later centuries. It would make them active and productive members of society again. Muhammad had advocated modesty of conduct and of appearance for both men and women, not the veiling and banning of women from their public duties.

Abduh's plans to take Islam back to the days of Muhammad and to change those laws that had been accrued in subsequent ages never materialized. Instead, the brand of revivalism nurtured by the Brotherhood movement in the twentieth century established itself as the mainstream ideology for radical Islam. The emphasis remained on the Sharia Law and on Jihad, the resort to arms to achieve the creation of an Islamic state.

Following its foundation in 1928, the Brotherhood rapidly developed into a well-knit guerrilla organization whose members underwent systematic military and ideological training. Its first act of violence in 1949 was to set the tone for a whole series of guerrilla attacks on Western and pro-Western targets for years to come. In 1949 members of the Brotherhood assassinated King Farouk's Prime Minister Nukrashi Pasha. The organization was banned and an estimated one million Brothers went underground. Shortly afterwards their founder, Al Banna, was assassinated by government agents in Cairo. In 1954 the Egyptian revolutionary leader, and president of the new republic of Egypt, Gamal Abdul Nasser, tried to compromise with the Brotherhood, but they plotted to kill him too, because he refused to establish an Islamic state or to share power with them. However, while Nasser banned the Brotherhood and had many of its key leaders imprisoned, another plot was uncovered by his security forces in mid-1965. This led to further widespread arrests and imprisonments. Three prominent Brothers, including the organization's old theoretician, Seyyid Qutb, were hanged.

A new opportunity for the Brothers' return presented itself in the aftermath of the Arab–Israeli War in 1967. The colossal defeat of the Arabs and the annexation of further territories by Israel sent tremors through all Muslim societies, especially Egypt, triggering a new wave of self-criticism and introspection unmatched in recent history. It was generally recognized that the ideological solutions of the past and the adoption of Western systems, as indeed Abduh had warned at the turn of the century, were inadequate for the regeneration, mobilization and uniting of the Muslim community against the common enemy. Only a return to Islam could restore their lost pride and power to the embattled and humiliated Muslim world.

And so it was that Islamic militancy began to be tolerated not only in Egypt but throughout the Muslim spectrum. Secularist leaders of Muslim countries began to tint their speeches with references to Islam, God, Muhammad and the Qur'an. After Nasser's death in 1970, the Brothers were released from jail by Nasser's successor, Anwar Sadat, who decided to tolerate them as a useful antidote to left-wing Marxist opposition. For this, he had to pay a heavy price when the Brothers turned against him for irreligiosity, pro-Western outlooks and above all for his peace treaty with Israel. This coincided with the Islamic Revolution in Iran and Sadat's hospitality to the deposed Shah in 1979. The Shah of Iran was regarded by radical Muslims as a friend of Israel. In 1980 riots broke out in the southern city of Assyut, spreading into

Cairo in the summer of 1981 and culminating in the assassination of Sadat by five members of al-Gamaa al-Islamia .

The Brotherhood, who had managed to win sixteen parliamentary seats in the 1982 Egyptian elections, have been pressing ever since for a return to the strict application of the Sharia Law as Egypt's only legal code. But entry into the parliamentary arena has not removed the Brotherhood from the scene of militant activism, nor has it deterred its support for subversive Islamist groups in the Near and the Middle East. In fact the Brothers continue to inspire a whole range of anti-Western, anti-Israeli organizations. The most familiar of these organization to the Western mass media are Hamas and Hizb Allah, the Party of God, active in southern Lebanon, a region also occupied by Israel.

Sadat was the victim of precisely this new Islamic radicalism which is ideologically and physically intertwined with the Arab–Israeli conflict. His fatal mistake in the eyes of the extremists was twofold: he had sought a settlement with the arch enemy Israel, but he had also offered sanctuary to a man regarded in Iran, a non-Arab, Islamic country, as the suppressor of Islamic traditional values, namely Mohammad Reza, the Shah of Iran. For while many of the Arab countries, including Egypt, Algeria, Syria, Iraq, Morocco, Tunisia and Lebanon, had followed a degree of compromise between westernizing reforms and Islam in the difficult post-independence years, Iran had been subject to rapid and uncritical westernization. This kind of pro-Western administration, which actively sought the removal of Islam from public life, had first begun in Turkey many years before, after the defeat of the Turkish Sultan in the First World War. Unlike Arabia, the birthplace of Muhammad and Islam, where Ibn Saud had resisted British pressures and had founded an orthodox Islamic state based on the Sharia Law in 1923, Turkey, the core of the Ottoman Empire, had opted for a diametrically opposed model. Ironically neither of these two countries had become a colony or a direct mandate.

In 1918 British and French troops had occupied Anatolia. In 1922 the Turkish nationalist leader, Kemal Atatürk had managed to drive them out of Turkey by mobilizing a liberating army. The following year he had declared Turkey a republic with him as its first president. Turkey's secular revolution had been fairly unproblematic, compared with the experience of similar liberation movements in the Arab world. There, the British and French hegemony had proved to be far more stubborn and long-lasting. Although a form of nominal independence had been granted to Egypt in 1922, other Arab states had to go through a tough and persistent struggle to achieve independence. The first country after Egypt to arrive at this goal was Iraq with its independence acknowledged in 1931. And in 1943 Lebanon, in 1944 Syria, and in 1946 Jordan declared their independence, But British and French indirect control remained practically unaltered. Tunisia, did not acquire independence until 1962. And Algeria's liberation as late as 1960 was the result of a protracted bloody war with France.

In Turkey, Atatürk was determined to restore Turkey's lost dignity by embarking on a whole catalogue of audacious revolutionary measures to create a prosperous Western style society. This involved a radical break with Islam, including the elimination of the Sharia Law, the introduction of European legislation, the abolition of Islam as Turkey's state religion, the banning of the Qur'an from school curricula, the eradiction of the Arabic script in favour of the Roman alphabet and the prohibition of the veil.

Atatürk's young neighbour and admirer, Iran's secularist monarch, Reza Shah, who came to power in 1926, aided by the British, also became convinced that the kind of westernizing reforms that were being forced on Turkey, were appropriate for Iran.

However, Reza Shah and later his heir Mohammad Reza, who became fascinated by the West and its technological progress, did not go as far as Atatürk. Although they saw Islam as a great obstacle to their westernizing reforms, they had reservations about abolishing it as Iran's state religion. They were fearful of the vociferous and traditionalist Iranian Shia clergy and their grass-root supporters amongst Iran's vast religious communities. Both Shahs had of course inherited a country already dissatisfied with Western, and particularly British imperialism. Although Iran, as an ancient non-Arab kingdom had not become an Ottoman territory, or a a British or French colony or mandate later on, it had not remained outside foreign imperialist rivalries. Throughout the early decades of this century Iran had witnessed British and Russian intervention in its political and public affairs. Concessions had for instance been made to Britain and Russia by the weak kings of the Qajar dynasty to improve Iran's post- and telegraph-systems. They had been given free access to Iran's forests and waterways. The British had also won the concession to explore and extract Iranian oil which had been discovered in 1906. This had enabled Britain to monopolize the Iranian oil fields during the First World War, in the inter-war period, throughout the Second World War and right up to 1951. In exchange for risibly low royalties paid to the Qajars, cheap Iranian oil poured into the British industry and transport sectors, contributing to the rise of living standards in Britain. Meanwhile, the Iranian economy and infrastructure were inhibited from being developed. The first uprising against the British and the Russians reached its heights in the 1906–11 constitutional revolution whose aim was to restrict monarchical and foreign power. The Iranian clergy had played a great part in this early expression of popular protest against foreign influence in Iran. They had fuelled anti-Western, anti-imperialist sentiments across a whole cross section of Iranian society.

It was these religious leaders who opposed Reza Shah's bold westernizing efforts from the very beginning. They were particularly angry about the abolition of the veil for women. Reza Shah had instructed his police to seize women in the streets and to tear their veils from their heads, and to prosecute those who persisted in wearing the veil. Although Islam had officially remained Iran's state religion, Reza Shah did not make a secret of what he thought of Islam and the Islamic clergy. They were in his view the greatest hindrance to modernization. During his reign Reza Shah did everything he could to remove the impact of Islam from Iran's public life. Rapid industralization, mechanization and the introduction of Western laws were to wrench Iranian society from its ancient Islamic roots and transplant it into the technological era of the twentieth century. Amongst the most ardent opponents to Reza Shah's westernizing projects was a young cleric by the name of Ruhollah Khomeini. He took every opportunity to attack Reza Shah in bitter terms for failing to govern in a manner which would foster Islam. Born in 1900 at Khomein near Isfahan, Khomeini had strong religious antecedents. Both his father and his maternal grandfather had been prominent religious figures, while his elder brother had become an Ayatollah, attaining the highest and the most prestigious rank in the Iranian clerical order. Khomeini's writings,in which he strongly opposed the westernization of Iran, were dominated by his sense of contempt for British imperial intentions. For he believed that the British had set Reza Shah on the throne to weaken the traditional power of Islam and the clergy. Khomeini thus became determined to free Iran from foreign influences and Reza Shah's absolutism. His solution for the country was not even the constitutionalism which had been championed by many clergy in the 1906 revolution, but an Islamic Republic. Constitutionalism was a concept imported from the West and was alien and incompatible with Islam.

Khomeini's opposition to the rapid social changes that were taking place in Iran did not cease when Reza Shah was deposed by western Allies following the events of the Second World War. With even greater vigour he continued to criticize the young Mohammad Reza who succeeded his father on the throne in 1946. The new Shah was seen from the outset by Iran's militant religious circles as contemptuous of religion. Reza Shah had sent him abroad to receive Western education to prepare him for the great task that lay ahead of him: the regeneration and modernization of Iran along the lines adopted by his father. This continued to be Mohammad Reza Shah's objective during his career as a strongly pro-Western monarch. Moreover, like Reza Shah who had not opted for a republic or a constitutional monarchy, he savoured absolute power as his style of government. But Mohammad Reza was aware that the clergy held a strong hold over Iranian society and that Shia Islam was the biggest single binding cultural influence amongst the majority of Iranians. Despite this awareness, the Shah placed religion in an ambivalent position. For nationalistic reasons Shia Islam was encouraged; yet his security agents sought to suppress the influence of the clergy when it conflicted with the process of westernization. No compromise was envisaged. Indeed the Shah even tried to create a new home-grown ideology based on pre-Islamic Iranian imperial history, with Cyrus the Great as a national hero and his ancient capital Persepolis (the City of the Persians) as a symbol of Iranian grandeur before the Arab invasion in the seventh century CE. It was an ideology designed to counter the influence of Islam. The Shah persisted in his campaign against the clergy, regarded as reactionaries who wanted to return the country to the unsophisticated society of the seventh century CE. Khomeini on the other hand claimed that kingdoms were against the Will of God and that only Islam could unite God, man and state in divinely-intended harmony.

Religious opposition was not directed against the Shah's strongly pro-Western and anti-Islamic outlooks only, but also against his despotism. There were causes of dissent of a different kind as well. Iranian Marxists and Western liberals who refused to accept the Shah's ideology and autocracy were also a major threat to the monarch and to British interests in Iran. Their activism ran parallel to and often coincided and coalesced with religious agitation.

Britain became the main target of attack in 1951 when Mossadegh was made Prime Minister. He soon rose to the status of national hero as he skilfully played on Iranian hatred of foreign domination, symbolized by the Anglo-Iranian Oil Company which was thought to be exploiting Iran's vital oil resources. The economic treaty that the British had imposed on the previous dynasty in May 1901 had granted Britain a sixty-year concession with exclusive exploration, production and oil refining rights over an area of 480,000 square miles. This comprised most Iranian provinces except for a few in the north of the country. High on Mossadegh's agenda was the nationalization of the Iranian oil industry. But it was also his intention to erode the power of the Shah, who was seen as a British puppet.

The decline of royal authority culminated on 16 August 1953 when the Shah abortively sought to replace Mossadegh. Mossadegh promptly announced that the Shah had attempted to overthrow him and instigated a popular uprising. The Shah was forced to flee the country. The British too left the oil fields in fear of their lives. Bent on teaching Mossadegh a lesson, they linked up with America's CIA. With the collaboration of Britain's MI6 they recruited mobs and royalist troops and engineered a coup d'état which returned the Shah to the throne. Mossadegh was arrested and put in prison. A few years later he was allowed to live in his country house near Tehran under what amounted to house arrest until he died in 1967. The British also returned to their oil fields, but. this time in the form of a consortium, with BP as its main shareholder.

As a secularist, Mossadegh may not have called the 1951 anti-British uprising of the Iranian people a religious Jihad, but there is no doubt that for the pro-Khomeini elements in the crowds the protest could have been anything other than a Holy War against the infidel exploiters of Muslim resources. Nevertheless, the focus from now on was to shift from the British to the American presence in Iran. Helping the Shah to overcome Mossadegh had paved the way for America to establish itself as the Shah's main protector and sponsor. American economic and technical assistance were instrumental in the creation of the Shah's notorious Security Police, the Savak. The latter was also largely assisted by Israel's intelligence agency, Mossad. The Shah even turned to the Israelis for the provision of his personal security as he believed that outsiders were more trustworthy than his compatriots. The Savak was to become the key institution of Iran in its aim to consolidate the Shah's position as absolute dictator. The Shah made particularly sure that a careful watch was kept on the clergy, and moved to suppress any power that they might wield. His increased use of police and suppression of free speech and political parties did not only intensify opposition to his regime from diverse quarters, but also obscured the merits of his modernizing efforts. This was especially true with regard to the emancipation of women.

After Mossadegh's crushing defeat, only one opposition remained that could claim grass-root support, namely the religiously-based alternative to the monarchy. Its spearhead, the fiery and uncompromising Khomeini, had in the meantime acquired the highly respected title of Ayatollah. Khomeini fiercely opposed the Shah's renewed plan to modernize Iran on a much larger scale. This was to happen under the banner of what the Shah and his associates had coined the White Revolution. Women's suffrage and the introduction of European family and personal codes regarding marriage and divorce, were amongst its major objectives. Another daring project was to change the Islamic calendar to a new royal calendar to mark Iran's pre-Islamic ancient monarchical tradition. Khomeini vigorously condemned these plans, arguing that they were offensive to Islam.

Although Khomeini's views were orthodox, especially with regard to women, his ability to express them with great passion and anti-imperialist, anti-Western sentiments, attracted a large following, even amongst women, mainly in the ranks of the disaffected urban proletariat, but also amongst intellectuals. Large sections of the population became increasingly convinced that the Shah was bent on destroying the Islamic basis of their country – making them completely dependent on the West.

In June 1963 Khomeini was arrested in Qum, the centre of religious seminaries near Tehran, provoking the worst riots of the century, which raged throughout the country's major cities for three days. In response, the Shah countenanced a bloody law-and-order operation by his army, which ferociously suppressed the riots, killing more than a thousand people. Amongst the protestors had been numerous veiled women, but also members of a cocktail of opposition organizations who used religion as a front for their own bitter exclusion from the country's political life. Khomeini, as the most ardent agitator of all, was exiled and had to take up forced residence in Najaf, in neighbouring Iraq. A wave of comprehensive arrests silenced, at least for a few years, other undesirable voices, religious and secular.

However, Khomeini was not to remain silent. His real Jihad against the Shah as the enemy of Islam was to take a fresh and more potent dimension. In Iraq he was able to link up with other Islamic activists who shared his views, including the Muslim Brothers. With the help of his supporters in various parts of the Islamic world, Khomeini launched a universal rally which was to mobilize and unite forces within Iran. His tough rhetoric, delivered from outside Iranian borders attacking the British and the Americans as the oppressors of Iran's national and religious identity, had a powerful impact. His fiery sermons were smuggled with increasing frequency into Iran, forming the basis for further religious unrest throughout the country. Khomeini proclaimed a new Islamic Era in which Islamic identity and self-respect could be restored. Western influences had to be thrust from the country. Only through the restoration of an Islamic state would Iran acquire complete self-determination.

The grounds for the acceptance of revolutionary Islam as Iran's only means to liberate itself from foreign domination were already being prepared inside the country by a group of disillusioned intellectuals. They were turning the mosques into places of political gathering and discussion. Long before Khomeini became known to the West, an Iranian writer, Jalal Al Ahmad, born in 1923, had sown the seeds of Iran's revolutionary identification with Islam. Similar to early proponents of Islamic Revivalism in the Arab World, Afghani and Abduh, Al Ahmad, born in 1923, mocked his own people for their aping of everything Western. He vehemently criticized the Western-trained intellectuals and educated elite who had penetrated the country's systems only to carry out the dictates of the West. Divorced from the customs and traditions of their own country they were helping it to sink into ever deeper servitude and dependency. Al Ahmad believed that home-grown Iranians whose minds had been moulded in traditional Islamic culture should revive the old values and restore the lost identity and the cultural character of the country. Al Ahmad, whose best-selling satire *The Disease of Westernism* was to be found in every Iranian's house in the 1960s, was not an Islamic reformist like Al Afghani, but an Islamic Revivalist. He was not imprisoned as was customary with writers whose works did not fit the state ideology, but his books were soon banned and could only be obtained through clandestine channels.

The man who set out to reform Islam in the revolutionary spirit of Al Afghani and who, like Khomeini, became a serious threat to the Shah's sovereignty, was Ali Shariati. Born in 1933 near Sabsevar in the province of Khorasan, he was the son of an expert in Qur'anic interpretation. He had spent his time as a student in and out of prison from 1957 to 1960 for his outspoken views on the uncritical westernization of Iran. In 1965 he founded a religious training centre in Tehran with the ostensible aim of teaching young Iranians the ideology of Islam as it had first been taught by Muhammad in the seventh century. But the the true purpose of the centre soon became transparent. Shariati was training a generation of Islamic warriors to be indoctrinated with the ideology of Jihad against all foreign influences. Unlike the clergy who were opposed to change, Shariati advocated a return to Muhammad's ideals, progressive in essence and open to reform. In fact in the late 1970s, as pressures on the Shah's regime from within and without became overwhelming, the Savak allowed Shariati (whose training centre had been closed down in 1973), to be freed from prison and to preach as an Islamic modernist in the hope that he would rid the country of its orthodox clergy. But in 1977 Shariati was exiled to Europe, where he soon died in London. The exact circumstances of his death have never been properly explained. It is thought that he died from the tortures that he had suffered while in prison in Iran.

Shariati never lived to see the culmination in 1978 of his large-scale teaching programme, when Iranians rose in unity to overthrow a political system that they believed had alienated them from their cultural roots. The regime of the Shah had systematically suppressed all dissenting voices, particularly those of Islam. By 1978 resistance had become all-pervasive, uniting all shades of opposition into one mighty and unpremeditated street protest which lasted several months, paralysed the country, and brought down the regime of the Shah. One of the astounding features of the revolution was the large-scale participation of women, who in their thousands if not millions donned the veil to symbolize their protest, their identification with Islam and their rejection of the westernizing processes that had, paradoxically, granted them Western-style civil and political rights.

Khomeini's triumphant return as the formidable leader of the Revolutionary Islamic Republic of Iran on 1 February 1979 was seen throughout the Muslim world by activist Islamists and radical groups as an amazing victory for Islam and a humiliating defeat for America, Israel and the continent of Europe which had supported the Shah and his regime for so many years. Amongst the first visitors to come to the Islamic Republic was Yasser Arafat, whose aim was to congratulate Khomeini and the Iranian nation on behalf of the PLO, the Palestinian Liberation Organization. Indeed, Khomeini's appeal was such that he acted as a magnet for groups throughout the Middle East that felt dispossessed and alienated by the inexorable encroachment of Western industrial, military and political power. And his vehement hatred of Israel made him doubly popular. In declaring a Jihad on all forms of neo-colonialism, he set out to make Islam a uniting force amongst Muslims, both Shia and Sunni, eradicating what he saw as puppet regimes in almost all Middle Eastern countries, includinq Saudi Arabia. Although an orthodox Islamic state, the birthplace of Muhammad was run by kings and princes and not by Islamic Jurists or Clerics, Khomeini declared.

Unlike the Shah and the westernized Iranian elites that had nurtured anti-Arab feelings, emphasizing a purely Iranian, pre-Islamic cultural identity, Khomeini saw himself and Iran as part of a universalist Islamic civilization. The divide between Sunni and Shia, which had separated the Muslims of Iran from their fellow Muslim Arabs, Turks and other Muslim nations, was not to stand in the way of the reconstructing of a strong and self-reliant Union of Islamic states.

Indeed, Khomeini attempted to remove all theological and dynastic barriers, albeit theoretically, by responding as a triumphant revolutionary Islamist to the profound crisis of identity that had gripped Islam since its decline in the nineteenth century. If Islam's historical strength, self-confidence and unity had been a sign of God's guidance of and pleasure at the Islamic community, symbolized by the Golden Age of Islam, modern history could also engender a sense of pride and self-esteem as a consequence of devotion to God and the law of God, the Sharia. Khomeini believed that he had set the example with his creation of the Islamic Republic of Iran.

A key element in Khomeini's attraction was his belief that an Islamic state must be run by Islamic clerics. And it is here too that there lay an implicit threat to the ruling dynasties of existing Islamic states, Saudi

Arabia and the Arab Emirates, as well as to the governments of secularist states such as Egypt, Algeria and conceivably even Turkey. Khomeini's doctrine of theocracy derived from his Shia background but bore close similarity to the ideal Sunni Islamic state advocated by the Muslim Brotherhood in Egypt. According to Khomeini, government emanates from God, who placed the Prophet at the head of the community. The members of this community are all equally subject to divine law or Sharia. No man can oppose this law since it emanates from absolute perfection. Moreover, although God has proclaimed all men equal with respect to the law, they are not all equal among themselves, since only one amongst them has been judged by the Lord as worthy of receiving the Message. Khomeini declared that upon God's commandment Ali, the designated successor to the Prophet, was given the same mission which he then delegated to his son, the next Imam. Thus divine designation became regarded as the only source of legitimacy for the state, passed from Imam to Imam.

Khomeini stressed that the Ulama or Islamic Theological Jurists, are also designated by God to carry on the task of the Imams as political leaders of Muslim nations. The Brotherhood's equivalent of an Imam was the Caliph who, as the Protector of the Sharia, had to be obeyed by his subjects.

Khomeini postulated the idea of *Velayat Faghih* or the Vice-Regency of the Islamic Jurists. In his book *The Theologians' Guardianship*, published in 1964 upon his exile to Iraq, he claims that the right to govern the Muslim community falls uniquely to the clerical authorities. These Jurists or experts on Qur'anic Laws are entitled to supervise and run society and state. Khomeini attributes the leadership of the community to those Jurists whose outstanding scholarship in Islamic Law, individual virtues, political and social insight, had elevated them to sufficiently high spiritual levels to represent the Prophet and his divine dictum.

Khomeini's Fundamentalism resembled that of the Brotherhood in so far as he also turned to the existing Sharia Law as the basis of his model Islamic state. He did not attempt to reform Islam by returning to the simple Medinan example that Muhammad had presented and that had been envisaged by the turn-of-the-century Islamic Reformists Afghani and Abduh. So even in its most revolutionary form, Islam remained as orthodox as in Saudi Arabia. The difference lay in who held power, the clergy or a monarchy.

Yet there was one further, crucial difference between Khomeini's perspective of how Islam should conduct itself in today's world, especially with regard to the West, and that of the conservative kings and princes of Saudi Arabia and the Arab Emirates. While these Islamic states have allied themselves with the United States and Europe in order to develop their economy and technology, Khomeini was against all compromise, denouncing their imperialist intentions and corrosive effects of their cultural values on the morals of Islamic societies. It was precisely this unyielding stance of Khomeini's Fundamentalism, which branded the United States as the 'Great Satan' and Europe, and particularly Britain, as the 'Small Satan', that has become associated with the image of Muhammad and his religion in modern Western eyes. Islam is now once again seen as a religion of fixed medieval views and uncompromising hostility to the West. The images of Islam created in the Christian Middle Ages when it had been an immediate military threat to Europe had been reawakened. The wheel of history seems to have turned full circle.

11

From Reverence to Travesty

Muhammad in the twentieth century

The Pen is Mightier than the Sword
Salman Rushdie, *The Satanic Verses*. 1988

On 14 February 1989 the Ayatollah Khomeini pronounced his Fatwa – which was effectively a death sentence – against Salman Rushdie, the author of *The Satanic Verses*, and his English publishers. A shocked West regarded this as an extreme attack on freedom of speech, a value dear to the hearts of a continent steeped in liberal secularist thinking. The idea of blasphemy, which was Khomeini's central motive for declaring the Fatwa, seemed remote and alien. Much of the intellectual establishment in Britain, in the rest of Europe and in America were dismayed by Khomeini's verdict and declared their solidarity with Rushdie. Influential novelists, writers and journalists joined forces in a concerted international campaign to condemn what seemed to them a savage medieval act. But a sense of outrage of equal intensity swept across the Muslim world, including moderate Muslim communities in Britain and other parts of the West, at Rushdie's daring novel which satirized the origins of Islam and the life of Muhammad. Some British Muslims even went as far as burning copies of *The Satanic Verses* in public. Western observers saw in this reaction a further demonstration of their traditional perception of Islam as a cruel and reactionary religion. The question of whether Rushdie had conciously used his freedom of speech to defame Muhammad and distort the origins of Islam was largely ignored, for people in the West were defending a principle, not a book. And although Ayatollah Khomeini died soon after pronouncing the Fatwa no subsequent religious leader in Iran has been able to lift a decree of a dead man of his exceptional religious authority.

For a Muslim world in which the figure of Muhammad is a supreme source of inspiration for restoring self-esteem and for counteracting the cultural and political impact of the West, Rushdie's attack on the most sacred foundations of Islam was explosively offensive and hurtful. It was especially offensive because it appeared to be so rigidly backed by the West – a West which was already blamed for all the troubles that the Muslims had been facing this century. In the previous centuries when Islam had been basking in power and success the vituperations of Western writings had been generally ignored. Now that the Muslim world felt itself to be highly vulnerable, the situation had changed. Islam sought to defend itself. Rushdie as an ex-Muslim who was educated in Britain, came to be seen not only by Islamic radicals and Khomeini supporters, but also by mainstream Muslims as a traitor to Islam and a servant of the West.

The verbal confrontation that ensued from the publication of *The Satanic Verses* deepened the political confrontation between the Islamic world and the West. The revival of the spirit of the medieval Crusades and of the Jihad that had been repeatedly ignited by the turbulence following the collapse of the Ottoman Empire in the 1920s, by the Palestinian conflict in the decades after 1948, and by the violent events in Iran and the Lebanon in the 1980s, culminated in a literary battle. Rushdie seemed to have brought new life to the dormant yet ancient Crusade of the Pen. Yet it was not at all the way the century had begun.

A hundred years before Khomeini's pronouncement of Fatwa, Nietzsche had proclaimed that God was dead, and in the intervening years spanning two world wars, a massive surge of industrialization and unprecedented advances in technology and science had critically diminished the appeal of orthodox religion for much of the people in Europe. While this had enabled writers to treat even their own religion with less respect and fear than in previous centuries, it had also allowed many others to look more objectively and with less prejudice at other religions. This trend had been particularly favourable in the reception of Muhammad and his religion. Indeed through much of the twentieth century and quite contrary to what was happening in the turbulent politics of the Islamic East, positive reassessments of Muhammad and Islam had begun to appear in European writings. Just as the military and political Crusades were returning in new guise, the Crusade of the Pen seemed to be gradually vanishing. The loosening of Christian thought had apparently paved the way for European writers to re-evaluate Islam as a reasonable alternative to the religion they had been brought up in.

The origins of this new approach lay in the fascination that the Orient had exercised over so many writers and painters in the nineteenth century. The simplicity of life untouched by industrialization, untrammelled by the restrained sexual ethic of Christianity, as they believed, brought Muslim life closer to nature and yet also to God than was possible in Europe. It was a closeness revealed in the mysticism that had already inspired Goethe in his West-östlicher *Divan* of 1819. One of German literature's greatest poets, the Prague-born Rainer Maria Rilke was also seized by this curiosity with the Orient and a desire to find an alternative to the purposelessness of modern Europe's mass urban living in the ancient realities of the East.

Long before he embarked on his 1910 journey to Egypt, Tunisia and Algeria, Rilke had felt a genuine affinity with Islam. But his longing to break free into the simplicity and informality of the Eastern way of life had been heightened when his wife Clara had returned from a visit to Egypt in 1907. Clara had showed him not only in words, but also in her drawings, the natural spirituality of the Muslim faith. Her sketches depicting potters on the banks of the Nile, basket-weavers and Bedouins whose lives were unaffected by outside influences and who radiated inner peace and contentment, in spite of their material poverty, had filled Rilke with a sense of profound nostalgia. They appeared still to be in touch with the source of life – with their inner beings – which Rilke believed the people of Europe had long been alienated from. He therefore turned his attention to Islam and began to marvel at Muhammad whose religion seemed to have provided a physical and spiritual equilibrium lacking in European man. Perhaps only the humble Bedouin of the desert, pure and untainted by the complexities of urban life could comprehend and evaluate the purpose of life? Perhaps the answer to happiness was not to display human arrogance and compete with God, but to submit to God's Will?

In the same year as Clara's return from Egypt, Rilke produced a poem entitled "*Mohammeds Berufung*" (Muhammad's Call). The poet depicted Muhammad as an unlettered man, as he had been described in the Qur'an, unable to write and read, and who acquired this ability only when the Word of God was revealed to him in his lonely cave high above the Meccan deserts. Muhammad's closeness to God, his ties with higher realities were in Rilke's view a product of his unaffectedness as a man of the desert. The poem conveys the awesome impact of Muhammad's vision of God brought to him through the Angel Gabriel.

But when there entered his lofty hideaway
The Instantly Recognisable, the Angel,
Upright, pure and gleaming with light
He renounced his every demand and begged

That he might remain, a mere merchant as he was,
Bewildered within from his travels:
He had never read – and now
Such a word, too much even for a wise man.

But the mighty imperious Angel pointed and pointed,
Showed him, what was written upon his sheet,
And would not give way and said again: Read!

Thereupon he read, read so that the Angel bowed.
And now he was a man who had read
And could read and obeyed and carried out the command.[1]

On 19 November 1910 Rilke set out on a journey to North Africa. On 26 November he wrote to Clara from Algiers:

There life comes from a Thousand and one Night.
Allah is great, and in the air there is no power beyond His power.[2]

In another letter addressed to his wife from Cairouan, Rilke once again expressed his admiration for Islam and its impact on the lives of the local population:

The flat white city stands there within rounded battlements like a vision ... It is a marvel how you can sense the simplicity and vibrance of this religion, it is as if the Prophet had been there only yesterday, and the city is his very realm[3]

On 28 December Rilke imparted with extreme modesty his thoughts on the Muslim way of life in a letter to Frau Hedwig Fischer:

---

1   Rainer Maria Rilke, *Sämtliche Werke*, edited by Ernst Zinn, Wiesbaden, 1955–66, Volume I, 'Muhammads Berufung', p. 638. (Translation by N. B. R. Reeves)
2   *Rilke, Chronik seines Lebens und Werkes*, Ingeborg Schnack, Frankfurt am Main, 1975, p. 359. (Translation by N. B. R. Reeves)
3   Rainer Maria Rilke, *Briefe 1897–1914*, edited by the Rilke Archive, Wiesbaden, 1950, p. 295. (Translation by N. B. R. Reeves)

As I travel I am hardly like an artist any more, faced as I am by this new world. I am like a beginner timidly and clumsily trying his hand at [depicting] an infinitely superior and wise reality.[4]

In 1912 Rilke spent a few months in Spain. And it was there that he was able to collect his impressions of the Islamic East. It was there, too, that he was encouraged to read the Qur'an once again and more intensively. On 4 December of that year he wrote to Fürstin Taxis about a converted mosque which he had visited in Cordoba:

This mosque; it is a concern, a worry, a disgrace what has become of it, churches twisted into the luminous inner space, I would like to comb them out like combing knots out of lovely hair . . . Christianity I could not help thinking is constantly slicing God up like some beautiful cake, but Allah is one, Allah is whole.[5]

Several days later, on 17 December 1912, he wrote again to the Fürstin, this time from Ronda, that he has become disillusioned with Christianity:

Incidentally I should tell you, Princess, that since Cordoba, I have been overcome by an almost fanatical anti-Christian feeling. I am reading the Qur'an, it is taking on, in places, a voice of its own, in which I am inside with all my powers like the wind in an organ. You really should not hand out these decaying rinds that are lying around as food. The juice has been sucked out, so, putting it crudely, you should spit out the rind ... In any case, Muhammad was immediate, like a river bursting through a mountain range, he breaks through to the one God with whom you can talk so wonderfully, every morning, without the telephone called 'Christ' into which people constantly shout 'Hallo, is anyone there?' and no one replies.[6]

Rilke's greatest goal in life was to capture in his poetry that very unity of existence which embraces the whole purpose of life. In his early work, before his acquaintance with Islam, he was still searching for

---

4 *Rilke, Chronik seines Lebens und Werkes*, Ingeborg Schnack, op. cit., p. 362. (Translation by N. B. R. Reeves)
5 *Rainer Maria Rilke/Marie von Thurn und Taxis, Briefwechsel*, edited by Ernst Zinn, Zurich 1951, p. 240. (Translation by N. B. R. Reeves)
6 Ibid., p. 245.

this unified essence of human life. In his novel *The Notes of Malte Laurids Brigge*, the author expressed, through his protagonist Malte his frustration at failing to grasp the contents and meaning of earthly existence in their totality. It was Rilke's journey to the East that finally helped him overcome the intellectual crisis that beset him after finishing *Malte*.

Rilke's experience of Islam and the Muslim way of thinking was to flourish into maturity in his highly acclaimed *Duino Elegies*. It took Rilke a whole decade to accomplish this remarkable work. In the *Duino Elegies*, he depicts European Man lost in his alienated environment. But at the same time an alternative existence is presented in which man, animals and plants are unified with their origins and in which both aspects of existence, life and death, are naturally dissolved into each other. It is a world in which there is no fear of death, because people live in a state of selflessness, in a transformed state of mind in which life and death are no longer opposites, but are complementary elements of a single entity. It is a world closely related to that of the Islamic mystic.

On the completion of the *Duino Elegies* on 10 March, 1922 Rilke wrote to clergyman Rudolf Zimmermann, confessing that he felt closer to both the Old Testament and the Qur'an than to the New Testament. Here he summed up in a few words what fascinated him so much about Islam:

> And once I tried to learn the Qur'an by heart. I didn't get far but what I did understand was that there you see a mighty index finger, pointing towards God, grasped in his eternal rise, in an Orient that will never be exhausted.[7]

In 1922, the year in which Rilke completed the Elegies, which he regarded as the ultimate task of his life, symbolizing the fruition of his mystic quest, one of Europe's most renowned experts on Islam and Islamic mysticism, Annemarie Schimmel – was born in the German town of Erfurt. She was to dedicate herself entirely to the study of Islam and to become one of Europe's rare advocates and campaigners for cooperation and understanding between the Islamic and the Christian cultures. If Rilke, as he himself had admitted on many occasions, had only touched the surface in his attempt to grasp the inner meaning

---

7 Rainer Maria Rilke, *Sämtliche Werke*, op. cit., Volume II, p. 1113. (Translation by N. B. R. Reeves)

of Muhammad's religious philosophy – Schimmel gained a unique and profound insight into the spirituality of Islam. And unlike Rilke, she saw affinities between Islamic and Christian mysticism. Her numerous publications and translations on different aspects of the Muslim faith won her several prizes in Europe and the Islamic East, particularly for promoting tolerance between Islam and Christianity. The latest of these awards was the prestigious German Peace Book Prize bestowed on her during the Frankfurt Book Fair in October 1995, but which caused a great deal of controversy. Annemarie Schimmel, who has taught as a professor of Islamic Studies at several universities, including Bonn, Ankara and Harvard, had sharply criticized Salman Rushdie in a television interview for injuring the feelings of Muslims 'in a very evil manner'.[8] She said that, although she did not support Khomeini's Fatwa or death edict, imposed on the author of *The Satanic Verses* in 1989, writers had a duty to respect the religious beliefs of others. She said she had seen 'grown men weep'[9] when they learned of the contents of Rushdie's book. Schimmel was misunderstood by many of her compatriots who thought that she had placed herself on the side of the Fundamentalists. One of her own colleagues, Gernot Rotter, professor of contemporary Middle Eastern studies at the University of Hamburg, called on the Börsenverein, the German Book Trade Association, which awarded the Prize, to review their decision. In an article in *Die Zeit*, Rotter said:

> A peace prize is for peace. When the winner is touched by even a shadow understanding for a death penalty then the decision should be reconsidered – by both sides.[10]

Rotter said it was shameful that while some Muslim clerics and intellectuals had the courage to condemn the death sentence on Rushdie, Germany's most famous scholar of the Islamic faith was demanding 'understanding for weeping Muslims'. His view naturally won sympathy in Germany where Islamic fundamentalism is a heated political issue. In January 1995 the German airline Lufthansa provoked wide public

---

8 *The Times Higher Education Supplement*, 13 October 1995, p. 19 (Perspective). The article is based on an interview with Professor Annemarie Schimmel by Jennie Brookman and is entitled: 'Fragile Figure in Eye of Storm'.
9 Ibid.
10 Ibid.

criticism because it refused to accept Rushdie as a passenger. But the Börsenverein stuck by Professor Schimmel and said that she deserved to be awarded the prize. This Book Prize is awarded each October Fair for 'literary, scientific or artistic work which supports the idea of peace'.

In one of her major works, *Mystische Dimensionen des Islam* (*Mystical Dimensions of Islam*), Annemarie Schimmel writes:

> Whoever studies Islam in the West and becomes accustomed to the traditional image of Muhammad as it has developed in the Christian world over centuries of hatred and hostility, will be amazed to witness the powerful mystical qualities that are ascribed to this man in the Sufi tradition, a man whom the ordinary European is used to regarding as a sly and sensual politician and at best as the founder of a heresy derived from Christianity. Even the most recent studies of the Prophet, which show his honesty and profoundly religious attitude, betray nothing of the msytical love that his followers feel for him. A Prophet who was so certain of being God's instrument must indeed have been a great man of prayer; for precisely through prayer he could sense over and over again the presence of the God who had sent him.[11]

Schimmel's effort throughout her work has been to illustrate the central importance of Muhammad's figure in Muslim thought and practice and how he is revered as the key religious image in Islam. For the scholars of Islamic law, the Prophet is the legislator-jurist who defined the rights and obligations of Muslim men and women; for the mystic, he is the ideal seeker on a journey to spiritual perfection; and for the philosopher and the statesman, he is the role-model for both a resolute leader and a just ruler. For most ordinary Muslims, the Prophet is a model for living, a source through whom flowed God's grace and salvation. And as the thirteenth century Islamic mystic Rumi had said, he was 'the evidence of God's existence'. Indeed, Schimmel analyses the works of several Islamic mystics, including Rumi's, in which the virtues and physical and spiritual beauty of the Prophet are extolled both in prose and poetry. At the same time the reader is reminded that this is an idealization and not an idolization, as Muhammad himself had forbidden any cult of personality. He had repeatedly said that nothing would upset him more than finding

---

11 Annemarie Schimmel, *Mystische Dimensionen des Islam*, München (Munich), 1995, pp. 51–2. (Translation by N. B. R. Reeves)

out that his people worshipped him instead of God. Muhammad's only objection to Christianity had been what he considered as worship of Man. For him only the Almighty God, the Creator of Heaven and Earth was worthy of worship and nobody beside Him.

Annemarie Schimmel was not the first European critic to defend Muhammad against his demonization in the West. But her apologia carried a much greater weight and credibility than that of the few others. This is due to her expertise in Islamic thought. Prior to her efforts in rehabilitating Islam and Muhammad, Comte de Boulainvilliers in the eighteenth century and Thomas Carlyle in the nineteenth century, both social critics, had condemned Christian theological, artistic and historical writings for defaming Muhammad and his religion. They had also stood up in defence of Muhammad's moral and spiritual qualities and profound quest for the betterment of human society. But it was not until the first decades of the twentieth century that the relentless search for both historical and spiritual Muhammad began to correct the vilifying stereotype propagated in Christian theology and which had been the basis for his general rejection in Europe. A whole array of apologetic volumes including revised biographies and new translations of the Qur'an began to appear in several European languages. Most biographers and translators of the Qur'an adopted a favourable approach to Muhammad, feeling the need to rebut his European image and to highlight his spiritual significance.

One of the first positive assessments of Muhammad's life and achievements was Dagohert von Mikusch's *Mohammed: Tragödie des Erfolgs* (*Muhammad: Tragedy of Success*). In his foreword Mikusch asks a straightforward question 'What motivated Mohammed, an honourable merchant in Mecca, from a noble family and affiliated by marriage to a wealthy widow, to see his true role in preaching a divinely inspired religion which was to unite Man with God?'[12] Mikusch found the core of his answer in Goethe's tribute to Muhammad's genius and his call to Prophethood, that had appeared in his autobiographical work *Dichtung und Wahrheit*. Here Goethe had said that Muhammad had simply been overwhelmed by the feeling that he had to let the wider world know about the divine message which was driving within him. For Goethe

---

12 Dagohert von Mikusch, *Mohammed: Tragödie des Erfolgs*, Leipzig, 1932, Vorwort (Foreword), pp. 7–8.

this irresistible need to impart what was within to others was the characteristic of genius. Mikusch decided that he had to return to the Qur'an and to the early sources with a fresh, unprejudiced eye. He discovered that the success and expansion of Muhammad's religion was the cause of hostility with which he was treated by the West. As a result, the essential character of Muhammad which emerges from Mikusch's biography is one of ardent piety and pure and elevated morality devoted to higher purposes of life.

Other European biographers lived for several years amongst the Bedouin Arabs in the desert to visualize and conjure up the feelings and thoughts that may have affected Muhammad. One such attempt was made by R. V. C. Bodley whose popular biography *The Messenger*, is one of the rare accounts of Muhammad's life written from a perspective close to that of Muslims themselves. Bodley depicts the religion of Arabia, between Mecca and Medina, where Muhammad lived and preached his beliefs. If a Muslim of the seventh century were to return to that region today, Bodley says, nothing would surprise him, because the Arabs lived in a kind of timeless reality. Bodley's depictions were similar to those of Rilke's who had also felt that it was as if the Prophet had been there only yesterday:

> The nomad Arabs in their black tents, the travellers on their camels, the pilgrims streaming over the desert from the Red Sea would all be there as he had left them. So would the people's clothes, so would their physical appearance. The way of dressing has hardly altered at all. The seventh century Moslem would even be able to recognise tribes pasturing around Mecca, with the same names as in the days of Mohammed. Among the tribesmen he would find men directly descended from the people of his time.[13]

Bodley's Arab friends spoke to him of the founder of their faith as someone they knew. He had been a shepherd, he had worn the same kind of robes, he had ridden identical camels, his diet had been similar to theirs. Everything they did, they could associate with him. Muhammad was alive to these nomads as if he were one of them still. It was therefore easier for Bodley to reconstruct the scene thirteen hundred years before. Bodley believed that most modern European biographies of Muhammad

---

13 R. V. C. Bodley, *The Messenger*, London, 1946, Introduction, p. 3.

lacked the background of desert life which had inspired Muhammad spiritually and had helped to bring Islam into being. Because the biographers did not want to venture into those desolate regions of Arabia and expose themselves to the discomfort of nomadic existence, they simply imagined from the luxury of their homes in Europe how Muhammad must have felt and acted. Bodley writes:

> My attempt, therefore has been to present Mohammed as he really was – an Arab like many I knew in the desert; a man of simple tastes, but of great personality, with the good of his people at heart; a man who was inspired, but thought out all he did logically: Mohammed's tastes were simple and aesthetic, but he was also a man of the world. Neither was it a world of the remote past. Mohammed would not have felt ill at ease in society. He married and had children. He was a fine horseman, he could make his own shoes and mend his own clothes. He had a good sense of humour. He knew himself to be a leader, but he was never boastful and never tried to create anything resembling a court. He never led anyone to believe that he had supernatural gifts.[14]

Bodley sums up his own attempt at producing a biography of Muhammad in these words:

> There is nothing startlingly new about Mohammed in this biography. All that may have been introduced which is fresh is to show how circumstances made Mohammed do some things which to Occidentals have remained obscure. This has been possible owing to my long association with Arabs, to my friendship with them.[15]

Bodley continues defending Muhammad against adverse European views by bringing to light his conviviality, his modesty and his kind and affectionate nature. He reproaches Europe for rejecting him as an impostor:

> The Muslims follow the example of the founder of their faith who ruled Arabia but had no compunction about dining with a slave or sharing his dates with a beggar.
> Could a man who was not inspired have brought such an international brotherhood into being?

14 Ibid., p. 8.
15 Ibid., p. 9.

Does not the scoffing of the anti-Moslems rather reflect on themselves? Why should an impostor have left a creed which has grown ever since he died? Today the number of followers of the Moslem faith increase by a quarter of a million every year! And this without any persuasive disciples to preach the message of Islam.

The biography reminds the reader that the misunderstandings and hostilities between Christianity and Islam were brought on by the Crusades. It was from then on that 'Mohammed' became practically synonymous with 'blasphemy' for the Christians of Europe. What these denouncers of the 'False Prophet' seem to have missed, Bodley points out, is that, in the advent of Islam there was little difference of opinion between Muslims and Christians. Throughout his ministry, Muhammad would not have been offended to be thought a Christian, Bodley argues. The best evidence for this, he says, was that when Muhammad was persecuted, he sought and found protection for his people with the King of Abyssinia who ruled over a Christian Kingdom.

The twentieth century has also seen a revival of academic research in the West, and Muhammad has been viewed from an array of critical perspectives, attempting to verify the authenticity of Muslim early sources. One such critical biography was written by Rudi Paret entitled *Mohammed und der Koran (Muhammad and the Qur'an)*. Paret also produced a new translation of the Qur'an. His investigations led him to believe that:

Mohammed was in the very essence of his being a religious man. The key to understanding his personality lies in his religiosity. If in the pages that follow a stance is taken on a number of disputed features of Mohammed's personality and character, I have done it to be as just as possible to this Arab prophet but at the same time in the conviction that all knowledge is fragmentary, and to a good extent subjectively coloured. Every historian approaches the matter of his investigation with basic views that are peculiar to him and to his Age, and from the perspective that he thinks are particularly important and revealing.[16]

To the age-old European claim that Muhammad was a deceiver, Paret's view is clear-cut and devoid of ambiguity:

16 Rudi Paret, *Mohammed und der Koran, Geschichte und Verkündigung des arabischen Propheten*, Stuttgart, 1957. p. 136.

The accusation of dishonesty which has been laid against the Prophet time and again over the centuries up to the most recent times with varying degrees of vehemence is relatively easy to refute. Mohammed was not a deceptor.[17]

Paret argued that historians should not make the error of judging the Arabian prophet by a Christian yardstick and by the model set by Jesus who said that his Kingdom was not of this world. Muhammad, in contrast to early Christendom, had lived in a community in which the individual regarded himself as part of an all-pervasive communal life. He explains:

In Mecca the realm of religion was not excluded, as in the world of early Christianity, from that of politics . . . On his emigration to Medina the opportunity opened up for him for the first time to bring his followers together in a closed, independent unit. From then on one step followed another almost inevitably until finally the all-embracing Arab-Islamic Umma had become real. During all this Mohammed was in no way driven by the thrust of power. On the contrary, as we were able to show, he gave God the credit for even the greatest military and political successes, in deep humility. Nothing had changed in his fundamental attitude. His sense of mission remained the same one might say, as in the good old days.[18]

But perhaps the most renowned of the biographers who treated Muhammed, his divine inspirations and his role as a spiritual as well as a temporal leader from a historical and analytical perspective was W. Montgomery Watt. Watt gained a positive picture of Muhammad through his research based on a thorough analysis of early sources and acceptance only of those accounts that are backed by strong evidence. His two volume biography *Muhammad at Mecca* and *Muhammad at Medina* published in 1953 and 1956 were a remarkable contribution to the rehabilitation of Muhammad's image in Europe.

Watt investigated amongst other issues the controversial story of the Satanic Verses in his volume *Muhammad at Mecca* and came to the conclusion that Muhammad, by virtue of not accepting the offer made to him by the leaders of powerful Meccan Quraysh tribe at the advent

---

17 Ibid., p. 136.
18 Ibid., p. 138. (Translations by N. B. R. Reeves)

of Islam, not only proved his integrity to his cause and detachment from worldly ambitions but also saved the fundamental religious and social reform upon which he had set his heart.

Montgomery Watt, formerly Professor of Arabic and Islamic Studies at the University of Edinburgh, who has published many scholarly volumes on Islam, confirms Muhammad's purely religious and spiritual motives in preaching Islam and not the worldly pleasures which have been attributed to him by his European critics: With regard to the alleged Satanic Verses, Watt declares:

> Thus it was not for any worldly motive that Muhammad eventually turned down the offer of the Meccans, but for a genuinely religious reason; not for example, because he could not trust these men nor because any personal ambition would remain unsatisfied, but because acknowledgement of the goddesses would lead to the failure of the cause, of the mission he had been given by God [19]

Watt takes up the issue of the vilification of Muhammad in European writings in an article entitled *'Muhammad in the Eyes of the West'*. His introductory remarks are revealing. They demonstrate the dilemma of objectivity and impartiality, when dealing with history and religion – which many historians have failed to overcome.

The Christian world, Watt stresses, has traditionally rejected Islam as the other religion and has felt unceasingly threatened by it:

> To spend some time looking at the various ways in which through the centuries our Western world has thought of Muhammad and conceived his significance is not simply to take a leisurely stroll through some of the byways of history. The topic raised profound questions about the nature of objectivity in the fields of history and religion, and matters of contemporary relevance are also involved. There are in the world about a thousand million Christians and half that number of Muslims, and some of the world's urgent political problems might be easier to solve if these two great religious communities had a deeper respect for each other's religion. Yet for Westerners none of the world's religious leaders is so difficult to

---

19 W. Montgomery Watt, *Muhammad at Mecca*, Oxford, 1953. 'The Growth of Opposition', p. 105.

appreciate as Muhammad, since the West has a deep-seated prejudice against him.[20]

After providing a brief overview of the history of the demonization of Muhammad in Europe, Watt turns his attention to modern biographers who in his view have dealt with Muhammad inevitably only from the angle they have been interested in. Watt asks a crucial question whether it is at all possible to have an objective estimate of Muhammad and his achievements, if everyone sees in him just what he wants to see? And he answers the question thus:

> The answer appears to be that while pure objectivity in an abstract sense is impossible in the case of a man like Muhammad, since any judgement about him is bound to be relative to the writer's whole culture and system of values, yet a measure of objectivity is attainable in practice by adopting, or at least approximating, what might be called 'the standpoint of the whole'. This conception is to be understood against the background of a world rapidly becoming 'one world' at the physical level (travel and communication) and also, though more slowly, at the intellectual, cultural and religious level. In the religious sphere it is difficult at the moment to envisage a take-over by any one religion. The next step would appear to be mutual recognition and mutual appreciation of one another by the world religions.[21]

Watt recognizes that the attainment of such tolerant attitude is a painful process, since it requires the revision of some basic beliefs and values within oneself. But he definitely regards the process as absolutely vital in the present situation of the world. He believes that it is necessary for each religion to see itself as part of the total religious experience of mankind.

In France, it was Maxime Rodinson who adopted a similar universalist approach to religion as Watt's while producing his biographical account of Muhammad published in Paris in 1969. An English translation by Anne Carter of his *Mahomet* appeared in 1971. Rodinson, who drew his knowledge of Muhammad and of Islam from many years of study

---

20 W. Montgomery Watt, 'Muhammad in the Eyes of the West', Boston University Journal 22, No. 3, (Fall 1974). p. 61.
21 Ibid., p. 69.

and research, mostly in the Islamic lands themselves, is one of France's leading experts in the field. He expresses his own stance in his foreword:

> Muhammad was a religious genius, a great political thinker – and a man like you or me. He was not these things on three separate levels; they are three aspects of a total personality, and can only be seen in distinction by a careful analysis. Everything he did or said involved something of all these aspects of the man. Those whose main interest is in the religious man and his message have a lot to gain from understanding the non-religious motivations and repercussions of his actions. Those who see him primarily as a historical force should think carefully about the importance of the ideology which made him that kind of force; and indeed of that ideology itself.[22]

Perhaps the most honest confession of why the Europeans were still incapable of accepting Muhammad as an inspired leader of a world religion was expressed in the 1978 edition of *The Cambridge History of Islam* under a chapter on Muhammad: it demonstrates that in spite of the attempt made by writers to rid themselves of the persistent influence of medieval thinking on the modern perspectives of Muhammad and Islam, Muhammad was still unconsciously measured against the purely Christian distinction between what is 'religious' and what is 'secular', what 'temporal' and what 'spiritual':

> For the occidental reader there are grave difficulties in attaining a balanced understanding of the historical role of Muhammad. The most serious of these is that the dominant conception of religion as a private and individual matter leads men to expect that a religious leader will be a certain kind of man; and it is disconcerting to find that Muhammad does not conform to this expectation. He was undoubtedly a religious leader; but for him religion was the total response of his personality to the total situation in which he found himself. He was responding not only to what the occidental would call the religious and intellectual aspects of the situation, but also the social, economic and political pressures to which contemporary Mecca was subject. Because he was great as a leader his influence was important in all these spheres and it is impossible for any occidental

---

22 Maxime Rodinson, *Mahomet*, translated by Anne Carter, London, 1971, Foreword to the Second edition, p. xvii.

to distinguish within his achievement between what is religious and what is non-religious and secular.[23]

The article stresses another difficulty facing Europeans when assessing Muhammad:

> Another difficulty is that some occidental readers are still not completely free from the prejudices inherited from their medieval ancestors. In the bitterness of the Crusades and other wars against the Saracens, they came to regard the Muslims, and in particular Muhammad, as the incarnation of all that was evil, and the continuing effect of the propaganda of that period has not yet been completely removed from occidental thinking about Islam.[24]

Just two decades after the publication of *The Cambridge Encyclopedia of Islam* article on Muhammad, decades that had witnessed two oil crises, the toppling of the Shah of Iran, the emergence of the Islamic Republic in that country and a war in the Lebanon, there burst upon the world a work that was to ignite religious passions in East and West, already sensitized by the militancy of Islam and the onslaught on the Western way of life led by the Ayatollah Khomeini. It was Salman Rushdie's novel *The Satanic Verses*.

Like many satirical works *The Satanic Verses* takes earlier materials, motifs, tales, images, and recasts them, juxtaposes them, relativizes them in the time-honoured manner of all caricatures, lampoons or travesties. But like all caricatures it also magnifies, it distorts and it makes the serious laughable. In a word, satire is mischievous. It can be mischievous in the way naughty boys are. But it can also be mischievous in its effect, playing with what serious-minded people hold to be sacred. Satire can be cruel because it can trample with impunity upon feelings dear to people's hearts. It possesses the amorality of detached art. Ironically the outright attacks of the earlier opponents of Muhammad, the epithets of Dante, the fulminations of Luther and other men of the Church, the vituperations of Marlowe, the mockery of Rabelais, the blood and thunder

---

23 *The Cambridge History of Islam*, Volume I. 'The Central Islamic Lands', edited by P. M. Holt, Ann K. S. Lambton and Bernard Lewis, Cambridge, 1978, Chapter 2, 'Muhammad' p. 30.

24 Ibid., p. 30.

of Voltaire may have been easier to cope with. They can be dismissed as the frenzy of fanatical opponents. But the pen of a satirist, however playful, however subtle in its use of paralleled action, of analogy and ambivalence, can seem more insidious, more threatening because it is almost impossible to answer in kind. For a vulnerable Muslim world, fuelled by historical grievance, by economic difficulties, by an overriding sense of helplessness in a world in which the figure of Muhammad is serving as comfort and a supreme source of inspiration Rushdie's satirization of Muhammad's life and deeds were explosively offensive and hurtful.

The Satanic Verses is a highly complex psychodrama and although narrated in a comic style, it poses serious and pertinent questions. Its main preoccupation may appear at first glance to be nothing but the vilification of Islam and its founder, 'the Prophet Mahound' in the novel, as the crusading demonologists knew him! But on a deeper level it depicts the trauma of the transformations of cultural identity that affects the Muslim migrant on the one hand and the Muslim sceptic at home on the other. They share the same inner conflict. The migrant protagonist of the novel leaves his homeland and is compelled to assimilate values, attitudes and habits that are alien to him. He gradually loses faith in his own religion and his own culture in order to please the people of his adopted country. The sceptic re-evaluates the religious beliefs into which he has been born in the course of his own struggle for existence. His eyes gradually open up to new realities, as he is compelled in today's society to rely increasingly on himself alone. His daily experiences begin to cast doubts on the benevolence of a God that has promised happiness and contentment to the faithful.

The Satanic Verses is about belief and unbelief, about theology and myth, about spirituality and physicality, about reality and dream. it is about the loss of faith and loss of identity. It is in a sense the world of Salman Rushdie himself, displaced and uprooted through his British upbringing and schooling. But the doubts of a man disillusioned about his cultural and religious background are expressed in violent, obscene and often gratuitously offensive imagery and language. Rushdie's travestied biographical novel outraged a Muslim world from which he himself has been alienated and which he felt able to satirize with detachment.

The author questions Islam's claim to Truth, not as a straightforward atheist, but as someone who is still emotionally involved yet seeks to distance himself from that involvement through satire. His assault on the image of Muhammad was seen as an assault on a man who is firmly lodged in the psyche of Muslims for whom life without Muhammad would lose its entire meaning. The use of the name 'Mahound' for the travestied depiction of the fictional prophet – the medieval epithet by which people of Europe swore and which was synonymous with the name of the Devil in the Middle Ages – highlights this assault.

The themes of religion and identity are carried with a relentless narrative impulse across the entire novel by the portrayal of lives, thoughts and actions of the two protagonists Ismail Najmuddin and Saladin Chamcha. Gibreel Farishta, meaning Gabriel Angel, is an endearing nick-name given Ismail by his late mother, because he had been such a good child! Chamcha on the other hand is Saladin's abbreviated Indian surname which is intended to facilitate his integration into British life as a migrant. As it transpires, Saladin is the son of a Bombay magnate who has been sent to Britain to receive a Western education and who, contrary to his father's bourgeois ambitions, decides to become an actor. Gibreel is already a superstar in the Indian movies with numerous fans who worship him like God. He is a flamboyant schizophrenic dreamer who believes in reincarnation. His hallucinatory Alter Ego, his Archangelic Other-Self, is the Angel Gabriel, the bearer and revelator of the Qur'an to Muhammad.

Fate eventually brings the two men together, not through their acting careers, but through a far more dramatic accident. They are the only survivors of the wreck of a plane, scheduled for a flight from Bombay to London but which is hijacked and blown up by three Muslim extremists; two men and one woman. It is the woman who detonates the bomb when they reach the skies above the British Isles. In the crash everyone is killed, including the hijackers themselves. Only Gibreel and Chamcha are saved. Their fall from the skies is symbolically coined 'the Angelic-devilish Fall' by the author and is assisted by Gibreel's celestial Other Self who as Chamcha's guardian Angel provides him with wings similar to his own. While they float in the air as in Heaven, Gibreel sings his favourite reincarnation song encouraging Chamcha to learn and grasp its inner meaning: 'To be born again, first you have to die'. This is clearly a metaphor intentionally used by Rushdie who is familiar with Islamic mystic thought. It is a metaphor that in effect constitutes the narrative thread right through the novel to the very end and is the core concept of the spirituality of Islam, satirically distorted here. It is based on a commonly quoted saying attributed to Muhammad: 'I had died before I was born'.

But the song of Muhammad is sung in Rushdie's *Satanic Verses*, not by a pious mystic, but by a cynic, a psychotic hallucinator, Gibreel Farishta, this dubious character with a shady identity. He does not exactly know who he really is, God incarnate or Devil incarnate? In his hallucinations he does not recognize whether he hears the voice of God or the promptings of the Devil. In his waking life he reminds himself of his mother's picture of himself; heavenly, sweet-tempered, kind, sincere, 'a Goddamn Gold', as he confides to Chamcha after their fantastic fall from the skies. He also relates that he has been the epitome of absolute goodness (as Muhammad is known to his followers!). Just to lay eyes on him made his mother's dreams come true. He was her personal Angel, her Divine blessing, for which she was more than grateful to the Almighty. His change of name from Ismail Najmuddin to Gibreel Farishta, he confesses, had been a tribute to his dead mother's memory. But in reality, Gibreel was not the man that his mother had idolized and worshipped. He was not in the least angelic. As a matter of fact, he was often the Devil Incarnate, driven by all the devilish desires that anyone could think of. His insatiable lust for women for whom he did not feel any love, affection or respect, his self-obsession, his cunning, his ruthlessness – characteristics which had enabled him to rise to wealth and fame – were completely unholy. But he had an excuse for all of these, a justification for turning into the monster he had become. Life itself had shown him that being a servant of God was not such a good idea as it had seemed to his mother. God had often been indifferent, oblivious to his plight when he had badly needed help. During his wrestling with life, God had proved to be unreliable. He had let Gibreel down, had deserted him and had made him lose faith in the existence and benevolence of an omnipresent, omnipotent and omniscient God who rewarded the good and punished the evil. As a result Gibreel became in every way the caricatured opposite of his namesake, the Angel Gabriel, who he imagines himself to be. But the Muslim reader knows the Angel Gabriel as the Angel who revealed God's Word to Muhammad. At the same time the ugly images of medieval Christian fabrications that Muhammad was deluded and suffered from epileptic fits and that his revelations were either hallucinations or promptings from the Devil spring to mind. Moreover, Gibreel's characteristics as licentious and ruthlessly ambitious are characteristics traditionally attributed to Muhammad by his Western opponents. In his character Rushdie's Gibreel has close resemblance to the age-old European caricature of Muhammad. But to make the caricature more plausible even biographical fact such as making Gibreel, like Muhammad, an orphan who is compelled to earn a living at an early age, is mixed in.

Gibreel reveals the story of his life and how he had lost faith in the divinity of the Qur'an and Muhammad's message. He reveals it to Chamcha, his companion and disciple whose life he has miraculously saved. They are now recovering on a British beach where Gibreel can talk about his dreams and the whole idea of reincarnation which had preoccupied him all his life.

In his secular reincarnation, to use Rushdie's own term, Gibreel Farishta had been born in British Poona. However, in his infancy, he had been taken to the 'Bitch City', to Bombay, where his father had found a job as a food delivery man. At thirteen Gibreel had been compelled to follow in his father's footsteps. Soon afterwards his mother had been hit by a bus in the city and had died instantly. Father and son had buried their sadness beneath constant hard work which had eventually worn down the father. One day, when Gibreel was hardly nineteen, a sudden stroke had finished his father off, leaving the orphaned boy to the futurelessness of the Bombay streets. A childless merchant of the metropolis's grand Bazaar, an awesome, fat Budda-like figure, Babasaheb, had taken pity on him and had persuaded his wife to look after him, as if he were their own child. But she had been unable to give Gibreel love. She had been harsh and uncaring, determined to make a man of him so that he could look after himself and leave. While she stuffed herself and her big fat husband so full that they could hardly walk, she practically starved the boy of food.

But Babasaheb was basically a kindly man himself, and Gibreel was grateful to him for having saved him from the nightmare of Bombay streets. Babasaheb was also a psychic who had introduced Gibreel to the idea of reincarnation. Once the merchant had recounted that during a séance his glass had been visited by a friendly spirit. So, Babasaheb had asked the spirit whether there was a God? At once, the glass which had been running round and round on the table had stopped. Not a twitch, completely dead, motionless. The room had been filled with silence. Then Babasaheb had asked the spirit whether there was a Devil? And to his absolute amazement the glass had instantly begun to shake and rattle – slowly at first but faster and faster thereafter, jumping up and down, backwards and forwards until it had smashed itself into a thousand and one pieces. The table had been covered by shattered particles of glass. The story had profoundly affected Babasaheb's young listener, because long before his mother's death Gibreel had become convinced of the existence of a supernatural, transcendental world beyond. He had in fact grown up believing in God, in Angels, Demons, Djinns and of course in Muhammad. From his mother he had heard a great many stories about the Prophet and his Greatness. 'What a Man!', he had thought, 'What Angel would not wish to speak to him?'[25] So Muhammad had become his role-model, he wanted to be like him. Sometimes, he even compared his own condition with that of the Prophet, how he had been orphaned and how he had to struggle with no funds through life. But he had made a great success of his career and of his job as the caravan leader of the wealthy Khadija and had ended up marrying her. And of course he had become the leader of Arabia through his insistence that there was only one God and that he was the Prophet of God and had married several women.

The episode of day-dreaming came to an end on the morning of Gibreel's twenty-first birthday, when he was summoned by his benefactor and protector and sacked for no reason at all. Babasaheb was even unprepared to listen to an appeal. 'You are fired', he commanded, 'Boy like you is too damn good looking to carry tiffins on his head all his life. Get gone now, go, be a homosexual movie actor. I fired you five minutes back'.[26] And so it was that Gibreel was put out on the streets again. Babasaheb's charity had reached its limits. Young Gibreel had to pack and leave, to get on with life on his own. He became Gibreel Farishta, the actor, but it took him four years to become a star. He decided to educate himself and catch up with what he had missed in his early youth. He began to read compulsively, devouring everything that came his way, from Greek and Roman mythology to the origins of monotheistic religions. But what fascinated him most was Muhammad's experience of Prophethood and his encounter with the Angel Gabriel. He was particularly impressed by the incident of the Satanic Verses in the early career of the Prophet, by his politics, his popularity, and his relationships with women. In his dreams he was tormented by women of unbearable

---

25 Salman Rushdie, *The Satanic Verses*, The Consortium Inc., Dover-Delaware, 1992 (paperback edition), p. 22.
26 Ibid., p. 23.

beauty and sweetness which he believed were the type of women who loved and pampered Muhammad in his 'harem'. In his waking life, he was frustrated too. Because he knew he had the capacity for love, but not the power and status that could win beautiful women's hearts. So, he went on envying Muhammad for his 'luck with women' and decided to put all his efforts into becoming a great star, so that women could admire and worship him like he thought they worshipped Muhammad. To fulfill his ambition, Gibreel became the most self-seeking member of the most self-seeking industry on earth, the film industry. Here, once again, Rushdie revived the old prejudice about Muhammad that he used religion to rise to power and to indulge in worldly pleasures, as Gibreel seeks to emulate him in the pursuit of his desires.

One day the breakthrough came for Gibreel. He was offered the script of his life by Bombay's greatest film director. He wanted Gibreel to act in a highly popular series known as *Theologicals*, involving the ancient religions and their leaders. Suddenly Gibreel was a superstar. His anguish vanished. Power and fame soon embraced him. He found himself in an avalanche of approaches from women, young, old, married, unmarried. They all wanted to be loved by him and appear in public beside him. Rushdie again uses analogy here to the myth that when Muhammad moved from Mecca to Medina all his hardship vanished and he rose to a position of wealth and power and above all of self-indulgence and libertanism. This is indeed a libertanism in which the author engages his hallucinating protagonist, as wine, food and women become his vocation in life. But Gibreel's world eventually collapses in doubts about himself, about love, about the purpose of life, about God. During the filming of one of his theological movies he is injured in a mock flight and has to go to hospital. For months on end he does not stop bleeding from all his cavities. In his distress and helplessness for having been rejected by God he declares that God is dead. To prove it, upon his release, he goes straight to the city's famous hotel, where he orders a whole feast of the forbidden food, pork, in all its possible variations, fillets, chops, bacon, sausages, ham, ribs, loin. Under the gaze of photographers and reporters the filmstar stuffs the dead pig meat into his face so rapidly and with such eagerness that bacon rashers hung out of the sides of his mouth. It is clear that he has utterly changed, he has lost faith in Islam. It is also the end of his stardom. God is dead but also the star, the idol.

At this point in the novel the apostate disappears from Bombay. But the reader finds him aboard the aircraft which is destroyed in mid-air by terrorists in what may be a parodistic version of Muhammad's legendary night flight assisted by the Angel Gabriel from Mecca to Jerusalem and from the Temple Mount to the Throne of God. But at the same time it is a parody of the Christian fall from grace, the story of the Fallen Angel, Lucifer. The two protagonists Gibreel and Chamcha come floating down on to a British beach. During their fall they had encountered yet another caricature from Muhammad's life, the Goddess Al Lat, one of the three pagan deities whom Muhammad had banned in favour of his only and one God, Allah. But in this case she is disguised as Rekha, the rich Bombay carpet dealer, a beautiful married woman, whom Gibreel the filmstar, has jilted and who had commited suicide in despair. She is filled with vengeance and throws oaths at her former lover while also floating in the skies.

Sitting on the cold beach Gibreel narrates a dream, in effect a satire within a satire. The dream is of himself, reincarnated in another age when he was the Angel Gabriel. It is a rebirth that occurs in a parodistic reversal of time. Those cold sands of the British beach vanish, to give way to the burning sands of the Arabian desert. They are in Mecca, the birthplace of Muhammad and of Islam. From his vantage-point above the Meccan valley, here named Jahilia (the Arabic for the Age of Ignorance prior to the Rise of Islam), the Angel observes a businessman called Mahound, trekking to a mountain cave. The readers are told directly that he has assumed the swear-name given him by his enemies as a token of his identity, yet that Mahound was the medieval name for the Devil, the children's bogeyman. We watch Mahound receive his revelations as a businessman turned prophet. But Abu Simbel, the Ruler of Jahilia, (Abu Sufyan) and his wife Hind, have already turned against him, because his message 'One, One, One' threatens the many gods, the 360 idols and especially the three goddesses Al Lat, Al Uza and Manat that they worship. Moreover, the House of the Black Stone is a source of wealth for Abu Simbel and the inhabitants of Jahilia since the House is visited each year by flocks of pagan pilgrims. To stem Mahound's appeal, Abu Simbel has employed a satirist, Baal, to write malicious verse slogans to discredit and ridicule Mahound – slogans that are hung around the House of the Black Stone, a reference to Islam's most revered shrine, the House of God. Hind, the power behind Abu Simbel, is the protectress of the old goddesses, an habitual adultress and a lover of Baal. Indeed, Jahilia is renowned as a den of vice, with gambling, gangsterism, kidnapping and prostitution the norm. It is reminiscent of Bertolt Brecht's imaginary city of corrupt capitalism, Mahagonny, and indeed we find that Mahound's tribe is the Shark tribe. His three first converts and disciples are Bilal, the slave, Khalid, the water-carrier, and Salman, the Persian migrant. They are easy targets for Baal who gives them obscene nicknames.

But Abu Simbel also tried to change Mahound's mind about the One and Only God, Allah, by offering him power within the tribe provided that he acknowledged the three goddesses as daughters of Allah. Mahound attends a meeting with the pagans. He recites to the joyful audience the Satanic Verses. Immediately Abu Simbel and his supporters proclaim the words Allah Akbar, Allah is Great, and are thus 'converts' to Islam – to much confusion and bewilderment on the part of Mahound's own disciples. And subsequently Mahound, having slept, finds himself awaking in Hind's bed. Hind now negotiates for the equal treatment of her three goddesses whom Mahound had recognized in his recitation of the Satanic Verses as daughters of God. To ascertain whether the three goddesses can be Allah's equals or only his daughters Mahound, in confusion, goes to his cave.

Intensely worried, he begins now to draw Gibreel deeper and deeper into his realm, pressing him more and more for the Truth, for Revelation, though Gibreel, as he protests to himself, is really no more than an actor in a former existence. So fervent is Mahound's effort to try and squeeze more knowlege out of Gibreel, that the latter imagines they have become conjoined, a single entity, while in a grotesque and obscene further twist the two men even engage in a wrestling match in the nude, after which Mahound, rising from his exhaustion declares that the Angel had really been Shaitan, Satan, the Devil. So Gabriel recounts his experience of wrestling with Mahound;

> It happens: revelation, like this. Mahound, still in his notsleep, becomes rigid, veins bulge in his neck, he clutches at his centre. No, no, nothing like an epileptic fit, it can't be explained away that easily; what epileptic fit ever caused day to turn night, caused clouds to mass overhead, caused the air to thicken into soup . . . now the miracle starts in his my our guts, he is straining with all his might at something, forcing something, and Gibreel begins to

feel that strength that force, here it is at my own jaw working it, opening shutting; and the power, starting within Mahound, reaching up to my vocal cords and the voice comes.... Mahound's eyes open wide, he is seeing some kind of vision.[27]

Later, Mahound goes back to the House of the Blackstone and abrogates what the Devil had whispered in his ear before the pagan audience. The three goddesses are denounced in a direct quotation from the Qur'an. 'These are but names you have dreamed of, you and your fathers, Allah vests no authority in them'.[28]

Abu Simbel and Hind become Mahound's arch-enemies. Mahound's converts on the other hand find an explanation for the Satanic Verses that Mahound had initially pronounced – its purpose was to show them the Devil. In a highly ambiguous response Mahound says: 'Yes' – with the author interspersing the words, 'bitterness', 'cynicism' before Mahound's words continue: 'It was a wonderful thing I did. Deeper Truth bringing you the Devil'. 'Yes, that sounds like me!'.[29] And soon after, to escape the death sentence of the vengeful Abu Simbel and Hind, Mahound slips away from Jahilia (Mecca) to Yathrib (Medina). And Gabriel reflects:

> ... it was me both times, baba, me first and second also me. From my mouth, both the statement and the repudiation, verses and converses, universes and reverses, the whole thing, and we all know how my mouth got worked.[30]

The novel then returns to England and the experiences of Gibreel and Chamcha there, where problems of identity, religion and emigration are foregrounded. But Gibreel never stops dreaming; in a further chapter entitled Aysha (the name of one of Muhammad's wives) he imagines an Imam in European exile planning a revolution in an imaginary city called Desh. It is a revolution that will overthrow the ruler, Empress Aysha, put an end to the lax customs – to the rule of science and progress – the great Shaitan – and start time again. The disciples of Mahound, Salman and Bilal appear again as the Imam's assistants, with Bilal as the broadcaster

27   Ibid., p. 112.
28   Ibid., p. 124.
29   Ibid., p. 125.
30   Ibid., p. 123.

in the repeated radio messages transmitted to Desh. And in culmination, the Imam summons Gibreel as the Archangel and sitting on his back, makes the Night Flight to Desh, where the rebellious people are being massacred in cold blood by the Empress's troops. But the people are so many that they crush the troops. Gibreel is commanded by the Imam to kill Aysha. He engages in a deadly airborne battle with her, the White fighting the Black Angel, until she, revealed as the pagan goddess Al Lat, falls to earth and dies. Time is reborn, the Imam is triumphant. The episode is of course a thinly disguised version of Iran's Islamic Revolution, the Imam is Ayatollah Khomeini.

The novel proceeds with further hallucinations by Gibreel, in India and in England, involving again issues of identity, religious disbelief and culture. In the sixth chapter, 'The return to Jahilia', the narrative takes the reader back to Mahound's triumphant return to the city of his birth. Twenty-five years have elapsed. Hind now old, had ruled without challenge, since Mahound's escape to Yathrib. Her armies, sent out in repeated campaigns to destroy Mahound, have been defeated. Jahilia has surrendered. Hind surrenders too, but in a grotesque fashion. Dressed in veil and covered from head to toe, she comes to submit to Mahound. The Submission, the sign of conversion to Islam, takes the form of a protracted obscene physical obeisance between her and Mahound.

Jahilia houses another, closer, enemy, Salman, who had acted as Mahound's scribe for the continuing revelations in Yathrib, but had gradually begun to fabricate Mahound's utterances. The words became fiction, but what began as a test of Mahound's sincerity turns out to be Salman's downfall. For Mahound cannot distinguish between his words and those deliberately altered by the scribe, who wilfully exchanges the word of God for the Word of the Devil and vice-versa. Salman thinks to himself that he has seen through Mahound's 'tricks'. Thus the theme of the Satanic Verses is picked up again in new guise. Finally fearful of retribution, Salman escapes to Jahilia and seeks refuge with none other than the satirist opponent of Mahound, Baal. For Salman, the Persian, had got to:

> Wondering what manner of God this was that sounded so much like a businessman. This was when he had the idea that destroyed his faith, because he recalled that of course Mahound himself had been a businessman, and a damned successful one at that, a person

to whom organization and rules came naturally, so how excessively convenient it was that he should have come up with such a business-like archangel, who handed down the management decisions of this highly corporate, if non-corporal God.[31]

When Mahound re-enters the city and Abu Simbel and Hind have submitted to him, he declares not only the abolition of the temple of the three goddesses but the closure of all the dens of vice, including the brothels. But Abu Simbel argues for a gradual transition period, to which Mahound agrees, and settles in a tent beside the House of the Black Stone, now purged of pagan idols and renamed the House of Allah. He lives with his twelve wives.

The period of transition is to prove a fatal time. Mahound sends his men to seek out Salman. Salman is soon found but slips out of his guilt by declaring Baal, the poet, to be the real culprit, Mahound's real enemy. In a statement that was to be of fateful impact in reality, Salman argues that 'The pen is mightier than the sword'. Baal hides in one of the city's brothels, where he is disguised as a black eunuch, having coloured his skin with black paint, guarding the women, of whom there are twelve. In mocking defiance of Mahound, the brothel-keeper has accepted Baal's suggestion that the twelve prostitutes should be renamed after Mahound's twelve wives. One of the clients had in fact complained that Mahound could have twelve women while they could only have one. He particularly fancied Mahound's youngest wife, Aysha, and was terribly envious of the Prophet. To the brothel-keeper this seemed like a potent way of setting up a counter-weight to the House of God and Baal's suggestion is taken up. The women assume new identities, even to the point of believing they are Mahound's proper wives. They assume the names of The Mothers of the Faithful. Baal himself takes on Mahound's identity as their husband. This is a huge success and the men of Jahilia flock to the Curtain, the Purdah or the Veil (as the brothel is provocatively called), rotating the Fountain of Love in the courtyard, as pilgrims rotate the House of Allah as their token of reverence. The most popular of the women is the fifteen-year old Aysha.

At the end of the transition period, Mahound's soldiers storm the Curtain. Baal is not found and is only discovered when he serenades the

---

31 Ibid., p. 364.

prostitutes from outside their prison. Finally, growing tired of simulating and disguising his true identity, he tears off his turban, washes the paint off his skin and delivers himself to the soldiers. He declares however that he recognizes no jurisdiction but his own Muse – or to be precise The Twelve Muses – the female prostitutes and inspirations of his poetry.

Face to face with Mahound in the tent of judgement, Baal depicts how in the brothel he had become the literal husband of the twelve prostitutes, imitating Mahound. The audience begin to laugh. Baal's earnestness only causes more mirth. Mahound is furious and sees this as the final mockery. Baal is taken away by the soldiers to be executed for his insults. He leaves the tent with the words: 'Whores and writers, Mahound. We are the people you can't forgive'[32] To which Mahound replies: 'Writers and whores. I see no difference here.'[33]

Gibreel's dream ends soon. He sees Mahound dying of a sudden illness in Aysha's bed while Hind sits in solitude at a banquet to which no one comes. But Hind, the witch, has conjured up powers that finally overcome Mahound. For a while she becomes a recluse mourning the destruction of her beloved Al Lat's temple, but succeeds in reviving the goddess's powers. For as darkness engulfs the dying Mahound, he recognizes the work of Al Lat, her final revenge. He calls upon her to light the lamp. Light returns. Mahound's last words are 'Still, I thank Thee, Al Lat, for this gift'.[34]

In Rushdie's complex satire, the parody of Muhammad, Mahound, finally succumbs to the pagan Devil. As in a hall of mirrors, reality and illusion are inextricably mixed, the playfulness of the imagination and the wickedness of the satirist's tongue are inseparably linked. Vice and virtue are intertwined, the sacred represented as profane, the angelic and the devilish portrayed as inter-dependent, indeed identical. God and Devil seem to be manifestations of one another. Concepts of good and evil are relativised. Clear-cut identity is lost. But it is not only the loss of identity of the human being that lies at the heart of this perturbing work; it is the loss of identity of religion itself.

Muhammad's life, the people he encountered, his disciples, companions and allies, his enemies, his wives, his doctrines, the story of

---

32 Ibid., p. 392.
33 Ibid., p. 392.
34 Ibid., p. 394.

his prophethood, all appear here in grotesque and travestied guise. The whole amalgam of myths that had been conjured up in Europe from the Middle Ages by bellicose crusaders, by generations of churchmen fearful of a threatening and all-powerful Islam, by reforming men of the Christian Church, by flamboyant writers of the Renaissance, by champions of Reason in the Enlightenment, by writers, poets and painters intoxicated by the imagined charms of the exotic Orient, by serious biographers unable to shake off their own Christian view of the world, all flash by, all are echoed in this provocative work: the Venerable Bede, John of Damascus, Paul Alvarus, William Langland, William Dunbar, Higden, Mandeville, Dante, Lydgate, Rabelais, Marlowe, Luther, Prideaux, Pitts, Abbé de Vertot, Voltaire, Hugo, Diderot, Gibbon, Muir, Byron, Shelley, Southey, Delacroix, Thackeray, the spirit of their words are revived in Rushdie's pages. It is truly Mahound re-born.

But there is another tradition that lives on, the tradition of Roger Bacon, of John of Segovia, of Lessing, of young Goethe, of Boulainvilliers, of Bolingbroke, of Carlyle, of Dawson, of Reland, of Rilke, of Paret, of Sprenger, of Tor Andrae, of Bodley, of Montgomery Watt, of Rodinson, of Schimmel. They have sought to understand Muhammad's cause, Muhammad's message, Muhammad's social and political reforms, Muhammad's personality and character in the context of his times and with an open mind. They have sought to dispel the myths and the stereotypes and to show how Islam embraces values dear to religions that have regarded it as their sworn enemy, while Muhammad himself saw his Faith as the continuation and enhancement of those very religions. Let us hope that their pens will be mightier than the sword for years to come, dispelling the myths that have surrounded Muhammad in Europe for the past millennium.

Bibliography

Works consulted on the Life of Muhammad (Biographies by Muslims and Europeans)

Ahmad, Ahmad. Bashii-ud-Din Mahmud *The Life of Muhammad*, Rabwah, 1959.

Al-Tabari, Abu Jafar. *Tarikh al-Rusul wa'l-Muluk* ed. M. de Goeje (15 vols) Leyden 1879-1901, volume 3.

Andrae, Tor. *Muhammad. The Man and His Faith*, translated by Theophil Menzel, London, 1936.

Boulainvillier, Comte Henri. *The Life of Mahomet*, anonymous translator, London, 1731.

Caetani, Leone. *Annali dell'Islam*, Milan, 1905.

Dashti, Ali. *Twenty Three Years*, A study of prophetic career of Muhammad, translated by T. R. C. Bagley, London, 1985.

Hisham, Ibn. *Kitab Sirat Rasul Allah* (Das Leben Muhammeds nach Ibn Ishak, bearbeitet von Ibn Hisham), edited by F. Wüstenfeld, Göttingen, 1859-60.

Hisham, Ibn. *Sirat Rasul Allah*, edited by Rafi al-Din Ishak Hamadani, Tehran, 1975.

Ishaq, Ibn. *Sirat Rasul Allah*, translated and edited by A. Guillaume, *The Life of Muhammad*, Oxford, 1978.

Lings, Martin. *Muhammad. His Life based on the Earliest Sources*, London, 1983.

Margoliouth, D.S. *Mohammad and the Rise of Islam*, London, 1905

Mikusch, Dogohert von. *Muhammad: Tragödie des Erfolgs*, Leipzig, 1932.

Muir, Sir William. *The Life of Muhammad*, Edinburgh, 1912.

Nasr, Seyyid Hossein. *Muhammad: Man of Allah*, London, 1982.

Nöldeke, Theodor. *Das Leben Muhammeds*, Hannover, 1863.

Paret, Rudi. *Muhammad und der Koran*, Stuttgart, 1967.

Payandeh, Abol. Qassem *Nahjol-Fussaha, A Collection of Muhammad's Sayings*, (based on *Al-Sahih Al Bukhari*), Tehran, 1993.

Rodinson, Maxime. *Mahomet*, translated by Anne Carter, The Penguin Press, 1971.

Rotter, G. *Ibn Hisham - Das Leben des Propheten,* Tübingen, 1976.

Saad, Ibn. *Kitab Al-Tabaqat- Al Kabir,* translated by S. Moinul Haq, Karachi, 1967.

Saad, Ibn. *Tabaqat,* (Ibn Saad Biographien), edited by E. Sachau, Leyden, 1905.

Sprenger, A. *Das leben und die Lehre des Mohammad,* Berlin, 1861.

Suhrawardy, Abdullah. *The Sayings of Muhammad* (selected from *Al-Sahih Al Bukhari*) with a foreword by Mahatma Gandhi, John Murray, London, 1954.

Wakidi, A. *Kitab al-Maghazi, edited by Marsden Jones, London, 1966.*

Washington, Irving. *The Life of Mahomet,* London, 1851.

Watt, W. Mongomery. *Muhammad at Mecca, Oxford, 1953. Muhammad at Medina,* Oxford, 1956. *Muhammad's Mecca in the Qur'an,* Edinburgh, 1988.

Works consulted on the History of Arabia and Islam

Cahen, Claude., Weltgeschichte, Fischer. *Der Islam vom Ursprung bis zu den Anfängen des Osmanenreiches,* (ed.) Frankfurt, 1968.

Gibbon, Edward. *Decline and Fall of the Roman Empire,* London, Frederick Warne, 1872.

Holt, P. M., Lambton, Ann K. S. and Lewis, Bernard. eds., *The Cambridge History of Islam,* Volume I, 1970.

Lammens, H. *L'Arabie Occidentale avant l'Hégire,* Beirut, 1924.

Lammens, H. *La Cité Arabe de Taif à la Veille de l'Hégire,* Beirut, 1922.

Lammens, H. *La Mecque à la Veille de l'Hégire,* Beirut, 1924.

Nicholson, R. A. *A Literary History of the Arabs,* Cambridge, 1930.

On the History of the Middle East

Mansfield, Peter. *The Ottoman Empire and its Successors.* London, 1973.

Steinbach, Udo. and Robert, Rüdiger. *Der Nahe und Mittlere Osten.* Band 1, Grundlagen, Strukturen und Problemfelder, Leverkusen, 1987 (ed.).

Dictionaries and Encyclopedias with entries of Islam and Muhammad

The Cambridge Encyclopedia of Islam, 1992.
The Dictionary of Islam, edited by Thomas Patrick Hughes, Lahore, 1964.
The Oxford Encyclopedia of Islam, 1992.

Translations of and commentaries on the Qur'an

Bell, Richard. *The Qur'an.* Translated, with a critical re-arrangement of the Surahs by Edinburgh, 1937.
Bodwell, J. M. *Bodwell's Koran.* Translated from Arabic by London, 1876
Burton, John. *The Collection of the Qur'an.* Cambridge, 1977.
Dawood, N.J. *The Koran.* Translated with Notes by Penguin Classics, Harmondsworth, 4th revised edition, 1974.
Montet, Édouard. *Le Coran.* Traduction Nouvelle Paris, 1929.
Paret, Rudi. *Der Koran.* Übersetzung von Stuttgart, 1962.
Sale, George. *The Koran or Alcoran of Muhammad.* Translated by with a Preliminary Discourse, London, Warne, n.d.
Sherif, Faruq. *A Guide to the Contents of the Qur'an.* London, 1985.

On the Sprituality of Islam

Boylan, Michael. *Hafez, Dance of Life.* A modern discovery of his greatest poems, Maze Publishers, Washington DC 1988. (transl.)
Nasr, Sayyid Hossein. *Islamic Spirituality: Foundation, London, 1987. Ideals and Realities of Islam,* London, 1966.
Nicholson, A. Reynold. *Rumi – Poet and Mystic* (Selections from his writings), translated by R. A. Nicholson, Washington DC 1950.
Schimmel, Annemarie. *Mystische Dimensionen des Islam,* 3rd edn, Munich, 1995.

Works consulted on the History of Europe and Christianity

Bainton, Ronald H. *The History of Christianity,* London, 1964.

Fischer, H. A. L. *A History of Europe,* Volume I – From the Earliest Times to 1713, London, 1970.

Hick, John. *The Metaphor of God Incarnate*, London, 1993.

Jones, Terry. *Crusades,* London, 1994.

Pirenne, Henri. Muhammad and Charlemagne, translated by Bernard Miall, New York, 1939.

Romer, John. *Testament, The Bible and History*, London, 1988.

On the History of European Thought

Aiken, Henry D. *The Age of Ideology.* The 19th Century Philosophers, London, 1956.

Berlin, Isaiah. *The Age of Enlightenment*, London, 1956. The 18th Century Philosophers.

Fink, Eugen. *Nietzsches Philosophie, Stuttgart,* 1960.

Hampshire, Stuart. *The Age of Reason.* The 17th Century Philosophers, London, 1956.

Hegel, G.W.F. *Lectures on the Philosophy of World History*, translated by H. B. Nisbet, Cambridge, 1975.

Hill, Christopher. *The Antichrist in Seventeenth-Century England*, London, 1969.

Hill, Christopher. *The World Turned Upside Down*, London, 1986.

Kaiser, Gerhard. *Geschichte der deutschen Literatur von der Aufklärung bis zum Sturm und Drang*, Guterlöh, 1966.

Manchester, William. *A World Lit Only By Fire.* The Medieval Mind and The Renaissance, Portrait of an Age, Boston, Toronto, London, 1992.

Nicolson, Harold. *The Age of Reason*, London, 1971.

Works consulted on the Reception of Muhammad and Islam in European Writings

Asin, Miguel. *Islam and the Divine Comedy*, translated by Courtney Langdon, London, 1926.

Bale, John. *Select Works of John Bale*, edited by Henry Christmas, Cambridge, 1849.

Beard, Thomas. *Antichrist the Pope of Rome,* London, 1625.

Dante Alighieri, *The Divine Comedy,* London, 1926.

Dunbar, William. *The Poems of William Dunbar,* translated by Courtney Langdon, Oxford, 1918.

Fowlie, Wallace. *A Reading of Dante's Inferno,* Chicago and London, 1976.

Langland, William. *Piers Plowman,* edited W. W. Skeat, Eets No. 54, 1873.

Luther, Dr Martin. *Dr. Martin Luther's Divine Discourses,* translated by Captain Henry Bell, London, 1652.

Marlowe, Christopher. *Tamburlaine The Great,* edited by J. S. Cunningham, London, 1981.

Porter Smith, Byron. *Islam in English Literature,* Beirut, 1939.

Rabelais, François. *Pantagruel,* Edition critique sur le texte original, edited by Verdun L. Saulnier, Genève et Paris, 1959.

Shakespeare, William. *King Henry V,* The Arden Shakespeare, edited by T.W. Craik, London, 1995.

Southern, R. W. *Western Views of Islam in the Middle Ages,* Cambridge Massachusetts, 1962.

Tyndale, William. *Doctrinal Treatises,* Parker Society, London, 1848.

Mongomery Watt, W. *Muhammad in the Eyes of the West,* Boston University Journal, 122, No. 3, Autumn, 1974

Works consulted on the Reception of Muhammad and Islam in European Writings

Besterman, Théodore. *Voltaire,* London, 1969.

British Journal for Eighteenth Century Studies. 'Images of Islam in some French writings of the First Half of the Eighteenth Century', British Journal for Eighteenth Century Studies, 14; ii (Autumn 1991).

Byron, Lord. *Selected Poems,* edited by Susan J. Wolfson and Peter J. Manning, Harmondsworth, 1996.

Byron, Lord. *Don Juan,* edited by T. G. Steffan and W. W. Pratt, Harmondsworth, 1966.

Byron, Lord. *Childe Harold's Pilgrimage,* 2nd edition, London, 1812.

Carlyle, Thomas. *On Heroes, Hero-Worship and the Heroic in History,* London, 1888.

Dawson, George. *Biographical Lectures,* edited by George St Clair, London, 1887.

Diderot et D'Alembert. *L'Encyclopédie ou Dictionnaire Raisonné des Arts et des Métiers,* (Supplément), Amsterdam, 1969.

Goethe, Wolfgang von. *Goethes Werke,* Hamburger Ausgabe, edited by Erich Trunz, 7th impression, 1964.

Günderode, Karoline von. *Der Schatten eines Traumes,* Gedichte, Prosa, Zeugnisse von Zeitgenossen und mit einem Essay von Christa Wolf, Darmstadt und Neuwied, 1979.

Heine, Heinrich. *Briefe,* edited by Friedrich Hirth, Mainz, 1950.

Heine, Heinrich. *Sämtliche Werke,* edited by Ernst Elster, Leipzig, Wien, 1890.

Hugo, Victor. *Oeuvres Complètes de Victor Hugo,* Paris, 1880.

Kant, Immanuel. 'Beantwortung der Frage Was ist Aufklärung' in *Was ist Aufklärung* Kant, Erhard, Hamann, Herder, Lessing, Mendelssohn, Riem, Schiller, Wieland. Thesen und Definitionen, edited by Erhard Bahr, Stuttgart, 1975.

Lamartine, Alphonse de. *Oeuvres de Alphonse de Lamartine, Souvenirs, Impressions, Pensées, Paysages pendant un Voyage en Orient,* Paris, 1832.

Lessing, Gotthold Iphraim. *Nathan der Weise,* edited by Peter Demetz, Frankfurt, 1966.

Luther, Dr Martin. *Luther's Works,* translated by Jaroslav Pelikan, Saint Louis, 1958–1967.

Montesquieu, Charles Louis. *Oeuvres Complètes de Montesquieu,* Tome Premier et Tome Second, *Lettres Persanes,* Paris, 1949.

Nietzsche, Friedrich. *Thus Spake Zarathustra,* translated with an introduction by R. J. Bollingdale, Harmondsworth, 1974.

Ockley, Simon. *History of the Saracens,* 3rd edition, Cambridge, 1757.

Pitts, Joseph. *A Faithful Account of the Religion and Manners of the Mahometans,* London, 1731.

Prideaux, Humphrey. *The True Nature of Imposture Fully Displayed in the Life of Mahomet,* 8th edition, London, 1723.

Rilke, Rainer Maria. *Sämtliche Werke,* edited by Ernst Zinn, Wiesbaden 1955–1966

Rilke, Rainer Maria. *Briefe 1897–1914,* edited by the Rilke Archive, Wiesbaden, 1950.

Rilke, Rainer Maria, Marie von Thurn und Taxis. *Briefwechsel,* edited by Ernst Zinn, Zurich, 1951.

Rushdie, Salman. *The Satanic Verses*, The Consortium Inc., Dover, Delaware, 1992 (paperback edition).

Schnack, Ingeborg. *Rilke, Chronik seines Lebens und Werkes*, Frankfurt am Main, 1975.

Seigel, Jules Paul. *Thomas Carlyle. The Critical Hertiage*, London, 1971.

Shelley, Percy Bysshe. *The Complete Poetical Works of Shelley*, edited by Thomas Hutchinson, Oxford, 1904.

Thackeray, Makepeace. William. *Notes of a Journey from Cornhill to Grand Cairo*, London, 1846.

Voltaire, François Marie. *Mahomet ou le Fanatisme*, précedé d'un extrait du Traité sur la Tolérance, Le Temps Singulier, Collection L'Immortel, Paris, 1979.

Webster, Richard. A Brief History of Blasphemy. Liberalism, Censorship and 'The Satanic Verses', London, 1989.

Works consulted on the Resurgence of Islam

Dekmejian, R. Hrair. *Islam in Revolution*, New York, 1985.

Esposito, John L. *Islam and Politics*, Second edition, New York, 1987.

Works consulted on Orientalist Paintings

Stevens, Mary Anne. *The Orientalists: Delacroix to Matisse*, European Painters in North Africa and the Near East, Royal Academy of Arts, London, 1984.